VAX COBOL ON-LINE
Interactive Programming Concepts and Examples

Related Titles of Interest from Wiley

VS COBOL II: Highlights and Techniques, by Jim Janossy, is a companion to Gary Brown's *Advanced ANSI COBOL with Structural Programming* (second edition). Gary Brown's book is reference in nature; Jim Janossy's book is designed for you to use for rapid, focused learning of crucial differences between VS COBOL II and IBM's workhorse compiler VS COBOL.

Structured COBOL Programming (sixth edition), by Robert and Nancy Stern, is an excellent beginner's textbook for learning the COBOL language.

Jim Janossy has also written several other books, published by John Wiley & Sons, dealing with the mainframe environment:

Practical MVS JCL (1987, 1992)

Practical VSAM For Today's Programmer (1988)

Practical TSO/ISPF For Programmers and the Information Center (1988)

VAX COBOL ON-LINE
Interactive Programming Concepts and Examples

JAMES G. JANOSSY

De Paul University, Chicago

John Wiley & Sons, Inc.
New York • Chichester • Brisbane • Toronto • Singapore

Library of Congress Cataloging-in-Publication Data
Janossy, James G. (James Gustav), 1947-
    VAX COBOL on-line: interactive programming concepts and examples
/ by James G. Janossy.
        p.   cm.
    Includes index.
    ISBN 0-471-55196-1 (alk. paper)
    1. VAX computer—Programming. 2. COBOL (Computer program language) 3. On-line data processing. I. Title.
QA76.8.V32J36 1992
005.2'45—dc20   91-26811

Printed in the United States of America.
10 9 8 7 6 5 4 3 2 1

This book is dedicated to the memory of
Grace Murray Hopper (1906–1992)
fama semper vivat

PREFACE

In this book I explain to you the background of interactive (on-line) processing and show you how to do it using VAX COBOL. You can use this book to quickly become proficient in on-line work using the VAX family of computers. I wrote this "hands on" book for two audiences:

- *Programmers, consultants, IBM-oriented personnel "branching out" to the VAX environment, and VAX end users.* You can benefit from a stable, workable on-line system model. DEC provides fine information retrieval tools but you can see from the examples in this book that VAX COBOL is also easy to use. It may meet some of your application needs better than "higher overhead" software.
- *Students completing an information systems curriculum using a VAX.* If this includes you, you may need to apply on-line programming skills quickly to implement a systems project.

I show you the essential logic building blocks of on-line inquiry, record add/change file access, and on-line record deletion. I've also fully illustrated how to create and load an indexed file on the VAX and how to use the indexed file READ, WRITE, REWRITE, DELETE, and START verbs. I show you how to program advanced features such as an indexed file alternate key browse, a simple but workable access security mechanism, how to archive deleted records to a file, enhancements for direct transfer between screens, and how to build (and test) a system incrementally using stub programs. You can do all of this easily on the VAX!

Prerequisite Knowledge

I assume only that you know the basics of COBOL and are comfortable with it. If you have taken an introductory course in COBOL (on a VAX or any other computer system), you will find this book easy to use. If you know COBOL but have never used a VAX, Chapters 5 and 6 give you concise information about VAX system commands and show you how to use the VAX EDT text editor.

If you are new to COBOL, you will find either *Structured COBOL Programming*, 6th Edition, by Stern and Stern (John Wiley & Sons, Inc.,

1991) or another of my books, *COBOL: A Software Engineering Introduction* (Dryden Press, 1989) an excellent companion to this book.

About VAX COBOL . . .

VAX COBOL is an ANSI-standard implementation of the COBOL language. In the IBM mainframe environment, CICS is often used to achieve on-line business data processing. VAX COBOL implements on-line processing without a product such as CICS, using simple but powerful extensions to the COBOL ACCEPT and DISPLAY verbs. This book shows you how to program computer terminal screens using ACCEPT and DISPLAY.

Digital Equipment Corporation is second only to IBM in size. Since founding it in 1967, Ken Olson and DEC have pioneered in the field of interactive processing. VAX machines span the entire spectrum of power from desktop machines to the powerful VAX-6000 series. All members of the VAX computer family run the same operating system (VMS) and use the same text editor (EDT). All support the same version of VAX COBOL. You will find the many examples and illustrations in this book an enjoyable way to explore the interactive power of the VAX.

For Professionals and Students

The best way to become productive in VAX COBOL and interactive programming is to actually run programs and see how they work. You could key-enter all of the programs in this book but that's tedious. I have arranged to make all of the programs (including my complete VAXDEMO system) available to you as ASCII files on diskette as described in Appendix E. Upload them and run them to "animate" your readings. Copy and use them as models if you like them.

For Instructors

I designed this book to help you teach interactive programming concepts to students as part of an undergraduate or graduate CIS/MIS curriculum. Here is how I arranged the contents for programming and "project" classes:

Chapters 1–4:	Introduce essential on-line concepts.
Chapters 5–6:	Show how to use VMS file commands and the VAX EDT text editor.
Chapters 7–9:	How to design screens.
Chapter 10:	How to create and load indexed files.
Chapters 11–15:	A complete VAX COBOL on-line system demonstration including incremental construction and testing.
Chapter 16:	Advanced topics: direct transfer between functions and concurrent (multiple terminal) access.
Appendix A:	Questions and exercises for class use.
Appendix D:	How to convert VAX COBOL programs to the microcomputer-based RM/COBOL-85 compiler as supplied with *Structured COBOL Programming*, 6th edition, by Stern & Stern (Wiley, 1991).

See Appendix E for information about a student workbook that parallels *VAX COBOL On-Line.*

With thanks . . .

I'd like to thank Dr. Helmut Epp, Chairman of the Department of Computer Science and Information Systems of DePaul University, for his support in my restructuring of our CSC360 On-Line Concepts course. Work invested there played a major role in shaping the content of this book. I would also like to thank Dr. L. Edward Allemand for his suggestions for book content and class exercises. I thank Steve Samuels, Director of the DePaul University Computer Career Program, for giving me the opportunity to refine interactive VAX COBOL techniques as a part of the CCP curriculum. Thanks also to Norm Noerper of Northeastern Illinois University, to Caliber Data Training who helped shape this book in many ways, and to Dr. Lynn H. Solomon for his help in reviewing page proofs.

Special thanks to Dawn Tortorella, director of DePaul's Academic Computing Services, and Bob Dameron, chief systems programmer. Dawn and Bob provide outstanding support on the VAX 6410, on which all of the programs in this book were developed and tested!

Jim Janossy
Chicago, Illinois

SUMMARY CONTENTS

Appendixes

CONTENTS

11   VAXDEMO: A COMPLETE MENU-BASED ON-LINE SYSTEM

12   INTERACTIVE INQUIRY: PROGRAM CINQU1

Chapter One

INTRODUCTION TO INTERACTIVE PROCESSING

In this first chapter I explain the background of interactive ("on-line") processing and tell you why this is easier and more direct on the VAX than on IBM mainframes. It's easiest for you to see the reason for this by understanding a little recent history.

1.1 Computing Machine Generations

We chronicle the progression of computer technology according to machine and software generations. Four generations of computer hardware have existed:

First generation, 1950 to 1959:

- Slow vacuum tube circuit elements
- Paper tape or punched card input and output
- Memory capacity less than 32,000 bytes

Second generation, 1959 to 1964:

- Separate transistors as circuit elements
- Punched card and hardcopy (printing) terminal interfaces
- Magnetic tape data storage, limited amounts of disk
- Memory capacity less than 128,000 bytes

Third generation, 1964 to 1972:

- Moderate scale integrated circuitry (a few hundred transistors per circuit board component)
- High speed tape and disk storage

1

- Expensive and relatively slow video terminals
- Memory capacity rises to a few megabytes

Fourth generation, 1973 to present:

- Large scale and very large scale integrated circuitry (thousands or millions of transistors per circuit board element)
- Very high speed, high capacity disk storage
- Inexpensive video terminals
- Memory capacity explodes to hundreds of megabytes.

I have mapped these machine generations for you on a timeline in Figure 1.1.

Applying computer horsepower to the immediate processing of information is known as *interactive* processing. Interactive processing was unknown in the first two computing machine generations. Today's mainframe computers have their roots in those first two generations, while

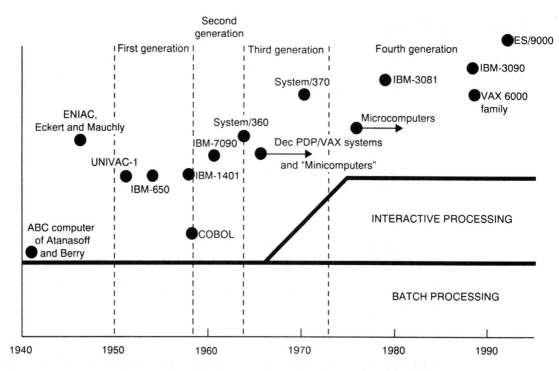

Figure 1.1   There have been four generations of computing machinery since the commercialization of digital computers; interactive (on-line) processing became available in the third generation.

minicomputers and microcomputers date from the late third and fourth generations. This has a decisive influence on how interactive processing is done on different types of computers. It's also the reason that COBOL doesn't provide a standard method for handling program-to-terminal communication: COBOL was invented in 1959!

1.2 Batch and Interactive Processing Modes

First and second generation computers were *batch* machines that followed an *input/process/output* work flow. They were designed to input program instructions, read data from punched cards or magnetic tape, and output new files or reports.

In a **batch processing mode**, work for the computer is done at the computer's convenience. Some types of work, such as handling accounting data and printing reports, are well served by batch processing. Much of the work to which computers were applied in the early era was of this type. For batch processing, data can be conveyed to the computer system as bundles of punched cards or as files of records stored on tape or disk.

Batch processing is still applied to many business data processing applications when these factors apply:

1. A high volume of work exists to be done.
2. The work can be grouped ("batched") to increase machine efficiency.
3. Completion time measured in hours or days is acceptable.

High volume file updates such as credit card payment processing are well served by batch processing. Batch processing is very machine efficient and therefore costs much less per update transaction than on-line processing. It's the type of processing you probably learned first.

Third generation computers (1964 to 1972) came about when a new kind of business data processing became vital. **Interactive processing** supports the immediate completion of small units of work, called *transactions*, and is sometimes called *transaction processing*. Information inquiry, immediate file update, and many other time-critical tasks require interactive support. Under interactive processing, the completion of a task is scheduled at the convenience of a computer user, not at the convenience of the computer. The lower part of the Figure 1.1 timeline maps the period in which interactive processing became available.

Batch and interactive processing modes coexist in support of modern business data processing systems, as depicted in Figure 1.2. The files

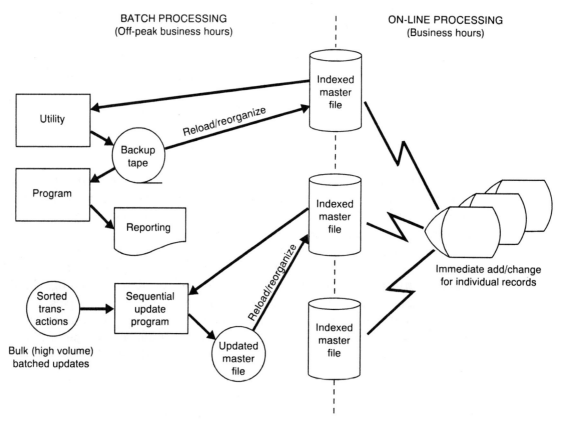

Figure 1.2   Batch and interactive processing modes coexist in support of modern business data processing systems by sharing access to indexed files or a database.

supporting a data processing system are typically shared by interactive and batch processes. Interactive processing is usually given priority during business hours. Batch processing gains priority or sole access to the files during nonbusiness (often night) hours.

1.3 Real-Time, Interactive, and On-Line Processing

By the late 1960s advancing manufacturing technology made it possible to integrate whole electronic circuits in single semiconductor "microchips." Breakthroughs in magnetic disk technology provided a way to store and retrieve data quickly and flexibly. Video technology was adapted to provide a human-to-machine interface with a typewriterlike keyboard.

The progress of the late 1960s combined to make it possible to construct "mini" computers for purposes very different from batch processes. The 1960s saw the introduction of *real-time* computers such as the Digital Equipment Corporation PDP family, the ancestor of today's VAX.

"Real-time" means that information is input to a computer electronically and is acted upon immediately instead of being grouped with other data to be processed. In real-time processing information enters a computer system as a stream of characters represented by electronic signal pulses, not as a file of records.

One of the first applications of real-time computing was the automation of factory processes and oil refineries. A real-time computer system can be programmed to accept data from pressure and temperature sensors in chemical tanks and use the data to make decisions. Such a computer decides which pipe valves to open or close to fill (but not overflow) each tank. The computer system generates electrical signals to control other equipment. This was the type of work for which early minicomputers were developed. Other real-time applications include controlling elevators, heating and ventilation equipment, and medical monitoring gear.

In the late 1960s and early 1970s we quickly realized that not only machine control but many types of information inquiry and manipulation would benefit from immediate computer access. When the stimulus to a program comes from a sensor or mechnical device, it is called a *process control* application. When the stimulus comes from a human using a computer terminal, such as the modern VAX workstation shown in Figure 1.3, we use the term *interactive* to describe the processing situation.

Information storage on magnetic disk is necessary to support interactive processing. This information access requires disk drives to be "on-line," as opposed to "off-line." Interactive processing has also become known as *on-line processing.* In this book, I use the terms *interactive processing* and *on-line processing* to mean the same thing.

1.4 Teleprocessing

Interactive processing made it possible to automate activities that could never have received adequate treatment in a batch mode. Airline reservation systems pioneered the use of interactive capabilities. Multiple computer terminals, in different locations, can access the same disk-stored data and immediately store or change reservations for airline tickets.

Figure 1.3   On-line access to source code revolutionized the way programmers work. On-line real-time computing was pioneered by the Digital Equipment Corporation minicomputer ancestors of the VAX, which were among the first systems to take advantage of modern integrated circuitry, disk, and video terminal technology. *(Photograph by Flip Chalfant, courtesy of DePaul University Department of Academic Publications, Gwyn Friend, Director.)*

A computer terminal might be on a different floor in the same building as the computer, a few miles from the computer, or on the other side of the world. When a computer terminal is "remote" from the computer, telephone lines are often used to connect them. But the telephone network was not designed to handle digital computer signals.

As you can see in Figure 1.4 digital signals are pulses (on-off signals) representing the bits making up bytes of data. Signals that represent speech and music vary more smoothly. A **modem** (**mo**dulator/**dem**odulator) is used at each end of a remote terminal connection to convert digital signals to tones that the telephone network can handle and to convert these tones back into digital signals at the receiving end. Without the sig-

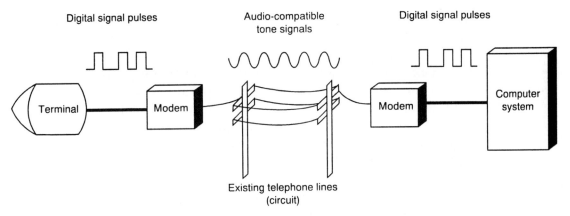

Figure 1.4 A *modem* (*mo*dulator/*dem*odulator) is used at each end of a remote terminal connection to convert digital signals to tones that the telephone network can handle and to convert these tones back into digital signals at the receiving end.

nal conversion performed by modems, terminals and computers could not use ordinary telephone lines. Interactive processing with this kind of connection is called **teleprocessing** ("process at a distance").

1.5 Data Transmission Speed

The speed at which a computer system and terminal can transfer information over a circuit to each other is measured in bits per second. The limiting factor in teleprocessing is usually the speed of the modem you use for the terminal/telephone line and telephone line/computer connections. In the 1970s modems were often as slow as 300 bits per second (30 characters per second). In the 1980s technological progress made 1200 bit per second modems generally affordable. Now 2400 bit per second modems are quite common, and modems as fast as 9600 bits per second are appearing.

Each character (byte) is represented by eight bits. For data transmission purposes an additional bit may exist at the beginning and end of each series of eight signal pulses for a character. A modem capable of transmitting 2400 bits per second (bps) is handling 240 characters of data per second, 10 bits per byte.

How long will it take for a computer screen with 600 characters of data to be transmitted using a 2400 bits per second modem? 600 characters ÷ 240 characters per second = 2.5 seconds. A 1200 bps modem—half the speed—would require 5 seconds to transmit the screen. A 2400 bps modem might cost less than $100 today; 1200 bps modems are obsolete.

The maximum data transmission speed over telephone lines depends on the amount of electrical noise and spurious signals affecting the circuit. Ordinary telephone connections can typically support 2400 bits per second transmission. Modern FAX machines achieve higher data transmission rates by compressing data and using more sophisticated modulation techniques. Special telephone circuits arranged by leasing a telephone line for continuous use can support much higher data transmission speeds, such as 56,000 bits per second (5600 characters per second).

Microwave, earth satellite, and modern fiber optic communication circuits can transport data at enormously higher rates, up to millions of bits per second. The Integrated Services Digital Network (ISDN) now being developed by major telephone companies will ultimately provide high speed digital transmission over ordinary telephone lines without the use of modems. ISDN reengineers the entire telephone system to handle voice transmissions in digitized form. This makes it possible for voice and data signals to be handled in the same way. ISDN service is available now in some cities and will be expanded over the next two decades. With ISDN you can throw away your modem. You will enjoy 64,000 bps data transmission (yes, 64,000 bits per second) directly at your telephone connection!

1.6 Data Storage on Magnetic Disk

In modern business data processing almost all applications are serviced by a combination of business-hours (daytime) on-line access and update, and off-hours (nightly) batch processing as depicted in Figure 1.2. The batch processing cycle typically includes disk file backup, file reorganization, high volume batch updating, and reporting.

The disk storage supporting this dual mode of operation often relies on indexed files. Indexed files provide the ability to retrieve a single record from a file without having to read all of the records that physically preceed it.

In the IBM mainframe environment ISAM (Indexed Sequential Access Method) provided early indexed file support. ISAM's successor, VSAM, was released by IBM in 1973. In the VAX environment Record Management Services (RMS) is the system software component that supports indexed file processing. I show you how to create and access indexed files on the VAX in Chapter 10.

1.7 Where the VAX Fits In

Digital Electronics Corporation pioneered the development of dedicated real-time computer systems in the 1960s with the "PDP" family of computers. These were 16 bit machines; they communicated between internal components 16 bits at a time.

DEC introduced the VAX series in the 1970s. The VAX was the first major line of 32 bit minicomputers. Until it was developed, only mainframes could boast of manipulating data in 32 bit chunks. The VAX could process data fast enough to support scores of on-line terminals. VMS, its operating system, was designed to support interactive processing. Thus the VAX makes it relatively easy to do on-line programming.

In the next chapter we'll take a look at the major difference between VAX on-line processing and on-line processing on IBM's mainframe System 370/3090/9000 computers, which stem from earlier batch operating system architectures.

1.8 Chapter Summary

The ancestry of the 32 bit VAX minicomputer lies entirely in the machine generations developed for real-time, interactive processing. IBM and other mainframes have their roots in earlier machine generations in which batch processing was the sole mode of operation.

Batch processing involves grouping data so that it can be processed at the timing convenience of the computer system. *Real-time processing* demands that the computer give attention to a stimulus immediately on demand. Real-time computer systems were developed in the late 1960s. *Process control applications* involve a dedicated computer monitoring sensors to make real-time judgments and control other machinery. The distinction between *process control* and *interactive applications* is simply where the stimulus for the computer comes from. Interactive implies that a human supplies the stimulus.

The development of hard disk drives, inexpensive integrated circuitry, and video terminals made it possible for companies such as Digital Equipment Corporation to develop *minicomputers* in the 1960s. With the development of *modems* to modulate digital signals into tones that the telephone network could carry, *teleprocessing* ("processing at a distance") became possible.

1.9 Important Terms

You can review these terms to check your understanding of this chapter:

Computing machine generations Four distinct technological categories of business data processing computer, beginning with the first commercial computers produced in 1950.

Interactive The acceptance and immediate processing of commands from a computer terminal operator.

ISDN Integrated Services Digital Network, the telephone system of the future, which will carry both voice and data in digitized form and eliminate the need for modems.

Modem A device that converts digital signals into audio tones capable of transmission over ordinary telephone lines and converts incoming audio tones representing a digital signal into digital form.

On-line A synonym for *interactive* in the business data processing environment.

Process control The immediate processing of a sensor-generated signal input by a computer to control other machinery.

Real-time Immediate processing of a stimulus by a computer, directly causing production of an appropriate output signal or update of machine-stored data.

Teleprocessing Interactive processing that takes place with a distance between the terminal and the computer, often using telephone lines to carry the data transmission.

You can find additional questions and exercises for this chapter in Appendix A.

Chapter Two

COMPARING VAX AND IBM/CICS ON-LINE PROCESSING

2.1 Variations among Computing Systems

Interactive processing developed after COBOL was invented. For this reason COBOL provides no interactive processing language standard. Software and hardware manufacturers have extended COBOL to handle interactive processing. You will find that interactive processing varies considerably from one type of computer to another.

Interactive processing puts a program in the position of being a middleman between a computer terminal user and information stored on disk. Two approaches have evolved to allow a COBOL program to play this role: One approach—*conversational*—is used by mini- and microcomputer architectures; the other approach—called *pseudoconversational*—is used by large IBM mainframes.

2.2 VAX On-Line Support

Minicomputer system vendors such as Digital Equipment Corporation were founded in the late 1960s after the advent of the third computing machine generation. This was well after pure batch processing had been joined by interactive processing.

Minicomputer vendors had no experience in the batch processing era. They created whole new machine architectures and operating systems to suit real-time and interactive processing. UNIX, the popular multimachine operating system, developed entirely in the interactive era and has no roots in batch processing. Neither does RSX, DEC's operating sys-

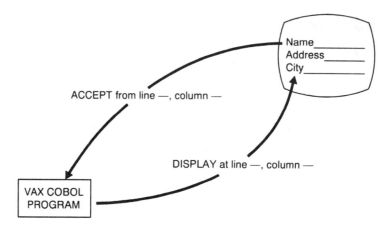

Figure 2.1 Interactive processing in the VAX environment relies on extensions to the COBOL DISPLAY and ACCEPT verbs such as LINE and COLUMN.

tem for the PDP family of computers, or VMS, the successor to RSX as the operating system for the VAX.

Mini- and microcomputer operating systems give your programs the support they need to access terminals. Interactive processing in the VAX environment relies on extensions to the COBOL DISPLAY and ACCEPT verbs (such as LINE and COLUMN) as shown in Figure 2.1. As I'll show you in Chapter 7 these extensions give you many screen formatting, numeric input conversion, cursor positioning, and screen control options.

2.3 "Conversational" VAX COBOL ACCEPT/DISPLAY Verbs

The VAX operating system VMS (much like UNIX) was developed from scratch with the intention of supporting interactive processing. This makes it possible for you to write interactive VAX COBOL programs with the ACCEPT and DISPLAY verbs using software external to COBOL.

In VAX COBOL the ACCEPT verb lets a program receive data entered at a computer terminal. The DISPLAY verb sends information to the computer terminal. You can achieve *conversational* program operation because the computer system "converses" with the terminal operator character by character. Each keystroke is received immediately by the VAX operating system and "echoed" back to the terminal to appear on its screen. Your interactive VAX COBOL program is continuously active.

VMS hands over a field of keyboard-entered data to your program when you press the *<Return>* key.

Options you code with DISPLAY let you put the cursor at specific positions on the screen. You can DISPLAY information with normal intensity, bright, dark (unseen), blinking, underlined, or "reversed."

An interactive VAX COBOL program can open and access files in the same way that a batch program does. You "graduate" to on-line work in the VAX COBOL environment in a straightforward progression from batch programming. Beyond indexed files, you need only understand ACCEPT/DISPLAY syntax and on-line program logic to write an interactive VAX COBOL program.

2.4 How IBM/CICS On-Line Processing Differs From VAX

We started to shift some work to on-line processing in the late 1960s. But IBM's premier System/360 computer line and its operating systems (OS and DOS, the ancestors of MVS and DOS/VSE) were developed in 1963 and 1964. (Yes, they really are that old!) By 1968 IBM faced the task of fitting on-line processing into the existing batch-oriented environment of the System/360. Contemporary IBM mainframes such as the 3090 and ES/9000 are direct descendants of the System/360 (they use the same operating system and job control language). The mechanism IBM chose in the 1960s to support on-line processing is still the way that on-line processing is handled on mainframes.

IBM adapted mainframes running ancestors of the MVS and DOS/VSE operating systems to on-line business data processing by providing CICS (Customer Information and Control System). CICS is a *teleprocessing monitor program*. It is entirely separate from the MVS and DOS/VSE operating systems and separate from languages such as COBOL.

CICS is a large assembler program designed to run continuously. The batch-oriented MVS and DOS/VSE operating systems "see" CICS as a single large program. Like any program, CICS begins running when job control language for it is submitted—a task typically handled once per day (or even less frequently) by the computer operations personnel of a mainframe installation. CICS continues to execute throughout the business day, and most interactive programs on the mainframe interact with it.

As I have shown in Figure 2.2, the ACCEPT and DISPLAY verbs don't play any role in IBM mainframe interactive programming and you can't use them in a program associated with CICS. Each on-line program is actually run by CICS within memory it allocates to the program. The program communicates with the terminal screen by forming a record of the data to be sent. CICS "expands" this record into the stream of characters understood by the terminal. In the same way, CICS "packages" communication from the terminal to the program as a record.

In the IBM mainframe environment all interactive programs are written as subprograms that CALL (and are CALLed by) CICS. You accomplish interactive processing on IBM mainframes using special CICS commands imbedded within COBOL programs. Certain CICS commands send information to a terminal and others receive information from it.

An IBM mainframe interactive program does not "converse" with the terminal operator in the same direct way that a VAX COBOL program

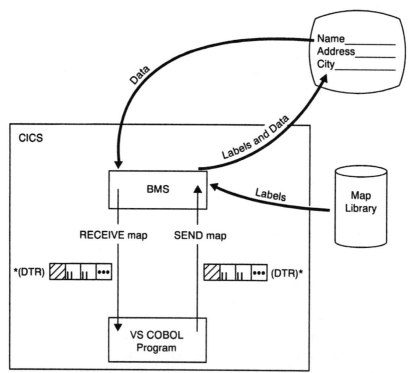

*Data transmission record

Figure 2.2 ACCEPT and DISPLAY verbs don't play any role in IBM mainframe interactive programming; a program communicates with the terminal by forming a record of the data, which is "packaged" and sent by CICS as a data stream to the terminal by the Basic Mapping Support (BMS) subsystem.

COMPARING VAX AND IBM/CICS ON-LINE PROCESSING   15

does. Instead, you program CICS using *pseudoconversational* techniques. A CICS program is activated only briefly to send or receive a full screen of data. It becomes inactive again while the terminal operator "fills out" a whole screen of data. CICS is used in this way to gain processing efficiency, but it makes your programs much more complicated.

No program associated with CICS can directly access any file, because CICS "owns" all of the files used by any on-line program. In the IBM mainframe environment you have to learn to use non-COBOL CICS commands to do file input/output actions.

CICS is governed by many tables that tell it the names of programs, screen images, files, and terminal operators. As a programmer you cannot directly change these control tables. Only a designated system programmer can update them to include new programs and files. If this seems bureaucratic, keep in mind that the large organizations that use mainframes and CICS are accustomed to spreading responsibility for specialized tasks among several people.

If you already know how to write interactive programs in the CICS environment you will be amazed at the relative ease of VAX COBOL interactive programming. Interactive programming on the VAX involves much less coordination of things external to a program. Because the VAX operating system is inherently interactive, you can write an on-line program without anyone making control table entries on your behalf.

2.5 Chapter Summary

Interactive processing is a more recent development than COBOL. COBOL provides no language standard for it and various computer systems implement it in different ways.

The VAX gives you *conversational* interactive programming because its operating system was designed to provide this support. VAX COBOL programs use the ACCEPT and DISPLAY verbs (with extensions to syntax) to handle communication from and to a terminal.

IBM mainframes are usually programmed using *pseudoconversational* techniques, under which a program is active only briefly to service communication with a terminal. IBM mainframes predate interactive processing. The MVS and DOS/VSE operating systems are batch-oriented and don't directly support terminal communication. On IBM mainframes the large CICS teleprocessing monitor program supplements the operating system to provide on-line system support.

Interactive programming on a mainframe using CICS is much more complicated than interactive programming on the VAX. An interactive program in the mainframe environment is really a subroutine to CICS. The program must use special commands to ask CICS to do terminal and file access. CICS is controlled by external tables that can be updated only by a systems programmer, and much coordination is required to develop a new CICS program or interactive system. On the VAX, you don't face the complexity of pseudoconversational logic, special commands, or external tables controlling on-line processing.

2.6 Important Terms

You can review these terms to check your understanding of this chapter:

CICS   Customer Information and Control System. A software product required to support interactive data processing on IBM mainframes; not used for interactive programming on the VAX.

Conversational programming   An interactive program that remains active while the person at a computer terminal enters data on the screen; typical of the VAX and microcomputers. You receive keyed data field by field.

Pseudoconversational programming   An interactive program that becomes inactive while the terminal operator enters data; typical of IBM/CICS mainframe on-line software. You receive keyed data a full screen (all fields) at a time.

Teleprocessing monitor   A program, such as CICS, that is capable of running continuously under a batch operating system to handle computer terminal communication; not used on the VAX.

You can find additional questions and exercises for this chapter in Appendix A.

Chapter Three

MENU-BASED INTERACTIVE SYSTEMS

3.1 Functions of an Interactive Business System

An interactive system accesses one or more indexed files or a database, providing a terminal operator with the ability to accomplish these functions:

- Add records to disk storage
- Change or "update" existing records
- Make immediate inquiries into stored data
- Delete records

If you use the first letter of the words *Add*, *Change*, *Inquiry*, and *Delete* to form a word you get the acronym ACID. This summarizes the general capabilities of an interactive business data processing system.

The most commonly used interface provided to the terminal operator to accomplish add, change, inquiry, and delete functions is menu-based. This means that the computer terminal operator selects the action to be performed from a listing—a *menu*—of possible actions. I've illustrated the menu of my VAXDEMO interactive system (which I'll show you how to program in Chapters 11–15) in Figure 3.1.

The VAXDEMO menu lets you choose between inquiring about a record (seeing it), adding/changing a record, deleting a record, or viewing the contents of a file in an alternate key, sequential "browse" mode beginning at a specified customer name. The fifth option ends execution of the on-line system.

Figure 3.2 illustrates how you can depict the structure of a menu-based system using a hierarchical chart. The box at the top of this chart is the menu. Boxes under the menu each represent one of the menu-selectable functions. In many cases each function is accomplished by one program, but it is possible that a function, represented by a box, may involve several separately coded programs. The menu itself is usually coded in a single program.

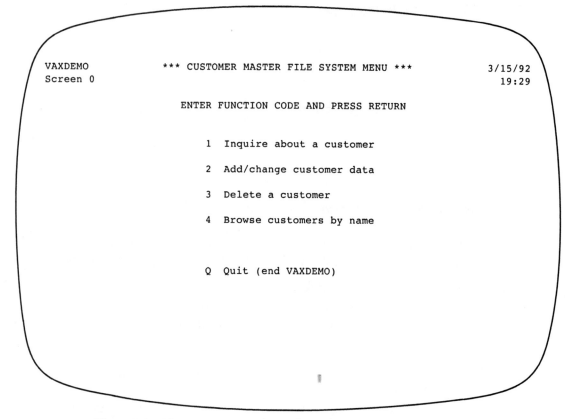

Figure 3.1   The most commonly used interface provided to the terminal operator to accomplish add, change, inquiry, and delete functions is menu-based. This is the menu screen of the VAXDEMO demonstration system I've illustrated in Chapters 11–15.

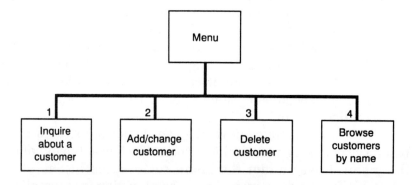

Figure 3.2   How you can depict the structure of a menu-based system using a hierarchical chart. The box at the top of this chart is the menu; boxes under the menu each represent one of the menu-selectable functions.

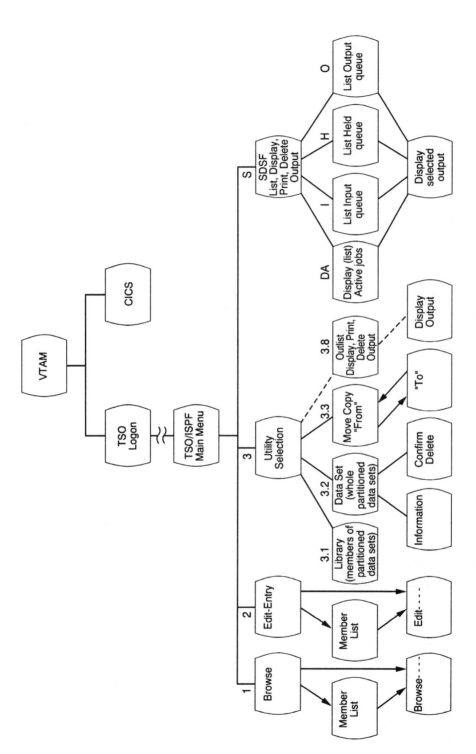

Figure 3.3 A large on-line system is often composed of a main menu and several levels of submenus. This is a part of IBM's Time Sharing Option TSO/ISPF, the programmer's workbench of the IBM mainframe. (Adapted by permission of the publisher from Janossy, *Practical TSO/ISPF*, John Wiley & Sons, Inc., 1988.)

A function selectable from a menu might itself present another menu. In such a case the selection is called a **submenu**. Menu-based systems of broad functional scope are often organized with submenus. You may already be familiar with IBM's Time Sharing Option TSO/ISPF, the programmer's workbench of the mainframe. It's typical of a menu-based system organized into a menu and submenus, as I illustrate in Figure 3.3, which is adapted from another of my books (Janossy, *Practical TSO/ISPF*, John Wiley & Sons, Inc., 1988).

3.2 Formatted Screen "Geography"

You can access each of the functional choices on an on-line menu by entering the selection value associated with it. In the on-line screen of

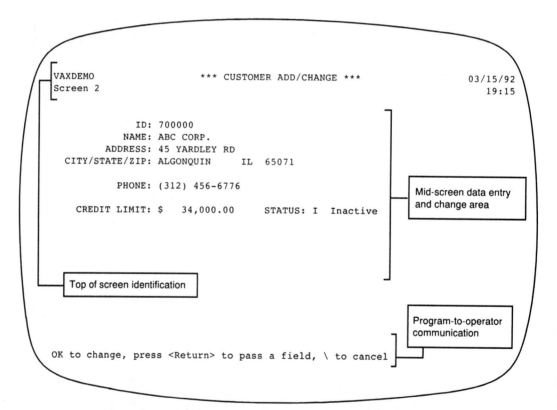

```
VAXDEMO                *** CUSTOMER ADD/CHANGE ***              03/15/92
Screen 2                                                          19:15

            ID: 700000
          NAME: ABC CORP.
       ADDRESS: 45 YARDLEY RD
CITY/STATE/ZIP: ALGONQUIN      IL   65071

         PHONE: (312) 456-6776

  CREDIT LIMIT: $   34,000.00      STATUS: I   Inactive
```

Mid-screen data entry and change area

Top of screen identification

Program-to-operator communication

```
OK to change, press <Return> to pass a field, \ to cancel
```

Figure 3.4   The geography of a functional on-line screen is usually divided into three areas: the top is used for identification, the central part is used for data display or entry, and the bottom is used for program communication to the operator ("prompts").

Figure 3.1 you can enter 2 and press the **<Return>** key to "go into" the customer file inquiry function.

The screen that results when you select a function from a menu usually provides a formatted working area as illustrated in Figure 3.4. Different parts of the screen "geography" are dedicated to specific purposes:

- The top is used for identification, titling, and date and time information.
- The central part is used for data display or entry.
- The bottom is used for program communication to the operator (prompts).

In using a formatted screen you move the cursor from field to field entering or changing information to complete the processing. In the case of inquiry-only screens the display itself represents completion of processing. One unit of completed work for the terminal operator is called a *transaction*.

After completing a transaction you have the option of remaining in a function to process additional records. At some point you enter a designated quit value to end work within the function and return to the menu.

3.3 Direct Transfer between Menu Functions

Training people to use an on-line system is usually simple with a menu structure because menu screens act as guides to functional selections. But once a terminal operator becomes experienced, having to navigate "up and down" a hierarchy through menus can become an irritation. The time needed for data transmission to present a menu and receive the operator response becomes a stumbling block. A *direct transfer* software feature provides the means for you to jump directly from one function to another without having to go through a menu. Logic for direct transfer is an interesting advanced subject that I'll show you in Chapter 16.

3.4 Scrolling versus Paging Screens

The formatted screens associated with menu-based systems are similar to the windows of modern microcomputer software packages. Formatted screens follow one another in whole screen images. When you choose a menu selection the interactive system replaces the menu screen with another formatted screen. This form of screen transition is called **paging** and is typical of modern VAX on-line systems. In the VAX environment formatted screens are sometimes referred to as **forms**.

An older, more primitive form of screen management is known as **scrolling**. A scrolled display is like the display of a word processor. It mimics the paper in a typewriter. With a scrolled display the screen is not formatted; you enter new lines at the bottom of the screen. As the end of each new line is reached and you press the **<Return>** key all the information on the screen moves up a line and the top line scrolls off the screen.

Scrolling is associated with unformatted screens and has its origin in the days of mechanical hardware terminal devices. Early interactive mini- and microcomputer software often used scrolling displays but modern business data processing systems do not.

3.5 On-Line System Security

An interactive business data processing application accessed by an end user operates apart from the computer accounts used by programmers. Most interactive applications provide some form of password entry by an operator to protect the interactive system from access by unauthorized parties. Besides confining access to intended personnel, on-line system security may also require the terminal operator to enter an identifier. You can record this identifier in a special nondisplayed field in records added or changed by the operator. This lets you document who added or changed records.

Interactive system security is usually placed at the point of operator entry to the system. This may be in the program that presents and manages the system menu. Security logic may exist in a special program that is invoked even before the menu program is given control.

You can also put security logic and password entry actions into your especially sensitive interactive programs, such as a program that handles deletion of records from a file. I show you how to build a simple security mechanism into an interactive VAX COBOL program in Chapter 14.

3.6 On-Line Help Screens

Until the 1980s people who used an interactive business data processing system ("end users") were usually required to undergo extensive training. Each interactive system was typically documented with a large printed manual describing how to use the system and what its error messages meant.

Modern on-line systems usually provide assistance to the terminal operator within the system itself. General on-line help may provide an illustration of the keyboard layout and key meanings. This primitive form of help may consist of little more than on-line access to a text file containing the system reference manual.

Context sensitive on-line help provides computer terminal operator assistance on the action underway when a help command is entered (or the "help" key is pressed). This is a real benefit to the people who use the interactive system because it gives information about the specific action underway at the time help is requested. With context sensitive on-line help you don't have to search a long time for the specific assistance you need.

Providing on-line help involves placement of help information within a file accessible to the system. Each program must contain logic identifying the action underway as the operator moves through the system.

3.7 Command-Based Interactive Systems

Command-based interactive systems are less common than menu-based interactive systems. Command-based systems do not provide menus. Instead, you must compose and key in a precise character string to directly initiate a processing action—for example:

```
16APR/CF/ORD/LAX
or
16APRCFORDLAX
```

A freight clerk might key this in to obtain information on the flights scheduled for April 16 (16APR) by Consolidated Freight Airlines (CF) between Chicago O'Hare (ORD) and Los Angeles International airport (LAX). The entry would be made on a completely blank screen.

A command-based on-line system sacrifices the legibility and ease of use of menus to gain data transmission efficiency. Command-based systems are faster for experienced operators to use but require that operators receive much more training. On-line systems that must process an especially high volume of transactions, such as airline reservation systems, often use a command-based structure. They may present data in abbreviated, unlabeled format on a scrolled display, or even on a typewriter-style printer.

The interactive programs I have created for this book illustrate menu-based rather than command-based techniques. A command-based interactive system structure employs only a primitive subset of available screen facilities. Menu-based systems are by far the more prevalent in modern business data processing.

3.8 Common User Access (CUA) Standards

In 1987 IBM announced its initial set of comprehensive standards known as Systems Application Architecture or SAA. The goal of these standards is to help make new application systems similar enough in appearance and operation to be transportable between different levels of computers (3090 and ES/9000 mainframes, mid-range AS/400 machines, and microcomputers).

IBM's SAA standards apply only to its own hardware and software products, but many manufacturers such as DEC are expressing interest in following some of the standards or formulating similar standards. One part of SAA standards is *Common User Access*, or *CUA*, which sets the standards for screen geography usage and operation. CUA describes screen operation similar to the Microsoft Windows 3.0, Apple Macintosh and OS/2 environments. CUA suggests standard ways to arrange pull-down menus, movable pop-up windows, a mouse (on-screen pointing device), and standard use of colors.

Implementation of CUA is just beginning. It's not possible yet to predict how readily and to what extent CUA will actually function as a standard. Almost all business data processing software at present does not operate as CUA describes. Neither VAX COBOL nor IBM's CICS teleprocessing monitor inherently provide support for CUA standards. The programs I show you in this book are intended to help you learn how to implement user-friendly, modern on-line programs as a first step. As support for CUA materializes you could adapt these programs to the screen format that might be required to make them "CUA compliant."

3.9 Chapter Summary

An *interactive* application system accesses one or more indexed files or a database, providing a terminal operator with the ability to add, change, see (*inquire* about), and delete records. The most commonly used people-to-terminal interface is *menu-based*. Under this mode of operation you select the action to be performed from a listing (menu) of possible actions. You can represent the menu structure of a system with a hierarchical chart much like an organization chart.

Screens in a menu-based system are usually formatted so that the top is used for identification and titling, the central part is used for data display or entry, and the bottom is used for program communication to the operator in the form of *prompts*. You get to the screen for a function by selecting it from a menu. If the system supports it you can also get to a screen for a function directly from another, without going through a menu, by using a *direct transfer* command.

Menu-based systems use paging screens rather than scrolling displays. *Paging screens* completely replace one another and are sometimes called *forms* in VAX literature. *Scrolling* or *unformatted screens* act like word processor screens. New lines appear at the bottom, lines move upward as the screen is used, and lines eventually scroll off the top of the screen.

Most interactive applications provide some form of *password entry* by an operator to protect the interactive system from access by unauthorized parties. This may be placed at the point of operator entry to the system or may protect some critical functions of the system such as record deletion.

Modern on-line systems usually provide assistance to the terminal operator within the system itself. *General on-line help* may show keyboard layouts and key meanings. *Context sensitive on-line help* provides assistance on the action underway at the time a help command is entered or the help key is pressed.

Command-based systems do not provide menus but instead require you to key in a precise character (command) string to initiate a processing action, such as `16APR/CF/ORD/LAX`. Command-based on-line systems sacrifice ease of use to gain data transmission efficiency. They require more terminal operator training and are less commonly used than menu-based systems.

IBM's *Systems Application Architecture* (*SAA*) provides standards for a screen appearance called *Common User Access*, or *CUA*. At present neither VAX COBOL nor IBM's CICS teleprocessing monitor inherently support CUA standards.

3.10 Important Terms

You can review these terms to check your understanding of this chapter:

Application system   A collection of related programs that support a specific business function.

Business Information System   An application system that serves a purpose such as accounting, payroll, order entry, inventory control, or similar task of a business enterprise.

Command-based on-line system   An interactive system under which you must enter a command to access a function.

Formatted screen display   A computer terminal screen produced with VAX COBOL DISPLAY verb options so that screen fields are labeled and all remain in fixed locations.

Menu-based on-line system   An interactive system that guides a terminal operator to make processing function selections from a list.

Paging   The replacement of a formatted computer screen by another full screen.

Scrolling   New lines of terminal screen output appear at the bottom of the screen and the contents of the screen move upward as each new line is presented.

Prompt   A message from an interactive program to the computer terminal operator.

Transaction   A unit of work to the terminal operator such as the entry of one record, inquiry into one record, or the deletion of a record.

You can find additional questions and exercises for this chapter in Appendix A.

Chapter Four

DESIGNING COMPUTER TERMINAL SCREENS

4.1 Generality of Screen Design Concepts

Despite differences in programming approaches between IBM mainframes and mini- and microcomputers most elements of interactive screen design apply to all environments. Similar factors include screen size, field display characteristics, and field labeling. You need to address nearly identical considerations of data placement and program-to-operator communication regardless of whether you use IBM mainframe, VAX, or microcomputers.

4.2 Screen Size

Computer terminal screen size is measured by the number of lines on a terminal display and the number of characters (columns) on each line. In the early days (pre-1980s) these sizes varied among different types of equipment. A screen size of 24 lines of 80 characters is now the common denominator.

A screen size of 80 × 24 displays 1,920 characters. The screen size of IBM PC microcomputers and compatible equipment is one line larger, providing an 80 × 25 display of 2,000 characters. When you use a microcomputer to emulate VAX or IBM computer terminals the "extra" 25th line is used by your terminal emulator software but not by the VAX or IBM system. Both Digital Equipment Corporation VT family terminals and IBM mainframe terminals may provide a 25th line for terminal status information. If present, this line is formed by the terminal hardware itself, not by the computer system.

You can achieve a screen width of 132 columns on some DEC and IBM terminals. I have oriented all of the examples in this book to an 80 × 24 display size, which is much more common.

4.3 Screen Field Attributes

Standard among all modern lines of computer terminals is the ability to display fields with three different levels of brightness. Normal intensity presents characters at a readable level of brightness. BOLD intensity presents characters brighter so they stand out. NO ECHO in VAX COBOL does not present characters visually at all and is of limited use (it's most helpful for the entry of passwords).

DEC VT-100 and more modern terminals include additional screen attribute capabilities such as reverse video (dark character against its lighted rectangular screen cell), underlined, and blinking. Most terminal emulators for PCs and Macintosh microcomputers also support this wide range of screen handling capabilities.

Designing an on-line screen involves deciding where to place labels and fields and how to use screen field attributes. I follow a common convention of using bold intensity for screen field labels and normal intensity for data entered at the terminal. I brighten data fields that fail to meet validation requirements to better identify them on add or change screens.

4.4 Terminal Screen Design with Paper Grid Form

You can use a paper grid form such as the one in Figure 4.1 to plan the layout of an on-line screen before you program it. This kind of form is labeled with line and column numbers. In VAX COBOL you specify the location of any field on the screen by its line and column location.

Designing a screen is a trial-and-error process. You usually have to pencil sketch a layout, then erase and rewrite parts of it to reposition fields as you work out your final design. Figure 4.1 is an example of a paper-and-pencil design I drew for the screen of the add/change program I show you in Chapter 13. It is a "final" layout. You don't see all of the trials and reworkings I did to finalize the screen.

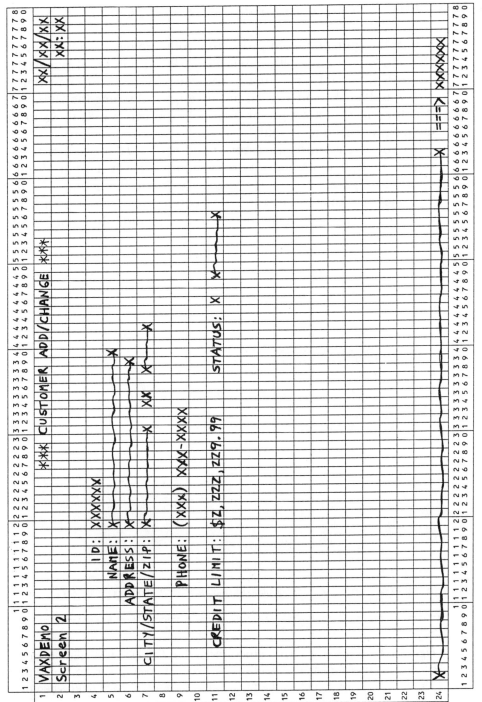

Figure 4.1   You can use a paper grid form like this to plan the layout of an on-line screen before you program it. In VAX COBOL you specify the location of any field on the screen by its line and column location.

4.5 Using a Word Processor to Design Terminal Screens

Screen design using word processing software has become popular as an alternative to design with paper forms. Word processed screen design is more flexible and convenient. You can "try out" different field placements and labels, and you get the advantage of seeing the layout much as it will appear on a computer terminal. You can use Xs or 9s to indicate the length of each data field.

If you use a word processor or the VAX EDT text editor to design a screen, include a manually typed column ruler at the top of the text as shown in Figure 4.2. You can also copy this to the bottom of the layout. This makes it easy to determine the column location of each field when the screen is to be programmed. You can include line numbers on your

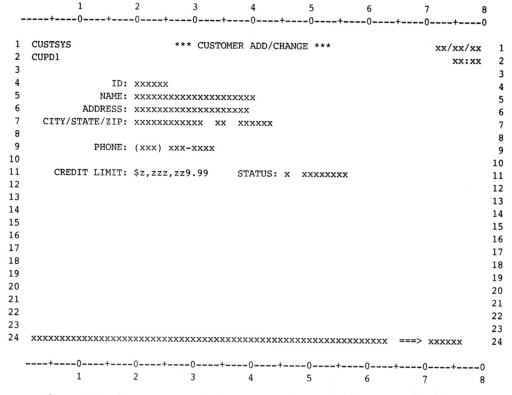

Figure 4.2   If you use a word processor or the VAX EDT text editor to design a screen, include a manually typed column ruler at the top and bottom of the layout. This makes it easy to determine the column location of each field when the screen is to be programmed.

word processed design layout or count the lines manually for programming. A paper print of the screen is as good as a grid form for programming purposes and has the benefit of looking neater as design documentation.

4.6 Screen Painting Software

Screen painting software goes a step beyond screen layout design on a word processor. Screen painters let you work out the layout of a screen and then generate all or most of the code to implement the screen. Screen painting software is an optional product, not a part of VAX COBOL or IBM CICS, and it is not standardized. In the examples in this book, I show you paper grid designs.

4.7 Top of Screen Layout: Keep It Simple!

Response time is defined as the elapsed time between the pressing of the *<Return>* key by the terminal operator and the interactive program's completion of processing. A response time of one second or less is usually quite acceptable. Response time greater than a few seconds becomes irritating and wastes the operator's time.

You have to transmit every character on an on-line screen from the computer to the terminal at least once. Since data transmission takes time, it's important to avoid including ornaments in screen layouts like those you might have used in printed reporting. In particular, don't use borders of asterisks or lines of hyphens to segregate parts of the screen. The transmission of these nonessential characters can unnecessarily slow the response time of an interactive system.

Each installation usually develops a standard for the type of information presented at the top of formatted interactive screens. This often specifies a program or screen identifier at the upper left corner, a descriptive title in the middle top line, and the date and system time at the upper right corner.

4.8 Designing the Data Area of a Terminal Screen

When you design the middle (data) area of a formatted screen you need to put a short label in front of each field to describe it. Allow enough positions following the label to accommodate the size of the field. You should follow a few simple rules in forming screen labels:

- *Arrange fields like whatever paper form is used* to record the information being entered.

- *Avoid abbreviations,* but if they are necessary for spacing reasons abbreviate consistently and without eliminating too many vowels (a,e,i,o,u). For example, "number" should not be abbreviated NUM in one place and NO in another; either of these is more readable than NMBR or NBR.

- *Avoid punctuation* except in messages. Punctuation such as periods after abbreviations introduces visual clutter.

- *Consider displaying dates without slashes*; 101890 is easier to enter correctly than 10/18/90 on screens with many date fields.

- *Align field starting positions vertically* where possible, rather than scattering fields over the screen; this is easier to read.

If no paper form exists—perhaps the information being entered is taken over the telephone from a caller—arrange screen fields in common and ordinary formats. For example, arrange address fields such as name, address, city, state, and zip code as on an envelope.

Figure 4.3   IBM CICS requires that the the cursor move in a left-to-right, top-to-bottom sequence of fields. VAX COBOL does not require this, but it makes screens operate more naturally for terminal operators in English-speaking countries.

Under IBM CICS the information entry point of an interactive screen—the cursor—must move in a left-to-right, top-to-bottom sequence of fields. I have depicted this motion in Figure 4.3. VAX COBOL does not require that the cursor move like this. But you should still follow this convention (at least for screens to be used in English-speaking countries). This cursor motion makes screen operation more natural for terminal operators because it matches the way you read English.

4.9 Designing Your Prompts

The last line on the terminal display is usually reserved for program communication with the terminal operator. A message that gives the terminal operator instructions to enter information is known as a **prompt**. A prompt may contain information about a data field entry error and request its correction. Since the screen is only 80 characters wide your prompts must be brief and concise. Composing the text of each prompt is the job of a systems analyst, although programmers must accomplish this if the content of each prompt is not otherwise specified.

The text of your prompts has to be be businesslike and understandable to the nontechnical people who will use your system. Your prompts should be free of computer jargon. As with any technical writing you should always use words consistently. Two rules help guide you to form good prompts:

- A given word should always have the same meaning.
- A given thing should always be referred to with the same word.

In my examples in this book I always refer to the key pressed to end an action as the **<Return>** key. The operator is instructed to

```
Fill in data and press <Return>
```

when the entry of data is necessary. If an entry is incorrect and must be changed, I send a message such as:

```
Credit limit must be numeric,>1000, correct and <Return>
```

I strongly suggest that you do not include words in your prompts that ridicule or criticize the terminal operator. A message that gives the impression of chastising the terminal operator can easily cause insult, and it makes your interactive system appear unprofessional. (It's also unlikely to hasten the entry of correct information, but it will probably make the terminal operator more critical of any shortcomings in your system.)

4.10 Windows and Pull-Down Menus

Overlaid windows and side-by-side "tiled" windows have been popularized by microcomputer software. Coupled with the use of a mouse as a pointing device, these *graphical user interfaces (GUIs)* have begun to gain acceptance.

Neither VAX COBOL nor IBM CICS provide direct support for windows. Pull-down menus are not as yet commonly associated with COBOL business data processing programming. In this book I give you a straightforward introduction to capable interactive programming using VAX COBOL. But the examples in my VAXDEMO system don't address the complex memory management and library issues involved in supporting a windowing environment.

4.11 Chapter Summary

Considerations such as screen size, field display characteristics, and field labeling apply to screen design in all environments. Computer terminal screen size is measured by the number of lines on a terminal display and the number of characters (columns) on each line. A screen size of 24 lines of 80 characters is now the standard.

Screen attributes describe the way in which a field on a screen is presented. Modern computer terminals let you display fields at normal intensity, bright (BOLD) and dark (NO ECHO). Modern terminals such as the DEC VT-100 also support reverse video, underlined, and blinking screen fields.

When you design an on-line screen you decide where to place fields on it and how to use screen field attributes. To design a screen, you can use a paper grid form, a word processor, or (if available) *screen painting software*. Include a column ruler on your word-processed screen designs to make programming easier.

Response time is important in interactive systems. Design screens to minimize data transmission by eliminating or making sparse use of ornamentation and borders. Include a screen identifier at the upper left corner, a descriptive title in the middle top line, and the date and system time at the upper right corner of each screen. Design the data area (middle) of screens to resemble the paper forms on which the data is printed. Avoid using punctuation and abbreviations if possible; when they are necessary, use abbreviations consistently. Aligning fields so that they start in the same column makes them easier to read.

Reserve the last line on the terminal display for *prompts* from the program to the terminal operator. Make your prompts clear, concise, businesslike, and free of computer jargon. Avoid language that might cause offense.

4.12 Important Terms

You can review these terms to check your understanding of this chapter:

Screen field display attribute   A controlling specification that dictates how a terminal screen field will be presented; three standard choices are normal intensity, BOLD intensity, and NO ECHO, meaning the field is not visible.

Response time   The elapsed time between the instant you press the **<Return>** key and the moment that the intended action occurs on your computer terminal screen.

Screen design grid   A paper layout form having 24 lines of 80 columns each that you use to work out the placement of screen labels, data entry fields, and prompts.

Screen labels   Literal characters on the screen in front of data fields that tell what the content of each field represents.

Screen painter   A software product that allows you to design a screen on a terminal using specified codes to represent intended screen field display attributes. The product generates program code to produce the screen.

You can find additional questions and exercises for this chapter in Appendix A.

Chapter Five

VAX FILE COMMANDS AND THE EDT TEXT EDITOR

With very little acclimation to the VAX environment you can create source code and data files, compile, linkage edit, and run programs. In this chapter I show you how to use VMS commands, DCL (*Digital Command Language*—the interactive job control language of the VMS operating system) and the VAX text editor EDT.

5.1 How to Log On to the VAX

Starting logging on by turning on your terminal (or activating your communication program if you are using a microcomputer). If you need to establish a connection to a VAX with a dial-up via a modem, do this now. Then press the *<Return>* key to gain the attention of the VAX. If your installation uses communication switching equipment tied to several computers you may be prompted to enter the local name of the computer system you wish to access. After you make that entry and press the *<Return>* key the VAX will prompt you to enter an account ID as illustrated in Figure 5.1. (*Note*: I'll refer to the carriage return key as the *<Return>* key as it is labeled on VT family terminals. On microcomputers emulating a terminal you will see this key labeled as the *<Enter>* key. Regard *<Return>* and *<Enter>* as the same in this book.)

After entering your account ID the VAX will request that you enter your password. This will not be visible on the screen. When you reach the dollar sign prompt, the VAX awaits your command.

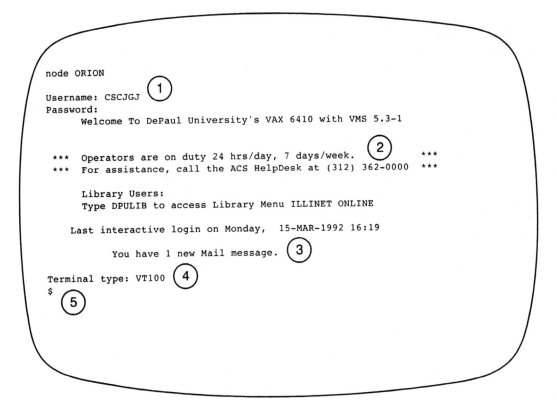

```
node ORION

Username: CSCJGJ   (1)
Password:
        Welcome To DePaul University's VAX 6410 with VMS 5.3-1


  ***   Operators are on duty 24 hrs/day, 7 days/week.  (2)    ***
  ***   For assistance, call the ACS HelpDesk at (312) 362-0000  ***

        Library Users:
        Type DPULIB to access Library Menu ILLINET ONLINE

     Last interactive login on Monday,  15-MAR-1992 16:19

           You have 1 new Mail message.  (3)

Terminal type: VT100  (4)
  $  (5)
```

Figure 5.1   (1) To log on to the VAX you enter your assigned username and password. (2) You may receive broadcast messages and (3) notification of mail messages awaiting. (4) The VAX automatically interrogates your terminal to see if it is a member of the VT terminal family. (5) You are "on" the system when you reach the dollar sign prompt.

5.2 Logging Off

To log off enter logout or its abbreviation lo at the dollar sign prompt (note that VMS makes no distinction between uppercase and lower case letters):

$ logout *<Return>*

or

$ LO *<Return>*

5.3 Changing Your Password

You should change your assigned password the first time you log on. The password is entirely under your control. By changing it to something only you know, you prevent anyone else from logging onto your account and tampering with your files. To change your password enter the command:

    $ set password <Return>

In response the VAX will ask that you enter your current password and press <Return>. The password will not appear on the screen. You will then be asked to enter a new password and to repeat the entry of the new password to confirm it. The new password will then replace your old password. You must remember your new password and use it the next time you log on. There is no way anyone else can determine your password once it is accepted by the VAX, so don't forget what you made it!

Digital Command Language is not case sensitive. You can mix upper- and lowercase letters in your password, in DCL commands, and in filenames.

From this point on I won't clutter my examples with the <Return> symbol after VMS system commands. Just remember that you press <Return> after entering a command to send it to VMS.

5.4 Files on the VAX

Characters (bytes) are grouped into fields, fields are grouped into records, and records are housed physically in files. You can name files with one to nine letters or numbers, a period, and a suffix of up to three letters or numbers in this format:

    CALC1.COB
    JIMUPDATE.COB
    CALC1.OBJ
    CALC1.EXE

You can see the contents of any file by using the DCL command TYPE:

    $ TYPE CALC1.COB   *Lists contents of file on screen*

According to VAX naming conventions the suffix of the filename identifies the type of information in the file:

COB   COBOL source code.

OBJ   An object file created by the COBOL compiler.

EXE   An executable "load module" created by linkage editing.

LIS   A file of printlines containing the COBOL compiler's listing of the source code and any error messages.

DAT   Files containing data.

You can list the names of all your files with the DIR command at the dollar sign prompt. When I entered this command it produced the list shown in Figure 5.2.

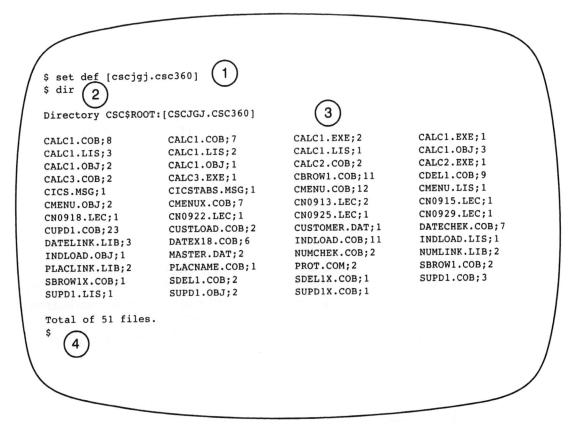

```
$ set def [cscjgj.csc360]   ①
$ dir   ②

Directory CSC$ROOT:[CSCJGJ.CSC360]     ③

CALC1.COB;8         CALC1.COB;7         CALC1.EXE;2         CALC1.EXE;1
CALC1.LIS;3         CALC1.LIS;2         CALC1.LIS;1         CALC1.OBJ;3
CALC1.OBJ;2         CALC1.OBJ;1         CALC2.COB;2         CALC2.EXE;1
CALC3.COB;2         CALC3.EXE;1         CBROW1.COB;11       CDEL1.COB;9
CICS.MSG;1          CICSTABS.MSG;1      CMENU.COB;12        CMENU.LIS;1
CMENU.OBJ;2         CMENUX.COB;7        CN0913.LEC;2        CN0915.LEC;1
CN0918.LEC;1        CN0922.LEC;1        CN0925.LEC;1        CN0929.LEC;1
CUPD1.COB;23        CUSTLOAD.COB;2      CUSTOMER.DAT;1      DATECHEK.COB;7
DATELINK.LIB;3      DATEX18.COB;6       INDLOAD.COB;11      INDLOAD.LIS;1
INDLOAD.OBJ;1       MASTER.DAT;2        NUMCHEK.COB;2       NUMLINK.LIB;2
PLACLINK.LIB;2      PLACNAME.COB;1      PROT.COM;2          SBROW1.COB;2
SBROW1X.COB;1       SDEL1.COB;2         SDEL1X.COB;1        SUPD1.COB;3
SUPD1.LIS;1         SUPD1.OBJ;2         SUPD1X.COB;1

Total of 51 files.

$   ④
```

Figure 5.2   (1) The SET DEF command sets your default subdirectory. (2) You can list the names of all your files with the DIR command at the dollar sign prompt. (3) All the file names in your current default directory are listed. (4) You return to the dollar sign prompt when DIR finishes.

You can enter parameters after the DIR command to request not only filenames but space usage (in 512 byte blocks) and last update time and date:

```
$ DIR/size/date
```

Files of all types exist separately on the VAX. (This is different from an IBM mainframe under MVS, which uses "partitioned data sets" for libraries. The mainframe equivalent of an .EXE file is a "load module" that must exist as a member of a partitioned data set.)

5.5 Subdirectories and File Security

VMS supports subdirectories. You can create a subdirectory with the CREATE/DIRECTORY command:

```
$ CREATE/DIRECTORY [CSCJGJ.CSC360]
```

In this example I logged on as CSCJGJ, which puts me into my root directory [CSCJGJ]. I used the CREATE/DIRECTORY command to create a subdirectory named [CSCJGJ.CSC360]. When I do a directory listing of [CSCJGJ] I will see CSC360.DIR shown as a file.

To go into a subdirectory you set your default directory to that subdirectory with the SET DEF command:

```
$ SET DEF [CSCJGJ.CSC360]
```

From this point on (until I change the default directory again) I will be "positioned" in the subdirectory. Subdirectories can be housed within subdirectories to as great a depth as you wish. You can use subdirectories to segregate files for different projects. I use [CSCJGJ.CSC360] at DePaul University to house all of the files associated with our undergraduate course CSC360, "On-Line System Concepts."

The full name of a file includes the root and subdirectory it is in and the filename, stated in this form with no spaces within it:

```
[CSCJGJ.CSC360]CALC1.COB
```

Once it is created and populated with files you can't delete a subdirectory until you delete all of the files in it. Then, to remove the subdirectory, you have to set its protection level to allow deletion. Do this in the next high level directory (the directory in which the subdirectory exists):

```
$ SET DEF [CSCJGJ]
$ SET PROT=(o:d) CSC360.DIR
```

```
$ DELETE CSC360.DIR;*
```

The SET PROT command alters security so that you as the "*owner*" have delete authorization for the subdirectory.

VMS "sees" four kinds of users of the computer system: *system*, *group*, *owner*, and *world*. You are the owner of your files; generally speaking others cannot access your files unless you let them. Four access privileges exist: read, write, execute, and delete. As owner you have maximum access to your files, but as a measure of protection VMS does not give even the owner automatic delete authority on subdirectories. That's why you have to use the SET PROT command to gain this authority when you want to delete a subdirectory. Here is the command to give all other users (the "*world*") the authority to read my file named CALC1.COB:

```
$ SET PROT=(w:r) CALC1.COB
```

You can see the file security applied to files with the DIR command using the /prot parameter:

```
$ DIR/prot
```

5.6 Copying, Renaming, and Appending Files

You can copy a file from one file name using COPY:

```
$ COPY CALC1.COB WHOPPER.COB
```

This copies CALC1.COB to create a new file named WHOPPER.COB. CALC1.COB is not changed. I can copy a file from directory [CSCJGJ] to subdirectory [CSCJGJ.CSC360]:

```
$ COPY [CSCJGJ]CALC1.COB  [CSCJGJ.CSC360]CALC1.COB
```

You can also rename a file:

```
$ RENAME CALC1.COB  MONGO.COB
```

Here I have changed the name of CALC1.COB to MONGO.COB. The contents of the file have not changed, but CALC1.COB does not exist after this action.

If you use the **APPEND** command you can copy one file to the "back" of another. For example:

```
$ APPEND FOES.DAT  FRIENDS.DAT
```

Here FOES.DAT has not been changed but a copy of it has been put immediately after the last record in FRIENDS.DAT. Now FRIENDS.DAT is larger.

5.7 File Version Number

Every file carries a semihidden number as a part of its name called the version number. The version number appears after a semicolon following the name:

```
CALC1.COB;3
```

When you copy to a filename or edit and save a file, a new file is created with the next higher version number for that name. The older versions of the file remain on the system until you delete them. (If your background is in the IBM mainframe environment you can think of this as if a generation data group were established for every filename you create.)

When you refer to a file by just its common name, such as CALC1.COB, VMS automatically accesses the file of this name with the highest version number. You can access files with a version number lower than the current (highest) one by specifying the version number as a part of the name:

```
$ TYPE CALC1.COB;2    Lists contents of file on screen
```

5.8 Using PURGE to Delete Old Versions of Files

If you want to delete all the older versions of a file leaving only the most recent version on the system use the PURGE command:

```
$ PURGE CALC1.COB    Deletes old versions of CALC1.COB
```

If you use the PURGE command without a filename all of the older versions of all files will be eliminated:

```
$ PURGE    General purge command
```

5.9 Checking Your Space Allocation

When your account was created on the VAX a space limit was established for you. You can check on how much space your files are taking up and the amount of additional space available to you with the SHOw QUOta command:

```
$ SHO QUO        Tells how much disk space you can use
```

Figure 5.3 was produced when I used the SHO QUO command. If you are

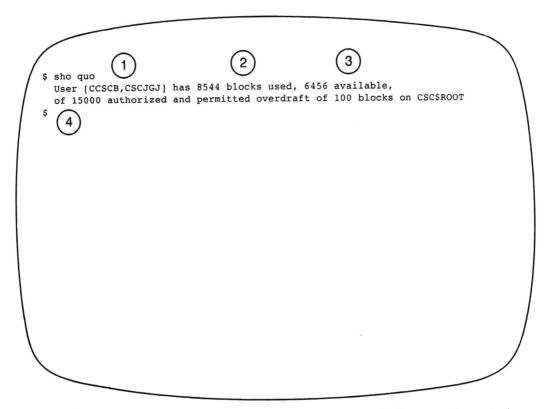

Figure 5.3   (1) The SHO QUO ("show quota") command tells you (2) how much disk space your files now occupy and (3) how much additional space you are permitted to use. (4) You return to the dollar sign prompt when SHO QUO finishes.

close to running out of space, delete any files you no longer need and issue the general PURGE command to delete obsolete versions of files that you wish to keep. VMS automatically reclaims space from deleted files. (There is no programmer library "reorganization" or "compress" function as on an IBM mainframe under MVS.)

5.10 Deleting Files with the DELETE Command

To delete all versions of a file you have to specify the *wildcard symbol* ✶ as the version number with DELETE:

    $ **DELETE** CALC1.COB;✶   *Deletes all versions of file*

You can use the wildcard character in other commands too, to selectively process some of your files:

```
$ DIR *.COB   Lists names of all .COB files
$ DELETE CALC1.*;*   Deletes all CALC1 files
```

5.11 VMS Control Keys

If you hold down the **<Ctrl>** key and press one of these letter keys you send a special control (command) value to the VAX:

<Ctrl/S>   Stops sending characters to the screen.

<Ctrl/Q>   Restarts sending characters (reverse of **<Ctrl/S>**).

<Ctrl/I>   Tab (you can use this instead of the **<Tab>** key).

<Ctrl/C>   Cancels a program now being executed.

<Ctrl/Y>   Interrupts processing and returns control to the VMS.

Pressing **<Ctrl/S>** is handy if you used the TYPE command to show the contents of a file on the screen and the screen is scrolling too fast to see it. **<Ctrl/S>** stops the screen. Pressing **<Ctrl/Q>** starts the screen again.

5.12 Starting EDT Text Editing

The EDT text editor is a part of the VAX environment. You can think of EDT as a moderately capable word processor useful for preparing source code. You start EDT by entering EDT and the name of a file:

```
$ EDT CALC1.COB <Return>
```

Once you start EDT the cursor changes to the EDT prompt, the asterisk *. When the file you have indicated you want to edit is a new one, with no content, EDT presents the message illustrated in Figure 5.4. If the file has one or more lines in it already EDT lists the first line as shown in Figure 5.5.

5.13 EDT Line Editing and Keypad Modes

You can use EDT in two different modes of operation. One mode is called *line editing;* the other is called *keypad* or *full screen* mode.

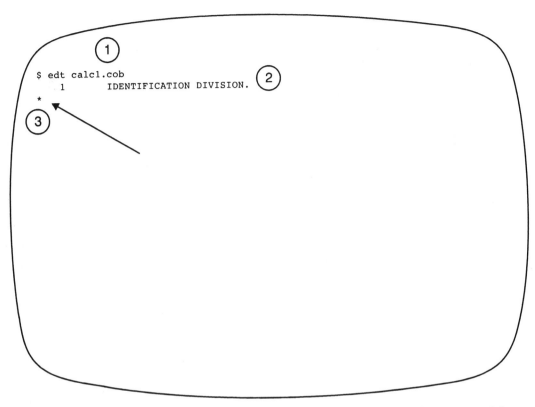

Figure 5.4   (1) You start the EDT text editor by entering EDT *filename.* (2) *If the file already exists, EDT lists the first line.* (3) The asterisk is the EDT prompt.

Line editing is the most primitive editing mode. You can use this with any type of terminal, even a hardcopy printing terminal. In line editing mode you do not have full screen access to the contents of a file. Instead, you issue commands to work with one or a group of lines at a time. Line editing is not very handy, but you may be limited to it if you use a terminal that does not provide VT terminal features.

The more capable keypad mode of EDT operation provides access to a file a full screen at a time using the screen as a "moving window" into the file. Keypad mode allows you to use the arrow keys and numeric keypad keys to move the cursor around the screen, insert characters into the middle of lines, delete lines, and scroll the screen forward and backward in the file. You can use keypad mode only on DEC VT family terminals or a microcomputer emulating a VT-100. For keypad mode to be practical you also need a connection to the VAX running at least as fast as 1200 bps.

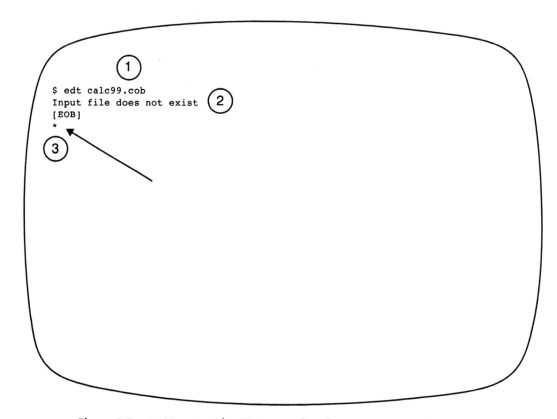

```
    (1)
$ edt calc99.cob
Input file does not exist  (2)
[EOB]
*
  (3)
```

Figure 5.5   (1) You start the EDT text editor by entering EDT *filename.* (2) *If the file does not exist, EDT tells you;* [EOB] *means "end of block."* (3) The asterisk is the EDT prompt.

You will most likely use EDT in keypad mode, so I describe that for you here. If you would like to explore EDT line editing mode skip ahead to topic 5.19 at the end of this chapter.

5.14 Starting EDT Full Screen Keypad Mode

EDT begins operation in line editing mode. Figures 5.4 and 5.5 illustrate how your screen will look when EDT starts running. To use keypad mode enter the letter C at the asterisk prompt and press *<Return>*:

    C <Return>

You will branch into keypad mode. To return to line editing mode from keypad mode at any time press *<Ctrl/Z>*.

5.15 Editing in Keypad Mode

Once you have begun keypad mode with the C command at the asterisk prompt, EDT clears the screen. If the file is empty only [EOB], for "end of block," will show on the screen. Put the cursor before this and start entering characters. If the file already contains source code, its first 22 lines will appear as in Figure 5.6. You can move the cursor to any location using the *<Arrow>* keys and insert characters.

Figure 5.6 shows you a special format for COBOL source code called *terminal format.* VAX COBOL does not require you to enter any COBOL line numbers. The first column you enter is treated as either column 7 or 8 on the COBOL statement depending on whether it is a * comment or a compilable statement. Source code you enter in terminal format is

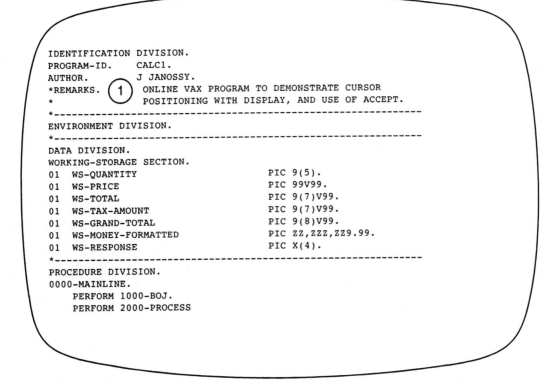

```
IDENTIFICATION DIVISION.
PROGRAM-ID.      CALC1.
AUTHOR.          J JANOSSY.
*REMARKS.    (1)      ONLINE VAX PROGRAM TO DEMONSTRATE CURSOR
*                     POSITIONING WITH DISPLAY, AND USE OF ACCEPT.
*-----------------------------------------------------------------
ENVIRONMENT DIVISION.
*-----------------------------------------------------------------
DATA DIVISION.
WORKING-STORAGE SECTION.
01   WS-QUANTITY              PIC 9(5).
01   WS-PRICE                 PIC 99V99.
01   WS-TOTAL                 PIC 9(7)V99.
01   WS-TAX-AMOUNT            PIC 9(7)V99.
01   WS-GRAND-TOTAL           PIC 9(8)V99.
01   WS-MONEY-FORMATTED       PIC ZZ,ZZZ,ZZ9.99.
01   WS-RESPONSE              PIC X(4).
*-----------------------------------------------------------------
PROCEDURE DIVISION.
0000-MAINLINE.
     PERFORM 1000-BOJ.
     PERFORM 2000-PROCESS
```

Figure 5.6   When you enter C at the EDT asterisk prompt, you enter "keypad" (full screen) mode. This screen shows you what VAX terminal format looks like for COBOL source code. You don't enter line numbers. (1)The first column is interpreted as column 7 if it is a comment or column 8 if it's not a comment.

adjusted in column placement by the compiler when it is listed in .LIS file output. (If you obtain the source code for the programs in this book on diskette as described in Appendix E you will find that they are in VAX terminal format.)

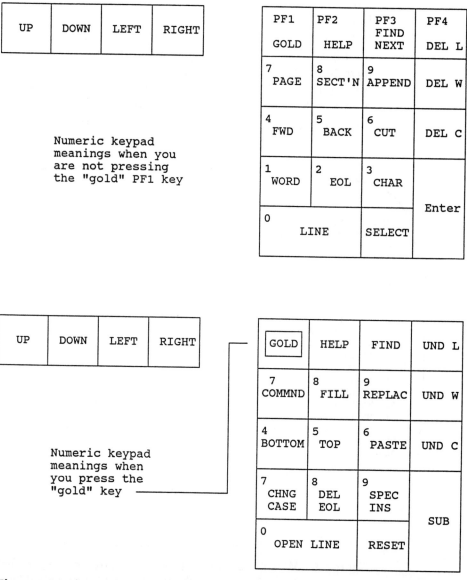

Figure 5.7 The numeric keypad keys on a VT-100 terminal perform special editing functions when you are in EDT "keypad" mode. PF1 is not really colored gold. It acts like a shift key to change the meaning of other numeric keypad keys.

In keypad mode the *<Backspace>* key moves the cursor to the beginning of each line and the *<Delete>* key deletes one character at a time left of the cursor. EDT is always in "pushright" mode. There is no overstrike mode in EDT. Letters, numbers, and punctuation that you enter always cause new characters to be inserted and push the line of text to the right.

In keypad editing mode, the keys on the numeric keypad on VT-100 terminals are transformed into edit function keys, most of which have two functions. Figure 5.7 shows you the functions of the numeric keypad keys on VT-100 terminals. You access the primary function of a key when you press it by itself. If you press the key while you are holding down the "gold" key (usually labeled PF1) you get the alternate function of the key. (The PF1 key is not really colored gold. This is old terminology that has come to resemble a DEC inside joke, just as is the less common reference to PF1 as the "blue" key.)

You access the handiest of the keypad keys without pressing the "gold" PF1 key:

Number	Meaning	What it does
7	PAGE	Moves forward or backward one screen
8	SECTION	Moves forward or backward to the next page eject character
4	FWD	Changes movement direction to forward
5	BACK	Changes movement direction to backward
1	WORD	Moves cursor forward or backward one word
2	EOL	Moves cursor to the end of the line

But on a microcomputer emulating a VT-100 your numeric keypad may not have these same meanings! Your emulator may provide a key redefinition capability to assign key meanings matching those on VT family terminals.

Quite frankly, once you go beyond the handy keypad keys I've listed you'll face a much longer learning curve in becoming comfortable with EDT. If you want to go beyond those editing keys you can use the following list of key meanings, which also refer to the labels on the keys shown in Figure 5.7. I have grouped these into functional categories (something, unfortunately, that most manuals don't do!):

Cursor movement:

CHAR   Moves the cursor one character at a time in the current cursor movement direction.

TOP   Moves the cursor to the beginning of the file.

BOTTOM   Moves the cursor to the end of the file.

Search and replace:

FIND   Allows entry of a character string that will be searched for in the file. After you enter the character string you use the FWD or BACK key to search in either direction from the cursor position.

REPLAC   Replaces the text in the SELECT range with the material in the paste buffer (you put things in the paste buffer with the SELECT key).

FINDNEXT   Repeats the previous FIND action.

SUB   With the cursor positioned at a character string located with a FINDNEXT function, SUB performs two actions: it issues a REPLAC, and then a FINDNEXT.

Cut and paste (block move or copy):

SELECT   Marks the start of a portion of text to perform a special operation. You can then move the cursor to the end of the part of the text to be processed and press the APPEND, CHNGCASE, CUT, FILL, or REPLAC keys. The RESET key eliminates the "block marking" caused by SELECT.

CUT   Deletes the text in the SELECTed range and stores the text in a "paste" buffer, replacing any text already stored in this buffer.

PASTE   Inserts the contents of the paste buffer into the file at the point where the cursor is located.

APPEND   Deletes the SELECT range and stores the text at the end of the paste buffer.

FILL   Reformats the text lines in the SELECT range.

Deletion of text:

DEL EOL   Deletes the remainder of the line on which the cursor is positioned up to the line terminator character **<Return>** and places these characters into the "line" buffer.

DEL C   Deletes the character at which the cursor is positioned and puts it in the "character" buffer.

DEL L   Deletes the remainder of the line on which the cursor is positioned up to and through the line terminator character and places these characters into the line buffer.

DEL W   Deletes the next word and stores the characters in the "word" buffer.

Undelete:

UND C   Inserts a character from the character buffer into the file at the cursor position.

UND L   Inserts the material in the line buffer into the file at the cursor position.

UND W   Inserts the material in the word buffer into the file at the cursor position.

Miscellaneous:

CHNGCASE   Changes the case of the text within the SELECT range; makes capital letters lowercase and vice versa.

SPECINS   SPECial INSert allows entry of the ASCII decimal equivalent of a nonprinting character for placement into text. You position the cursor, press the "gold" key and SPECINS and enter the decimal value.

5.16 Ending Your Keypad Editing Session

To end keypad editing mode enter *<Ctrl/Z>* with the cursor positioned at any point in the screen display. EDT will drop out of full screen mode and revert to line editing mode. You will see the asterisk prompt at the bottom of the screen. Then enter the word EXIT and press *<Return>*. This automatically saves the next higher version number of the file to disk for you and returns you to the dollar sign prompt.

You can leave your editing session by entering QUIT at the asterisk prompt instead of EXIT. QUIT ends the editing session without saving the file to disk. If you end with QUIT, none of the work you did during the editing session will be saved.

5.17 Recovering from an Interruption to EDT

As EDT operates it automatically builds a file with the suffix .JOU as a "journal" of your editing actions. If your editing session is interrupted, EDT can recover almost all of your work if you start the next edit session of the file properly. If you do not start the next session with recovery in mind, you lose the .JOU file and the ability to recover!

If you're interrupted in an EDT editing session (for example, if you accidentally press the terminal *<Break>* key, shut off your terminal, or your dial-up telephone line connection is disrupted) log on again and do a $ DIR *.JOU listing. If you see a file of the same name as the one you were editing with a suffix of .JOU, start an EDT edit of the file using this command:

$ EDT/RECOVER name.suf *<Return>*

where name.suf is your file name. The /RECOVER option tells EDT to apply the journal of changes in the name.JOU file. You will see the screen animate as all of your editing keystrokes are rapidly "played back" to affect the file.

5.18 Documentation and On-Line Help

VMS provides extensive on-line help facilities you can access by stating the word HELP at the dollar sign prompt:

$ HELP *<Return>*

VMS gives you instructions and topic listings to let you narrow your search for help to a specific area. You can also get help in the same way at the asterisk prompt while you are in an EDT editing session.

5.19 EDT Line Editing Mode

Most people prefer to use EDT full screen keypad mode for editing since it resembles a word processor. But line editing mode can be productive

and rapid for dial-up work since it minimizes the amount of data transmitted. If you are limited to a modem speed of 1200 bps or less, you may
find line edit mode more productive than full screen keypad mode.

5.19.1 STARTING LINE EDITING MODE

To use line editing mode, get into EDT as usual by entering EDT and a
file name at the system prompt (the file does not have to exist before you
do this):

```
$ EDT little1.cob
```

Then to start entering lines into a new file specify the "insert" command
(abbreviated I) at the EDT asterisk prompt (see below).

5.19.2 STARTING TEXT ENTRY ("INSERT")

To start entering text into a new file, enter the "insert" command at the
asterisk prompt:

```
*I
```

EDT will indent the cursor. Keys you enter at this time will be captured
and made a part of the file:

```
$ edt little1.cob
Input file does not exist
[EOB]
*I
            IDENTIFICATION DIVISION.
            PROGRAM-ID.  LITTLE1.
            *AUTHOR.    J JANOSSY.
            *INSTALLATION. DEPAUL UNIVERSITY.
            *REMARKS.
                  -
                  -
                  -
```

Lines of COBOL source code on a VAX can be as long as 255 bytes. If you
enter a line longer than 68 characters EDT will wrap the cursor around to

```
$ edt alice.dat
Input file does not exist
[EOB]
*i
            0123456789
            The time has come,
            the walrus said,
            to talk of many things.
            Sailing ships, and
            sealing wax, and
            cabbages and kings.
            ^z
[EOB]

*t w
     1      0123456789
     2      The time has come,
     3      the walrus said,
     4      to talk of many things.
     5      Sailing ships, and
     6      sealing wax, and
     7      cabbages and kings.
[EOB]
*
```

```
Line numbers are
shown by EDT on
the screen only
when you use the
TYPE or T command.
W means "whole."
```

Figure 5.8   Line insertion (shown here in EDT line editing mode, not keypad mode) does not assign line numbers. EDT supplies line numbers when you list the lines in a file with the TYPE WHOLE (T W) command. The line numbers on the screen are not a part of the file.

the next line automatically. This does not actually break the line in two, it's just the way that EDT presents lines on the screen. When you have completed entering the line, press **<Return>**. This denotes the end of a line.

Line insertion does not assign line numbers. EDT supplies line numbers when you list the lines in a file as shown in Figure 5.8. The line numbers are not a part of the file.

When you do line insertion **<Backspace>** moves the cursor to the front of the line. To move to the right you can use the **<Right arrow>** up to the end of a line. Both **<Left arrow>** and **<Delete>** keys move the cursor leftward, deleting one character at a time. **<Up arrow>** and **<Down arrow>** keys don't work in line editing mode.

To end entry into a file press **<Ctrl/Z>** which will return you to the asterisk prompt.

5.19.3 LISTING A FILE IN LINE EDIT MODE

To see what you have already entered into a file use the line edit mode "type" command at the asterisk prompt as illustrated in Figure 5.8:

*TYPE WHOLE   "Type" or list the whole file to the screen. Suspend the scrolling with the combination of keys **<Ctrl/S>**, resume it with **<Ctrl/Q>**, end it with **<Ctrl/C>**.

*T W   Same as above; T and W are acceptable abbreviations for the full commands.

*T 12   Type EDT line number 12.

*T 8:45   Type EDT line numbers 8 through 45.

*T .   Type the line on which EDT is now positioned. You can also see this line by just pressing **<Return>** at the asterisk prompt.

*T E-5:E   Type the last five lines of the file; the E-5 is an arithmetic expression and you can use any number in place of 5. The expression after the colon can also be arithmetic. E indicates the end of file.

*T ALL "abc"   Display all lines with "abc" in them; "abc" can be a character string of any length. Only the lines containing the exact character string will be presented. (This *is* case sensitive.)

5.19.4 RESUMING TEXT ENTRY

To begin entering text again at the end of an existing file start the line insertion process with:

*I E

To begin insertion of more text at a point within the file enter:

*I nn

where nn is the EDT number of a line *before* which you want to insert more lines. For example,

*I 8

indicates you wish to begin the entry of lines *before* line 8. The new lines will go into the file between existing lines 7 and 8, and will carry assigned line numbers such as 7.1, 7.2, and so forth, with decimal point values to distinguish them.

5.19.5 RESEQUENCING LINE NUMBERS

EDT automatically applies nonimbedded line numbers so you can reference lines in EDT commands. Your insertions create line numbers that are more complex to reference because they carry decimal portions. You can renumber or "resequence" line numbers at the asterisk prompt by entering the command:

*RES

This applies new EDT line numbers to all lines, giving the first line the number 1 and each line following the next higher integer line number. Line numbers are not stored in the file but are generated and presented each time EDT is used to edit the file. Even if you do not resequence during your edit, the file will appear with fresh line numbers in your next edit session.

5.19.6 LINE EDIT TEXT DELETION

You can delete individual lines in a file using the "delete" or D command. Several variations are possible:

*D 5   Deletes line number 5.

*D 9:14   Deletes lines 9 through 14.

*D 5:E   Deletes lines 5 through the end of file.

*D W   Deletes the whole file content, making it empty, but does not delete the filename.

5.19.7 EDITING AND MODIFYING TEXT IN LINE EDIT MODE

To correct a line you can either delete and replace the line or make a change to a character string within the existing line. "Delete/replace" is simpler to learn but involves more key entry:

*R 17   Delete line 17 and begin inserting one or more lines here. This places EDT into line insertion mode at the point of the deletion. End insertion with *<Ctrl/Z>*.

To modify a line in a file rather than deleting and replacing it use the "substitute" command, abbreviated S:

    *S/abcd/efgh/17

This substitutes the character string efgh for the existing character string abcd in line 17 only. EDT automatically shows the change in the affected line. You can type the line with the command T 17 to confirm it.

You don't have to specify the line number to be affected by a substitution. Instead, you can position EDT to the beginning of the file using the "find" or F command and specifying line 1. The substitution command can then be issued specifying WHOLE:

    *F 1
    *S/abcd/efgh/WHOLE

This causes a search of the whole file; all occurrences of the abcd character string are replaced with the efgh string. To perform the string substitution over just a range of lines specify the line number range in the last part of the command. Here is how to replace abcd with efgh on lines 23 through 35 only:

    *S/abcd/efgh/23:35

5.19.8 FINDING A CHARACTER STRING IN LINE EDIT MODE

You can easily search a file for the occurrence of a character string and display the lines on which it is found. To make a complete search of the file, first position to its beginning with a find for line 1:

    *F 1

Then find and display the desired line:

*F "abcedf"   Find the first occurrence of "abcedf" in the file and display the line.

*F ""   Find the next occurrence of the specified string (no space between the two quotation marks).

5.19.9 LINE EDIT MOVE AND COPY

You can move one or more lines of text or copy one or more lines of text from one location to another in a file:

```
*COPY 1:8 TO END   Copies lines 1 through 8 to the end of the file.
*COPY 12:25 TO 67   Copies lines 12 through 25 to a position
```
immediately before line 67.

The MOVE command is a COPY automatically combined with "delete." This command:

```
*MOVE 3:8 TO END
```

accomplishes the same thing as these two commands:

```
*COPY 3:8 TO END
*D 3:8
```

5.19.10 ENDING TEXT ENTRY AND SAVING THE FILE

Enter <*Ctrl/Z*> while in "insert" to escape from the insert process. This returns you to the asterisk prompt. When you are at the asterisk * prompt enter EXIT <*Return*> and the file will automatically be saved. Ending with the word QUIT will not save the file.

5.20 Printing Material

Each installation can tailor the command file it provides to allow you to send files to a printer. Most often this command is the word PRINT, which can usually be abbreviated PR:

```
$ PR CALC1.LIS
```

If your installation requires additional parameters, such as print destination and bin number for this command, the command will usually prompt you for their entry.

5.21 Setting Your Terminal to 132 Character Width

It's handy to see more than 80 characters per line on a screen when viewing print output. If your terminal supports it you can set it to display 132 characters per line (VT-100s support this). In DCL you do it this way:

```
$ set term/width=132
```

You can set the terminal back to 80 character display with a similar command using 80 instead of 132.

In EDT you set the terminal to display 132 characters per line with:

```
*set screen 132
```

A similar EDT command involving the number 80 will return the screen to 80 character display.

5.22 Chapter Summary

Digital Command Language (*DCL*) is the interactive job control language of the VAX VMS operating system. You use it after logging on to the system to communicate commands to VMS. Its prompt is the dollar sign $.

Filenames, such as CALC1.COB, under VMS consist of one to nine letters or numbers, a period, and a suffix of up to three letters or numbers. Common filename suffixes are .COB, .OBJ, .EXE, .LIS, and .DAT. VMS automatically maintains a file version number as the third part of the filename: CALC1.COB;3 is a full filename. You gain access to the highest file version number when you don't specify version in the name. The $ PURGE command deletes obsolete file versions. VMS commands let you:

- Change your password (SET PASSWORD).
- See the contents of a file (TYPE).
- List all your filenames (DIR).
- Create subdirectories (CREATE/DIRECTORY).
- Change file security [SET PROT=(w:r)].
- Copy files (COPY).
- Rename files (RENAME).
- Append files to one another (APPEND).
- Check space allocation (SHO QUO).
- Delete files (DELETE).
- Print a file (usually PR).

Certain combinations of keys let you control VMS in these ways:

<Ctrl/S>   Stops sending characters to the screen.

<Ctrl/Q>   Restarts sending characters (reverse of *<CTRL/S>*).

<*Ctrl/C*>   Cancels a program now being executed.

<*Ctrl/Y*>   Interrupts current process and returns control to VMS.

EDT is the text editor provided with the VAX. EDT has two modes of operation: *line editing* and *keypad* or *full screen editing*. To use keypad mode you have to be using or emulating a VT family terminal such as the VT-100. When you are in EDT the prompt changes to the asterisk *. Using EDT in keypad mode involves these types of commands:

$ **EDT** CALC1.COB **<*Return*>**   Start editing session.

*C **<*Return*>**   Get into keypad (full screen mode).

<*Arrows*>   Cursor movement.

<*Ctrl/Z*>   End keypad mode.

*EXIT   End edit, saving file.

*QUIT   End edit without saving.

Line editing mode offers a full range of text insertion, deletion, replacement, searching ("find"), changing, moving, and copying. You may find it more convenient than keypad mode if you use a 1200 bps or slower modem since line editing mode minimizes data transmission. This chapter provides a concise reference for you on both EDT keypad and line editing modes as topics 5.12 through 5.19.

EDT automatically records your keystrokes in a *journal file* named with the suffix .JOU. If you are interrupted when using EDT you may be able to recover most of your work by starting the next EDT edit of the file with the command $ EDT/RECOVER.

Both VMS and EDT offer *on-line help*. To access it you just enter the word HELP at either the $ or * prompt.

5.23 Important Terms

You can review these terms to check your understanding of this chapter:

VMS   The operating system of the VAX.

DCL   Digital Command Language, consisting of interactive VMS commands that let you list filenames and file contents, copy, rename, delete and otherwise manipulate your files.

Control keys   Combinations of keys such as *<Ctrl/S>* that you enter by holding down the *<Ctrl>* key and pressing the letter indicated, such as *<S>*. Control keys communicate requests for special services to VMS.

File   A collection of records.

File version   A number at the end of a filename managed by VMS. Every time a file is created under a given name a new file with a version number one higher is created. Older file versions are kept. You must use the $ PURGE command to eliminate obsolete file versions.

Subdirectory   A new directory capable of housing files, created within an existing directory.

EDT   VAX system text editor, which provides keypad (full screen) mode as well as more primitive line editing mode; your means of creating files of source code and data on the VAX.

Keypad mode   The full screen mode of the EDT text editor, which requires that you use or emulate a VT terminal.

"Gold" key   The PF1 key on a VT terminal in EDT keypad mode.

Line editing mode   A primitive mode of EDT text editor operation that lets you insert lines in a file one by one and change or delete them with brief commands. This mode of EDT can be accessed by any video or hardcopy terminal.

You can find additional questions and exercises for this chapter in Appendix A.

Chapter Six

COMPILING, LINKAGE EDITING, AND RUNNING ON THE VAX

To process your source code into an executable "image" (machine language) on the VAX you need to compile it, then linkage edit the result of the compile. Then you can execute the machine language representation of the program with the RUN command. I have sketched out these steps in Figure 6.1.

6.1 VAX COBOL Terminal Format

VAX COBOL accepts source code in a special format designed to make it easier to code. You can prepare programs in this "terminal"format directly on the VAX using the EDT text editor as I described in Chapter 5. You can also prepare source code on a microcomputer in this format in an ASCII file and then upload it to your VAX for compilation.

Figure 6.2 shows you how terminal format looks on the screen. You don't need to provide COBOL line numbers in the first six positions of each line. The first column you enter is treated as either column 7 or 8 on the COBOL statement depending on whether it is an * comment or a compilable statement.

I prepared the source code for all of the programs in this book in terminal format. The listings published here were produced by the COBOL compiler in .LIS files. As you can see in those listings the code is perfectly normal COBOL code and the compiler has adjusted the placement so that comment lines (with *) start in column 7 while all other lines start in column 8.

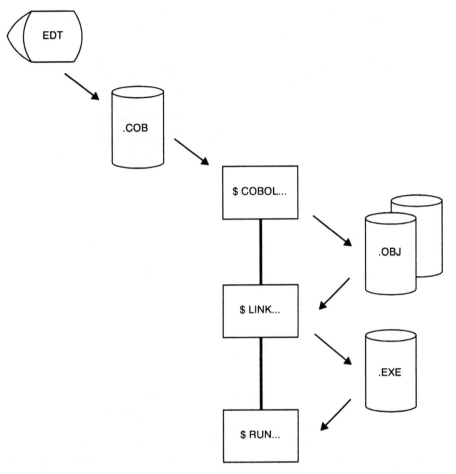

Figure 6.1   Compiling, linkage editing, and running in the VAX COBOL environment.

6.2 Compiling a COBOL Program

After entering source code for a COBOL program into a file with a suffix of .COB using EDT (or by uploading the code from a microcomputer) you can compile it by entering:

    $ **COBOL** CALC1

This invokes the VAX COBOL compiler. It automatically looks for your source code in a file of the name you specified with a suffix of .COB. In

```
IDENTIFICATION DIVISION.
PROGRAM-ID.    CALC1.
*AUTHOR.        J JANOSSY   INTERNET: JANOSSY@CSCVAX.DEPAUL.EDU
*INSTALLATION.  DEPAUL UNIVERSITY, CHICAGO, ILLINOIS, USA
*================================================================
*    First "CALC" Demonstration Program in VAX COBOL ON-LINE!
*
*    Demonstrates cursor positioning with DISPLAY and the use
*    of ACCEPT.  Crude; does not redisplay input after the
*    program receives it.  See CALC3 for best example!
*================================================================
ENVIRONMENT DIVISION.
*----------------------------------------------------------------
DATA DIVISION.
WORKING-STORAGE SECTION.
01   WS-QUANTITY                     PIC 9(5).
01   WS-PRICE                        PIC 99V99.
01   WS-TOTAL                        PIC 9(7)V99.
01   WS-TAX-AMOUNT                   PIC 9(7)V99.
01   WS-GRAND-TOTAL                  PIC 9(8)V99.
01   WS-MONEY-FORMATTED              PIC ZZ,ZZZ,ZZ9.99.
01   WS-RESPONSE                     PIC X(4).
*----------------------------------------------------------------
PROCEDURE DIVISION.
0000-MAINLINE.
    PERFORM 1000-BOJ.
    PERFORM 2000-PROCESS
      UNTIL WS-RESPONSE = 'QUIT' OR 'quit'.
    PERFORM 3000-EOJ.
    STOP RUN.
```

Figure 6.2 VAX "terminal format" for COBOL statements is designed to make your entry of source code as easy as possible. You don't enter any COBOL line numbers. The first column is treated as column 7 by the compiler if it contains the comment asterisk. This position is treated as column 8 if it does not contain an asterisk. The VAX COBOL compiler automatically adjusts the placement of lines on your source code (.LIS) listings.

this example it will compile CALC1.COB. The compiler will show you on the screen any source code lines that contain errors, each followed by an error message. No error messages are produced if a program compiles successfully. Either way you'll eventually get back to the VMS dollar sign prompt.

Compilation is handled immediately by the VAX, and small programs may compile within seconds. Your compile may take a minute or more if your program is large or if many terminal users are active. The compile produces a file named with the suffix .OBJ as an *object file* for the linkage editor.

6.3 VAX COBOL Compiler Options

Practically speaking you usually need to specify at least the LIST and COPY_LIST options with your VAX COBOL compiles. You will benefit greatly from also using the CROSS_REFERENCE and CHECK options:

- The LIST option causes the compiler to produce a file containing a source code listing, including errors, which you can print or examine with EDT. If your program size is medium to large, you'll need this listing to be able to analyze the compiler's error messages. This file is automatically named with the suffix .LIS, such as CALC1.LIS.
- The COPY_LIST option causes the compiler to list any lines you bring into the program with the COPY compiler directive. If you don't specify this option, lines copied in will be compiled but you won't see them in the .LIS file.
- CROSS_REFERENCE causes the compiler to create a sorted cross reference listing of data names within a program in your .LIS file, handy for program modification.
- The CHECK option helps you in locating PERFORM statement and subscript/index errors.

I strongly recommend that you use at least this form of compile command:

```
$ COBOL/LIST/COPY_LIST   CALC1
```

or even better, this:

```
$ COBOL/LIST/COPY_LIST/CROSS_REFERENCE/CHECK   CALC1
```

See topic 6.6, where I show you how to create a short "synonym" for this command.

6.4 Linkage Editing a Program

When you successfully compile a VAX COBOL program the compiler creates a nonexecutable object file with the name of the source code file and a suffix of .OBJ. You linkage edit this file to turn it into a *machine language "image"* by entering the LINK command:

```
$ LINK CALC1
```

The linkage editor automatically looks for a file with the name you specify and the suffix .OBJ. When the link edit ends successfully you will find that the linkage editor has created a file of machine language named with the filename and a suffix of .EXE, for example CALC1.EXE.

If your program uses the CALL verb (it CALLs subprograms) you have to take special steps. You first need to separately compile each of the subprograms and the main (CALLing) program so that their object (.OBJ) files exist. Then you use the LINK command, naming the main program first and the subprograms following, separated by commas and with no spaces in between:

```
$ LINK   VAXDEMO,CUPD1,PLACNAME,NUMCHECK,SDEL1,SBROW1
```

In this example VAXDEMO is the main program, CUPD1 is a subprogram it calls, PLACNAME and NUMCHEK are subprograms called by CUPD1, and SDEL1 and SBROW1 are subprograms called by VAXDEMO. The result will be one single file named VAXDEMO.EXE containing the machine language of all of the modules.

6.5 Running a Program

You can execute a program that you have successfully compiled and linkage edited using the RUN command and the program name:

```
$ RUN CALC1
```

To stop the program before it ends on its own press *<Ctrl/C>*. With either a normal ending or this interruption you will get back to the VMS dollar sign prompt.

6.6 Viewing Program Outputs

You can view files of printlines such as the .LIS file produced by the compiler using the TYPE command or with EDT in either its line editing or keypad editing mode. *If you use EDT to view a compile listing (or any report file), end your viewing with QUIT instead of EXIT so that no new version of the file is created.* EXIT saves a new version of the file. Since EDT writes files with a format different from normal carriage control conventions a new .LIS file saved by EDT will not print properly.

Interactive programs don't ordinarily write reports, but you'll need to write batch VAX COBOL programs to produce some types of reports from the files you maintain on-line. Files to be written by a COBOL program are named in SELECT/ASSIGN statements:

```
SELECT MY-INPUT-FILE ASSIGN TO 'PAYROLL.DAT'.
```

If this statement had been coded as

```
SELECT MY-INPUT-FILE ASSIGN TO PAYROLL.
```

VMS would create the next higher version number of a file named PAYROLL.DAT.

6.7 Command Files to Streamline Your Tasks

Anything you might enter into the dollar sign prompt can instead be entered as keystrokes in a file. You can feed this keystroke file into VMS as if you were at that moment entering those same keystrokes individually. Such a file is called a *command file*.

All VMS command filenames must end with the suffix .COM. (On microcomputers such a file might be called a ".BAT" file.) You invoke a command file by entering its name prefaced by an @ sign. For example, if you had a command file named BONK.COM you would execute it by entering:

```
$ @BONK
```

One command filename is special: LOGIN.COM. If this command file is present in your root directory the VAX executes it automatically when you log on. You can code a synonym in your LOGIN.COM file to set up a convenient way to invoke the compiler with options. Create a file named LOGIN.COM and enter this statement in it *including* the dollar sign:

```
$ C :== COBOL/LIST/COPY_LIST/CROSS_REFERENCE/CHECK
```

The :== "equates" the abbreviation at the left—I have coded just the single letter C—to all of the keystrokes to the right. The next time you log on, C will be recognized as a synonym for the entire COBOL compile command. (Right now you can make the synonym take effect by entering @LOGIN at the dollar sign prompt). With this synonym in effect you can compile a program invoking the four desirable VAX COBOL compiler options by just entering:

```
$ C CALC1
```

6.8 Redirecting Screen Output

You can house another useful pair of synonyms in your `LOGIN.COM` command file to let you reroute screen output from your terminal to a file:

```
$ TODISK :== ASSIGN SCREEN.DAT SYS$OUTPUT
$ TOTUBE :== DEASSIGN SYS$OUTPUT
```

Once these synonyms are active entering `TODISK` (pronounce it "to disk") will send subsequent transmissions from the system to a file named `SCREEN.DAT`:

```
$ TODISK
```

Entering `$ TOTUBE` (pronounce this "to tube") will route subsequent transmissions to your terminal ("tube") screen.

These synonyms are useful if you have no local printer attached to your terminal yet want to make a paper copy of your file directory or of the `DISPLAY` output of a program. You can use them to make screen prints for documentation of an interactive system. Try `$ TODISK` and then do a `DIR` listing. Then do `$ TOTUBE` to again get communication to go to your screen and use EDT to view the contents of `SCREEN.DAT`.

6.9 A Handy Command File for Logging Out

Every time you edit a file using EDT and end the edit session with `EXIT` a new version of the file is stored. All of the older versions of the file remain and take up some of your disk space. Every time you run a program that creates a report or file new versions of those files are created. Every compile and link edit creates new `.OBJ` and `.EXE` file versions, too. Until you begin dealing with callable modules, you should eliminate `.OBJ` files in your directory at the end of a session.

It's handy to delete unnecessary files as you log out. If you create a small command file named `OFF.COM` you can take care of some file deletions automatically and then log out:

```
$ PURGE
$ LOGOUT
```

Create such a file using EDT. Make sure you put the dollar signs as well as the commands themselves within the command lines. Now you can log off by entering:

```
$ @OFF
```

This executes the command file named OFF.COM. You'll get rid of your old file versions and log off all in one action.

6.10 Command Retrieval and Repetition

VMS stores the last 20 commands you have used in your present logon session. You can retrieve these and reexecute them one by one in last-in, first-out sequence by pressing the *<Up arrow>* key. You can move the cursor backward with the *<Delete>* key to edit a retrieved command and resubmit it by then pressing *<Enter>*. This can often save you the effort of reentering a long LINK command.

6.11 Chapter Summary

You invoke the VAX COBOL compiler using the command **$ COBOL/LIST name**, which automatically looks for your source code in name.COB. Error messages are presented on the screen and in a file named name.LIS. The compile produces a file named with the suffix .OBJ. Access important compiler options with this command:

```
$ COBOL/LIST/COPY_LIST/CROSS_REFERENCE/CHECK   name
```

Create a LOGIN.COM file for yourself and put this synonym in it:

```
$ C :== COBOL/LIST/COPY_LIST/CROSS_REFERENCE/CHECK
```

The next time you log on, C will be recognized as a synonym for the entire COBOL compile command so that you can compile by entering:

```
$ C name
```

Linkage edit an object file with the LINK command:

```
$ LINK name
```

which automatically seeks a file named name.OBJ. If your program CALLs subprograms your LINK command has to name the main program object file first and the subprogram object files following:

```
$ LINK name,CUPD1,PLACNAME,NUMCHECK,SDEL1,SBROW1
```

The linkage edit produces a single file name.EXE (also called an *image*), which you can execute with the RUN command:

```
$ RUN name
```

To stop the program before it ends normally press *<Ctrl/C>*.

You can view the compiler's `.LIS` file with the VMS `TYPE` command or with EDT. If you use EDT to view a listing, end your viewing with `QUIT` instead of `EXIT` so that no new version of the file is created.

You can house a series of VMS commands in any file named with a suffix of `.COM`. It's handy to use EDT to create a file named `OFF.COM` with these commands in it (including the $):

```
$ PURGE
$ LOGOUT
```

You can log off by executing this command file and automatically purge obsolete file versions (to conserve disk space) before you leave the system:

```
$ @OFF
```

VMS stores the last 20 commands you have executed. You can retrieve these by pressing the *<Up Arrow>* key.

6.12 Important Terms

You can review these terms to check your understanding of this chapter:

$ COBOL name   The command to invoke the VAX COBOL compiler without any special options. `Name` is the front part of your source code filename. This process creates an object file name.`OBJ`.

$ LINK name   The command to invoke the VAX linkage editor. This process reads a file name.`OBJ` and creates a machine language file name.`EXE`.

$ RUN name   The command to execute a program. This process gives control to a file name.`EXE`.

Command file   A file named with a suffix `.COM` containing VMS system commands, such as `BONK.COM`. You can invoke all the commands it contains by entering the front part of the name prefaced by @ at the dollar sign prompt: `$ @BONK`.

Image   A VMS term for executable machine language file. In the IBM mainframe environment this is known as a *load module*.

You can find additional questions and exercises for this chapter in Appendix A.

Chapter Seven

ACCEPT AND DISPLAY IN VAX COBOL

The VAX VMS operating system is inherently interactive and directly supports conversational program-to-terminal communication. You can receive keystrokes entered at a terminal using the ACCEPT verb, and you can send information to a terminal screen with the DISPLAY verb. You do not need to invoke any special compiler or operating system features to use these verbs.

In this chapter I show you how ACCEPT and DISPLAY options work. I'll apply these verbs first to some simple demonstration programs named CALC1, CALC2, and CALC3 in Chapters 8 and 9. Then I'll recommend a subset of these options for your day-to-day use and demonstrate them in the complete VAXDEMO example in Chapters 11 through 15.

By the way, none of the examples in this book use any DEC software other than the VAX COBOL compiler and Record Management System (RMS) file handler. You do not need DEC's Terminal Data Management System (TDMS) software to handle terminal-to-program communication, and I don't use it in any of my examples.

7.1 Terminal-to-Program Communication

ACCEPT transfers a field of information from the terminal keyboard to the operating system character by character. The input is given to your program when the *<Return>* key is pressed. DISPLAY transfers information from your program to the terminal screen. In VAX COBOL, both verbs give you many options, making it possible to control the position of the cursor on the screen and the display intensity, and to erase all or parts of the screen.

You should understand that the ACCEPT and DISPLAY extensions described here apply only to VAX COBOL and to other minicomputer and microcomputer compilers patterned on it. ACCEPT and DISPLAY are not used in the IBM mainframe environment for interactive programming. In the IBM mainframe environment, you can use ACCEPT only in batch programs, to obtain the system date and time. On IBM mainframes, DISPLAY sends debugging messages to print. So although VAX COBOL and IBM VS COBOL are identical for batch programming they differ enormously for interactive programming.

7.2 ACCEPT and VAX COBOL Extensions

You can use the ACCEPT verb in its most primitive form to get the date or time from the operating system:

```
ACCEPT WS-DATE FROM DATE.
```

But when you code ACCEPT with FROM and LINE and COLUMN, it seeks data from the terminal running the program:

```
ACCEPT WS-QUANTITY FROM LINE 7 COLUMN 21 WITH CONVERSION.
```

Keystrokes entered at the terminal are placed into the receiving field such as WS-QUANTITY when you press the **<Return>** key. If you don't enter any data into a field before you press **<Return>**, a PIC X(nn) field receives spaces while a PIC 9(nn) field receives the value zero.

I have sketched the format of the ACCEPT verb in Figure 7.1. All of the specifications cited in brackets are optional and can be used in combination; no single statement would use them all.

7.3 DISPLAY and VAX COBOL Extensions

The DISPLAY verb directs its output to the computer terminal running the program. A simple DISPLAY cites a data name or literal value:

```
DISPLAY WS-QUANTITY.
DISPLAY 'THIS IS A MESSAGE'.
```

With optional DISPLAY specifications you can position the item being output at a specific LINE and COLUMN. You can also clear the screen before outputting begins, control the intensity of the item on the screen, and sound a bell (beep). For example:

```
DISPLAY 'HELLO' AT LINE 1 COLUMN 1 ERASE TO END OF SCREEN.
```

ACCEPT data-name

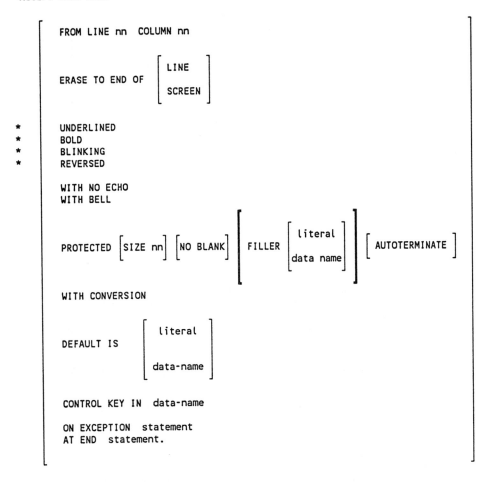

```
ACCEPT data-name

┌                                                                              ┐
│   FROM LINE nn  COLUMN nn                                                    │
│                                                                             │
│                         ┌         ┐                                         │
│                         │  LINE   │                                         │
│   ERASE TO END OF       │         │                                         │
│                         │  SCREEN │                                         │
│                         └         ┘                                         │
│                                                                             │
* │   UNDERLINED                                                              │
* │   BOLD                                                                    │
* │   BLINKING                                                                │
* │   REVERSED                                                                │
│                                                                             │
│   WITH NO ECHO                                                              │
│   WITH BELL                                                                 │
│                                                                             │
│                ┌        ┐ ┌          ┐ ┌   ┌           ┐ ┐ ┌              ┐ │
│                │        │ │          │ │   │  literal  │ │ │              │ │
│   PROTECTED    │ SIZE nn│ │ NO BLANK │ │ FILLER        │ │ │ AUTOTERMINATE│ │
│                │        │ │          │ │   │ data name │ │ │              │ │
│                └        ┘ └          ┘ └   └           ┘ ┘ └              ┘ │
│                                                                             │
│   WITH CONVERSION                                                           │
│                                                                             │
│                    ┌           ┐                                            │
│                    │  literal  │                                            │
│   DEFAULT IS       │           │                                            │
│                    │ data-name │                                            │
│                    └           ┘                                            │
│                                                                             │
│   CONTROL KEY IN  data-name                                                 │
│                                                                             │
│   ON EXCEPTION  statement                                                   │
│   AT END   statement.                                                       │
└                                                                             ┘
```

* These features are available only with VT-100 and later model terminals; they are not supported on the VT-52 terminal

Figure 7.1   ACCEPT verb and VAX COBOL extensions.

clears the terminal screen and displays the word HELLO at the upper left corner. This statement:

DISPLAY '' AT LINE 1 COLUMN 1 **ERASE TO END OF SCREEN.**

also clears the screen but leaves it completely empty; the two apostrophes with nothing between them cause no data transmission and the cursor remains in the first position of the screen. The following DISPLAY

```
DISPLAY data-name
```

```
┌                                                      ┐
│   AT LINE nn  COLUMN nn                              │
│                                                      │
│                          ┌ LINE   ┐                 │
│   ERASE TO END OF        │        │                 │
│                          └ SCREEN ┘                 │
│                                                      │
*│   UNDERLINED                                        │
*│   BOLD                                              │
*│   BLINKING                                          │
*│   REVERSED                                          │
│                                                      │
│   WITH BELL                                          │
│                                                      │
│   WITH CONVERSION                                    │
│                                                      │
│   WITH NO ADVANCING.                                 │
└                                                      ┘
```

* These features are available only with VT-100 and later model terminals; they are not supported on the VT-52 terminal

Figure 7.2   DISPLAY verb and VAX COBOL extensions.

outputs a value at BOLD intensity (bright) at a specific location and sounds a brief warning beep:

```
DISPLAY WS-QUANTITY
    BOLD
    WITH BELL
    AT LINE 7 COLUMN 21.
```

My sketch of the format of the DISPLAY verb is shown in Figure 7.2. All of the specifications in brackets are optional. You can use them in combination; no single statement would use them all.

7.4 Typical ACCEPT and DISPLAY Option Usage

You can execute ACCEPT and DISPLAY one after another to receive data from a computer terminal and redisplay it in a formatted way. The data you receive might also be used for computation or record updating. In the following example I receive a value into a numeric field, MOVE it to a formatted numeric field suitable for presentation, and DISPLAY the formatted field in the same screen location:

```
WORKING-STORAGE SECTION.
  01 WS-QUANTITY                PIC 9(5).
  01 WS-QUANTITY-FORMATTED      PIC ZZ,ZZ9.
  -
  -

PROCEDURE DIVISION
  -
  -
  ACCEPT WS-QUANTITY
      REVERSED
      PROTECTED NO BLANK
      WITH CONVERSION
      FROM LINE 7 COLUMN 21.
MOVE WS-QUANTITY TO WS-QUANTITY-FORMATTED.
DISPLAY WS-QUANTITY-FORMATTED AT LINE 7 COLUMN 21.
```

> REVERSED gives a reverse video display (dark characters on light backgroud)

The **REVERSED** option makes the entry field appear in reverse video with dark characters on a light background. Because spaces in reverse video appear as solid bright areas, this makes the length of the field apparent to the terminal operator for the entry process.

ACCEPTing a field REVERSED, moving the value received to a numeric formatted PICture, then DISPLAYing the formatted field in the same location without REVERSED removes the reverse video effect. The next statement could be an ACCEPT for another field at a different location, which would then "light up" in reverse video as the field active for data entry. I'll show you a consistent way to use this technique in Chapter 9.

ACCEPT provides two options that automatically accomplish some data validation:

- **PROTECTED** limits the quantity of characters that can be received into a field to the size of the specified receiving field.
- **WITH CONVERSION** converts entered data to match the receiving field PIC and automatically rejects invalid entries; with some limitations it does numeric field "de-editing" for you.

7.5 ACCEPT *Option: PROTECTED*

PROTECTED makes sure that the terminal operator doesn't key in more data than a field can handle. What it really protects is the screen image. Unless you use PROTECTED the terminal operator can go past the end of the field and destroy the label of the next field (compare

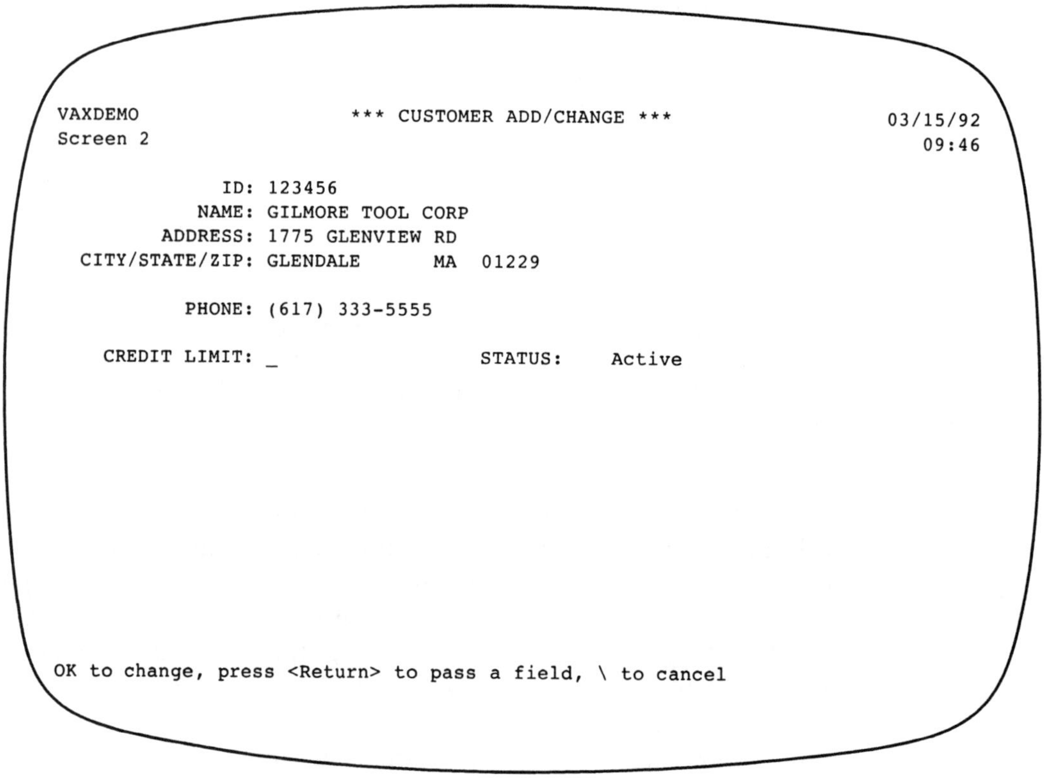

```
VAXDEMO                *** CUSTOMER ADD/CHANGE ***               03/15/92
Screen 2                                                           09:46

            ID: 123456
          NAME: GILMORE TOOL CORP
       ADDRESS: 1775 GLENVIEW RD
 CITY/STATE/ZIP: GLENDALE       MA  01229

         PHONE: (617) 333-5555

  CREDIT LIMIT: _                     STATUS:    Active




OK to change, press <Return> to pass a field, \ to cancel
```

Figure 7.3a Add/change screen of VAXDEMO function 2. I show you how to program this screen and function in Chapter 13. You see it here before the operator has begun entering credit limit and customer status information.

Figures 7.3a and 7.3b!). You can code the PROTECTED option as a single word, which protects a field at its coded field length:

```
ACCEPT WS-QUANTITY
    REVERSED
    PROTECTED NO BLANK
    WITH CONVERSION
    FROM LINE 7 COLUMN 21.
```

Alternatively, you can code PROTECTED SIZE nn. This overrides the field definition and establishes the number of characters that can be entered:

```
PROTECTED SIZE 12 NO BLANK
```

```
 VAXDEMO                   *** CUSTOMER ADD/CHANGE ***              03/15/92
 Screen 2                                                             09:46

            ID:  123456
          NAME:  GILMORE TOOL CORP
       ADDRESS:  1775 GLENVIEW RD
 CITY/STATE/ZIP: GLENDALE       MA   01229

         PHONE:  (617) 333-5555

  CREDIT LIMIT:  123456789123456789123456789123456789123456789...




 OK to change, press <Return> to pass a field, \ to cancel
```

Figure 7.3b   Potential screen damage that a terminal operator could cause if you didn't use PROTECTED on the ACCEPT that obtains credit limit information. Without PROTECTED the operator could continue keying beyond the end of the field.

I'll explain to you when to use PROTECTED as a single word and when to use SIZE nn as we apply this in programs in the next several chapters.

What is the effect of PROTECTED? If more keystrokes are attempted in the field than are allowed by the field length or SIZE, the cursor does not advance and a warning beep is automatically sounded.

What about NO BLANK? PROTECTED ordinarily displays spaces in the field immediately prior to beginning ACCEPT processing. This interferes with the display of an existing field when record update is underway. The **NO BLANK** clause of PROTECTED delays its blanking action until after you enter the first keystroke in the field. This way the terminal operator can see what is in the field already, which he or she may not wish to change. NO BLANK is a useful clause of PROTECTED that I use in the example programs that follow.

7.6 ACCEPT *Option:* WITH CONVERSION

On a terminal screen you might enter a number value into a field without leading zeros. In addition, you might enter a period—which is not a numeric symbol—for a decimal point. For example, you might enter the value $1.23 into a PIC 999V99 (5 byte) receiving field on the screen in this way:

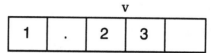

But COBOL requires that this value be present purely as a number to consider it valid numeric data:

```
          v
| 0 | 0 | 1 | 2 | 3 |
```

A very important point:

> "De-editing" a number entered at the terminal into the purely numeric form that COBOL requires is a chore common to all interactive systems, whether they are programmed on the VAX or on IBM mainframes.

Different software systems handle this de-editing chore in different ways. Unfortunately, neither VAX COBOL nor CICS does de-editing in quite the way you would consider truly useful.

The **WITH CONVERSION** option of ACCEPT transforms a number entered with trailing spaces or a decimal point into a purely numeric value with implied decimal point, right justified in the receiving field with leading zeros. WITH CONVERSION automatically rejects non-numeric characters (including the comma) when you press *<Return>* to end field entry.

WITH CONVERSION allows entry of one decimal point and automatically removes it, so you need to allow a screen field that will receive a decimal number with one more position than required by the size of the numeric PIC. For example, allow six screen positions for entry of an unsigned PIC 9(3)V99 field because an entered decimal point will take up one position of the field on the screen.

WITH CONVERSION also accepts a leading or trailing hyphen to indicate a negative number. If you intend to receive a signed number allow an extra position in the screen field to accommodate it. For example, to receive a signed PIC S9(3)V99 value allow 7 positions on the screen for it. A terminal operator might enter −123.45 for it (count them—that's seven positions!).

But WITH CONVERSION has its weaknesses. A dollar sign and commas are not considered valid input. My simple CALC1, CALC2, and CALC3 example programs in the next chapters use WITH CONVERSION for the entry of numeric data. But the full-scale VAXDEMO application I show you in Chapters 11 through 15 illustrates how to use a numeric field validation subprogram named NUMCHEK instead of WITH CONVERSION. I programmed NUMCHEK to de-edit numbers you might enter with a dollar sign, commas, and a decimal point. (You can see the source code for NUMCHEK in Appendix B. Like all the other programs in this book you can get this source code on diskette for uploading as described in Appendix E.)

7.7 Chapter Summary

You can receive keystrokes entered at a terminal using ACCEPT. You can send data to a terminal screen with DISPLAY. No special compiler or operating system features are needed to communicate with terminals. ACCEPT transfers a field of information from the terminal keyboard to the program when the **<Return>** key is pressed. You can use the LINE and COLUMN options to position the cursor on the screen with either of these verbs.

DISPLAY allows you to erase the screen before you present new information on it, present information in bright (BOLD) as well as normal intensity, and sound a beep with the BELL option.

ACCEPT provides several options such as REVERSED, PROTECTED, and WITH CONVERSION:

- **REVERSED** makes the entry field appear in reverse video so it appears with dark characters on a light background.
- **PROTECTED** limits the quantity of characters that can be received into a field, saving the screen image from the entry of too many characters in a field.
- **WITH CONVERSION** de-edits data entered into a numeric field to provide "pure" number data for COBOL (with some limitations).

These give you the tools to you need to handle the entry and presentation of data at computer terminals.

7.8 Important Terms

You can review these terms to check your understanding of this chapter:

ACCEPT   The VAX COBOL verb to receive data entered at a terminal keyboard.

DISPLAY   The VAX COBOL verb to send data to a computer terminal screen.

ACCEPT/DISPLAY extensions   Optional clauses such as LINE, COLUMN, WITH CONVERSION, PROTECTED, BOLD, REVERSED, BLINKING, UNDERLINED, and DARK.

ERASE TO ...   A DISPLAY extension to clear the remainder of a line or the screen.

LINE nn, COLUMN nn   An ACCEPT or DISPLAY extension to position the cursor on the screen to a specific location.

PROTECTED   An ACCEPT extension that controls the length of the entry permitted in a field on the screen.

NO BLANK   An optional clause of ACCEPT PROTECTED that delays blanking of the field until the terminal operator makes a keystroke in it.

WITH CONVERSION   An ACCEPT extension that causes input data to be converted to the format of the receiving field.

You can find additional questions and exercises for this chapter in Appendix A.

Chapter Eight

CALC1: YOUR FIRST CONVERSATIONAL PROGRAM

In this chapter I show you the screen layout for a calculation-only demonstration program and the source code that drives it. When you finish this chapter you will be able to design and write this type of program yourself.

8.1 A Simple Interactive Screen

Figures 8.1 and 8.2 depict a screen with two enterable fields: QUANTITY and PRICE. You can picture a sales clerk using this screen to enter the quantity of an item bought by a customer and the unit price of the item (the price "each"). After the entry of QUANTITY and PRICE the program calculates three fields and presents them automatically on the screen. The interactive program "behind" the screen computes the "extended" price of the purchase by multiplying quantity times unit price. Then it calculates 8% sales tax, and finally the total charge to the customer (extended price + sales tax). For example, for quantity 10 of an item that costs $2.50 each, the TOTAL is computed as $25.00, TAX is computed as (.08 × 25.00) = 2.00, and the GRAND TOTAL is computed as 25.00 + 2.00 = $27.00.

Figure 8.2 depicts how the CALC1 screen appears when you have entered QUANTITY and PRICE but the program has not yet done the calculations. Figure 8.3 shows the result after the calculations.

8.2 CALC1: A Simple Interactive Program

My VAX COBOL source code for program CALC1 is listed in Figure 8.4. Brief as it is, CALC1 demonstrates many essential aspects of VAX inter-

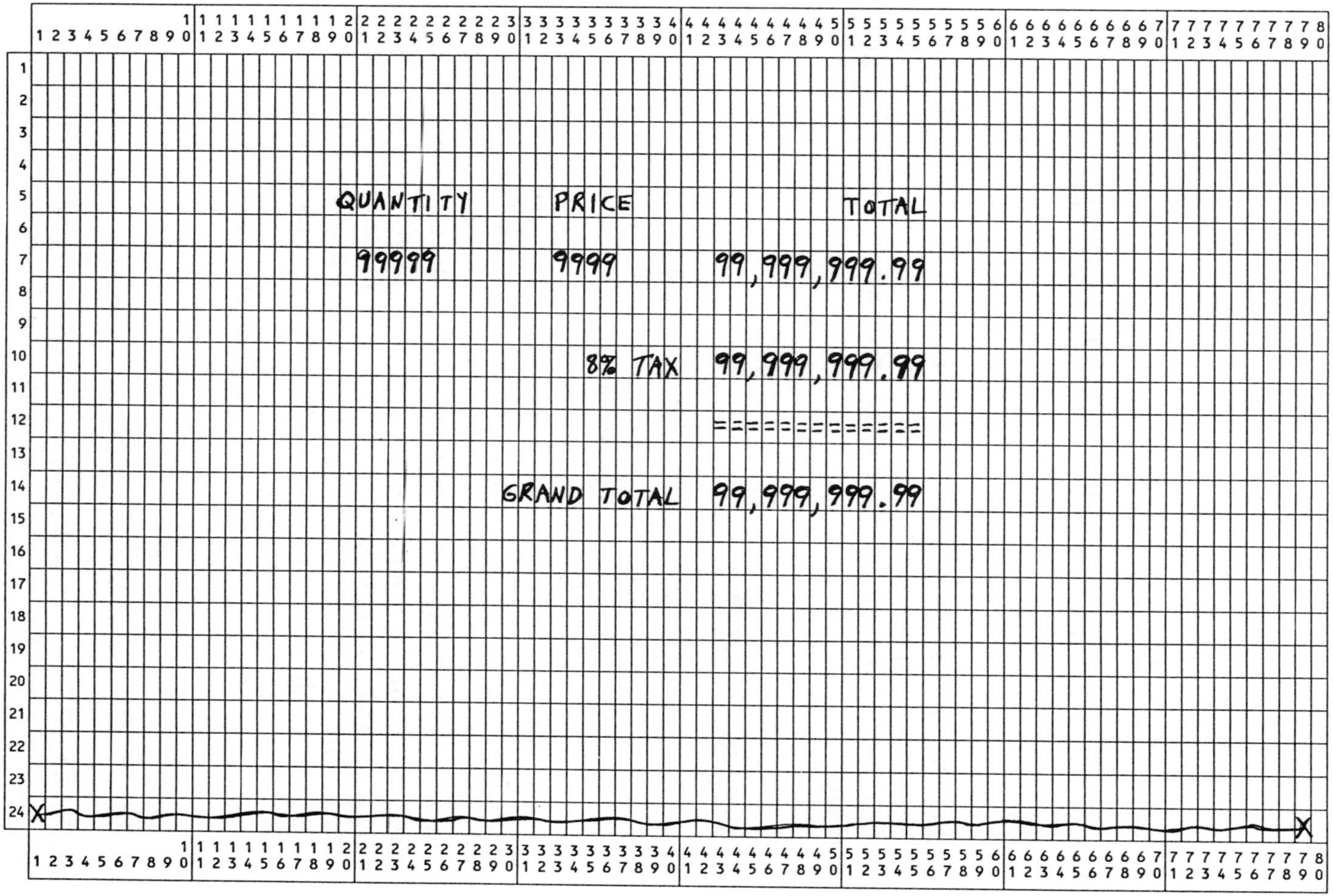
QUANTITY
PRICE
TOTAL
99999
9999
99,999,999.99
8% TAX
99,999,999.99
==============
GRAND TOTAL
99,999,999.99

Figure 8.1 Screen design for CALC1, an interactive program that lets you key in two numbers, QUANTITY and PRICE. After you enter these values the program computes and shows you TOTAL (the product of quantity and price), 8% sales TAX, and the GRAND TOTAL of a purchase.

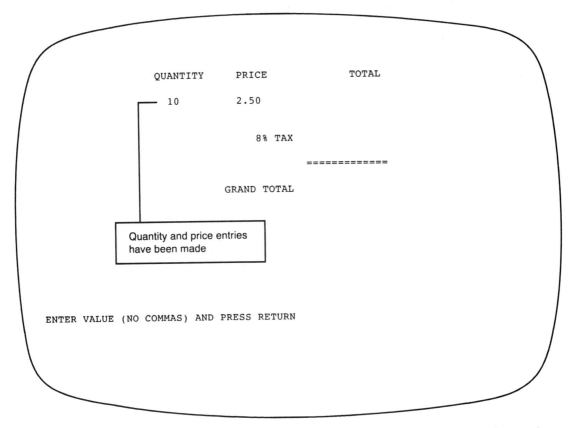

```
        QUANTITY     PRICE              TOTAL

          10         2.50


                        8% TAX

                        =============

        GRAND TOTAL


   ┌─────────────────────────┐
   │ Quantity and price entries │
   │ have been made           │
   └─────────────────────────┘




ENTER VALUE (NO COMMAS) AND PRESS RETURN
```

Figure 8.2 The CALC1 screen after you have entered QUANTITY and PRICE but the program has not yet done the calculations for TOTAL, TAX, and GRAND TOTAL.

active programming, including conversational logic structure. (Review Chapter 2 if you have forgotten how a conversational interactive program differs from a pseudoconversational program!)

8.3 Action Diagrams for Program Logic

I planned the source code for CALC1 using the diagram shown in Figure 8.5. This is called an *action diagram*. It provides a simple summary of the logic of a program. I highly recommend that you think of program logic using action diagrams as you look at my examples and develop your own interactive programs. They are a simple way to depict program

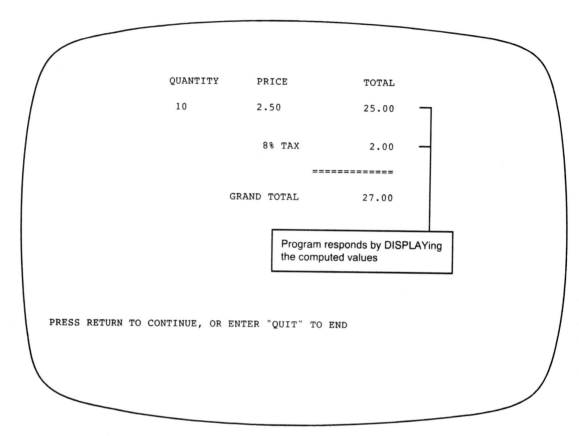

```
          QUANTITY          PRICE              TOTAL

             10              2.50              25.00  ┐
                                                     │
                        8% TAX                 2.00  ┤
                                                     │
                        ============                 │
                                                     │
                     GRAND TOTAL                27.00│
                                                     │
                     ┌─────────────────────────────┐│
                     │ Program responds by DISPLAYing││
                     │ the computed values          ││
                     └─────────────────────────────┘│


  PRESS RETURN TO CONTINUE, OR ENTER "QUIT" TO END
```

Figure 8.3 CALC1 screen after the program completes calculation of TOTAL, TAX, and GRAND TOTAL.

logic using a "graphic pseudocode." They are not specific to one programming language, but they work especially well with COBOL, C, Pascal, PL/I, FORTRAN, and even Assembler.

On an action diagram such as Figure 8.5 every bracket represents one paragraph of COBOL code. The diagram shows how you plan to use the three structured programming building blocks of sequence, selection, and iteration. You position a bracket to the right of where it is performed most frequently. You jot pseudocode, spelling out what is to happen in a paragraph, within its bracket. The diagram shows the highest level of logic at the left and the lowest level of logic detail at the right. You start reading the diagram at the upper left corner and move down to get the big picture. You can use an action diagram for a logic design walkthrough before you start coding a program.

```
CALC1                     15-Mar-1992 23:30:57   VAX COBOL V4.3-57
Source Listing            15-Mar-1992 23:20:50   CSC$ROOT:[CSCJGJ.VAXCO]CALC1.COB;1

     1          IDENTIFICATION DIVISION.
     2          PROGRAM-ID.    CALC1.
     3          *AUTHOR.         J JANOSSY    INTERNET: JANOSSY@CSCVAX.DEPAUL.EDU
     4          *INSTALLATION.  DEPAUL UNIVERSITY, CHICAGO, ILLINOIS, USA
     5          *==================================================================
     6          *    First "CALC" Demonstration Program in VAX COBOL ON-LINE!
     7          *
     8          *    Demonstrates cursor positioning with DISPLAY and the use
     9          *    of ACCEPT.  Crude; does not redisplay input after the
    10          *    program receives it.  See CALC3 for best example!
    11          *==================================================================
    12          ENVIRONMENT DIVISION.
    13          *------------------------------------------------------------------
    14          DATA DIVISION.
    15          WORKING-STORAGE SECTION.
    16          01  WS-QUANTITY                      PIC 9(5).
    17          01  WS-PRICE                         PIC 99V99.
    18          01  WS-TOTAL                         PIC 9(7)V99.
    19          01  WS-TAX-AMOUNT                    PIC 9(7)V99.
    20          01  WS-GRAND-TOTAL                   PIC 9(8)V99.
    21          01  WS-MONEY-FORMATTED               PIC ZZ,ZZZ,ZZ9.99.
    22          01  WS-RESPONSE                      PIC X(4).
    23          *------------------------------------------------------------------
    24          PROCEDURE DIVISION.
    25          0000-MAINLINE.
    26              PERFORM 1000-BOJ.
    27              PERFORM 2000-PROCESS
    28                  UNTIL WS-RESPONSE = 'QUIT' OR 'quit'.
    29              PERFORM 3000-EOJ.
    30              STOP RUN.
    31          *
    32          1000-BOJ.
    33              DISPLAY '' AT LINE 1 COLUMN 1 ERASE TO END OF SCREEN.
    34              DISPLAY 'QUANTITY       PRICE            TOTAL'
    35                  AT LINE 5 COLUMN 20.
    36              DISPLAY '8% TAX'        AT LINE 10 COLUMN 35.
    37              DISPLAY '=============' AT LINE 12 COLUMN 43.
    38              DISPLAY 'GRAND TOTAL'   AT LINE 14 COLUMN 30.
    39          *
    40          2000-PROCESS.
    41              DISPLAY '        '      AT LINE  7 COLUMN 21.
    42              DISPLAY '        '      AT LINE  7 COLUMN 33.
    43              DISPLAY '            '  AT LINE  7 COLUMN 43.
    44              DISPLAY '            '  AT LINE 10 COLUMN 43.
    45              DISPLAY '            '  AT LINE 14 COLUMN 43.
    46              DISPLAY 'ENTER VALUE (NO COMMAS) AND PRESS RETURN'
    47                  AT LINE 24 COLUMN 1 ERASE TO END OF LINE.
    48          *
    49              ACCEPT WS-QUANTITY
    50                  PROTECTED
    51                  WITH CONVERSION
    52                  FROM LINE 7 COLUMN 21.
    53              ACCEPT WS-PRICE
    54                  PROTECTED
    55                  WITH CONVERSION
    56                  FROM LINE 7 COLUMN 33.
    57          *
    58              COMPUTE WS-TOTAL = WS-QUANTITY * WS-PRICE.
    59              MOVE WS-TOTAL TO WS-MONEY-FORMATTED.
    60              DISPLAY WS-MONEY-FORMATTED AT LINE 7 COLUMN 43.
    61          *
    62              COMPUTE WS-TAX-AMOUNT = WS-TOTAL * .08.
    63              MOVE WS-TAX-AMOUNT TO WS-MONEY-FORMATTED.
    64              DISPLAY WS-MONEY-FORMATTED AT LINE 10 COLUMN 43.
    65          *
    66              COMPUTE WS-GRAND-TOTAL = WS-TOTAL + WS-TAX-AMOUNT.
    67              MOVE WS-GRAND-TOTAL TO WS-MONEY-FORMATTED.
    68              DISPLAY WS-MONEY-FORMATTED AT LINE 14 COLUMN 43.
    69          *
```

(Continued)

Figure 8.4   Source code for CALC1, a simple interactive program in VAX COBOL.

```
70              DISPLAY 'PRESS RETURN TO CONTINUE, OR ENTER "QUIT" TO END '
71                  AT LINE 24 COLUMN 1.
72              ACCEPT WS-RESPONSE
73                  PROTECTED
74                  FROM LINE 24 COLUMN 60.
75          *
76           3000-EOJ.
77              DISPLAY 'QUITTING AS REQUESTED' AT LINE 1 COLUMN 1
78                  ERASE TO END OF SCREEN.
```

Figure 8.4   *(Continued)*

The form of procedure chart I've drawn in Figure 8.5 was described by Henning Nelms in his book *Thinking With a Pencil* (Barnes and Nobel, 1957). Diagrams like these were independently described by Jean-Dominique Warnier in France and refined by Kenneth Orr in the United States. I wrote about them in a book in 1985 and in numerous articles (*Data Training* magazine, 1986–1987) and called them "program profiles." James Martin and Carma McClure varied some of the nomenclature and shape of the brackets and identified them as action diagrams in their book *Diagramming Techniques for Analysts and Programmers* (Prentice Hall, 1985). "Action diagram" seems an appropriately descriptive name. Action diagrams play a significant role in modern computer aided software engineering but they are excellent logic picturing tools in pencil-and-paper form.

You'll see all of my example interactive VAX programs both in source code and action diagram form in this book.

8.4 BOJ/Process Until/EOJ Conversational Logic Structure

A conversational interactive program has a structure resembling that of a batch program. It has a beginning that is performed once to start processing. It has a PERFORM . . . UNTIL that repeatedly executes a processing loop. The program remains continuously active until the terminal operator doesn't want to process any more transactions. When the transaction-processing loop ends, the program executes its end of job logic once to sign off.

Every iteration of the processing loop (2000) in a conversational interactive program is called a **transaction**. When you invoke the program you process one transaction at a time and may handle many transactions one after another. In CALC1 one transaction consists of the entry of QUANTITY and PRICE information, the computation of three values, and their DISPLAY on the terminal screen.

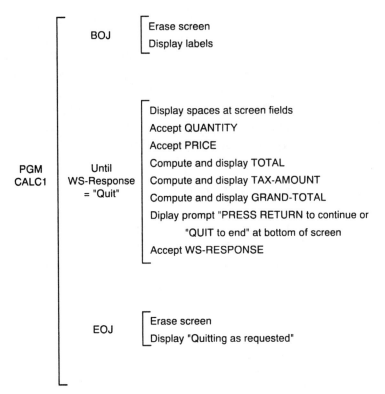

Figure 8.5 Action diagram showing the logic of CALC1. I map out program logic with these diagrams before coding. Each bracket is a paragraph of COBOL code. The language inside the bracket is pseudocode.

8.5 The Terminal Operator Controls Processing

The terminal operator determines if, after the completion of processing for one transaction, another transaction exists to be processed. The processing loop (2000) is performed until the operator indicates that it is time to stop. How do you provide the operator with the ability to indicate this?

In batch processing you seek a new record to process at the bottom of the processing loop (the process you PERFORM . . . UNTIL in your mainline); you eventually hit end-of-file. In a conversational interactive program you seek the operator's intention at the bottom of the processing loop. In the logic diagram in Figure 8.5 I prompt the operator with the end-of-transaction message at the bottom of the "until" bracket (2000).

In source code (Figure 8.4) I issue the end of transaction prompt at lines 70 and 71, where I display a message asking the operator to press *<Return>* to continue processing or enter QUIT *<Return>* to terminate the program. The PERFORM . . . UNTIL condition that drives the transaction processing loop is satisfied if WS-RESPONSE assumes a value of "QUIT". It takes on this value if the operator enters it at the ACCEPT coded at lines 72–74. If the operator presses *<Return>* here immediately, WS-REPONSE receives spaces, the loop-terminating condition is not satisfied, and you process another transaction.

8.6 ACCEPT and DISPLAY in CALC1

Program CALC1 contains three ACCEPT statements and several DISPLAY statements. Since the ACCEPT statements for QUANTITY and PRICE expect to receive numeric values and place them in numeric fields, I coded WITH CONVERSION on them at lines 51 and 55. I didn't code WITH CONVERSION at the ACCEPT at line 72 for WS-RESPONSE, because it expects to receive alphanumeric (not numeric) input. All of my ACCEPTs have PROTECTED on them to prevent the operator from overshooting the field on the screen (entering too many characters).

I put the DISPLAY statements in CALC1 into groups. The first group, at lines 33 through 38, clears the screen and then places literal characters on it called *screen labels*. Since these labels need to be written to the screen only once, I put these DISPLAYs in beginning of job.

At the start of the transaction processing loop (2000) I use another set of DISPLAY statements to write spaces to all data entry fields on the screen. This blanks out data from a previous transaction.

My third set of DISPLAY statements are at lines 60, 64, and 68. These DISPLAYs each follow a COMPUTE that develops a value. I move each computed value to a formatted field (PIC ZZ,ZZZ.99) to eliminate leading zeros and insert commas and the decimal point. I then DISPLAY the formatted field on the screen. My final DISPLAY presents the end-of-loop prompt to the operator.

8.7 ACCEPT When No Data Is Entered

If no data is entered when ACCEPT is executed—you press the *<Return>* key immediately—and the receiving field is numeric WITH CONVERSION, the field assumes a value of zero. The computation that results in Figure 8.6 shows that each of the computed values in this case becomes zero.

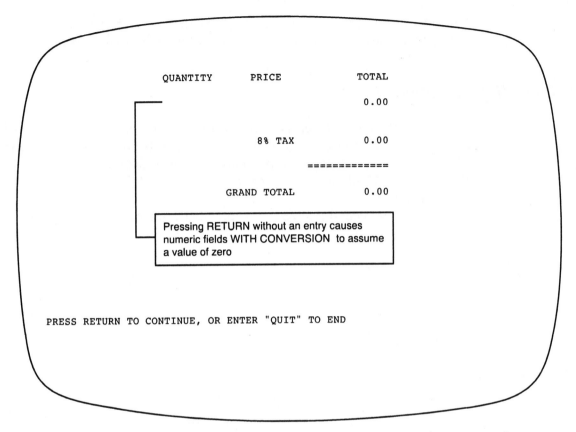

Figure 8.6   If no data is entered when ACCEPT is executed—you press the *<Return>* key immediately—and the receiving field is numeric WITH CONVERSION, the field assumes a value of zero.

If the receiving field in an ACCEPT is an alphanumeric (PIC X) field and you enter no data before pressing the *<Return>* key, the receiving field is filled with spaces.

8.8 *<Arrow>* Keys and *<Backspace>* Not ACCEPTed!

The *<Arrow>* cursor positioning keys and *<Backspace>* are not regarded as valid entries when ACCEPT is executed. But you might make a mistake entering data to a field and want to move the cursor backwards in the field to correct it. To do this you have to use the *<Delete>* key. This is "destructive" delete. Each time you press *<Delete>* you delete a character to the left of the cursor. You have to reenter characters you have deleted leftward after you correct the part of the field that is wrong.

8.9 Ending Execution of CALC1

Figure 8.7 illustrates the entry of the word QUIT by the terminal operator at the end-of-loop prompt. In response to this entry the condition at the PROCESS . . . UNTIL loop is satisfied. Control passes to 3000-EOJ in the program, which erases the screen and DISPLAYs the message shown in Figure 8.8.

Notice that I coded line 28 to accept either uppercase "QUIT" or lower-

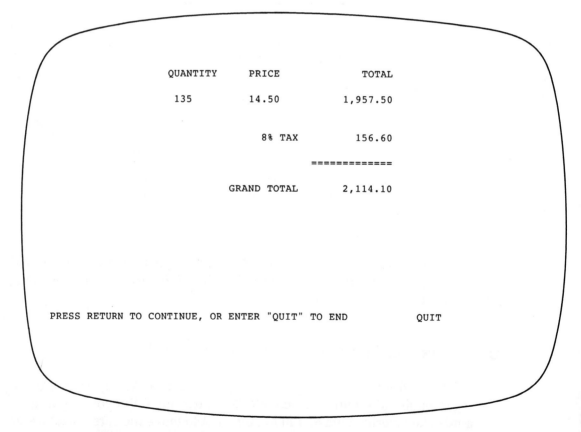

Figure 8.7   You end execution of CALC1 by entering "QUIT" at the operator prompt after completion of a transaction.

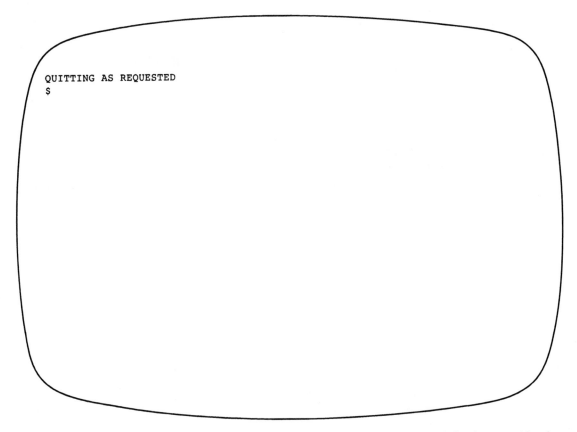

```
QUITTING AS REQUESTED
$
```

Figure 8.8 When you end execution of CALC1 you receive a final screen like this from its end-of-job logic.

case "quit." Unless you take case into account terminal users can become quite frustrated, since most end-users expect case distinctions not to matter.

8.10 Demonstrating CALC1

The best way to see how a conversational interactive VAX COBOL program works is to actually run CALC1. You can key in its source code from Figure 8.4 using EDT, and compile, linkage edit, and run it as described in Chapter 6. But a more convenient way to work with the program is to obtain its source code on diskette and upload it to your VAX system. The source code for CALC1, and for all of the other programs in this book, is available on diskette as described in Appendix E.

8.11 Other ACCEPT Options

ACCEPT presents three options that I do not suggest you use:

- DEFAULT
- PROTECTED FILLER (literal)
- WITH EDITING

I will describe each option here and tell you why I suggest you not use it.

DEFAULT changes the default zero or spaces value for "no data entered" to some other value. It assigns a value to a field when **<Return>** is pressed and no data has been entered:

```
ACCEPT WS-QUANTITY
    FROM LINE 7 COLUMN 21
    WITH CONVERSION
    DEFAULT . . .
```

You can code DEFAULT as a literal, a data-name, or the words IS CURRENT:

DEFAULT 1.	For an integer field
DEFAULT 15.00.	For a PIC 9(5)V99 field
DEFAULT 'MORE'.	For an alphanumeric field
DEFAULT WS-PREV-NAME.	As a data-name
DEFAULT IS CURRENT.	As present value of WS-QUANTITY

Unfortunately DEFAULT affects only the receiving field. It doesn't put anything visible on the screen to show what the default value for the field will be. This leaves the terminal operator "blind," and this is troublesome.

PROTECTED has an option name **FILLER** that appears similar to DEFAULT but is not the same. PROTECTED FILLER '-' fills the field with specified literal contents (such as hyphens) that are shown on the screen but don't affect field contents. I don't recommend that you use change the default filler values from spaces.

ACCEPT . . . **WITH EDITING** allows the terminal operator to use the **<Left arrow>** and **<Right arrow>** in addition to **<Delete>** to change the contents already keyed into a field, but it hides from view what the field received by the program actually contains. You can make an error in entering a field, correct it as allowed by WITH EDITING, and still have the corrected entry fail because the behind-the-scenes actual contents of the field includes invalid data. Experiment with it as you wish, but be warned about its use!

8.12 *ACCEPTing Control Keys*

VAX COBOL does not ordinarily support the entry of keys such as function keys, arrows, and combination keys such as *<Ctrl/A>* with ACCEPT. You can arrange to ACCEPT these keys with the **CONTROL KEY IN** option.

When you code CONTROL KEY IN you establish a separate field, apart from the data being ACCEPTed, in which any control value entered is stored. To interpret the control key you need to establish definitions for keys based on decimal ASCII key values.

Frankly I don't recommend that you try to use the CONTROL KEY IN option of ACCEPT until you are quite familiar with VAX COBOL interactive programming. Since the use of control keys is not essential and complicates conversational interactive programming, I haven't included this in my example programs. If you would like to pursue control key handling see the bibliography in Appendix C, where I cite the DEC publication you can use as a guide in this area.

8.13 Chapter Summary

Conversational interactive logic is readily represented using an *action diagram*, a simple graphic pseudocode. On an action diagram, every bracket represents one paragraph of COBOL code. The diagram shows how you plan to use the three structured programming building blocks of sequence, selection, and iteration in implementing logic. You can use an action diagram for design walkthrough before starting program coding.

A *transaction* is a unit of work to the terminal operator. A *conversational program* remains continuously active until the terminal operator doesn't want to process any more transactions. The program has a structure that resembles that of a batch program except that instead of seeking another record at the bottom of its processing loop, it seeks the operator's intentions. Does the operator wish to continue with more transactions or quit?

Program CALC1 ACCEPTs two numeric values. It computes and DISPLAYs three other values from those entered. This small program demonstrates conversational interactive logic, the basic syntax of ACCEPT and DISPLAY, and use of the PROTECTED and WITH CONVERSION options.

If no data is entered when ACCEPT is executed and you have coded WITH CONVERSION, a numeric receiving field will receive a value of zero. An ACCEPT for an alphanumeric field will receive spaces. *<Arrows>* and

<Backspace> keys are not considered legitimate input to a common ACCEPT. You can use only the *<Delete>* key to correct a field entry.

ACCEPT syntax provides additional options including DEFAULT, PROTECTED FILLER (literal), and WITH EDITING. These options all have subtle pitfalls that make them problematic. The examples in this book do not use these options but instead provide functionality in more open and reliable ways. Accepting control keys likewise involves more complex programming techniques that are not explored in these examples.

8.14 Important Terms

You can review these terms to check your understanding of this chapter:

Action diagram   A compact way of mapping out program logic using brackets and pseudocode to show sequence, selection, and iteration.

Control key   The cursor movement *<Arrow>* keys, *<Tab>*, *<Backspace>* and combination keys such as *<Ctrl/S>*; not handled by ACCEPT unless you code the CONTROL KEY IN option.

DEFAULT   An option of VAX COBOL's ACCEPT verb that gives a receiving field a standard value if nothing is entered into it on the screen; it does not automatically show on the screen.

PROTECTED FILLER . . .   An ACCEPT option that fills a field with a specified value when ACCEPT is executed; it appears on the screen but does not get into the program receiving field.

Chapter Nine

CALC2 AND CALC3: MORE EFFECTIVE SCREEN HANDLING

You have many ACCEPT and DISPLAY options at your disposal with VAX COBOL. You need to make effective choices in using them. In this chapter I show you how to code ACCEPT and DISPLAY options to provide terminal operator convenience and make your conversational interactive programs easy to use.

9.1 VT-100 Terminal Video Screen Attributes

Terminals in the Digital Equipment Corporation VT family contain circuitry providing several screen field display attributes beyond those normally associated with IBM mainframe terminals. These characteristics are supported by several manufacturers and are readily emulated by microcomputers. The following field attributes became available with the model VT-100 terminal:

BOLD   Presents a field at bright intensity.

REVERSED   Shows the field as dark characters on a bright background.

BLINKING   Flashes the field on and off.

UNDERLINED   Presents a field with underscores.

NO ECHO   Used with ACCEPT, receives the keystrokes entered in the field but does not display them.

Except for NO ECHO you can use these attributes in combination with both
ACCEPT and DISPLAY and with the PROTECTED option, as shown:

```
DISPLAY 'Enter your birth date as 6 numbers'
    BOLD
    REVERSED
    AT LINE 4 COLUMN 10
    ERASE TO END OF LINE.

ACCEPT WS-OP-ID FROM LINE 4 COLUMN 63 WITH NO ECHO.

ACCEPT WS-OP-ENTRY
    REVERSED
    PROTECTED
    AT LINE 24 COLUMN 71.
```

Video screen presentation attributes can enhance screen legibility if you
use them carefully. Screen labels DISPLAYed with BOLD stand out from
data entry fields. If you display a screen field to be entered by the operator with REVERSED or UNDERLINED the operator can see the length of the
field. BLINKING, used sparingly for very important messages, can help
draw attention to an error. But overuse of any special screen presentation
attribute lessens its ability to draw attention and creates visual clutter.

9.2 Program CALC2: Enhanced Screen Field Treatment

In Program CALC1 in Chapter 8 I demonstrated for you the essential flow
of control in a conversational interactive program. That primitive program made minimal use of ACCEPT and DISPLAY options. In program
CALC2 (an enhancement of CALC1), listed in Figure 9.1, I incorporate
additional features:

- Screen labels are presented BOLD (bright intensity), with source
  code at lines 33 through 38
- WITH BELL has been used on the prompts at line 47 and 90
- The ACCEPT statements for QUANTITY and PRICE have been
  expanded to specify REVERSED at lines 53, 59, 65, 71, and 77
- WITH CONVERSION has been specified for DISPLAY statements at
  lines 64 through 79
- BLINKING has been used (overused?) for the DISPLAY at line 82.

Figure 9.2 shows you the screen produced by CALC2. I have applied
reverse video to all fields, but you will probably agree that this overdoes it.

```
CALC2                  15-Mar-1992 23:23:24    VAX COBOL V4.3-57
Source Listing         15-Mar-1992 23:21:26    CSC$ROOT:[CSCJGJ.VAXCO]CALC2.COB;1
     1          IDENTIFICATION DIVISION.
     2          PROGRAM-ID.    CALC2.
     3          *AUTHOR.        J JANOSSY   INTERNET: JANOSSY@CSCVAX.DEPAUL.EDU
     4          *INSTALLATION.  DEPAUL UNIVERSITY, CHICAGO, ILLINOIS, USA
     5          *=========================================================
     6          *    Second "CALC" Demonstration Program in VAX COBOL ON-LINE!
     7          *
     8          *    This program overdoes the use of reverse video and blinking
     9          *    to show you things to avoid in your interactive programs.
    10          *    It's easy to create visually unappealing screens if you
    11          *    misuse the wealth of VAX and VT terminal family features!
    12          *=========================================================
    13          ENVIRONMENT DIVISION.
    14          *---------------------------------------------------------
    15          DATA DIVISION.
    16          WORKING-STORAGE SECTION.
    17          01   WS-QUANTITY                    PIC 9(5).
    18          01   WS-PRICE                       PIC S99V99.
    19          01   WS-TOTAL                       PIC S9(7)V99.
    20          01   WS-TAX-AMOUNT                  PIC S9(7)V99.
    21          01   WS-GRAND-TOTAL                 PIC S9(8)V99.
    22          01   WS-RESPONSE                    PIC X(4).
    23          *---------------------------------------------------------
    24          PROCEDURE DIVISION.
    25          0000-MAINLINE.
    26              PERFORM 1000-BOJ.
    27              PERFORM 2000-PROCESS
    28                  UNTIL WS-RESPONSE = 'QUIT' OR 'quit'.
    29              PERFORM 3000-EOJ.
    30              STOP RUN.
    31          *
    32          1000-BOJ.
    33              DISPLAY '' AT LINE 1 COLUMN 1 ERASE TO END OF SCREEN.
    34              DISPLAY 'QUANTITY       PRICE            TOTAL' BOLD
    35                  AT LINE 5 COLUMN 20.
    36              DISPLAY '8% TAX'      BOLD AT LINE 10 COLUMN 35.
    37              DISPLAY '==============' BOLD AT LINE 12 COLUMN 43.
    38              DISPLAY 'GRAND TOTAL'  BOLD AT LINE 14 COLUMN 30.
    39          *
    40          2000-PROCESS.
    41              DISPLAY '        '              AT LINE  7 COLUMN 21.
    42              DISPLAY '        '              AT LINE  7 COLUMN 33.
    43              DISPLAY '           '           AT LINE  7 COLUMN 43.
    44              DISPLAY '           '           AT LINE 10 COLUMN 43.
    45              DISPLAY '           '           AT LINE 14 COLUMN 43.
    46              DISPLAY 'ENTER VALUE (NO COMMAS) AND PRESS RETURN'
    47                  WITH BELL
    48                  AT LINE 24 COLUMN 1
    49                  ERASE TO END OF LINE.
    50          *
    51              ACCEPT WS-QUANTITY
    52                  PROTECTED
    53                  REVERSED
    54                  WITH CONVERSION
    55                  FROM LINE 7 COLUMN 21.
    56          *
    57              ACCEPT WS-PRICE
    58                  PROTECTED
    59                  REVERSED
    60                  WITH CONVERSION
    61                  FROM LINE 7 COLUMN 33.
    62          *
    63              COMPUTE WS-TOTAL = WS-QUANTITY * WS-PRICE.
    64              DISPLAY WS-TOTAL
    65                  REVERSED
```

(Continued)

Figure 9.1   Source code for program CALC2 with BOLD, WITH BELL, REVERSED, WITH CONVERSION on DISPLAY, and BLINKING options. This program overuses some of these options. When you run it, the appearance is not visually pleasing!

```
66                    WITH CONVERSION
67                    AT LINE 7 COLUMN 43.
68          *
69                COMPUTE WS-TAX-AMOUNT = WS-TOTAL * .08.
70                DISPLAY WS-TAX-AMOUNT
71                    REVERSED
72                    WITH CONVERSION
73                    AT LINE 10 COLUMN 43.
74          *
75                COMPUTE WS-GRAND-TOTAL = WS-TOTAL + WS-TAX-AMOUNT.
76                DISPLAY WS-GRAND-TOTAL
77                    REVERSED
78                    WITH CONVERSION
79                    AT LINE 14 COLUMN 43.
80          *
81                DISPLAY 'PRESS RETURN TO CONTINUE, OR ENTER "QUIT" TO END '
82                    BLINKING
83                    AT LINE 24 COLUMN 1.
84                ACCEPT WS-RESPONSE
85                    PROTECTED
86                    FROM LINE 24 COLUMN 60.
87          *
88          3000-EOJ.
89                DISPLAY 'QUITTING AS REQUESTED' AT LINE 1 COLUMN 1
90                    WITH BELL
91                    ERASE TO END OF SCREEN.
```

Figure 9.1   *(Continued)*

9.3 *DISPLAY . . . WITH CONVERSION for Numeric Data: Problems!*

A number stored in memory, such as the TOTAL, TAX, and GRAND TOTAL, may have an implied decimal point indicated with a PICture such as PIC 99V99. When you DISPLAY such a value on the screen you have to format it. At a minimum you need to insert a period at the decimal point location. Leading zero suppression, a dollar sign for monetary amounts, commas every three digits left of the decimal point, and a sign are also desirable and you usually have to provide them.

You have already seen WITH CONVERSION on the ACCEPT statement. It "de-edits" what the you enter into a numeric field, making it into a pure number so COBOL can do arithmetic with it. You can also use WITH CONVERSION on the DISPLAY of a numeric field to gain some elements of formatting. When used on DISPLAY, however, the result with WITH CON-VERSION is not entirely satisfactory, and I don't recommend you follow the pattern of CALC2 to use it. WITH CONVERSION accomplishes some of what you need to do when displaying numeric data, but not enough. If you use it on DISPLAYs your screens can appear sloppy and amateurish through no fault of your own!

If you display a numeric field WITH CONVERSION you do not get commas; the TOTAL value in Figure 9.2 is presented as 1957.50 rather than 1,957.50. WITH CONVERSION cannot provide a dollar sign to you if you want it. WITH CONVERSION operates field-by-field. It has no ability to for-

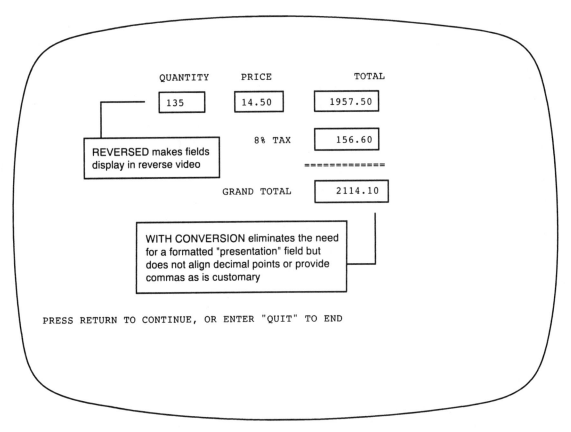

Figure 9.2   Screen produced by CALC2. The boxes around the five fields depict reverse video. The prompt line blinks. Note that the decimal points for TOTAL, TAX, and GRAND TOTAL are not aligned in the same column, making the sum look messy (WITH CONVERSION on DISPLAY is responsible for that.)

mat a column of numbers so that all of the decimal points line up in the same column to make a more readable display. (The GRAND TOTAL in Figure 9.2, 2114.10, is offset to the right in relation to the fields above it, making it appear as a sloppily presented sum.)

If you use WITH CONVERSION to DISPLAY a signed negative value, it formats the field with a floating leading sign as shown in Figure 9.3. While this reveals the sign of the value, it's more customary in business and accounting to display a sign trailing after the final digit of a number. When presented trailing, the signs of numbers always appear in the same location rather than appearing in different positions for numbers of differing magnitude. WITH CONVERSION doesn't do this.

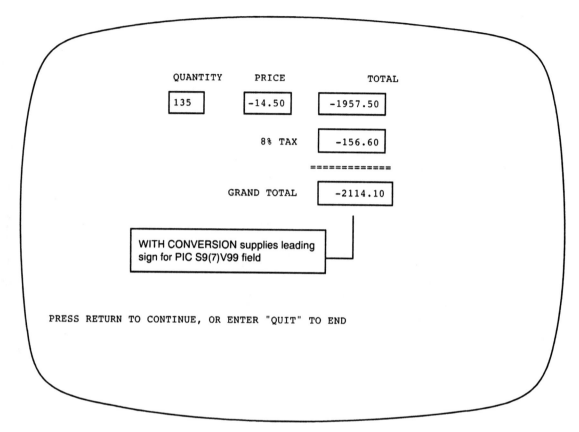

Figure 9.3 WITH CONVERSION on DISPLAY presents negative signs leading. This is not in keeping with common accounting conventions under which the sign of a negative number is presented after it (trailing). You have more control over field format if you move a value to a numeric-edited field such as PIC Z,ZZZ,ZZ9.99- and DISPLAY that field.

9.4 Program CALC3: A Good Pattern for Field Handling

Figure 9.4 lists the source code for program CALC3, my final version of an interactive VAX COBOL demonstration program. Unlike CALC2, CALC3 makes better use of video presentation attributes, including traditional numeric formatting field techniques instead of DISPLAY . . . WITH CONVERSION. Unlike CALC1 or CALC2, CALC3 redisplays the value received in a field after receiving it. This lets the you see the value "cleaned up" by the formatting action. And it gives you total control over things like the alignment of fields.

```
CALC3                    15-Mar-1992 23:26:07     VAX COBOL V4.3-57
Source Listing           15-Mar-1992 23:00:29     CSC$ROOT:[CSCJGJ.VAXCO]CALC3.COB;1

    1            IDENTIFICATION DIVISION.
    2            PROGRAM-ID.      CALC3.
    3            *AUTHOR.         J JANOSSY   INTERNET: JANOSSY@CSCVAX.DEPAUL.EDU
    4            *INSTALLATION.   DEPAUL UNIVERSITY, CHICAGO, ILLINOIS, USA
    5            *================================================================
    6            *   Best "CALC" Demonstration Program in VAX COBOL ON-LINE!
    7            *
    8            *   Enhances CALC2.  Continues use of screen attributes but
    9            *   uses formatted working-storage fields to display/redisplay
   10            *   numeric values.  This provides more control over number
   11            *   formats than DISPLAY ... WITH CONVERSION and uses reverse
   12            *   video only on the active data entry field.
   13            *================================================================
   14            ENVIRONMENT DIVISION.
   15            *----------------------------------------------------------------
   16            DATA DIVISION.
   17            WORKING-STORAGE SECTION.
   18            01  WS-QUANTITY                    PIC 9(5).
   19            01  WS-QUANTITY-Z                  PIC ZZ,ZZ9.
   20            01  WS-PRICE                       PIC S99V99.
   21            01  WS-PRICE-Z                     PIC Z9.99-.
   22            01  WS-TOTAL                       PIC S9(7)V99.
   23            01  WS-TAX-AMOUNT                  PIC S9(7)V99.
   24            01  WS-GRAND-TOTAL                 PIC S9(8)V99.
   25            01  WS-RESPONSE                    PIC X(4).
   26            01  WS-MONEY-Z                     PIC ZZ,ZZZ,ZZ9.99-.
   27            *----------------------------------------------------------------
   28            PROCEDURE DIVISION.
   29            0000-MAINLINE.
   30                PERFORM 1000-BOJ.
   31                PERFORM 2000-PROCESS
   32                    UNTIL WS-RESPONSE = 'QUIT' OR 'quit'.
   33                PERFORM 3000-EOJ.
   34                STOP RUN.
   35            *
   36            1000-BOJ.
   37                DISPLAY '' AT LINE 1 COLUMN 1 ERASE TO END OF SCREEN.
   38                DISPLAY 'QUANTITY      PRICE             TOTAL' BOLD
   39                    AT LINE 5 COLUMN 20.
   40                DISPLAY '8% TAX'        BOLD AT LINE 10 COLUMN 35.
   41                DISPLAY '============='  BOLD AT LINE 12 COLUMN 43.
   42                DISPLAY 'GRAND TOTAL'   BOLD AT LINE 14 COLUMN 30.
   43            *
   44            2000-PROCESS.
   45                DISPLAY '         '              AT LINE  7 COLUMN 21.
   46                DISPLAY '         '              AT LINE  7 COLUMN 33.
   47                DISPLAY '         '              AT LINE  7 COLUMN 43.
   48                DISPLAY '         '              AT LINE 10 COLUMN 43.
   49                DISPLAY '         '              AT LINE 14 COLUMN 43.
   50                DISPLAY 'ENTER VALUE (NO COMMAS) AND PRESS RETURN'
   51                    AT LINE 24 COLUMN 1
   52                    ERASE TO END OF LINE.
   53            *
   54                ACCEPT WS-QUANTITY
   55                    PROTECTED
   56                    REVERSED
   57                    WITH CONVERSION
   58                    FROM LINE 7 COLUMN 21.
```
                                                              (Continued)

Figure 9.4   Source code for CALC3, my final version of this program. I suggest you use this as a model for further work as I do in the VAXDEMO demonstration system in this book. The screens presented by the program are shown in the next several figures. This program makes better use of video presentation attributes than CALC1 or CALC2 does. It shows only the current field in reverse video. It uses traditional numeric formatting field techniques instead of DISPLAY ... WITH CONVERSION and redisplays entered data formatted without reverse video.

```
59              MOVE WS-QUANTITY TO WS-QUANTITY-Z.
60              DISPLAY WS-QUANTITY-Z AT LINE 7 COLUMN 21.
61      *
62              ACCEPT WS-PRICE
63                 PROTECTED
64                 REVERSED
65                 WITH CONVERSION
66                 FROM LINE 7 COLUMN 33.
67              MOVE WS-PRICE TO WS-PRICE-Z.
68              DISPLAY WS-PRICE-Z AT LINE 7 COLUMN 33.
69      *
70              COMPUTE WS-TOTAL = WS-QUANTITY * WS-PRICE.
71              MOVE WS-TOTAL TO WS-MONEY-Z.
72              DISPLAY WS-MONEY-Z AT LINE 7 COLUMN 43.
73      *
74              COMPUTE WS-TAX-AMOUNT = WS-TOTAL * .08.
75              MOVE WS-TAX-AMOUNT TO WS-MONEY-Z.
76              DISPLAY WS-MONEY-Z AT LINE 10 COLUMN 43.
77      *
78              COMPUTE WS-GRAND-TOTAL = WS-TOTAL + WS-TAX-AMOUNT.
79              MOVE WS-GRAND-TOTAL TO WS-MONEY-Z.
80              DISPLAY WS-MONEY-Z AT LINE 14 COLUMN 43.
81      *
82              DISPLAY 'PRESS'
83                 AT LINE 24 COLUMN 1.
84              DISPLAY ' RETURN'
85                 BLINKING
86                 AT LINE 24 COLUMN 6.
87              DISPLAY ' TO CONTINUE, OR ENTER "QUIT" TO END '
88                 AT LINE 24 COLUMN 13.
89              ACCEPT WS-RESPONSE
90                 PROTECTED
91                 FROM LINE 24 COLUMN 60.
92      *
93          3000-EOJ.
94              DISPLAY 'QUITTING AS REQUESTED' AT LINE 1 COLUMN 1
95                 ERASE TO END OF SCREEN.
```

Figure 9.4   *(Continued)*

9.5 Traditional PIC Number Formatting

The way a terminal operator enters a number is often not the way it is best presented on the screen. An operator might, for example, most conveniently enter a number as 1234. We would like to have it appear on the screen as 1,234. You can use traditional numeric formatting PICs for screen presentation. You code numeric formatted fields such as PIC $Z,ZZZ,ZZZ.99- in WORKING-STORAGE and MOVE data to such a field before displaying it.

For example you can move a number stored in a PIC 9(5) field to a field defined with PIC ZZ,ZZ9. You can then redisplay the formatted PIC field at the same location on the screen as that where data was entered. Move a signed field with implied decimal to a field such as PIC Z,ZZZ,ZZ9.99- for formatting.

In CALC3 I have defined WS-QUANTITY-Z, WS-PRICE-Z, and WS-MONEY-Z at lines 19, 21, and 26. I use these fields to format the values for screen presentation. You can think of these fields as **screen format fields** because they are used to explicitly format number values for screen display.

9.6 Field Redisplay after Entry

Figure 9.5 depicts the entry of a value into the QUANTITY field of program CALC3. Since the ACCEPT at lines 54 through 58 is coded with REVERSED, the entry field appears as a bright bar indicating the length of the field. Let's say that the operator keys in 9657 without a comma, as required by WITH CONVERSION on an ACCEPT statement.

Figure 9.6 shows how the screen appears after the operator presses

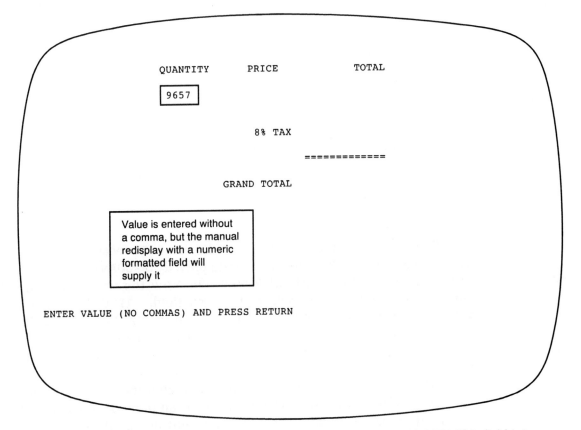

Figure 9.5   CALC3 screen when you are entering QUANTITY. This field is in reverse video when it is active for entry.

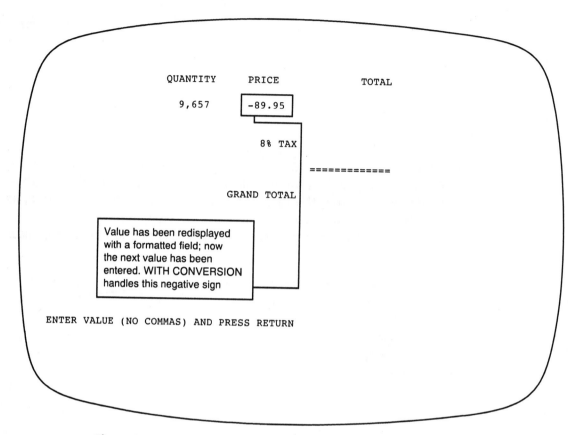

Figure 9.6 CALC3 screen after you have entered QUANTITY and pressed *<Return>*. PRICE is now the active data entry field.

the *<Return>* key. I've moved the entered value 9657 received for QUAN-TITY to WS-QUANTITY-Z and have redisplayed WS-QUANTITY-Z at the same screen location without REVERSED. Now the value no longer appears in reverse video. Instead, the next field, PRICE, is in reverse video due to the ACCEPT I coded for it at lines 62 through 66. This vividly shows the operator the active field. It's a touch of graphic convenience that can make your VAX interactive screens much easier for the terminal operator to use.

In Figure 9.7 the terminal operator has entered the value −89.95 in the PRICE field and pressed *<Return>*. This is an unusual price, but let's assume it covers the return of merchandise and represents a credit. The value has been transformed by WITH CONVERSION to a signed numeric

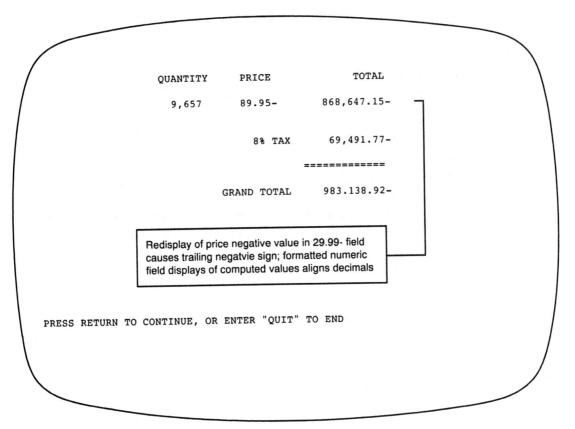

```
        QUANTITY        PRICE              TOTAL

         9,657          89.95-         868,647.15-

                        8% TAX          69,491.77-

                                      =============

                   GRAND  TOTAL         983.138.92-


         ┌──────────────────────────────────────────┐
         │ Redisplay of price negative value in 29.99- field │
         │ causes trailing negatvie sign; formatted numeric  │
         │ field displays of computed values aligns decimals │
         └──────────────────────────────────────────┘


PRESS RETURN TO CONTINUE,  OR ENTER  "QUIT"  TO END
```

Figure 9.7 CALC3 screen after completion of one transaction. I redisplay entered data by passing it through a numeric edited field. This lets me control how the field will appear on the screen, including placement of decimal point and sign.

value in WS-PRICE. I have moved WS-PRICE to WS-PRICE-Z and then redisplayed WS-PRICE-Z at the same screen location without REVERSED. The field no longer appears in reverse video. Due to the numeric formatting I coded for WS-PRICE-Z the sign of the value is presented trailing, in the way customary for accounting information.

My explicit numeric formatting of the TOTAL, TAX, and GRAND TOTAL fields is also shown in Figure 9.7. CALC3 has computed these values. As each was computed I MOVEd it to WS-MONEY-Z, which I then DISPLAYed. I needed only one formatted field to handle all three values because the logic at lines 70 through 80 did the computations and DISPLAYs one after another.

9.7 Chapter Summary

Terminals in the VT family contain circuitry providing several screen field display attributes: BOLD, REVERSED, BLINKING, UNDERLINED, and NO ECHO. You can use these in combination with both ACCEPT and DIS-PLAY, in combination with each other, or in combination with other options such as PROTECTED, WITH CONVERSION, and WITH BELL.

While you can simply ACCEPT data into a field, it's beneficial to reDISPLAY the value received on the screen. This standardizes the appearance of the field on the screen and confirms to the terminal operator what was received. If you ACCEPT with REVERSED the terminal operator can see the field length for the entry. Subsequent reDISPLAY without REVERSED can remove this "highlighting" of the field.

You can reDISPLAY numeric data on the screen WITH CONVERSION but it is a poor substitute for explicit (PIC $ZZ,ZZZ.99-) formatting. WITH CONVERSION can't insert commas, can't line up columns of decimal points, and can't provide a leading dollar sign. It puts the sign in front of negative numbers, not behind them as is common in accounting work.

Program CALC3 in this chapter concludes my demonstration of a simple interactive VAX COBOL program. It shows you a workable selection of VT terminal attributes that provide a convenient interface for computer terminal operators.

9.8 Important Terms

You can review these terms to check your understanding of this chapter:

Screen field display options (attributes) VAX COBOL DISPLAY options that control the way a field is shown on the screen:

BOLD Shows a field at bright intensity.

REVERSED Shows the field as dark characters on a bright back ground.

BLINKING Flashes the field on and off.

UNDERLINED Presents a field with underscores.

NO ECHO Used with ACCEPT, receives the keystrokes in the field but does not display them.

Screen format field A field to which data is moved to format it for DISPLAY on the screen with commas, dollar sign, decimal point, and numeric sign.

Traditional PIC numeric formatting   Moving a number value received from keyboard entry to a formatted field such as PIC $ZZ,ZZZ.99 to have it made into a field to be displayed on the screen.

You can find additional questions and exercises for this chapter in Appendix A.

Chapter Ten

CREATING AND USING INDEXED FILES

It's quite likely that you have used sequential files in your previous programming, but you may not have used indexed files. In this chapter I give you the background you need to create and use indexed files on the VAX. *Indexed files* (called VSAM "key sequenced data sets" on IBM mainframes) provide the capability to access individual data records on disk by symbolic key. I'll explain to you why this is critical to interactive systems.

10.1 Disk Devices

The bits making up bytes (characters) of information are just electrical charges. In memory they are stored in transistors that are either "on" (carrying an electrical charge) or "off" (not carrying a charge). Eight tiny transistors among the hundreds of thousands of transistors on an integrated circuit represent the binary 0s and 1s of a character in memory. "On" and "off" can also be represented by magnetized spots on a tape or disk recording surface. This is how we record information electronically.

A magnetic tape such as a cassette or videotape is long and narrow. This is a fine configuration for sequential storage and access of information. But we have to arrange the magnetic surface in a different way if we want to quickly get (physically) to any point on the surface. A *magnetic disk* (either floppy or hard) has the same magnetic recording surface as tape but is arranged as a *platter*. As shown in Figure 10.1 several disk platters are usually stacked on the same shaft. The *read/write head assembly* (disk "arm") can swing across the disk surface. The combination of disk

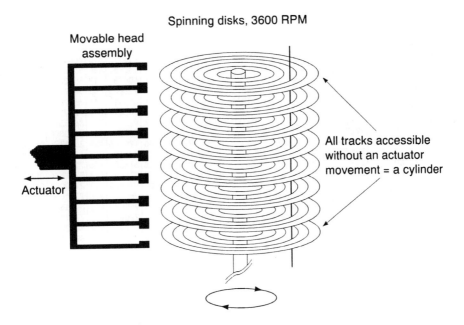

Spinning disks, 3600 RPM

Movable head assembly

All tracks accessible without an actuator movement = a cylinder

Actuator

Figure 10.1 A magnetic disk stores data by storing binary bits as magnetized spots on recording surfaces arranged as platters. This supports *direct access* to the data.

rotation and disk head assembly movement makes much of each recording surface accessible.

Disk devices are critical to interactive systems. Because of their construction they permit **direct access** to individual records. **Random access** is often used as a synonym for direct access but can be a confusing term, because it implies that you don't know which record you will receive when you read the file. That's not the correct interpretation. *Random access* means that input/output software cannot predict what record you will ask for next. The files we discuss in the chapter to support interactive systems all make use of disk storage devices for direct access.

10.2 The Primary Key Field

When you store information in a file and you expect to access individual records in the file, you have to be able to uniquely identify each record.

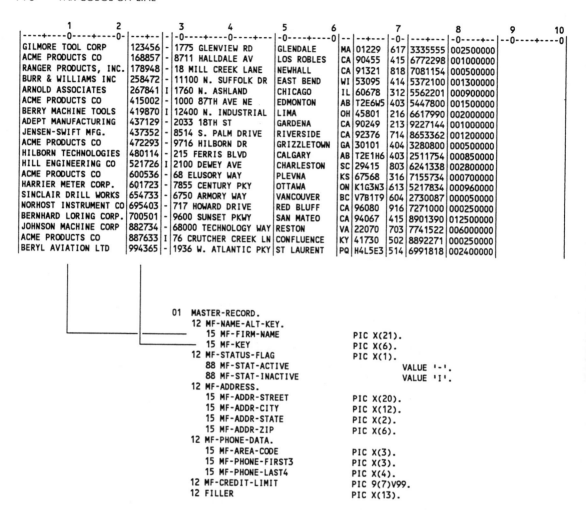

```
                1             2         3           4         5          6         7              8          9         10
        ----+----0----+----0-  ---+--  -  -0----+----0----+---  -0----+----0  --  --+----  -0-  ---+----  -0----+--  --0----+----0
        GILMORE TOOL CORP     123456  -  1775 GLENVIEW RD       GLENDALE    MA 01229  617 3335555  002500000
        ACME PRODUCTS CO      168857  -  8711 HALLDALE AV       LOS ROBLES  CA 90455  415 6772298  001000000
        RANGER PRODUCTS, INC. 178948  -  18 MILL CREEK LANE     NEWHALL     CA 91321  818 7081154  000500000
        BURR & WILLIAMS INC   258472  -  11100 N. SUFFOLK DR    EAST BEND   WI 53095  414 5372100  001300000
        ARNOLD ASSOCIATES     267841  I  1760 N. ASHLAND        CHICAGO     IL 60678  312 5562201  000900000
        ACME PRODUCTS CO      415002  -  1000 87TH AVE NE       EDMONTON    AB T2E6W5 403 5447800  001500000
        BERRY MACHINE TOOLS   419870  I  12400 N. INDUSTRIAL    LIMA        OH 45801  216 6617990  002000000
        ADEPT MANUFACTURING   437129  -  2033 18TH ST           GARDENA     CA 90249  213 9227144  001000000
        JENSEN-SWIFT MFG.     437352  -  8514 S. PALM DRIVE     RIVERSIDE   CA 92376  714 8653362  001200000
        ACME PRODUCTS CO      472293  -  9716 HILBORN DR        GRIZZLETOWN GA 30101  404 3280800  000500000
        HILBORN TECHNOLOGIES  480114  -  215 FERRIS BLVD        CALGARY     AB T2E1H6 403 2511754  000850000
        HILL ENGINEERING CO   521726  I  2100 DEWEY AVE         CHARLESTON  SC 29415  803 6241338  002800000
        ACME PRODUCTS CO      600536  -  68 ELUSORY WAY         PLEVNA      KS 67568  316 7155734  000700000
        HARRIER METER CORP.   601723  -  7855 CENTURY PKY       OTTAWA      ON K1G3N3 613 5217834  000960000
        SINCLAIR DRILL WORKS  654733  -  6750 ARMORY WAY        VANCOUVER   BC V7B1T9 604 2730087  000050000
        NORHOST INSTRUMENT CO 695403  -  717 HOWARD DRIVE       RED BLUFF   CA 96080  916 7271000  000250000
        BERNHARD LORING CORP. 700501  -  9600 SUNSET PKWY       SAN MATEO   CA 94067  415 8901390  012500000
        JOHNSON MACHINE CORP  882734  -  68000 TECHNOLOGY WAY   RESTON      VA 22070  703 7741522  006000000
        ACME PRODUCTS CO      887633  I  76 CRUTCHER CREEK LN   CONFLUENCE  KY 41730  502 8892271  000250000
        BERYL AVIATION LTD    994365  -  1936 W. ATLANTIC PKY   ST LAURENT  PQ H4L5E3 514 6991818  002400000
```

```
              01  MASTER-RECORD.
                  12  MF-NAME-ALT-KEY.
                      15  MF-FIRM-NAME          PIC X(21).
                      15  MF-KEY                PIC X(6).
                  12  MF-STATUS-FLAG            PIC X(1).
                      88  MF-STAT-ACTIVE                      VALUE '-'.
                      88  MF-STAT-INACTIVE                    VALUE 'I'.
                  12  MF-ADDRESS.
                      15  MF-ADDR-STREET        PIC X(20).
                      15  MF-ADDR-CITY          PIC X(12).
                      15  MF-ADDR-STATE         PIC X(2).
                      15  MF-ADDR-ZIP           PIC X(6).
                  12  MF-PHONE-DATA.
                      15  MF-AREA-CODE          PIC X(3).
                      15  MF-PHONE-FIRST3       PIC X(3).
                      15  MF-PHONE-LAST4        PIC X(4).
                  12  MF-CREDIT-LIMIT           PIC 9(7)V99.
                  12  FILLER                    PIC X(13).
```

Figure 10.2 Customer records in a sequential file that will be loaded to an indexed file and accessed by the VAXDEMO system.

You can do this by regarding one field in the record as the *key field*, sometimes called the *primary key*. No two records in the file will be allowed to have the same key value. There are two categories of record keys:

- **Pointer or "location" key**: The key value tells where (physically) the data is stored on disk.

- **Symbolic key**: The key value is just a unique identifier and has nothing to do with where the data is stored.

Pointer keys are easiest for an operating system to handle, but most of the time you don't have the luxury of being able to use a pointer key. The key field of a file is usually something like a government-assigned identification number (social security number in the United States or social insurance number in Canada) or a unique stock number or account ID. Such values do not have anything to do with where you can store a record on disk.

Suppose I run a small manufacturing company that makes nuts and bolts and other metal fasteners. Figure 10.2 lists 20 records in my customer master file. Each record carries name, address, and credit limit information on one of my customers. (My customers are mostly other firms that use my fasteners to make the products that they sell.) I uniquely identify each of my customers with a six-character account number that I will call the *key*. The key field is located in positions 22 through 27 of each record.

I created the customer file to use with my VAXDEMO demonstration system. You'll see much more of it in the next several chapters in which I call it the *master file*. Figure 10.3 shows you how a customer record appears on my interactive inquiry and add/change screens.

10.3 Sequential Files

Sequential files are the simplest form or "organization" of stored data. In a *sequential file* records are written to disk or tape one after another in ascending order of their key field value. You might think of these records as rows in a table copied out row by row for storage outside of memory. The listing shown in Figure 10.2 looks exactly like the records in a sequential file.

A sequential file is fine for applications that always process all the records in a file. Reporting programs usually do this; paper-based reporting is a batch operation. But in an interactive application you usually want to access just one or a few records in a file. If you used a sequential file to support an interactive application the response time of your system would be very poor.

Suppose your customer master file contained a record for each of your 500,000 customers and the data for the customer you wanted to

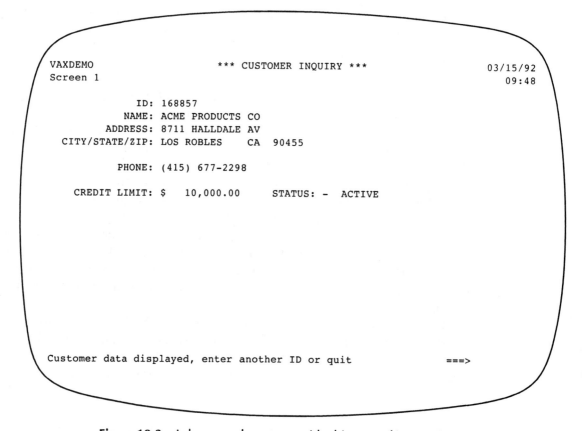

```
VAXDEMO                   *** CUSTOMER INQUIRY ***                03/15/92
Screen 1                                                            09:48
                  ID: 168857
                NAME: ACME PRODUCTS CO
             ADDRESS: 8711 HALLDALE AV
       CITY/STATE/ZIP: LOS ROBLES    CA  90455

               PHONE: (415) 677-2298

        CREDIT LIMIT: $   10,000.00     STATUS: -  ACTIVE




   Customer data displayed, enter another ID or quit              ===>
```

Figure 10.3   I show you how to provide this type of interactive access to customer records in the inquiry and add/change functions of my VAXDEMO system (Chapters 11-15).

bring to the screen happened to be about 400,000 records into this file. Physical input/output (I/O) actions take a relatively long time. You might wait hours for 400,000 READs to be done to finally get to the record you wanted! Interactive systems demand a way to get to the record directly with as few physical I/O actions as possible.

10.4 Relative Files

You can think of a *relative file* as a special form of sequential file. It's always stored on disk and contains fixed-length records. Since the oper-

01	GILMORE TOOL CORP	123456	-	1775 GLENVIEW RD	GLENDALE	MA	01229	617	3335555	002500000
02	ACME PRODUCTS CO	168857	-	8711 HALLDALE AV	LOS ROBLES	CA	90455	415	6772298	001000000
03	RANGER PRODUCTS, INC.	178948	-	18 MILL CREEK LANE	NEWHALL	CA	91321	818	7081154	000500000
04	BURR & WILLIAMS INC	258472	-	11100 N. SUFFOLK DR	EAST BEND	WI	53095	414	5372100	001300000
05	ARNOLD ASSOCIATES	267841	I	1760 N. ASHLAND	CHICAGO	IL	60678	312	5562201	000900000
06	ACME PRODUCTS CO	415002	-	1000 87TH AVE NE	EDMONTON	AB	T2E6W5	403	5447800	001500000
07	BERRY MACHINE TOOLS	419870	I	12400 N. INDUSTRIAL	LIMA	OH	45801	216	6617990	002000000
08	ADEPT MANUFACTURING	437129	-	2033 18TH ST	GARDENA	CA	90249	213	9227144	001000000
09	JENSEN-SWIFT MFG.	437352	-	8514 S. PALM DRIVE	RIVERSIDE	CA	92376	714	8653362	001200000
10	ACME PRODUCTS CO	472293	-	9716 HILBORN DR	GRIZZLETOWN	GA	30101	404	3280800	000500000
11	HILBORN TECHNOLOGIES	480114	-	215 FERRIS BLVD	CALGARY	AB	T2E1H6	403	2511754	000850000
12	HILL ENGINEERING CO	521726	I	2100 DEWEY AVE	CHARLESTON	SC	29415	803	6241338	002800000
13	ACME PRODUCTS CO	600536	-	68 ELUSORY WAY	PLEVNA	KS	67568	316	7155734	000700000
14	HARRIER METER CORP.	601723	-	7855 CENTURY PKY	OTTAWA	ON	K1G3N3	613	5217834	000960000
15	SINCLAIR DRILL WORKS	654733	-	6750 ARMORY WAY	VANCOUVER	BC	V7B1T9	604	2730087	000050000
16	NORHOST INSTRUMENT CO	695403	-	717 HOWARD DRIVE	RED BLUFF	CA	96080	916	7271000	000250000
17	BERNHARD LORING CORP.	700501	-	9600 SUNSET PKWY	SAN MATEO	CA	94067	415	8901390	012500000
18	JOHNSON MACHINE CORP	882734	-	68000 TECHNOLOGY WAY	RESTON	VA	22070	703	7741522	006000000
19	ACME PRODUCTS CO	887633	I	76 CRUTCHER CREEK LN	CONFLUENCE	KY	41730	502	8892271	000250000
20	BERYL AVIATION LTD	994365	-	1936 W. ATLANTIC PKY	ST LAURENT	PQ	H4L5E3	514	6991818	002400000

└── Record number (pointer key for a relative file)

Figure 10.4 Customer records arranged as a relative file with record number as the pointer key.

ating system knows where (physically on disk) the file starts it can compute the location of every record in the file. If you want to get, for example, the 51st record in the file, the operating system can find it by multiplying the record length by 50 and accessing data this far from the beginning of the file. You can picture a relative file as in Figure 10.4.

Relative files were the first form of random access file. You could use them to support an interactive system, but they have a critical shortcoming. The key of the records in a relative file is a pointer key that is not part of the record. When you store a record in such a file you say what record number you want to put it into. When you want to access that record you have to say the record number where it is located. For example, to retrieve the record for Sinclair Drill Works I could not say, "Get me the record with customer ID 654733." Instead I would have to say, "Get me record number 15." But there is nothing associated with Sinclair Drill Works that tells me that its data is located in this place.

Relative files are not practical when you need access to data by symbolic key. Almost all of the work to be done by interactive business data processing systems requires access to data by symbolic key.

10.5 Indexed Files

An **indexed file** is more complicated than either a sequential file or a relative file because it requires two related structures. One of these structures is the data itself, such as the records in a file of customers. But the indexed file also requires a form of "road map" to the data called an *index*. The index is shown in Figure 10.5 as one of the items within the dashed line. The indexed file is *everything* within the dashed line.

The index is like the index to a book. If you want to look up something in a book you scan the index to find the topic you are looking for. Finding the location of the item via the index, you then go directly to the right page for the information.

You can think of the index for an indexed file as if it contained very short records. There is one index record for each data record. The index record has only two fields in it: the primary key value and a pointer to where the record is stored. The records in the index are always kept in ascending order of the key field. When you want to get a particular record the index can be scanned quickly (by system software, not your program) to find the symbolic key value of the record you want. When this index record is found, the pointer value in it indicates exactly where the record is physically located on the disk. System software then gets that record for you.

Building the index for a file and keeping it up-to-date as records are added to or deleted from the file is a complicated process. System software called an **access method** handles these tasks so that no locally writ-

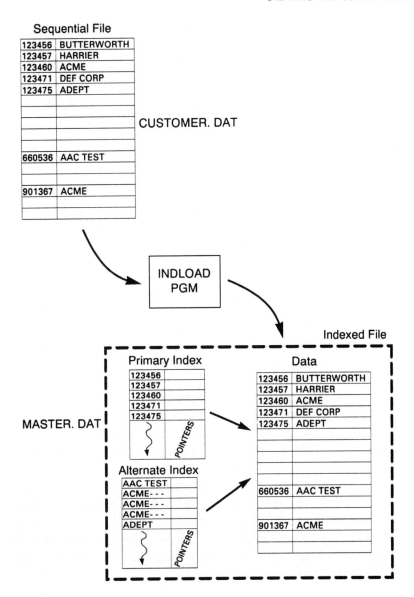

Figure 10.5   When customer records are copied to an indexed file by the INDLOAD program, the indexed file access method automatically builds the primary and alternate indexes. (The indexed file is the entire collection of components within the dashed line.)

ten program has to worry about them. On IBM mainframes this system software was formerly called ISAM and is now called VSAM. On the DEC VAX it's called Record Management Services or RMS. Neither VSAM or RMS indexed files are actually as simple internally as the illustration I just gave you, but they act exactly as if they were constructed that simply.

10.6 Creating an Indexed File on the VAX

When you create an indexed file on the VAX you simply copy records from a sequential file to the indexed file as shown in Figure 10.5. Record Management Services handles the creation of the index as well as the storage of the data itself. The only thing you have to guarantee is that each record you load to the file has a unique key and that the records you are loading are sorted in ascending key sequence.

Figure 10.6 shows you a program named INDLOAD that I wrote to create and load my customer master file. This program reads records from a sequential file named CUSTOMER.DAT and creates an indexed file named MASTER.DAT. The programs in my VAXDEMO system (Chapters 11 to 15) will access this indexed file.

Creating an indexed file on an IBM mainframe involves "defining" the file before loading it. This lets you design the internal arrangement of the indexed file to optimize its efficiency. But it also makes the process of creating every indexed file more complicated since you have to understand the product, named IDCAMS, that handles the definition process.

System software on the VAX called File Definition Language (FDL) provides a capability similar to IDCAMS/VSAM on an IBM mainframe. Using FDL you can define the characteristics of an indexed file to make it as efficient as possible given the data record length and volume for a particular file. If you work with large indexed files on the VAX consult Appendix C for information on DEC publications that can help you use FDL to design them efficiently.

10.7 Alternate Keys

You'll notice that "inside" the indexed file enclosed by a dashed line in Figure 10.5 there are actually two index files and the data file. The second index I have illustrated is optional and is called an **alternate index.**

Alternate indexes are like the several card catalogs of a public library. You can usually find a book by knowing its subject matter, or by knowing

```
INDLOAD              15-Mar-1992 12:10:21    VAX COBOL V4.3-57
Source Listing       15-Mar-1992 12:10:06
CSC$ROOT:[CSCJGJ.VAXCO]INDLOAD.COB;1

     1          IDENTIFICATION DIVISION.
     2          PROGRAM-ID.     INDLOAD.
     3          *AUTHOR.        J JANOSSY    INTERNET: JANOSSY@CSCVAX.DEPAUL.EDU
     4          *INSTALLATION.  DEPAUL UNIVERSITY, CHICAGO, IL
     5          *=================================================================
     6          *    Program to Create/Load Indexed File in VAX COBOL On-Line!
     7          *         General Purpose Indexed File Loader  3-1-92
     8          *
     9          *    Reads records from a sequential file and copies them to
    10          *    an indexed file.  Once this program has been run the
    11          *    indexed file exists and can be accessed.
    12          *=================================================================
    13          ENVIRONMENT DIVISION.
    14          INPUT-OUTPUT SECTION.
    15          FILE-CONTROL.
    16              SELECT SEQ-FILE                 ASSIGN TO CUSTOMER.
    17              SELECT IND-FILE                 ASSIGN TO MASTER
    18                  ORGANIZATION       IS INDEXED
    19                  ACCESS MODE        IS SEQUENTIAL
    20                  RECORD KEY         IS IR-IND-KEY
    21                  ALTERNATE RECORD KEY IS IR-ALT-KEY
    22                  FILE STATUS        IS WS-STATUS.
    23          *----------------------------------------------------------------
    24          DATA DIVISION.
    25          FILE SECTION.
    26          *
    27          FD  SEQ-FILE
    28              LABEL RECORDS ARE STANDARD
    29              RECORD CONTAINS 100 CHARACTERS.
    30          01  SEQ-RECORD                      PIC X(100).
    31          *
    32          FD  IND-FILE
    33              LABEL RECORDS ARE STANDARD
    34              RECORD CONTAINS 100 CHARACTERS.
    35          01  IND-RECORD.
    36              12 IR-ALT-KEY.
    37                  15 IR-FIRM-NAME             PIC X(21).
    38                  15 IR-IND-KEY               PIC X(6).
    39              12 FILLER                       PIC X(73).
    40          /
    41          *----------------------------------------------------------------
    42          WORKING-STORAGE SECTION.
    43          01  WS-STATUS.
    44              12 WS-STATUS-BYTE1              PIC X(1).
    45              12 FILLER                       PIC X(1).
    46          *
    47          01  WS-INPUT-COUNT                  PIC 9(5)    VALUE 0.
    48          01  WS-REC-LOADED                   PIC 9(5)    VALUE 0.
    49          01  WS-REC-NOT-LOADED               PIC 9(5)    VALUE 0.
    50          01  F1-EOF-FLAG                     PIC X(1)    VALUE 'M'.
    51          /
    52          PROCEDURE DIVISION.
    53          *----------------------------------------------------------------
    54          *   In VAX COBOL you need declaratives (even in dummy form) to
    55          *   avoid abends even when nonzero File Status values such as
    56          *   '23' are received for a key-not-found condition.  Since
    57          *   DECLARATIVES are a "section" MAIN-PROGRAM must be a section.
    58          *----------------------------------------------------------------
    59          DECLARATIVES.
    60          0000-ERROR    SECTION.
    61              USE AFTER STANDARD ERROR PROCEDURE ON IND-FILE.
```

(Continued)

Figure 10.6 Source code for the INDLOAD program that copies records from the CUSTOMER.DAT sequential file to an indexed file named MASTER.DAT. The SELECT/ASSIGN statement clauses tell the VMS operating system what it needs to know about the file to define and copy records to it.

```
62          0000-DUMMY.  EXIT.
63        *
64          END DECLARATIVES.
65        *-------------------------------------------------------------
66          0000-MAIN-PROGRAM    SECTION.
67          0000-MAINLINE.
68              PERFORM 1000-BOJ.
69              PERFORM 2000-PROCESS
70                  UNTIL F1-EOF-FLAG = 'E'.
71              PERFORM 3000-EOJ.
72              STOP RUN.
73        *
74          1000-BOJ.
75              DISPLAY '*** Start of program INDLOAD'.
76              OPEN OUTPUT  IND-FILE.
77              IF WS-STATUS-BYTE1 NOT = '0'
78                  DISPLAY '*** Error opening indexed file, program ended'
79                  DISPLAY '    File Status = ', WS-STATUS
80                  STOP RUN.
81              OPEN  INPUT  SEQ-FILE.
82              PERFORM 2700-READ.
83        *
84          2000-PROCESS.
85              WRITE IND-RECORD FROM SEQ-RECORD.
86              IF WS-STATUS-BYTE1 = '0'
87                  DISPLAY IND-RECORD(1:27)
88                  ADD 1 TO WS-REC-LOADED
89              ELSE
90              IF WS-STATUS = '21'
91                  DISPLAY '*** Error next record    File Status = ', WS-STATUS
92                  DISPLAY IND-RECORD(1:27)
93                  ADD 1 TO WS-REC-NOT-LOADED
94              ELSE
95                  DISPLAY '*** Loading failed!    File Status = ', WS-STATUS
96                  DISPLAY IND-RECORD(1:27)
97                  STOP RUN.
98              PERFORM 2700-READ.
99        *-------------------------------------------------------------
100         2700-READ.
101             READ SEQ-FILE
102                 AT END
103                     MOVE 'E' TO F1-EOF-FLAG.
104             IF F1-EOF-FLAG NOT = 'E'
105                 ADD 1 TO WS-INPUT-COUNT.
106       *
107         3000-EOJ.
108             CLOSE  SEQ-FILE  IND-FILE.
109             DISPLAY 'File Status at INDFILE close = ', WS-STATUS.
110             DISPLAY 'Seq file records read   ',
111                 WS-INPUT-COUNT.
112             DISPLAY 'Records loaded          ',
113                 WS-REC-LOADED.
114             DISPLAY 'Records not loaded      ',
115                 WS-REC-NOT-LOADED.
116             DISPLAY '*** Program ended normally'.
```

Figure 10.6   *(Continued)*

its title, or by knowing its author. Every one of these different card catalogs is an alternate index. The item written at the top of each index card (the topic, title, or author) is an alternate key. An alternate key does not have to be unique. (A single author may have written more than one book.)

An alternate index to an indexed file lets you find one or more records quickly when you do not know the primary key. Chapter 15 shows how I use an alternate key to support an on-line "browse." I regard the `MF-FIRM-NAME` field of the customer record as alternate key. The on-line browse I show you lists the customer records on the screen in name sequence, since the alternate index is used to access them and it is stored in this order.

An indexed file can have more than one alternate index. But every alternate index imposes extra overhead on the access method and makes change/update operations to the file slower. I have illustrated the use of just one alternate index with the customer file, which is typical of real life.

10.8 *SELECT/ASSIGN Statement for Indexed Files*

You need to know how to code a long `SELECT/ASSIGN` statement in order to access an indexed file. Here is the `SELECT/ASSIGN` statement (lines 17–22) of my INDLOAD program:

```
SELECT IND-FILE     ASSIGN TO MASTER
    ORGANIZATION IS INDEXED
    ACCESS MODE IS SEQUENTIAL
    RECORD KEY IS IR-IND-KEY
    ALTERNATE RECORD KEY IS IR-ALT-KEY
    FILE STATUS IS WS-STATUS.
```

An "ordinary" `SELECT/ASSIGN` statement for a sequential file would have only the first line. That first line establishes the name you want to use for the file within your program (`IND-FILE` here). The name on the right, called the *implementor name*, links to the physical name of the file managed by the operating system. Here the VAX will assume `MASTER.DAT` as the actual file name. This is what the other clauses of this statement do:

ORGANIZATION   Tells if the file is `SEQUENTIAL` or `INDEXED`. Since the default is `SEQUENTIAL` we don't code this clause for ordinary sequential files.

ACCESS MODE   Tells how the program will access the file. This can be `SEQUENTIAL`, `RANDOM`, or `DYNAMIC`. The default is `SEQUENTIAL`. `RANDOM` gives you direct access and `DYNAMIC` gives you both sequential and direct capabilities. Your choice here dictates how the `READ` and `WRITE` verbs work.

RECORD KEY   Tells the name of the primary key field in the file description (`FD`) for the indexed file. Notice that this field does not

have to be the first field. It can be a part of the alternate key (these are
lines 36–38 of my INDLOAD program):

```
FD IND-FILE
    LABEL RECORDS ARE STANDARD
    RECORD CONTAINS 100 CHARACTERS.
01 IND-RECORD.
    12 IR-ALT-KEY.
        15 IR-FIRM-NAME        PIC X(21).
        15 IR-IND-KEY          PIC X(6).
    12 FILLER                  PIC X(73).
```

ALTERNATE RECORD KEY   Tells the name of the alternate key in the
FD of the indexed file. Notice that in the preceding description I have
made the alternate key a group name that includes the firm name (my
real intended alternate key) and the primary key. This makes the
whole alternate key unique even though the firm name is not. (I tell
you more about the advantage of this in Chapter 15.) If your alternate
record key is not unique to one data record it "duplicates" on more
than one data record. The same firm name—ACME PRODUCTS—is
found on many records. You must include the phrase WITH DUPLI-
CATES if the alternate key is not unique:

```
ALTERNATE RECORD KEY IS . . . WITH DUPLICATES
```

FILE STATUS   Tells the name of the two-byte field in WORKING-
STORAGE where you want the access method to put the File Status
value after each input/output action. I recommend that you code this
field as two one-byte fields as I do in lines 43 through 45 of my IND-
LOAD program. Sometimes you have to test just the first byte, apart
from the second byte:

```
01 WS-STATUS.
    12 WS-STATUS-BYTE1         PIC X(1).
    12 FILLER                  PIC X(1).
```

10.9 ACCESS MODE and the READ and WRITE Verbs

You can access an indexed file as if it were an ordinary sequential file.
You code ACCESS MODE IS SEQUENTIAL to do this in the file's
SELECT/ASSIGN statement. The file itself is not changed by your choice
of access. In this mode the READ verb acts as it does with an ordinary
sequential file. Every READ obtains the next record in the file and you

eventually hit end-of-file. In sequential mode you can WRITE records to the file but they must be in ascending key sequence (this is what the INDLOAD program does.)

When you code ACCESS MODE IS RANDOM you make the READ verb operate in direct access mode. In this mode READ will not get the next record and it will never hit end-of-file. In random mode READ expects you to have put the key value you want in the FD key field because that is the key of the record it looks for in the indexed file. In direct access mode WRITE will let you write records to the file in any sequence.

Your choices for access mode also include DYNAMIC. This mode allows you to do both sequential and random processing. To distinguish between sequential and random (direct access) reading, DYNAMIC forces you to use two different versions of the READ statement. In DYNAMIC mode the READ verb does random reading. For sequential reading you have to code READ (filename) NEXT. I show you how to do this in the CBROW1 program in Chapter 15.

10.10 OPEN I-O

You can OPEN an ordinary sequential file for either INPUT or OUTPUT. If you open it INPUT you can use the READ verb but not the WRITE verb. If you open it OUTPUT you can use WRITE but not READ. You can OPEN an indexed file a new way: I-O. If you code:

```
OPEN I-O IND-FILE.
```

you can use both the READ and the WRITE verbs with the file as well as REWRITE and DELETE (see below). You can also open an indexed file with EXTEND:

```
OPEN EXTEND IND-FILE.
```

This lets you append records to existing data in the file, thereby "extending" it. EXTEND plays little role in interactive programming, and I don't illustrate its use in this book.

10.11 REWRITE and DELETE Verbs

Indexed files give you additional input/output verbs to supplement READ and WRITE:

REWRITE Puts a record back into the indexed file, replacing the copy of the record you previously obtained with READ. To use REWRITE you move the record you want to put back into the file to the FD of the indexed file, then:

```
REWRITE IND-RECORD.
```

DELETE Removes the record from the indexed file. To use DELETE you put the key of the record you want to delete in the FD key field of the indexed file and you:

```
DELETE IND-FILE.
```

This does not delete the whole file, just the record whose key is in the FD key field!

Interactive add/change and delete operations require I-O access to an indexed file. I demonstrate this for you in Chapters 12 and 13 in the CUPD1 and CDEL1 programs.

10.12 START: Current Record Pointer and Key of Reference

When you code ACCESS MODE IS SEQUENTIAL you can use the START verb. START positions an internal value named the **current record pointer** (CRP) maintained by the access method. You code START by defining a relation condition involving one of the indexed file key fields:

```
MOVE LOW-VALUES TO IR-IND-KEY.
START IND-FILE
    KEY NOT LESS IR-IND-KEY.
```

START does not obtain a record for you. It just sets the current record pointer, which tells where to get a record from when you next ask the READ verb to get it. (In the preceding action START positions the file at its very beginning based on primary key, since NOT LESS means "equal to or greater than" and LOW-VALUES is the lowest possible value.)

You can also use START to change the **key of reference** (KOR) from the primary key to an alternate key when an indexed file has alternate keys. To do this you involve the alternate key field with START instead of the primary key:

```
MOVE LOW-VALUES TO IR-ALT-KEY.
START IND-FILE
    KEY NOT LESS IR-ALT-KEY.
```

In this action START positions the file at its very beginning based on an alternate key. Because the key of reference has been changed from the primary key to the alternate key, sequential reading will now obtain the records in alternate key sequence.

I show you how to use the START verb in Chapter 15. The CBROW1 program uses an alternate key browse based on firm name.

10.13 Using File Status

The indexed file access method communicates the outcome of your OPEN, READ, WRITE, REWRITE, DELETE, START, and CLOSE actions to you using the File Status field. You must test the value in this field immediately after each action to see if the action succeeded. Here is how I test File Status after an OPEN (these are lines 76–80 in my INDLOAD program):

```
OPEN OUTPUT IND-FILE.
IF WS-STATUS-BYTE1 NOT='00'
    DISPLAY '*** Error opening indexed file, program ended'
    DISPLAY ' File Status=', WS-STATUS
    STOP RUN.
```

File Status is easy to check if you remember that '00' indicates a successful OPEN or CLOSE and just '0' in the first byte always indicates that your other actions were successful. (For all commands except OPEN or CLOSE the second byte gives additional information about the action and may not be zero even when your action succeeded.) I have listed all of the VAX COBOL File Status values for you in Figure 10.7.

Some actions such as a sequential WRITE involve three possible outcomes (these are lines 85–97 in my INDLOAD program):

```
WRITE IND-RECORD FROM SEQ-RECORD.
IF WS-STATUS-BYTE1='0'
    DISPLAY IND-RECORD(1:27)
    ADD 1 TO WS-REC-LOADED
  ELSE
IF WS-STATUS='21'
    DISPLAY '*** Error trying to load a record!'
    DISPLAY '*** File Status=', WS-STATUS
    DISPLAY IND-RECORD(1:27)
    ADD 1 TO WS-REC-NOT-LOADED
  ELSE
    DISPLAY '*** Loading processed failed!'
    DISPLAY '*** File Status=', WS-STATUS
    DISPLAY IND-RECORD(1:27)
    STOP RUN.
```

VAX COBOL File Status Values

Note: in this chart 'x' means the first byte of File Status only while 'xx' means both bytes of File Status tested together. "All" means all of the possible specifations for the item.

File Status	Received with statements:	Received with ORGANIZATION	Received with ACCESS MODE	Meaning
'00'	OPEN CLOSE	All	All	Action successful
'0'	READ WRITE REWRITE DELETE START	All	All	Action successful Note: you cannot check for '00' on these actions or you will regard some normal situations as errors!
'02'	REWRITE WRITE	INDEXED	All	Duplicate alternate key was created
'02'	READ	INDEXED	All	Duplicate alternate key was read and more records exist with this alternate key
'04'	READ	All	All	Record read is not the same size as program's buffer
'05'	OPEN	All	All	Optional file is not present on the system
'07'	OPEN CLOSE	All	All	Invalid file organization or device specified
'10'	READ	All	SEQUENTIAL	End of file
'14'	READ	RELATIVE	All	Relative record number exceeds highest record number of the file
'21'	REWRITE	INDEXED	SEQUENTIAL	Primary key was changed after READ
'21'	WRITE	INDEXED	SEQUENTIAL	Primary key of record is out of sequence
'22'	REWRITE	RELATIVE or INDEXED	All	Duplicate alternate key and WITH DUPLICATES was not specified
'22'	WRITE	INDEXED	RANDOM	Duplicate primary key
'23'	DELETE READ REWRITE START	RELATIVE or INDEXED	RANDOM	Record not in file; primary key not found or START condition not satisfied
'24'	WRITE	RELATIVE or INDEXED	All	File out of space or relative record number too large

Figure 10.7   File Status values for VAX COBOL and what they mean.

124

'30'	All	All	All	Permanent file error
'34'	WRITE	SEQUENTIAL	SEQUENTIAL	File out of space
'35'	OPEN	All	All	File not found
'37'	OPEN	All	All	Inappropriate device type
'38'	OPEN	All	All	File was last closed with lock and is inaccessible
'39'	OPEN	All	All	Record key in FD differs in position or length from that of the file
'41'	OPEN	All	All	You can't open this file because it is already open
'42'	CLOSE	All	All	You can't close this file because it is not open
'43'	DELETE REWRITE	All	SEQUENTIAL	You must do a START or READ before taking this action
'44'	REWRITE	All	All	Record size is invalid
'46'	READ	All	SEQUENTIAL	No valid next record
'47'	READ START	All	All	File not open or open for output only
'48'	WRITE	All	All	File not open or open for input only
'49'	DELETE REWRITE	All	All	File not open or not open for I-O
'90'	All	All	SEQUENTIAL	Record is locked by another user but you can read it; it's in your FD now. This is a "soft lock."
'91'	OPEN	All	All	File exists but is locked by another user
'92'	READ WRITE REWRITE DELETE START	All	All	Record is locked by another user and it is not available to you. This is a "hard" lock.
'93'	UNLOCK	All	All	No current record
'94'	UNLOCK	All	All	File is not open or is open in an incompatible way
'95'	OPEN	All	All	No file space on the device
'98'	CLOSE	All	All	CLOSE error; no further information available

Note: The meanings of some File Status values differ between VAX COBOL and IBM VS COBOL/VSAM. Consult IBM manuals for work on IBM mainframess.

Figure 10.7   *(Continued)*

125

When you are writing a record to an indexed file in sequential mode as the INDLOAD program does, the action may succeed. A first-byte File Status of '0' tells you this. (The 1:27 after IND-RECORD at line 87 is a 1985 COBOL feature called *reference modification*. It means, "Use 27 characters from the field starting with position 1." I use it here so that I display the front part of a record and not the whole record.)

If the primary key of the record you are trying to write in sequential mode is out of sequence (lower than the key of the record you last wrote) the WRITE will not succeed. You will get a File Status value of '21' after you try it. This is what I am anticipating in lines 90 through 93 of IND-LOAD. Look up this value in Figure 10.7 and see what it is telling you.

It's possible for the indexed file to fail. This means that the access method has detected a data integrity problem with the file. In such a case you cannot continue to access the file reliably. You must instead force your program to end in a way that helps you investigate what the problem with the file is. That's what I do in lines 95 through 97 of INDLOAD. When you encounter indexed file failure, the actual File Status value will help you identify what specific problem exists.

10.14 Declaratives

In COBOL language standards File Status was originally called the *status key*. It was coupled to the use of **declarative logic**. Declaratives contain logic that would be executed only under error conditions.

Declaratives have lost favor in modern structured programming because they must be located at the beginning of your PROCEDURE DIVISION and not modularized elsewhere. VAX COBOL still requires you to code a declaratives section if you want to house your File Status checking logic near the places where you take input/output actions. So in my programs you will see the following "dummy" declaratives code which is there just to please the compiler:

```
PROCEDURE DIVISION.

DECLARATIVES.
0000-ERROR SECTION.
    USE AFTER STANDARD ERROR PROCEDURE ON IND-FILE.
0000-DUMMY. EXIT.

END DECLARATIVES.
```

These declaratives don't do anything. While VAX COBOL and micro-

```
LISTALT               15-Mar-1992 12:16:03    VAX COBOL V4.3-57
Source Listing        15-Mar-1992 12:15:54
CSC$ROOT:[CSCJGJ.VAXCO]LISTALT.COB;1

 1          IDENTIFICATION DIVISION.
 2          PROGRAM-ID.    LISTALT.
 3         *AUTHOR.        J JANOSSY    INTERNET: JANOSSY@CSCVAX.DEPAUL.EDU
 4         *INSTALLATION.  DEPAUL UNIVERSITY, CHICAGO, IL
 5         *=============================================================
 6         *    List Records by Alternate Key in VAX COBOL On-line!  3/1/92
 7         *
 8         *    Uses START to change key of reference to alternate key and
 9         *    then lists records in the MASTER.DAT file.  Uses File Status
10         *    checking for end-of-file and error conditions.
11         *=============================================================
12          ENVIRONMENT DIVISION.
13          INPUT-OUTPUT SECTION.
14          FILE-CONTROL.
15             SELECT IND-FILE              ASSIGN TO MASTER
16                ORGANIZATION  IS INDEXED
17                ACCESS MODE   IS SEQUENTIAL
18                RECORD KEY    IS IR-IND-KEY
19                ALTERNATE RECORD KEY IS IR-ALT-KEY
20                FILE STATUS   IS WS-STATUS.
21         *
22          DATA DIVISION.
23          FILE SECTION.
24          FD  IND-FILE
25              LABEL RECORDS ARE STANDARD
26              RECORD CONTAINS 100 CHARACTERS.
27          01  IND-RECORD.
28              12 IR-ALT-KEY.
29                 15 IR-FIRM-NAME          PIC X(21).
30                 15 IR-IND-KEY            PIC X(6).
31              12 FILLER                   PIC X(73).
32         *
33          WORKING-STORAGE SECTION.
34          01  WS-STATUS.
35              12 WS-STATUS-BYTE1          PIC X(1).
36              12 FILLER                   PIC X(1).
37          01  WS-RECORDS-READ             PIC 9(5)    VALUE 0.
38         /
39          PROCEDURE DIVISION.
40         *-------------------------------------------------------------
41         *   In VAX COBOL you need declaratives (even in dummy form) to
42         *   avoid abends even when nonzero File Status values such as
43         *   '23' are received for a key-not-found condition.  Since
44         *   DECLARATIVES are a "section" MAIN-PROGRAM must be a section.
45         *-------------------------------------------------------------
46          DECLARATIVES.
47          0000-DUMMY    SECTION.
48              USE AFTER ERROR PROCEDURE ON IND-FILE.
49          0000-REAL-DUMMY.   EXIT.
50          END DECLARATIVES.
51         *
52          0000-MAINLINE-SECTION    SECTION.
53          0000-MAINLINE.
54             PERFORM 1000-BOJ.
55             PERFORM 2000-PROCESS
56                UNTIL WS-STATUS-BYTE1 = '1'.
57             PERFORM 3000-EOJ.
58             STOP RUN.
59         *
60          1000-BOJ.
61             DISPLAY '*** Start of Program LISTALT'.
62             OPEN INPUT IND-FILE.
```

(Continued)

Figure 10.8 Source code for the LISTALT program that prints the contents of the MASTER.DAT indexed file in alternate key sequence. The MOVE and START verbs at lines 71 through 77 change the key of reference to the alternate key and position the current record pointer at the beginning of the alternate index. (First-byte File Status of '1' means that READ in sequential mode has reached end-of-file.)

```
 63            IF WS-STATUS NOT = '00'
 64                DISPLAY '*** Error on OPEN, program ended'
 65                DISPLAY '*** File Status = ', WS-STATUS
 66                STOP RUN.
 67        *-------------------------------------------------------------
 68        *   This START involves the alternate key field and so positions
 69        *   the file access method to read sequentially on alternate key:
 70        *-------------------------------------------------------------
 71            MOVE LOW-VALUES TO IR-ALT-KEY.
 72            START IND-FILE
 73                KEY NOT LESS IR-ALT-KEY.
 74            IF WS-STATUS-BYTE1 NOT = '0'
 75                DISPLAY '*** Error on alt key START, program ended'
 76                DISPLAY '*** File Status = ', WS-STATUS
 77                STOP RUN.
 78        *
 79            PERFORM 2700-READ.
 80        *
 81         2000-PROCESS.
 82            DISPLAY IND-RECORD(1:27).
 83            PERFORM 2700-READ.
 84        *
 85         2700-READ.
 86            READ IND-FILE.
 87        *-------------------------------------------------------------
 88        *   For sequential reading (all standard COBOL compilers):
 89        *       File Status first-byte '0' means read succeeded
 90        *       File Status first-byte '1' means end of file
 91        *       Any other File Status value means access method failure
 92        *-------------------------------------------------------------
 93            IF WS-STATUS-BYTE1 = '0'
 94                ADD 1 TO WS-RECORDS-READ
 95            ELSE
 96            IF WS-STATUS-BYTE1 = '1'
 97                NEXT SENTENCE
 98            ELSE
 99                DISPLAY '*** Error on READ, program ended'
100                DISPLAY '*** File Status = ', WS-STATUS
101                STOP RUN.
102        *
103         3000-EOJ.
104            DISPLAY '*** RECORDS READ = ', WS-RECORDS-READ.
105            CLOSE IND-FILE.
106            IF WS-STATUS-BYTE1 = '0'
107                DISPLAY '*** Program ended normally'
108            ELSE
109                DISPLAY '*** Error on CLOSE, program ended'
110                DISPLAY '*** File Status = ', WS-STATUS
111                STOP RUN.
```

Figure 10.8 *(Continued)*

computer COBOL compilers still require them, IBM's mainframe VS COBOL compilers do not.

You will see many more examples of File Status checking in the CINQU1, CUPD1, CDEL1, and CBROW1 programs in Chapters 11 to 15.

10.15 Listing Contents of an Indexed File

On the VAX you can use the VMS command $ TYPE to see the contents of an indexed file. For example, after running INDLOAD to copy records from CUSTOMER.DAT to MASTER.DAT you can enter:

```
$ TYPE MASTER.DAT
```

```
$ run listalt
*** Start of Program LISTALT
ACME PRODUCTS CO      168857
ACME PRODUCTS CO      415002
ACME PRODUCTS CO      472293
ACME PRODUCTS CO      600536
ACME PRODUCTS CO      887633
ADEPT MANUFACTURING   437129
ARNOLD ASSOCIATES     267841
BERNHARD LORING CORP. 700501
BERRY MACHINE TOOLS   419870
BERYL AVIATION LTD    994365
BURR & WILLIAMS INC   258472
GILMORE TOOL CORP     123456
HARRIER METER CORP.   601723
HILBORN TECHNOLOGIES  480114
HILL ENGINEERING CO   521726
JENSEN-SWIFT MFG.     437352
JOHNSON MACHINE CORP  882734
NORHOST INSTRUMENT CO 695403
RANGER PRODUCTS, INC. 178948
SINCLAIR DRILL WORKS  654733
*** RECORDS READ = 00020
*** Program ended normally
$
```

Figure 10.9   Output produced by the LISTALT program. The customer records in the MASTER.DAT file are listed in alternate key (firm name) sequence rather than primary key due to the START verb in lines 71 through 77.

and see the contents of the file. You cannot use a $ PR command to print an indexed file, but you can reassign screen output to a file, use $ TYPE, then print the file of screen lines you have captured. (See Chapter 6, topic 6.8, "Redirecting Screen Output," to review how you can establish TODISK and TOTUBE commands to do this.)

You can also write a simple program to read the indexed file sequentially and print the records. I have listed the source code for program named LISTALT in Figure 10.8. This program uses START to change the key of reference to the alternate key field as a beginning-of-job action in lines 71 through 77. As you can see from its output in Figure 10.9 it lists the records in MASTER.DAT in alternate key sequence. To make it list records in primary key sequence just comment out lines 71 through 77.

10.16 Chapter Summary

Indexed files provide the capability to access individual data records on disk by symbolic key. This is critical to interactive systems. An indexed file must reside on disk because it provides direct physical access to individual records.

A *magnetic disk* has the same type of recording surface as tape but it is arranged as a *platter*. The *read/write head assembly* (disk "arm") can swing across the disk surface. The combination of disk rotation and disk head assembly movement makes most of each recording surface accessible.

The *primary key field* in a record must uniquely identify the record. No two records in the file can have the same key value. A *pointer key* tells where the data is physically stored on disk. A *symbolic key* is just a unique identifier and does not tell where the data is stored. While pointer keys are easiest for an operating system to handle, business data processing demands the use of symbolic keys. Symbolic keys include already-assigned government identification numbers, stock numbers, account IDs, and so forth.

In a *sequential file* records are written to disk or tape one after another. Records can be retrieved only one after another. Sequential files are fine for batch processing and reporting, since these processes often deal with all records in a file. Interactive systems demand more direct access to individual data records.

Relative files were the first form of direct access file. A *relative file* is a special form of sequential file. It is always stored on disk and contains records of fixed length. The *key* of the records in a relative file is a pointer key. When you store a record in such a file you say what *record number* you want to put it into. When you want to access that record you have to say the record number where it is located. Relative files are not practical when you need access to data by symbolic key. Relative files are not suitable for most business data processing systems.

An *indexed file* is more complicated than either a sequential file or a relative file because it requires two related structures: the data and an index. The index is like the index to a book. It helps system software locate a record directly. You can picture that an index contains one very short record for each data record. This index record has only two fields in it: the primary key value and a pointer to where the record is stored. System software called an "access method" creates and manages the index. The indexed file access method on IBM mainframes is called VSAM. On DEC minicomputers it is called RMS, Record Management Services.

When you create an indexed file on the VAX you copy records from a sequential file to the indexed file. Each record must have a unique key, and the records must be processed in ascending order of this key. The VAX doesn't require you to define the index file first.

Indexed files can have alternate indexes. An *alternate index* lets you find one or more records quickly when you do not know the primary key. Unlike the primary key value, which must be unique to each record, the value of the alternate index in any given record can duplicate that in another record. Duplicate alternate index key values are said to be *nonunique*.

SELECT/ASSIGN statements for indexed files are more complicated than those for sequential files. SELECT/ASSIGN clauses document how you want to access the file (sequential, random, or dynamic), the names of the primary and alternate keys, and the name of the File Status field.

READ gets the next record when you are processing in sequential access mode. But in random or dynamic access mode READ looks for the record whose key you have put into the FD key field of the indexed file. WRITE also acts differently in different access modes. In sequential mode you have to write records in ascending key sequence. In random mode you can write records to an indexed file in any sequence. (Both modes of WRITE fail if you try to write a record with a primary key that duplicates a key already in the file.)

File Status communicates to you the outcome of input/output actions. File Status '00' indicates success for OPEN or CLOSE. First-byte File Status '0' means success for READ, WRITE, REWRITE, DELETE, and START. Other File Status values indicate problems that a program can or cannot handle. You have to recognize what File Status is "telling" your program and act accordingly. You have to check File Status after every input/output action, since an indexed file may fail. If this happens you must force your program to end in a way that helps you investigate the problem (by displaying the File Status value).

You can OPEN an indexed file for INPUT, OUTPUT, I-O, or EXTEND. I-O lets you READ, WRITE, REWRITE, and DELETE records. REWRITE puts a record back into the indexed file, replacing the copy of it you previously obtained with READ. DELETE removes a record from the indexed file.

The START verb positions an internal value named the *current record pointer*, which tells where to get a record from when you next execute the sequential READ verb. You can also use START to change the *key of reference* from the primary key to an alternate key when an indexed file has alternate keys.

VAX COBOL still requires you to code a DECLARATIVES SECTION in your PROCEDURE DIVISION if you want to house your File Status checking logic near the places where you take input/output actions. Examples in this book satisfy this demand of the compiler with dummy declaratives code.

You can list the contents of an indexed file with the VMS command $ TYPE or by writing a simple program to read the indexed file sequentially and print the records. By using START to change the key of reference you can get a listing of the file in alternate key sequence.

10.17 Important Terms

You can review these terms to check your understanding of this chapter:

Disk device   A data storage device with magnetic surfaces arranged in platters so that a read/write mechanism can quickly reach any recorded data.

Access method   System software that manages the data, indexes, and your access to files, especially those stored on disk.

Direct access   Immediate access to stored data as provided by disk devices and a software access method.

Random access   A synonym for direct access but from the point of view of system software; it can't predict what record you will ask for next.

Pointer key   A unique identifier for each record in a file that tells where on disk the record is stored.

Symbolic key   A unique identifier for each record in a file that does not indicate anything about its physical location on disk.

Sequential file   Records stored on tape or disk one after another so that you can access them only by reading them the same way: one after another.

Relative file   The earliest form of direct access file, it provides pointer key direct access to stored data but not symbolic key access.

Indexed file   A type of record storage that lets you access individual data records on disk by symbolic key.

Primary key   A unique identifier for each record in a file.

Alternate Key   An optional key field in records stored in an indexed file that gives you direct access to one or more records when you don't know primary key values. Unlike the primary key value, alternate key values do not have to be unique to one data record, they can duplicate (be nonunique).

ACCESS MODE   Your choice of how you want to process an indexed file in a given program, coded as SEQUENTIAL, RANDOM, or DYNAMIC in the SELECT/ASSIGN statement for the file. This controls how the READ and WRITE verbs work in the program.

I-O   A way to open indexed files so that you can use the READ, WRITE, REWRITE, and DELETE verbs in the same program.

File Status   A two-byte value returned to your program by the access method as communication about the success or failure of the input/output action you just attempted.

Current record pointer (CRP)   A value internal to the access method that tells what record to get when you next execute the READ verb; you can set it with the START verb.

Key of reference (KOR)   A value internal to the access method that indicates what key (primary or secondary) your next input-output action will deal with. You can set it with the START verb.

Declaratives   Logic that would be executed only under error conditions, coded in a SECTION at the start of your PROCEDURE DIVISION.

FDL   File Definition Language, which you can use on the VAX to define the characteristics of an indexed file to make it more efficient (similar to IDCAMS control statements on IBM mainframes.)

You can find additional questions and exercises for this chapter in Appendix A.

Chapter Eleven

VAXDEMO: A COMPLETE MENU-BASED ON-LINE SYSTEM

In this chapter I will show you the menu program of VAXDEMO, an interactive demonstration system. You will see how I built this main program and tested it using program "stubs" for each of its functions. In the chapters that follow I'll show you the remainder of the programs in the system, and we'll replace each stub with functional code. By Chapter 15 you will have acquired all of the essential building blocks you need to build real interactive systems on the VAX.

The name of a menu program is often the name of the *application system*. (Do you recall Chapter 3? It defined an application system as a collection of related programs that support a specific business function.) You invoke the menu program by name to run the application. In this book VAXDEMO is the name of my menu program, the program I explain to you in this chapter.

11.1 Menu-Selectable Functions

Modern interactive systems provide a menu that the computer terminal operator views; from the menu, the operator selects the next action to be taken. The choice of actions almost always include indexed file *inquiry*, record *update*, record *deletion*, or alternate key *browsing* (limited-range searching for a specific record).

Figure 11.1 depicts the menu screen of the VAXDEMO system. The last choice, Q, is really just a way to end its execution.

11.2 Overview of Menu Program Logic Structure

An interactive menu program is a *main program*. It CALLs other programs but is not CALLed by any program. Programs given control by a

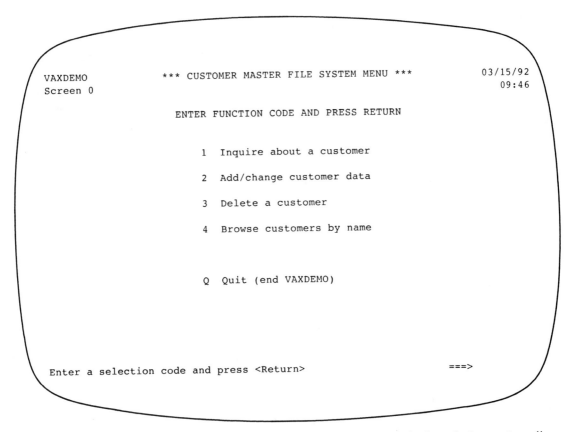

```
VAXDEMO              *** CUSTOMER MASTER FILE SYSTEM MENU ***        03/15/92
Screen 0                                                              09:46

                       ENTER FUNCTION CODE AND PRESS RETURN


                   1   Inquire about a customer

                   2   Add/change customer data

                   3   Delete a customer

                   4   Browse customers by name



                   Q   Quit (end VAXDEMO)




   Enter a selection code and press <Return>                        ===>
```

Figure 11.1 Menu screen of the VAXDEMO system. The last choice, Q, is really just a way to end execution of the application.

menu program are **subprograms**. You write subprograms with the source code features necessary for them to receive control and access shared data.

Figure 11.2 is the action diagram I developed for VAXDEMO. The logic of this program, as with any conversational interactive program, follows a "BOJ/process until/EOJ" pattern.

11.3 Menu Program Logic

In "beginning of job" (BOJ) the menu program does things that have to be done once to start processing. It obtains the system date, erases the screen, presents the initial operator prompt for a choice of menu selection, and seeks the operator's selection.

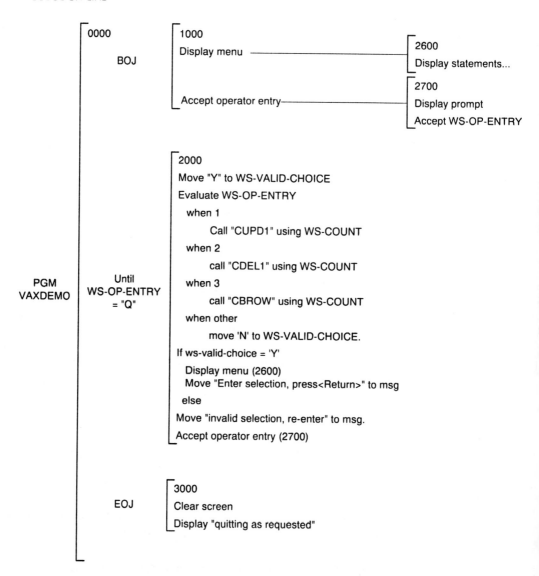

Figure 11.2   Action diagram for menu program VAXDEMO. The logic of this program, as with any conversational interactive program, follows a "BOJ/process until/EOJ" pattern. Each bracket on this chart shows in pseudocode the intended contents of a paragraph of source code.

The "process until" loop, like the processing loop of program CALC1, is controlled by the terminal operator. This loop will execute until the operator enters the value Q for WS-RESPONSE. If the operator enters Q at the very first prompt for a menu choice (in beginning of job) this loop will never execute.

When the terminal operator is finished using the VAXDEMO system he or she chooses the Q selection from the menu. When WS-RESPONSE assumes this value the condition of the PERFORM . . . UNTIL driving the loop is satisfied. Control passes to end of job logic (EOJ) and the VAXDEMO system ends execution.

11.4 The Menu Processing Loop in Detail

It's the job of the processing loop of a menu program to identify the choice made by the terminal operator and send control to the appropriate functional subprogram. In VAXDEMO a selection of 1, 2, 3, 4, or Q is a valid choice. Once VAXDEMO passes control to a functional subprogram with CALL, control remains in the CALLed subprogram until the operator finishes with it. An operator remains "in" a functional program ("in" the CALL) to process as many transactions as he or she wants.

Control reaches the bottom of the processing loop in VAXDEMO one of two ways:

1. When a menu choice was valid, a functional subprogram was given control, and its execution has ended.

or

2. If the operator entered an invalid selection code.

In the first case VAXDEMO redisplays the menu screen, since it will have been replaced by the functional subprogram that was CALLed. In the second case VAXDEMO doesn't have to redisplay the menu (let's save data transmission time!) because it's still on the screen. Either way VAXDEMO then prompts the operator at the bottom of its processing loop to make another menu selection.

11.5 Implementing VAXDEMO

The source code I composed for the VAXDEMO program follows my action diagram of Figure 11.2. I have listed it in Figure 11.3. Its highlights:

- **Beginning of job** ACCEPTs the date from the operating system, but not TIME; since time changes constantly I obtain it and display it more frequently than just once at beginning of job.

```
VAXDEMO              15-Mar-1992 11:54:14     VAX COBOL V4.3-57
Source Listing       15-Mar-1992 11:54:05
CSC$ROOT:[CSCJGJ.VAXCO]VAXDEMO.COB;1
     1           IDENTIFICATION DIVISION.
     2           PROGRAM-ID.      VAXDEMO.
     3          *AUTHOR.          J JANOSSY   INTERNET: JANOSSY@CSCVAX.DEPAUL.EDU
     4          *INSTALLATION.  DEPAUL UNIVERSITY, CHICAGO, ILLINOIS, USA
     5          *===============================================================
     6          *    Main Menu Program in VAXDEMO System in VAX COBOL ON-LINE!
     7          *
     8          *    Presents menu screen and allows terminal operator to
     9          *    select a function or quit.  Originally set to CALL stub
    10          *    programs for testing (see paragraph 2000-PROCESS).
    11          *===============================================================
    12           ENVIRONMENT DIVISION.
    13          *---------------------------------------------------------------
    14           DATA DIVISION.
    15           WORKING-STORAGE SECTION.
    16           01  WS-TRANS-COUNT                    PIC 9(7)  VALUE 0.
    17           01  WS-FORMATTED-COUNT                PIC Z,ZZZ,ZZ9.
    18           01  WS-OP-ENTRY                       PIC X(1)  VALUE SPACES.
    19           01  WS-VALID-CHOICE                   PIC X(1).
    20           01  SCR-MSG                           PIC X(58).
    21          *
    22           01  WS-DATE.
    23               12  WS-YR                         PIC X(2).
    24               12  WS-MO                         PIC X(2).
    25               12  WS-DA                         PIC X(2).
    26           01  WS-FORMATTED-DATE.
    27               12  WSF-MO                        PIC X(2).
    28               12  FILLER                        PIC X(1)  VALUE '/'.
    29               12  WSF-DA                        PIC X(2).
    30               12  FILLER                        PIC X(1)  VALUE '/'.
    31               12  WSF-YR                        PIC X(2).
    32          *
    33           01  WS-TIME.
    34               12  WS-HRS                        PIC X(2).
    35               12  WS-MIN                        PIC X(2).
    36               12  FILLER                        PIC X(4).
    37           01  WS-FORMATTED-TIME.
    38               12  WSF-HRS                       PIC X(2).
    39               12  FILLER                        PIC X(1)  VALUE ':'.
    40               12  WSF-MIN                       PIC X(2).
    41          *---------------------------------------------------------------
    42           PROCEDURE DIVISION.
    43           0000-MAINLINE.
    44               PERFORM 1000-BOJ.
    45               PERFORM 2000-PROCESS
    46                   UNTIL WS-OP-ENTRY = 'Q' OR 'q'.
    47               PERFORM 3000-EOJ.
    48               STOP RUN.
    49          *
    50           1000-BOJ.
    51               ACCEPT WS-DATE FROM DATE.
    52               MOVE WS-MO TO WSF-MO.
    53               MOVE WS-DA TO WSF-DA.
    54               MOVE WS-YR TO WSF-YR.
    55               MOVE 'Enter a selection code and press <Return>' TO SCR-MSG.
    56               PERFORM 2600-DISPLAY-MENU.
    57               PERFORM 2700-OP-PROMPT.
    58          *- - - - - - - - - - - - - - - - - - - - - - - - - - - - - - -
    59           2000-PROCESS.
    60               MOVE 'Y' TO WS-VALID-CHOICE.
    61          *
    62               EVALUATE WS-OP-ENTRY
    63                   WHEN '1'  CALL 'SINQU1'  USING WS-TRANS-COUNT
    64                   WHEN '2'  CALL 'SUPD1'   USING WS-TRANS-COUNT
    65                   WHEN '3'  CALL 'SDEL1'   USING WS-TRANS-COUNT
    66                   WHEN '4'  CALL 'SBROW1'  USING WS-TRANS-COUNT
    67                   WHEN OTHER
    68                       MOVE 'N' TO WS-VALID-CHOICE.
    69          *
```

Figure 11.3 Source code for program VAXDEMO. I built this directly from the action diagram design shown in Figure 11.2.

```
70            IF WS-VALID-CHOICE = 'Y'
71                PERFORM 2600-DISPLAY-MENU
72                MOVE 'Enter a selection code and press <Return>' TO SCR-MSG
73            ELSE
74                MOVE 'Invalid selection!  Re-enter a choice' TO SCR-MSG.
75        *
76            PERFORM 2700-OP-PROMPT.
77        * - - - - - - - - - - - - - - - - - - - - - - - - - - - - - -
78        2600-DISPLAY-MENU.
79            DISPLAY '' AT LINE 1 COLUMN 1 ERASE TO END OF SCREEN.
80            DISPLAY 'VAXDEMO' AT LINE 1 COLUMN 2.
81            DISPLAY '*** CUSTOMER MASTER FILE SYSTEM MENU *** '
82                BOLD AT LINE 1 COLUMN 21.
83            DISPLAY WS-FORMATTED-DATE AT LINE 1 COLUMN 72.
84            DISPLAY 'Screen 0' AT LINE 2 COLUMN 2.
85            DISPLAY 'ENTER FUNCTION CODE AND PRESS RETURN' AT LINE 4 COLUMN 23.
86            DISPLAY '1  Inquire about a customer' AT LINE  7 COLUMN 27.
87            DISPLAY '2  Add/change customer data' AT LINE  9 COLUMN 27.
88            DISPLAY '3  Delete a customer'        AT LINE 11 COLUMN 27.
89            DISPLAY '4  Browse customers by name' AT LINE 13 COLUMN 27.
90            DISPLAY 'Q  Quit (end VAXDEMO)'       AT LINE 17 COLUMN 27.
91        *
92        2700-OP-PROMPT.
93            ACCEPT WS-TIME FROM TIME.
94            MOVE WS-HRS TO WSF-HRS.
95            MOVE WS-MIN TO WSF-MIN.
96            DISPLAY WS-FORMATTED-TIME AT LINE  2 COLUMN 75.
97            DISPLAY SCR-MSG           AT LINE 24 COLUMN  2.
98            DISPLAY '===>'            AT LINE 24 COLUMN 66.
99            ACCEPT WS-OP-ENTRY   FROM LINE 24 COLUMN 71.
100           DISPLAY ''               AT LINE 24 COLUMN  2 ERASE TO END OF LINE.
101       *
102       3000-EOJ.
103           DISPLAY '' AT LINE 1 COLUMN 1 ERASE TO END OF SCREEN.
104           DISPLAY 'Quitting as requested'              AT LINE 1 COLUMN 2.
105           MOVE WS-TRANS-COUNT TO WS-FORMATTED-COUNT.
106           DISPLAY 'Number of transactions processed = ' AT LINE 2 COLUMN 2.
107           DISPLAY WS-FORMATTED-COUNT                    AT LINE 2 COLUMN 37.
108           DISPLAY 'Enter any VMS command now...'        AT LINE 4 COLUMN 2.
```

Figure 11.3   *(Continued)*

- **The processing loop** uses the EVALUATE verb of 1985 COBOL. EVALUATE clearly implements the "case" type of decision required here. (You can alternately use an older serial IF/ELSE structure here if you wish.)

- **Each CALL employs USING** to share a count field with each functional subprogram; each subprogram adds to this count, so I can accumulate a total of transactions processed. VAXDEMO displays this count when it ends.

- **Menu display** is housed in a paragraph by itself so that it can be invoked from BOJ and from the processing loop without redundant coding.

- **Prompt display and acceptance** operates in a standard way:
    - ACCEPTs the system time, formats it, and DISPLAYs it on the screen.

- DISPLAYs whatever prompt you have placed in SCR-MSG.
- ACCEPTs the operator's response.
- Erases the prompt field and operator response.

11.6 Testing the Menu Program with Stubs

Menu program VAXDEMO CALLs subprograms. To test it before those functional subprograms have been coded you can code small stub programs. A *stub program* simply provides a brief message confirming that it has received control and (after the terminal operator presses *<Return>*) gives control back to its CALLer, VAXDEMO.

Figure 11.4 lists the source code for Program SINQU1, one of four almost identical stub programs I used to test VAXDEMO:

SINQU1 stands in for CINQU1 before it is ready.

SUPD1 stands in for CUPD1 before it is ready.

```
SINQU1                  15-Mar-1992 11:51:09    VAX COBOL V4.3-57
Source Listing          15-Mar-1992 11:50:35    CSC$ROOT:[CSCJGJ.VAXCO]SINQU1.COB;1
     1          IDENTIFICATION DIVISION.
     2          PROGRAM-ID.    SINQU1.
     3         *AUTHOR.        J JANOSSY    INTERNET: JANOSSY@CSCVAX.DEPAUL.EDU
     4         *INSTALLATION.  DEPAUL UNIVERSITY, CHICAGO, ILLINOIS, USA
     5         *=================================================================
     6         *    Testing Stub for VAXDEMO Program CINQU1 in VAX COBOL ON-LINE!
     7         *
     8         *    This program receives control from the VAXDEMO menu program
     9         *    and just presents a simple message saying that it has been
    10         *    accessed.  After another <Return> it ends and control goes
    11         *    back to the menu program.
    12         *=================================================================
    13          ENVIRONMENT DIVISION.
    14         *----------------------------------------------------------------
    15          DATA DIVISION.
    16          WORKING-STORAGE SECTION.
    17          01   WS-OP-ENTRY                       PIC X(1).
    18          01   SCR-MSG                           PIC X(58).
    19         *
    20          LINKAGE SECTION.
    21          01   WS-TRANS-COUNT                    PIC 9(7).
    22         *----------------------------------------------------------------
    23          PROCEDURE DIVISION USING WS-TRANS-COUNT.
    24          0000-MAINLINE.
    25              ADD 1 TO WS-TRANS-COUNT.
    26              DISPLAY '' AT LINE 1 COLUMN 1 ERASE TO END OF SCREEN.
    27              DISPLAY 'Control passed to SINQU1'      AT LINE 1 COLUMN 2.
    28              DISPLAY 'Press <Return> to continue...' AT LINE 2 COLUMN 2.
    29              ACCEPT WS-OP-ENTRY                    FROM LINE 3 COLUMN 2.
    30          0000-EXIT.  EXIT PROGRAM.
```

Figure 11.4 Source code for program SINQU1, one of four almost identical stub programs I used to test VAXDEMO. This serves as the model for the other three testing "stubs" you need to test the VAXDEMO menu before writing the functional programs that handle customer file inquiry, add/change, delete, and browse functions.

SDEL1 stands in for CDEL1 before it is ready.

SBROW1 stands in for CBROW1 before it is ready.

After writing SINQU1 I made copies of it to create the last three. Each of these stub programs provides a LINKAGE SECTION to receive the count field passed by VAXDEMO and adds to that shared count field. This count is not especially important in my VAXDEMO demonstration system. I included this mainly to show you how to code shared data.

Each stub program erases the screen, then DISPLAYs a brief message as illustrated in Figure 11.5. When you press **<Return>** the stub program ends with EXIT PROGRAM (not STOP RUN, since that would end execution of the whole VAXDEMO system) and control returns to the menu.

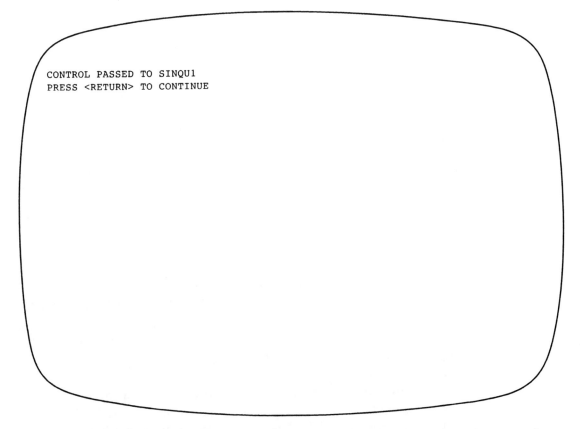

```
CONTROL PASSED TO SINQU1
PRESS <RETURN> TO CONTINUE
```

Figure 11.5   Screen presented by testing stub program SINQU1 when you select function 1 from the VAXDEMO menu. When you press **<Return>** this testing stub just sends control back to the VAXDEMO menu.

When you test a menu program with stubs, valid selections should cause passage of control to the appropriate subprogram. Invalid selections should cause the menu's error message to appear. Selecting Q should end menu execution.

11.7 Compiling and Linkage Editing Subprograms

To prepare a menu program and stub programs for testing you have to separately compile the source code for each program. You can do it with these commands:

```
$ COBOL/LIST vaxdemo
$ COBOL/LIST sinqu1
$ COBOL/LIST supd1
$ COBOL/LIST sdel1
$ COBOL/LIST sbrow1
```

This produces an object file for each program with the suffix .OBJ. You then linkage edit all of the modules together with the menu program name first:

```
$ LINK vaxdemo,sinqu1,supd1,sdel1,sbrow1
```

Linkage editing produces one machine language file. This file carries the name of the first program you stated in the LINK command and the suffix .EXE. To execute the system you run this file:

```
$ RUN vaxdemo
```

CAUTION ON SUBPROGRAM NAMES AND LINKAGE EDITING!

Caution! Let me save you some time and frustration. The LINK command reads files with the names you specify and the assumed suffix .OBJ. But when one program CALLs another the linkage edit does not use the filename where the .OBJ files are stored. **It uses the name you coded in the IDENTIFICATION DIVISION of each subprogram!** Be very careful to code your actual program names in the IDENTIFICATION DIVISION accurately. The best way to avoid problems is to make the filename and the IDENTIFICATION DIVISION name identical.

11.8 *LINK via a Command File*

At the end of Chapter 6 I showed you how to create command files (.COM files) to speed your work. The LINK command for a menu program and its functional subprograms is a candidate to be housed in its own command file. Using EDT, create a command file for yourself that has the LINK command I showed you in topic 11.7. This way you can relink all the components of your interactive system without having to rekey all of the subprogram names.

11.9 After Menu Testing . . .

A menu program is simple. You can test it quickly using program stubs. Once you test the menu you can use it to help test the functional subprograms that will replace each stub.

When the actual CINQU1 subprogram is created (in Chapter 12), I will replace the stub program for it with the real program. To do this I will change the VAXDEMO CALL statement at line 63 from CALL 'SINQU1' to CALL 'CINQU1' and compile VAXDEMO again. I will linkage edit the new .OBJ file from this compile with the .OBJ files for CINQU1 and the stub programs with this command:

```
$ LINK vaxdemo,cinqu1,supd1,sdel1,sbrow1
```

This way, I can phase in one functional subprogram at a time until (in Chapter 15) I complete the system. This isn't just a good way to introduce interactive VAX COBOL functionality to you. It's a standard way of integrating and testing the parts of any new interactive system one function at a time.

11.10 Chapter Summary

The name of a menu program is often the name of the application system. I show you VAXDEMO in this chapter, the menu program of my complete demonstration system. In a business data processing system the choice of actions you can select from a menu almost always include indexed file *inquiry*, record *update*, record *deletion*, and alternate key *browsing* (limited-range searching for a specific record).

An interactive menu program is a *main program*. It CALLs several *subprograms.* Each function you can select from the menu is usually implemented as a separate subprogram.

In "beginning of job" (BOJ) a menu program obtains the system date, erases the screen, presents the initial operator prompt for a choice of menu selection, and seeks the operator's selection. (If time of day appears on the screen it is not obtained once in BOJ because it changes continuously. Instead, you update the time field on the screen every time you give the terminal operator a prompt.)

The "process until" loop of the menu program is controlled by the terminal operator. He or she selects a function from the menu and can remain in it for several transactions before ending it and selecting another function from the menu. The system ends execution when the operator finally selects a "quit" action from the menu.

You can use stub programs to test a menu program before the subprograms it CALLs have been coded. A *stub program* is trivial. It just gives a brief indication that it has received control and then returns to the menu. In this chapter you see how I test the VAXDEMO menu program with four nearly identical stub programs, one each for the inquiry, add/change, delete, and browse programs I show you later in Chapters 12 through 15. In those later chapters I replace the stubs one by one with functional programs.

To prepare a menu program and stub programs for testing you have to separately compile the source code for the main program and for all subprograms. This creates an .OBJ file for each. Then you link these together, citing the menu (main) program name first. Since this command can be long, it is handy to put it into a command file as I showed you in Chapter 6.

11.11 Important Terms

You can review these terms to check your understanding of this chapter:

Main program   A program that CALLs another program. In an interactive system this is the highest-level menu program.

Subprogram   A program that is CALLed by another program. In an interactive system this usually how each menu-selectable function is housed.

Object file   The output of a compiler. This is a file named with a suffix of .OBJ. It contains instructions partially translated into machine language and is not executable.

Executable File   The output that the linkage editor builds from one or more object files, named with a suffix .EXE. This may be given control (executed) using the RUN command. The single .EXE file for an interactive system carries the menu program (main program) name.

You can find additional questions and exercises for this chapter in Appendix A.

Chapter Twelve

INTERACTIVE INQUIRY: PROGRAM CINQU1

12.1 Inquiry Screen Format

An **interactive inquiry** program gives you *"view"* access to information stored in an indexed file or database. In this chapter I show you the source code for CINQU1, an inquiry program that accesses the customer records that I loaded into an indexed file in Chapter 10. CINQU1 will replace the stub program SINQU1 that I used to test menu program VAXDEMO.

12.1 Inquiry Screen Format

Figure 12.1 shows you my design for the CINQU1 inquiry screen. This screen layout follows the guidelines I mentioned in earlier chapters. It has titling information at the top, including system date and time, and it uses the bottom line of the screen for a prompt. In the middle of the screen I have placed the fields that show the content of a record. By keeping the name, address, and city/state/zip information in familiar "mailing envelope" format it's easier to recognize and understand.

12.2 How the CINQU1 Screen Works

When you start CINQU1, you get the screen shown in Figure 12.2a. The screen labels are present but no data is on the screen. The prompt requests that you enter a record key at the bottom right side of the screen. I have entered the key 123456 at this point, but I haven't pressed **<Return>** yet. Figure 12.2b shows you how the screen looks after I press **<Return>**. Notice that the key has been shifted to appear in the middle of the screen and the area where I entered it on the prompt line has been

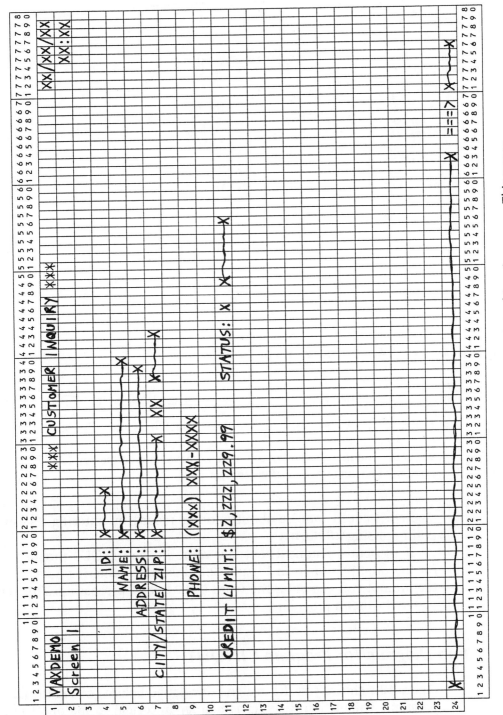

Figure 12.1 Layout for the CINQU1 customer record inquiry screen. This screen layout follows the guidelines I mentioned in earlier chapters.

147

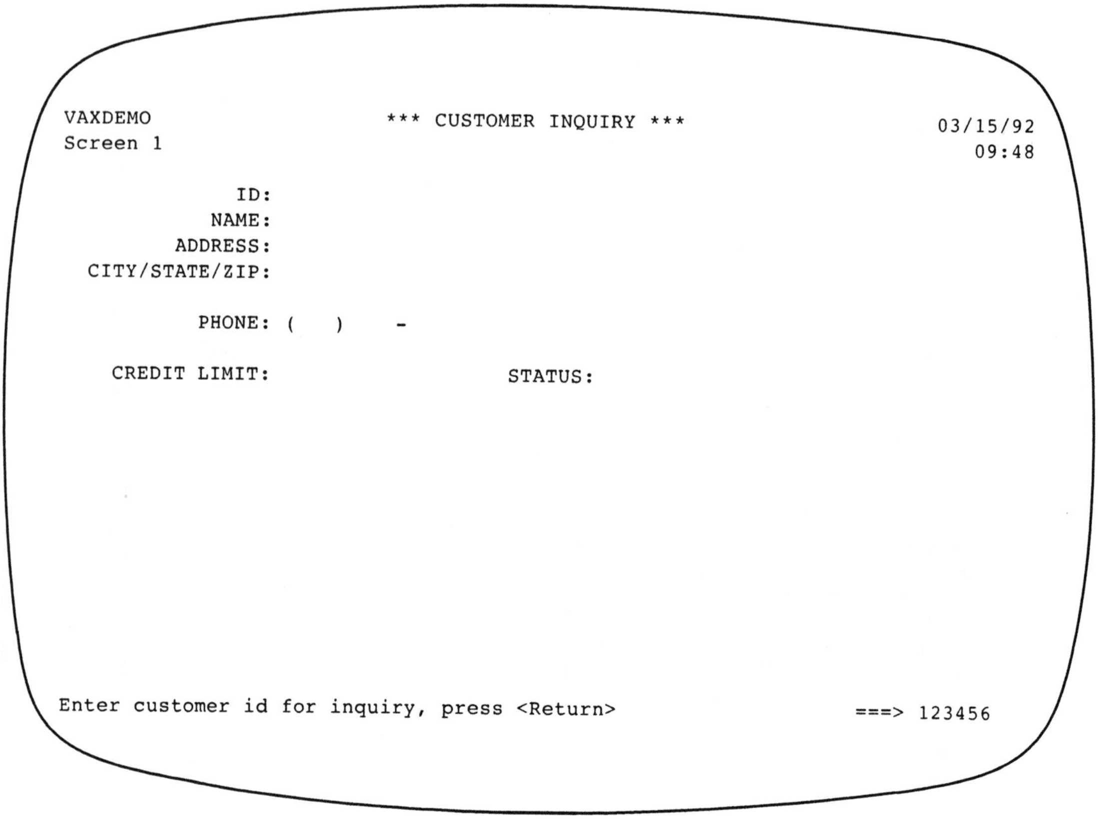

```
VAXDEMO                  *** CUSTOMER INQUIRY ***                03/15/92
Screen 1                                                          09:48

            ID:
          NAME:
       ADDRESS:
 CITY/STATE/ZIP:

         PHONE: (    )      -

  CREDIT LIMIT:                        STATUS:









 Enter customer id for inquiry, press <Return>            ===>  123456
```

Figure 12.2a   When you start CINQU1 you get this screen. The screen labels are present but no data is on the screen. The prompt requests that you enter a record key at the bottom right side of the screen. I have entered the key 123456 at this point but I haven't pressed *<Return>* yet.

cleared. I could inquire about another record by entering its key and again pressing *<Return>*.

If you enter a nonexistent key value in the CINQU1 program you'll get the prompt shown in Figure 12.3. Instead of entering a key value at the prompt you can enter the word QUIT to end processing. This returns you to the menu program.

12.3 Action Diagram for Program CINQU1

Figure 12.4 shows you the design I developed before I coded the CINQU1 program. This action diagram is similar in format to the one I mapped

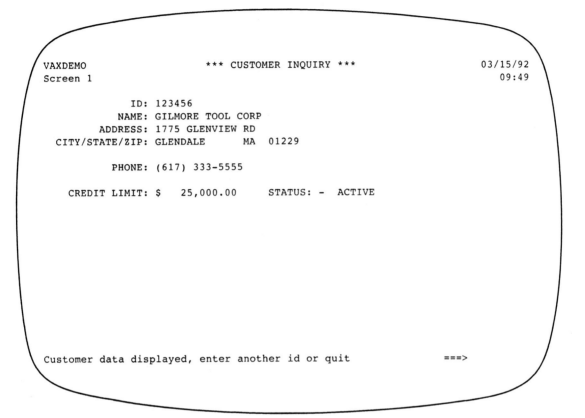

```
VAXDEMO                    *** CUSTOMER INQUIRY ***                03/15/92
Screen 1                                                          09:49

               ID: 123456
             NAME: GILMORE TOOL CORP
          ADDRESS: 1775 GLENVIEW RD
  CITY/STATE/ZIP: GLENDALE        MA   01229

           PHONE: (617) 333-5555

   CREDIT LIMIT: $   25,000.00      STATUS: -  ACTIVE
```

```
Customer data displayed, enter another id or quit              ===>
```

Figure 12.2b   How the CINQU1 screen looks after pressing *<Return>*. The key of the record requested for display has been shifted to appear in the middle of the screen, and the area where it was entered at the right of the prompt has been cleared.

out for the CALC1 program that you saw in Figure 8.5 in Chapter 8. Each bracket on this diagram represents one paragraph of source code. The highest level (mainline) of the program is at the left, and the lowest level is at the right. Brackets (paragraphs) are to the right of where they are performed most frequently.

I have provided this form of program logic map for every program in this book. You can compare the source code for CINQU1 to its action diagram and see the correspondence between the two. The diagram gives you the big picture and will help you see how the program does what it does.

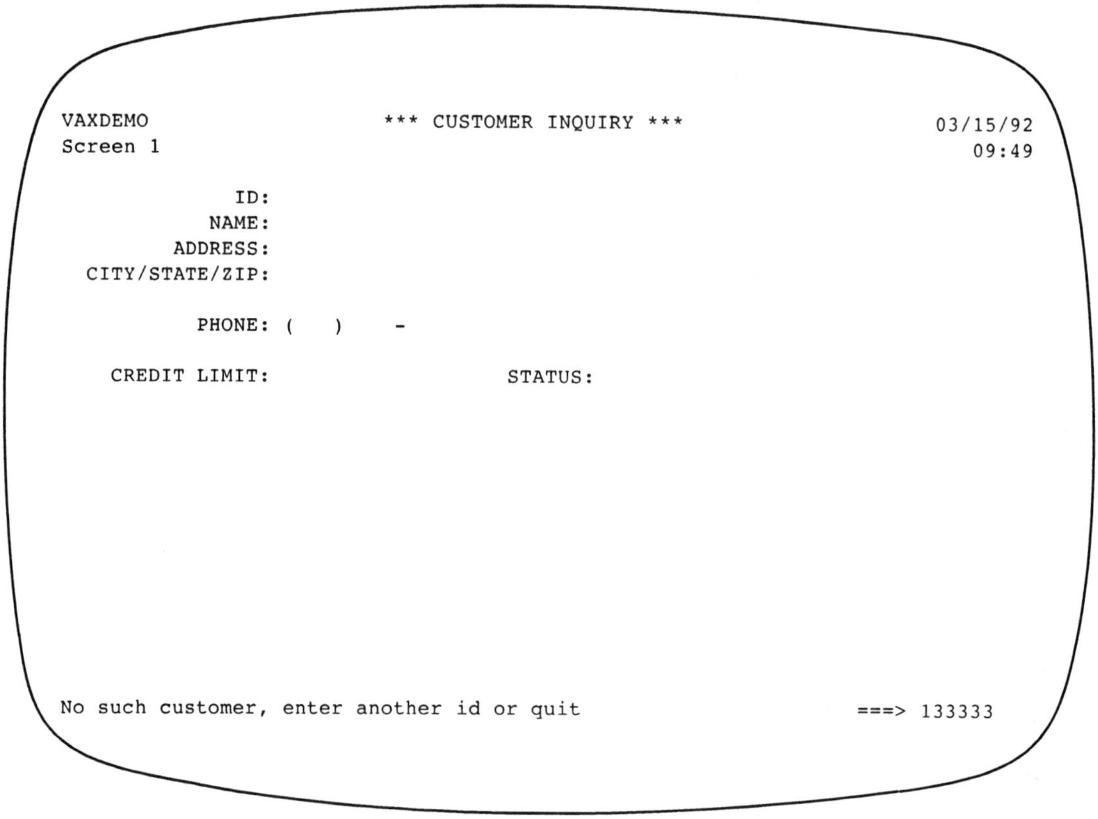

```
VAXDEMO                    *** CUSTOMER INQUIRY ***              03/15/92
Screen 1                                                          09:49

              ID:
            NAME:
         ADDRESS:
 CITY/STATE/ZIP:

           PHONE: (    )    -

  CREDIT LIMIT:                      STATUS:




No such customer, enter another id or quit                ===> 133333
```

Figure 12.3   If you enter a nonexistent key value when CINQU1 requests a key, you'll get this prompt.

12.4 CINQU1 Source Code

I have listed the source code for the CINQU1 program in Figure 12.5. This program is an ideal place to start your exploration of real-life conversational interactive programs because it's relatively short and highly modular.

12.5 Screen Labels and Data Display

Take a look at lines 125 through 137 of the source code for CINQU1. I display the screen labels at this point in beginning of job. All of the

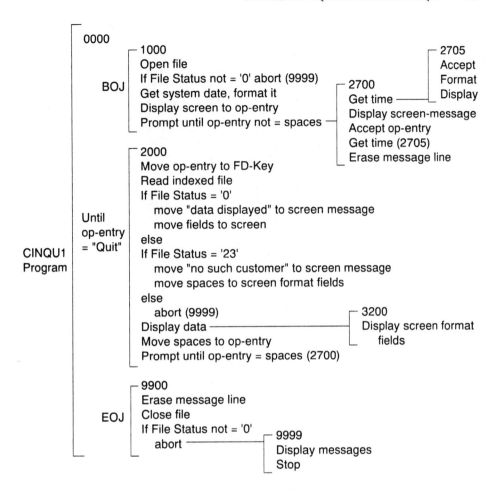

Figure 12.4 Action diagram for the logic of the CINQU1 program. Each bracket represents one paragraph of source code. The highest level (mainline) of the program is at the left and the lowest level is at the right. Brackets are to the right of where they are performed most frequently.

actions in this paragraph (1000) are the kinds of things that this program has to do only once when it starts running:

- Open the file.
- Obtain and format the system date.
- Set up the initial prompt.
- Give the terminal operator the initial prompt.

```
CINQU1                   15-Mar-1992 12:33:23   VAX COBOL V4.3-57
Source Listing           15-Mar-1992 12:33:09   CSC$ROOT:[CSCJGJ.VAXCO]CINQU1.COB;1
     1              IDENTIFICATION DIVISION.
     2              PROGRAM-ID.    CINQU1.
     3              *AUTHOR.        J JANOSSY   INTERNET: JANOSSY@CSCVAX.DEPAUL.EDU
     4              *INSTALLATION.  DEPAUL UNIVERSITY, CHICAGO, IL
     5              *=================================================================
     6              *   Function 1 of VAXDEMO system in VAX COBOL ON-LINE!  3/1/92
     7              *
     8              *   Performs inquiry in customer master file.  Before you can
     9              *   run this program you need to create an indexed file named
    10              *   MASTER.DAT with the INDLOAD program.
    11              *=================================================================
    12              ENVIRONMENT DIVISION.
    13              INPUT-OUTPUT SECTION.
    14              FILE-CONTROL.
    15                  SELECT MASTER-FILE              ASSIGN TO MASTER
    16                      ORGANIZATION  IS  INDEXED
    17                      ACCESS MODE   IS  RANDOM
    18                      RECORD KEY    IS  MF-KEY
    19                      ALTERNATE RECORD KEY IS MF-NAME-ALT-KEY
    20                      FILE STATUS   IS  WS-MASTFILE-FS.
    21              *-----------------------------------------------------------------
    22              DATA DIVISION.
    23              FILE SECTION.
    24              *
    25              FD  MASTER-FILE
    26                  RECORD CONTAINS 100 CHARACTERS
    27                  LABEL RECORDS ARE STANDARD.
    28              01  MASTER-RECORD.
    29                  12 MF-NAME-ALT-KEY.
    30                      15 MF-FIRM-NAME            PIC X(21).
    31                      15 MF-KEY                  PIC X(6).
    32                  12 MF-STATUS-FLAG              PIC X(1).
    33                      88 MF-STAT-ACTIVE                    VALUE '-'.
    34                      88 MF-STAT-INACTIVE                  VALUE 'I'.
    35                  12 MF-ADDRESS.
    36                      15 MF-ADDR-STREET          PIC X(20).
    37                      15 MF-ADDR-CITY            PIC X(12).
    38                      15 MF-ADDR-STATE           PIC X(2).
    39                      15 MF-ADDR-ZIP             PIC X(6).
    40                  12 MF-PHONE-DATA.
    41                      15 MF-AREA-CODE            PIC X(3).
    42                      15 MF-PHONE-FIRST3         PIC X(3).
    43                      15 MF-PHONE-LAST4          PIC X(4).
    44                  12 MF-CREDIT-LIMIT             PIC 9(7)V99.
    45                  12 FILLER                      PIC X(13).
    46              /
    47              *-----------------------------------------------------------------
    48              WORKING-STORAGE SECTION.
    49              01  WS-MASTFILE-FS.
    50                  12 WS-MASTFILE-STATUS-BYTE1    PIC X(1).
    51                  12 FILLER                      PIC X(1).
    52              01  WS-ABORT-PARAGRAPH             PIC X(4).
    53              01  SCR-MSG                        PIC X(64).
    54              01  WS-OP-ENTRY                    PIC X(6).
    55              *-----------------------------------------------------------------
    56              *   Screen format fields: a field is coded here carrying the
    57              *   display picture for each data field:
    58              *-----------------------------------------------------------------
    59              01  SCREEN-FORMAT-FIELDS.
    60                  12 SFF-KEY                     PIC X(6).
    61                  12 SFF-FIRM-NAME               PIC X(21).
    62                  12 SFF-ADDR-STREET             PIC X(20).
    63                  12 SFF-ADDR-CITY               PIC X(12).
    64                  12 SFF-ADDR-STATE              PIC X(2).
    65                  12 SFF-ADDR-ZIP                PIC X(6).
    66                  12 SFF-AREA-CODE               PIC X(3).
```

Figure 12.5 Source code for program CINQU1. I built this from the action diagram of Figure 12.4.

```
67              12 SFF-PHONE-FIRST3                 PIC X(3).
68              12 SFF-PHONE-LAST4                  PIC X(4).
69              12 SFF-CREDIT-LIMIT                 PIC $Z,ZZZ,ZZ9.99.
70              12 SFF-STATUS-FLAG                  PIC X(1).
71              12 SFF-STATUS-INTERP                PIC X(8).
72          *
73          01  WS-DATE.
74              12 WS-YR                            PIC X(2).
75              12 WS-MO                            PIC X(2).
76              12 WS-DA                            PIC X(2).
77          01  WS-FORMATTED-DATE                   PIC X(8).
78          *
79          01  WS-TIME.
80              12 WS-HRS                           PIC X(2).
81              12 WS-MIN                           PIC X(2).
82              12 FILLER                           PIC X(4).
83          01  WS-FORMATTED-TIME.
84              12 WSF-HRS                           PIC X(2).
85              12 FILLER                            PIC X(1)  VALUE ':'.
86              12 WSF-MIN                           PIC X(2).
87          *
88          LINKAGE SECTION.
89          01  WS-TRANS-COUNT                      PIC 9(7).
90          /
91          PROCEDURE DIVISION USING WS-TRANS-COUNT.
92          *----------------------------------------------------------------
93          *  In VAX COBOL you need declaratives (even in dummy form) to
94          *  avoid abends even when nonzero File Status values such as
95          *  '23' are received for a key-not-found condition.  Since
96          *  DECLARATIVES are a "section" MAIN-PROGRAM must be a section.
97          *----------------------------------------------------------------
98          DECLARATIVES.
99          0000-ERROR    SECTION.
100             USE AFTER STANDARD ERROR PROCEDURE ON MASTER-FILE.
101         0000-DUMMY.  EXIT.
102         *
103         END DECLARATIVES.
104         *----------------------------------------------------------------
105         0000-MAIN-PROGRAM    SECTION.
106         0000-MAINLINE.
107             PERFORM 1000-BOJ.
108             PERFORM 2000-PROCESS
109                UNTIL WS-OP-ENTRY = 'QUIT' OR 'quit'.
110             PERFORM 9900-EOJ.
111         0000-EXIT.  EXIT PROGRAM.
112         /
113         *----------------------------------------------------------------
114         *  Beginning of job
115         *----------------------------------------------------------------
116         1000-BOJ.
117             OPEN INPUT MASTER-FILE.
118             IF WS-MASTFILE-FS NOT = '00'
119                MOVE '1000' TO WS-ABORT-PARAGRAPH
120                PERFORM 9999-ABORT.
121             ACCEPT WS-DATE FROM DATE.
122             STRING WS-MO  '/'  WS-DA  '/'  WS-YR  DELIMITED BY SIZE
123                INTO WS-FORMATTED-DATE.
124         *
125             DISPLAY '' AT LINE 1 COLUMN 1 ERASE TO END OF SCREEN.
126             DISPLAY 'VAXDEMO'                  AT LINE  1 COLUMN  2.
127             DISPLAY '*** CUSTOMER INQUIRY *** '
128                                       BOLD AT LINE  1 COLUMN 28.
129             DISPLAY WS-FORMATTED-DATE       AT LINE  1 COLUMN 72.
130             DISPLAY 'Screen 1'              AT LINE  2 COLUMN  2.
131             DISPLAY 'ID:'            BOLD AT LINE  4 COLUMN 16.
132             DISPLAY 'NAME:'          BOLD AT LINE  5 COLUMN 14.
133             DISPLAY 'ADDRESS:'       BOLD AT LINE  6 COLUMN 11.
134             DISPLAY 'CITY/STATE/ZIP:' BOLD AT LINE  7 COLUMN  4.
135             DISPLAY 'PHONE: (   )   -' BOLD AT LINE  9 COLUMN 13.
```

(Continued)

Figure 12.5   *(Continued)*

```
136              DISPLAY 'CREDIT LIMIT:'        BOLD AT LINE 11 COLUMN  6.
137              DISPLAY 'STATUS:'              BOLD AT LINE 11 COLUMN 38.
138        *
139              MOVE 'Enter customer id for inquiry, press <Return>'
140                 TO SCR-MSG.
141              MOVE SPACES TO WS-OP-ENTRY.
142              PERFORM 2700-OP-PROMPT
143                 UNTIL WS-OP-ENTRY NOT = SPACES.
144        /
145        *----------------------------------------------------------------
146        *    Transaction processing loop
147        *----------------------------------------------------------------
148         2000-PROCESS.
149              MOVE WS-OP-ENTRY TO MF-KEY.
150        *
151              READ MASTER-FILE.
152              IF WS-MASTFILE-STATUS-BYTE1 = '0'
153                 MOVE 'Customer data displayed, enter another id or quit'
154                    TO SCR-MSG
155                 PERFORM 3100-MOVE-FIELDS-TO-SCREEN
156              ELSE
157              IF WS-MASTFILE-FS = '23'
158                 MOVE 'No such customer, enter another id or quit'
159                    TO SCR-MSG
160                 MOVE SPACES TO SCREEN-FORMAT-FIELDS
161              ELSE
162                 MOVE '2100' TO WS-ABORT-PARAGRAPH
163                 PERFORM 9999-ABORT.
164        *
165              PERFORM 3200-DISPLAY-DATA.
166              MOVE SPACES TO WS-OP-ENTRY.
167              PERFORM 2700-OP-PROMPT
168                 UNTIL WS-OP-ENTRY NOT = SPACES.
169        *
170        *================================================================
171        *
172         2700-OP-PROMPT.
173              PERFORM 2705-TIME.
174              DISPLAY SCR-MSG  AT LINE 24 COLUMN  2 ERASE TO END OF LINE.
175              DISPLAY '===>'   AT LINE 24 COLUMN 66.
176              ACCEPT WS-OP-ENTRY
177                 REVERSED
178                 PROTECTED
179                 FROM LINE 24 COLUMN 71.
180              PERFORM 2705-TIME.
181              DISPLAY ''        AT LINE 24 COLUMN  2 ERASE TO END OF LINE.
182        *
183         2705-TIME.
184              ACCEPT WS-TIME FROM TIME.
185              MOVE WS-HRS TO WSF-HRS.
186              MOVE WS-MIN TO WSF-MIN.
187              DISPLAY WS-FORMATTED-TIME AT LINE  2 COLUMN 75.
188        *
189         3100-MOVE-FIELDS-TO-SCREEN.
190              MOVE MF-KEY            TO  SFF-KEY.
191              MOVE MF-FIRM-NAME      TO  SFF-FIRM-NAME.
192              MOVE MF-ADDR-STREET    TO  SFF-ADDR-STREET.
193              MOVE MF-ADDR-CITY      TO  SFF-ADDR-CITY.
194              MOVE MF-ADDR-STATE     TO  SFF-ADDR-STATE.
195              MOVE MF-ADDR-ZIP       TO  SFF-ADDR-ZIP.
196              MOVE MF-AREA-CODE      TO  SFF-AREA-CODE.
197              MOVE MF-PHONE-FIRST3   TO  SFF-PHONE-FIRST3.
198              MOVE MF-PHONE-LAST4    TO  SFF-PHONE-LAST4.
199              MOVE MF-CREDIT-LIMIT   TO  SFF-CREDIT-LIMIT.
200              MOVE MF-STATUS-FLAG    TO  SFF-STATUS-FLAG.
201              IF MF-STATUS-FLAG = '-'
202                 MOVE 'ACTIVE'          TO SFF-STATUS-INTERP
203              ELSE
204              IF MF-STATUS-FLAG = 'I'
205                 MOVE 'INACTIVE'        TO SFF-STATUS-INTERP
```

Figure 12.5   (Continued)

```
206                ELSE
207                    MOVE ALL '*'            TO SFF-STATUS-INTERP.
208          *
209            3200-DISPLAY-DATA.
210                DISPLAY SFF-KEY             AT LINE   4 COLUMN 20.
211                DISPLAY SFF-FIRM-NAME       AT LINE   5 COLUMN 20.
212                DISPLAY SFF-ADDR-STREET     AT LINE   6 COLUMN 20.
213                DISPLAY SFF-ADDR-CITY       AT LINE   7 COLUMN 20.
214                DISPLAY SFF-ADDR-STATE      AT LINE   7 COLUMN 34.
215                DISPLAY SFF-ADDR-ZIP        AT LINE   7 COLUMN 38.
216                DISPLAY SFF-AREA-CODE       AT LINE   9 COLUMN 21.
217                DISPLAY SFF-PHONE-FIRST3    AT LINE   9 COLUMN 26.
218                DISPLAY SFF-PHONE-LAST4     AT LINE   9 COLUMN 30.
219                DISPLAY SFF-CREDIT-LIMIT    AT LINE  11 COLUMN 20.
220                DISPLAY SFF-STATUS-FLAG     AT LINE  11 COLUMN 46.
221                DISPLAY SFF-STATUS-INTERP AT LINE  11 COLUMN 49.
222                DISPLAY '' AT LINE 24 COLUMN 71 ERASE TO END OF LINE.
223          /
224          *------------------------------------------------------------
225          *   End of job
226          *------------------------------------------------------------
227            9900-EOJ.
228                DISPLAY '' AT LINE 1, COLUMN 1 ERASE TO END OF SCREEN.
229                CLOSE MASTER-FILE.
230                IF WS-MASTFILE-STATUS-BYTE1 NOT = '0'
231                    MOVE '9900' TO WS-ABORT-PARAGRAPH
232                    PERFORM 9999-ABORT.
233          *
234            9999-ABORT.
235                DISPLAY '' AT LINE 1, COLUMN 1 ERASE TO END OF SCREEN.
236                DISPLAY '**************************************************'
237                DISPLAY 'Program CINQU1 Error E99'.
238                DISPLAY 'Indexed file failure at paragraph ', WS-ABORT-PARAGRAPH.
239                DISPLAY 'File Status is ', WS-MASTFILE-FS.
240                DISPLAY 'Print this screen and contact programming group'.
241                DISPLAY '**************************************************'
242                STOP RUN.
```

Figure 12.5   *(Continued)*

But take a look also at lines 28 through 45 (the record layout for the customer file) and lines 59 through 71 (WORKING-STORAGE fields). Then look at paragraphs 3100 and 3200 (lines 189 through 222). You'll notice that the following sequence of actions occurs involving these fields every time a record is presented on the screen:

1. The record is obtained from the file and appears in MASTER-RECORD in the indexed master file FD.

2. Paragraph 3100 moves the data from the master file FDW to screen format fields to get it ready for DISPLAY.

3. Paragraph 3200 DISPLAYs the screen format fields.

12.6 How You Obtain Records from an Indexed File

The processing loop (2000) of CINQU1 is located at lines 148 through 168. I coded this in a very straightforward way. To obtain the record to be displayed on the screen I just move the key value that was entered at the bottom of the screen to the indexed file key field. Then I READ the file. Since the SELECT/ASSIGN statement was coded with ACCESS MODE IS RANDOM the READ verb will act as a random read and not as a sequential read.

Three outcomes are possible when you do a READ from an indexed file:

- You could be successful and get the record.
- You could be unsuccessful and not find a record with the key value you wanted in the file.
- The indexed file could fail.

Your program logic can certainly handle the first two cases; you will normally encounter them. But the last case is special. It means that your READ has failed but your program can't deal with the problem. All you can do in the third case is show as much as you can about the problem and stop the program ("abort" it). Why can an indexed file fail? It is a complicated structure. It can suffer an internal data integrity problem if this or another program accesses it but doesn't close it properly.

12.7 Using File Status

File Status is a two-byte field provided to you by the indexed file access method. Checking it is how you detect the outcome of any action you attempt with the file. Sometimes you have to test just the first byte of this field and sometimes both bytes together to find out the outcome. For a random mode READ these File Status values are relevant:

Value	Explanation	Random READ meaning
'0'	File Status first byte zero	You got the record
'23'	Two-byte value of 23	No such record key
Any other value	The value is an indication of the problem	File has failed

You can see in lines 152 through 163 how I test File Status to see if a record matching the key I wanted is in the file. This is just an IF/ELSE statement that has three possible outcomes. If the last outcome is the one that materializes, I perform 9999-ABORT to end the operation of the program. This paragraph displays messages telling the operator why the program is ending.

When you use File Status (not the obsolescent INVALID KEY option of the READ verb), VAX COBOL requires you to code DECLARATIVES at the start of the PROCEDURE DIVISION. But since I don't really want to handle file problems in DECLARATIVES this is "dummy" coding in CINQU1, at lines 98 through 103. It is present only to satisfy the compiler.

12.8 File Status for OPEN and CLOSE

Any action you take with an indexed file can reveal to you that the file has failed. You have to check File Status even when you OPEN or CLOSE an indexed file.

If you OPEN an indexed file and find that a two-byte File Status of value '00' is returned, the file opened successfully. Any other value indicates a problem that your program cannot resolve. You'll see that lines 117 through 120 in CINQU1 open the indexed file and check the File Status value. If, for example, I had miscoded CINQU1 and stated the key position of the record in the wrong location in the record, CINQU1 would abort (due to the logic in 9999-ABORT) with the screen illustrated in Figure 12.6. Look up this value in the File Status chart in Chapter 10 (Figure 10.7) and see what it is telling you.

After you CLOSE an indexed file a File Status value of '00' means the file closed successfully. Your work is not really done until you receive this value for your CLOSE. If the file has failed (as indicated by a File Status value other than '00' after the CLOSE) you need to know about it now, before any other program tries to use the file.

Actions other OPEN or CLOSE require that you check just the first byte of File Status for '0' for successful completion. Many actions, such as a successful READ, return File Status values starting with zero but with the second byte containing a number associated with supplementary information you often do not need.

12.9 LINK Command with Additional Subprograms

After developing a program like CINQU1 you need to test it. You replace a stub testing program with the "real" functional subprogram and test it with your already-proven menu program. To do this you have to do several things in sequence:

1. Compile the functional subprogram to create its .OBJ file.

2. Use EDT to change the CALL statement of the menu program so that it now calls the real program name instead of its testing stub.

3. Compile the revised version of the menu program, creating a new .OBJ file for it.

4. Linkage edit the programs together:

```
$ LINK VAXDEMO,CINQU1,SUPD1,SDEL1,SBROW1
```

After this command executes you can run the menu. When you select function "1" from the menu, the CINQU1 program will execute and test it. The EXIT PROGRAM coded at the end of its mainline returns control to VAXDEMO when you no longer want to do inquiries with it.

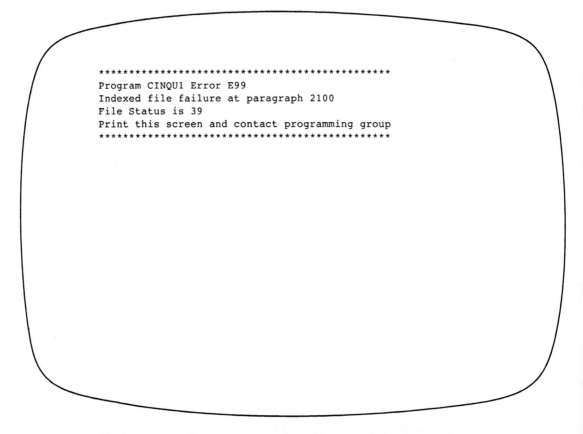

```
************************************************
Program CINQU1 Error E99
Indexed file failure at paragraph 2100
File Status is 39
Print this screen and contact programming group
************************************************
```

Figure 12.6 "Abort" screen produced by program CINQU1 if it cannot successfully OPEN the MASTER.DAT indexed file. This is produced by paragraph 9999-ABORT. Look up the value of the File Status chart in Chapter 10 (Figure 10.7) and see what this value is telling you.

12.10 Chapter Summary

An *interactive inquiry* program gives you *"view" access* to information stored in an indexed file or database. This type of program asks you to enter a record key. It then retrieves the record from an indexed file or database and shows you the contents on the screen.

As with any conversational program an inquiry program has three logical parts: beginning of job, process, and end of job. In beginning of job it opens the file, sets up the initial operator prompt, and issues this prompt. In its processing loop it does a random READ of the indexed file to get the record matching the operator's prompt response, presents it on the screen, then prompts the operator again. This transaction processing cycle repeats until the operator enters a quitting indication at the prompt.

READ seeks a specific record from an indexed file when you code its SELECT/ASSIGN statement with ACCESS MODE IS RANDOM. This type of READ seeks the record with the key value you have placed into the record key field in the FD of the indexed file. Random mode READ, unlike READ in sequential access mode, will never hit end-of-file.

Every time you do a random READ in an indexed file, three outcomes are possible: *successful* (got the record), *unsuccessful* (no record found with that key), or *indexed file failure*. You detect the outcome of your action by checking the File Status value immediately after the action. A '0' in the first byte of the two-byte File Status field indicates success. File Status '23' indicates the record was not found. Any other File Status value in response to a random mode READ indicates file failure. In this case you need to display File Status because its value will indicate what the problem with the file is.

You have to check for successful outcome for indexed file OPEN and CLOSE. In the case of these actions there is no middle ground: Either the action succeeded ('0') or file failure occurred.

To replace a testing stub in a menu-based system with a functional inquiry subprogram you need to compile the subprogram, change the menu program to CALL the subprogram name, compile it, and linkage edit the programs in the system.

12.11 Important Terms

Inquiry program   A program that gives you view access to information stored in an indexed file or database.

ACCESS MODE   A clause of the COBOL SELECT/ASSIGN statement that tells whether you want to process an indexed file sequentially or with random READs. Your choice for this clause dictates how the READ and WRITE verbs work.

Random mode READ   Execution of the READ verb when the SELECT/ASSIGN statement for an indexed file is coded with ACCESS MODE IS RANDOM. The READ seeks the record whose key you put into the record key field of the indexed file. (Unlike a READ in sequential access mode this type of READ will never reach end of file.)

Program abort   Forcing a program to end prematurely because it has detected a condition that it could not resolve, such as failure of an indexed file.

Access method failure   Inability to complete intended processing with the OPEN, READ, WRITE, REWRITE, DELETE, START, or CLOSE verbs as indicated by the operating system's input/output software. With indexed files you detect this by testing the File Status value after taking the action.

You can find additional questions and exercises for this chapter in Appendix A.

Chapter Thirteen

INTERACTIVE ADD/CHANGE: PROGRAM CUPD1

To create a new record in a file or change an existing one, you have to make the contents of the record visible and accessible to a terminal operator. In this chapter I show you how I arrange to do this for records in my customer master file. The CUPD1 program you see here is the most complex in this book. It uses two subprograms, NUMCHEK and PLACHEK, which I have listed for you in Appendix B.

13.1 An On-Line Update Screen

Figure 13.1 shows you the screen of my update program CUPD1. You'll note that this is the same screen layout I used in inquiry program CINQU1, covered in Chapter 12. On this copy of the layout I have identified each of the enterable fields with a number in a circle (this is not a part of the actual terminal screen). I'll describe to you in section 13.5 a technique for documenting your field validations and error messages using numbers such as these.

Full-scale file maintenance includes the deletion of records as well as the addition or change of records. Because record deletion is a serious matter and demands additional security, I put the record deletion function into a separate program in my VAXDEMO system. As you'll see in Chapter 14, my deletion program also uses the same screen format as the update and inquiry programs.

13.2 How Combined Add/Change Works

When you select the add/change function from the VAXDEMO menu the screen shown in Figure 13.2 appears. You are directed to enter the ID

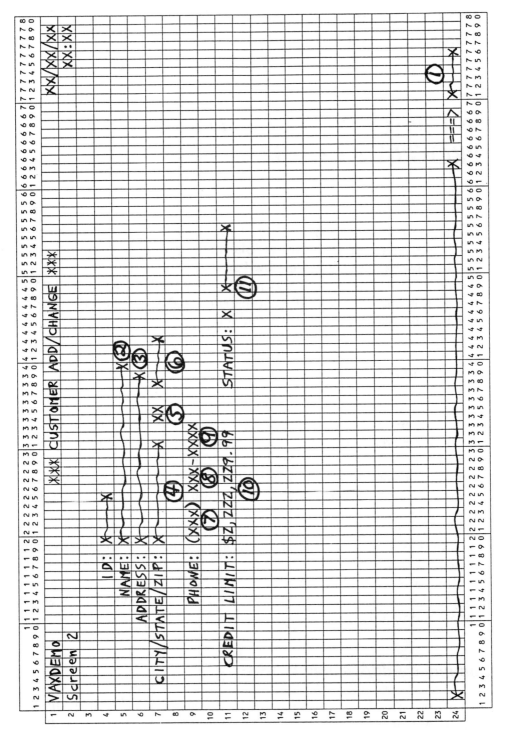

Figure 13.1 Screen layout of the CUPD1 customer file add/change update program. This is the same screen layout I used in the inquiry program CINQU1 (Chapter 12), but on this copy of the layout I have identified each of the enterable fields with a number in a circle (this is not a part of the actual terminal screen).

162

(key) of a record at the right of the prompt line. But you do not indicate if you want to add or change a record. Instead, the program assumes that you want to add a record if no record with the key you specified exists in the file. If a record with the key you specified is found in the file, its contents are DISPLAYed on the screen and a record change is assumed. In either case you can cancel the add or change if you do not want to proceed with it.

Figure 13.2 shows the add/change screen as it appears when a record

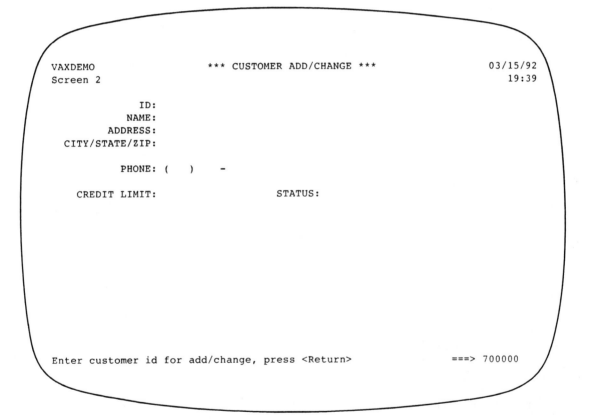

```
VAXDEMO                    *** CUSTOMER ADD/CHANGE ***                03/15/92
Screen 2                                                                19:39

            ID:
          NAME:
       ADDRESS:
 CITY/STATE/ZIP:

         PHONE: (    )    -

   CREDIT LIMIT:                          STATUS:




 Enter customer id for add/change, press <Return>              ===> 700000
```

Figure 13.2   When you select the add/change function from the VAXDEMO menu this screen appears. You are directed to enter the ID (key) of a record at the right of the prompt line, but you do not indicate if you want to add or change a record. The program assumes that you want to add a record if no record with the key you specified exists in the file. If a record with the key you specified is found in the file its contents are DISPLAYed on the screen and a record change is assumed.

with the key you entered is found in the file. The fields of the record are made accessible to you, and the cursor is positioned at the first enterable field, NAME. (The key field customer ID appears in the middle of the screen now but is not enterable. Can you explain why you can't change it once the transaction has begun?) This field appears in reverse video, whereas the other fields appear with normal intensity.

To accomplish a change you key in new contents for a field and press **<Return>**. Your entry is validated for correctness. If the entry is not correct, an error message relating to this field appears at the bottom of the screen. The cursor remains in the field until you enter valid data for it.

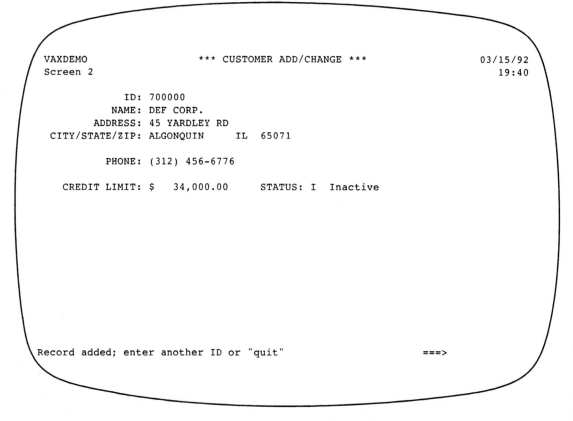

```
VAXDEMO                *** CUSTOMER ADD/CHANGE ***                03/15/92
Screen 2                                                             19:40

            ID: 700000
          NAME: DEF CORP.
       ADDRESS: 45 YARDLEY RD
 CITY/STATE/ZIP: ALGONQUIN      IL   65071

         PHONE: (312) 456-6776

  CREDIT LIMIT: $   34,000.00      STATUS: I   Inactive




Record added; enter another ID or "quit"                      ===>
```

Figure 13.3 When you press **<Return>** after entering data into the last field (STATUS), CUPD1 completes the transaction by writing the record or rewriting the record to the file. This represents completion of one transaction. You will then get the message shown to continue or "quit."

When you enter valid data for the field, it is redisplayed without reverse video and the cursor moves ahead to the next field.

When you are changing the contents of a record you might want to change only one or a few fields. To "tab through" a field without changing its contents you just press **<Return>**. As you know (from Chapter 8) this really sends spaces to the receiving field. I have arranged the logic of CUPD1 to save the original value of the field and restore it if you take this tab-through action. This makes the screen easy to use, since the tab-through action seems very natural.

When you press **<Return>** after entering data into the last field (the STATUS field here), CUPD1 completes the transaction by writing the record or rewriting the record to the file. Figure 13.3 illustrates the message you'll get. The prompt asks you to enter another record key or the word "quit" to end the add/change function.

13.3 Why You Should Combine Add/Change

Why should you combine the add and change functions? It's desirable to do this because:

- It's more convenient for end users.
- Program logic for each function is nearly identical; add and change use exactly the same data validations.
- Add and change programs are among the largest in a system, and combining them provides source code economy.
- The program itself can easily determine if an add or a change is intended based on its READ of the indexed file (or database). If the record is found, a change is assumed, if it's not, an add is assumed.

If you combine record add and change functions you also need to implement a *transaction cancellation* or *backout* capability. This handles the relatively infrequent instances where the terminal operator enters an incorrect key value and gets into an add or change unintentionally.

13.4 Transaction Cancellation

A terminal operator will occasionally have to cancel a transaction before completing it. This may be necessary because valid data for a certain field is not available but this fact becomes known only after an add or update action has been started. An operator might also enter an existing record key by mistake when a record addition was actually intended or vice versa.

My VAXDEMO on-line system provides for transaction cancellation in a simple and straightforward manner. I recommend that you use this method. You can cancel a transaction—either add or change—without affecting the master file by entering a backslash into any field. This symbol (\ ) is near the **<Return>** key on VT-100 family terminals. The backslash is ordinarily not used in data content, so it's a handy key to use as a transaction cancellation signal.

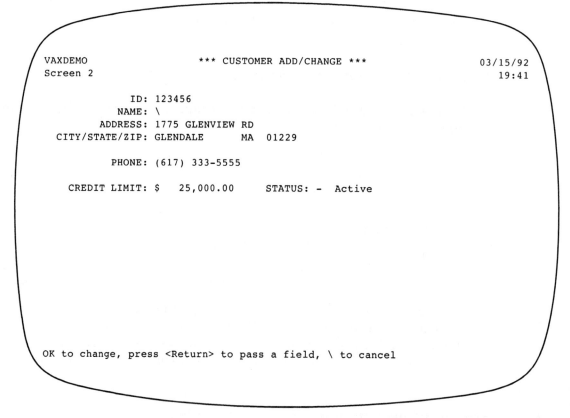

```
VAXDEMO                    *** CUSTOMER ADD/CHANGE ***              03/15/92
Screen 2                                                              19:41

               ID: 123456
             NAME: \
          ADDRESS: 1775 GLENVIEW RD
  CITY/STATE/ZIP: GLENDALE      MA   01229

            PHONE: (617) 333-5555

     CREDIT LIMIT: $   25,000.00     STATUS: -  Active









OK to change, press <Return> to pass a field, \ to cancel
```

Figure 13.4   The CUPD1 program lets you cancel a transaction. When you enter the backslash \ at the first position in a field and press the **<Return>** key, program CUPD1 abandons all further field entries. It clears the data from the screen, DISPLAYs a message advising that the transaction was cancelled, and prompts you to enter another customer ID or the word "quit".

Why didn't I use the **<*Escape*>** or a program function key for the transaction cancellation key? I chose the "\" key to keep my program as simple as possible. VAX COBOL lets you capture special function keys, but this requires much more complex coding (see section 8.12).

When you enter the backslash \ at the first position in a field and press the **<*Return*>** key, CUPD1 abandons all further field entries. It clears the data from the screen, DISPLAYs a message advising that the transaction was cancelled, and prompts you to enter another customer ID or the word "quit." Figure 13.4 illustrates this entry.

In real life the need to "back out" of an interactive transaction after starting it always eventually arises. Even if you don't combine add and change functions into one program you should include a transaction cancellation capability. If you forget to provide it, your end users will sooner or later ask for it and you will have to retrofit it into your programs anyway.

13.5 Add/Change Data Validation

Data entered at the terminal has to be validated for correctness by an add/change program. The requirements statement for this type of program has to include the criteria for checking data. The designer of the program should also clearly specify the text of the prompt that tells the terminal operator about any field error.

I have listed here the text of each prompt that I wanted to use in CUPD1. I made up this list *before* developing the program so that I would make sure the language was consistent:

E2	Firm name cannot be blank; reenter or \
E3	Address cannot be blank; reenter or \
E4	City cannot be blank; reenter or \
E5A	State/Prov cannot be blank; correct it or \
E5B	Abbrev invalid (must use CAPS); correct it or \
W6	Enter new zip or "#" to make zip spaces
E7	Area code must be entered, numeric, correct it or \
E8	Phone prefix must be entered, numeric; correct it or \
E9	Phone number must be entered, numeric; correct it or \
E10A	Credit limit must be specified; correct it or \

E10B   Must be => $1000 with decimal point; correct it or \

E11   Status flag must be – or I; correct it or \

"E" or "W" and a number is a handy way to summarize the nature of each event and relate each prompt to the field involved. "E" means *error* and "W" means *warning*. The number is the circled field number I documented in the screen layout of Figure 13.1. If you need to provide an end user with additional training materials or instructions about this screen, the "E" numbers in each prompt would make it easier to understand.

13.6 CUPD1 Source Code

I have listed the source code for Program CUPD1 in Figure 13.5. This is quite a large program compared to the others in this book, but it's my feeling that complete programs make it easier for you to see things in perspective. I have imbedded comments in the program to point out some of its most important features.

I ACCEPT and DISPLAY data using alphanumeric screen format fields in WORKING-STORAGE. I code these with a prefix of SFF- to best identify them. If you look at lines 68 through 82 of CUPD1 source code you will see these fields. I redefine fields that I will redisplay in numeric edited form with a suitable editing PIC such as $Z,ZZZ,ZZ9.99.

13.7 Subprograms for Data Validation (NUMCHEK and PLACNAME)

I recommend that you not use WITH CONVERSION to accept numeric data but that you instead use a ***de-editing subprogram*** such as NUMCHEK, which I have listed for you in Appendix B. WITH CONVERSION doesn't allow you to enter commas as a part of a number, but many people do want to enter numbers this way. Since I have already shown you how to use WITH CONVERSION in Chapter 9, I demonstrate for you here how to ACCEPT numeric data this alternative way.

Look at lines 92 through 96 of CUPD1 source code. You'll see these fields in WORKING-STORAGE:

```
01   WS-NUMCHEK-FIELDS.
     12 NUM-INPUT                PIC X(22).
     12 NUM-RIGHT-OF-DECIMAL     PIC 9(1).
     12 NUM-STATUS-FLAG          PIC X(1).
     12 NUM-OUTPUT               PIC 9(11)V9(6).
```

```
CUPD1                   15-Mar-1992 12:46:41    VAX COBOL V4.3-57
Source Listing          15-Mar-1992 12:46:31    CSC$ROOT:[CSCJGJ.VAXCO]CUPD1.COB;1

     1            IDENTIFICATION DIVISION.
     2            PROGRAM-ID.     CUPD1.
     3           *AUTHOR.         J JANOSSY   INTERNET: JANOSSY@CSCVAX.DEPAUL.EDU
     4           *INSTALLATION.   DEPAUL UNIVERSITY, CHICAGO, IL
     5           *================================================================
     6           *   Function 2 of VAXDEMO system in VAX COBOL ON-LINE!  3/1/92
     7           *
     8           *   Performs random access add/change update to customer file
     9           *      * Tab through a field with <Enter> for no change in it
    10           *      * Use <backslash> \ to cancel transaction at any field
    11           *   Uses subprogram 'NUMCHEK' for numeric field validation
    12           *   Caution: This version does not provide for concurrent use
    13           *   by multiple users!  See discussion on record locking you
    14           *   must arrange to allow multiple users to access same file!
    15           *================================================================
    16            ENVIRONMENT DIVISION.
    17            INPUT-OUTPUT SECTION.
    18            FILE-CONTROL.
    19                SELECT MASTER-FILE              ASSIGN TO MASTER
    20                    ORGANIZATION   IS   INDEXED
    21                    ACCESS MODE    IS   RANDOM
    22                    RECORD KEY     IS   MF-KEY
    23                    ALTERNATE RECORD KEY IS MF-NAME-ALT-KEY
    24                    FILE STATUS    IS   WS-MASTFILE-FS.
    25           *----------------------------------------------------------------
    26            DATA DIVISION.
    27            FILE SECTION.
    28           *
    29            FD  MASTER-FILE
    30                RECORD CONTAINS 100 CHARACTERS
    31                LABEL RECORDS ARE STANDARD.
    32            01  MASTER-RECORD.
    33                12 MF-NAME-ALT-KEY.
    34                    15 MF-FIRM-NAME                 PIC X(21).
    35                    15 MF-KEY                        PIC X(6).
    36                12 MF-STATUS-FLAG                    PIC X(1).
    37                    88 MF-STAT-ACTIVE                         VALUE '-'.
    38                    88 MF-STAT-INACTIVE                       VALUE 'I'.
    39                12 MF-ADDRESS.
    40                    15 MF-ADDR-STREET               PIC X(20).
    41                    15 MF-ADDR-CITY                 PIC X(12).
    42                    15 MF-ADDR-STATE                 PIC X(2).
    43                    15 MF-ADDR-ZIP                   PIC X(6).
    44                12 MF-PHONE-DATA.
    45                    15 MF-AREA-CODE                  PIC X(3).
    46                    15 MF-PHONE-FIRST3               PIC X(3).
    47                    15 MF-PHONE-LAST4                PIC X(4).
    48                12 MF-CREDIT-LIMIT                PIC 9(7)V99.
    49                12 FILLER                          PIC X(13).
    50           /
    51           *----------------------------------------------------------------
    52            WORKING-STORAGE SECTION.
    53            01  WS-MASTFILE-FS.
    54                12 WS-MASTFILE-STATUS-BYTE1         PIC X(1).
    55                12 FILLER                           PIC X(1).
    56            01  F1-FUNCTION-FLAG                    PIC X(3).
    57            01  F2-OP-STAT                          PIC 9(1).
    58            01  F3-INTERP-FLAG                      PIC X(1).
    59            01  WS-STATUS-FLAG                      PIC X(1).
    60            01  WS-ABORT-PARAGRAPH                  PIC X(4).
```

(Continued)

Figure 13.5 Source code for interactive add/change update program CUPD1.
This program is the largest in this book. It uses the same technique for screen entry
and redisplay I showed you in the CALC3 program in Chapter 9. (This program
CALLs the PLACNAME and NUMCHEK subprograms at lines 407 and 596. See
Appendix B for source code listings of these subprograms.)

```
 61         01  SCR-MSG                          PIC X(64).
 62         01  WS-OP-ENTRY.
 63             12 WS-OP-ENTRY-CHAR  PIC X  OCCURS 6 TIMES  INDEXED BY OP-IX.
 64         *-------------------------------------------------------------
 65         *   Screen format fields: a field is coded here carrying the
 66         *   display picture for each data field:
 67         *-------------------------------------------------------------
 68         01  SCREEN-FORMAT-FIELDS.
 69             12 SFF-KEY                       PIC X(6).
 70             12 SFF-FIRM-NAME                 PIC X(21).
 71             12 SFF-ADDR-STREET               PIC X(20).
 72             12 SFF-ADDR-CITY                 PIC X(12).
 73             12 SFF-ADDR-STATE                PIC X(2).
 74             12 SFF-ADDR-ZIP                  PIC X(6).
 75             12 SFF-AREA-CODE                 PIC X(3).
 76             12 SFF-PHONE-FIRST3              PIC X(3).
 77             12 SFF-PHONE-LAST4               PIC X(4).
 78             12 SFF-CREDIT-LIMIT              PIC $Z,ZZZ,ZZ9.99.
 79             12 SFF-CREDIT-LIMIT-X   REDEFINES
 80                SFF-CREDIT-LIMIT              PIC X(13).
 81             12 SFF-STATUS-FLAG               PIC X(1).
 82             12 SFF-STATUS-INTERP             PIC X(8).
 83         *-------------------------------------------------------------
 84         *   Fields to be shared with subprograms:
 85         *-------------------------------------------------------------
 86         01  WS-PLACNAME-FIELDS.
 87             12 PLC-PLACE-ABBREV              PIC X(2).
 88             12 PLC-COUNTRY                   PIC X(3).
 89             12 PLC-PLACE-NAME                PIC X(20).
 90             12 PLC-STATUS-FLAG               PIC X(1).
 91         *   ----------------------------------------------------------
 92         01  WS-NUMCHEK-FIELDS.
 93             12 NUM-INPUT                     PIC X(22).
 94             12 NUM-RIGHT-OF-DECIMAL          PIC 9(1).
 95             12 NUM-STATUS-FLAG               PIC X(1).
 96             12 NUM-OUTPUT                    PIC 9(11)V9(6).
 97         *-------------------------------------------------------------
 98         01  WS-DATE.
 99             12 WS-YR                         PIC X(2).
100             12 WS-MO                         PIC X(2).
101             12 WS-DA                         PIC X(2).
102         01  WS-FORMATTED-DATE                PIC X(8).
103         *
104         01  WS-TIME.
105             12 WS-HRS                        PIC X(2).
106             12 WS-MIN                        PIC X(2).
107             12 FILLER                        PIC X(4).
108         01  WS-FORMATTED-TIME.
109             12 WSF-HRS                       PIC X(2).
110             12 FILLER                        PIC X(1)  VALUE ':'.
111             12 WSF-MIN                       PIC X(2).
112         *
113         01  WS-COMP                          PIC S9(4) COMP  VALUE +0.
114         01  WS-TWOBYTE   REDEFINES   WS-COMP.
115             12 WS-CHAR                       PIC X(1).
116             12 FILLER                        PIC X(1).
117         *
118         LINKAGE SECTION.
119         01  WS-TRANS-COUNT                   PIC 9(7).
120         /
121         PROCEDURE DIVISION USING WS-TRANS-COUNT.
122         *-------------------------------------------------------------
123         *   In VAX COBOL you need declaratives (even in dummy form) to
124         *   avoid abends even when nonzero File Status values such as
125         *   '23' are received for a key-not-found condition.  Since
126         *   DECLARATIVES are a "section" MAIN-PROGRAM must be a section.
127         *-------------------------------------------------------------
128         DECLARATIVES.
129         0000-ERROR    SECTION.
```

Figure 13.5   *(Continued)*

```
130              USE AFTER STANDARD ERROR PROCEDURE ON MASTER-FILE.
131          0000-DUMMY.  EXIT.
132      *
133          END DECLARATIVES.
134      *----------------------------------------------------------------
135          0000-MAIN-PROGRAM    SECTION.
136          0000-MAINLINE.
137              PERFORM 1000-BOJ.
138              PERFORM 2000-PROCESS
139                  UNTIL WS-OP-ENTRY = 'QUIT' OR 'quit'.
140              PERFORM 9900-EOJ.
141          0000-EXIT.  EXIT PROGRAM.
142      *
143          1000-BOJ.
144              OPEN I-O MASTER-FILE.
145              IF WS-MASTFILE-STATUS-BYTE1 NOT = '0'
146                  MOVE '1000' TO WS-ABORT-PARAGRAPH
147                  PERFORM 9999-ABORT.
148              ACCEPT WS-DATE FROM DATE.
149              STRING  WS-MO  '/'  WS-DA  '/'  WS-YR  DELIMITED BY SIZE
150                  INTO WS-FORMATTED-DATE.
151              PERFORM 1100-DISPLAY-LABELS.
152              MOVE 'Enter customer id for add/change, press <Return>' TO SCR-MSG.
153              MOVE SPACES TO WS-OP-ENTRY.
154              PERFORM 2700-OP-PROMPT
155                  UNTIL WS-OP-ENTRY NOT = SPACES.
156      *
157          1100-DISPLAY-LABELS.
158              DISPLAY '' AT LINE 1 COLUMN 1 ERASE TO END OF SCREEN.
159              DISPLAY 'VAXDEMO'                 AT LINE  1 COLUMN  2.
160              DISPLAY '*** CUSTOMER ADD/CHANGE *** '
161                                        BOLD AT LINE  1 COLUMN 27.
162              DISPLAY WS-FORMATTED-DATE       AT LINE  1 COLUMN 72.
163              DISPLAY 'Screen 2'              AT LINE  2 COLUMN  2.
164              DISPLAY 'ID:'            BOLD AT LINE  4 COLUMN 16.
165              DISPLAY 'NAME:'          BOLD AT LINE  5 COLUMN 14.
166              DISPLAY 'ADDRESS:'       BOLD AT LINE  6 COLUMN 11.
167              DISPLAY 'CITY/STATE/ZIP:' BOLD AT LINE  7 COLUMN  4.
168              DISPLAY 'PHONE: (    )    -' BOLD AT LINE  9 COLUMN 13.
169              DISPLAY 'CREDIT LIMIT:'   BOLD AT LINE 11 COLUMN  6.
170              DISPLAY 'STATUS:'         BOLD AT LINE 11 COLUMN 38.
171      *
172      *===================================== PROCESS A TRANSACTION
173          2000-PROCESS.
174              PERFORM 2100-START-A-TRANS.
175      *----------------------------------------------------------------
176      *  Obtain each field from the screen field by field.  Handling of
177      *  a FIELD begins with F2-OP-STAT set to 0.  If operator supplies
178      *  required data F2-OP-STAT becomes = 1.  F2-OP-STAT is set > 1
179      *  if operator enters backslash \ to cancel transaction.
180      *----------------------------------------------------------------
181              MOVE 0 TO F2-OP-STAT.
182              PERFORM 2510-GET-NAME
183                  UNTIL F2-OP-STAT > 0.
184      *
185              IF F2-OP-STAT = 1
186                  MOVE 0 TO F2-OP-STAT
187                  DISPLAY '' AT LINE 24 COLUMN 2 ERASE TO END OF LINE
188                  PERFORM 2520-GET-ADDRESS
189                      UNTIL F2-OP-STAT > 0.
190      *
191              IF F2-OP-STAT = 1
192                  MOVE 0 TO F2-OP-STAT
193                  DISPLAY '' AT LINE 24 COLUMN 2 ERASE TO END OF LINE
194                  PERFORM 2530-GET-CITY
195                      UNTIL F2-OP-STAT > 0.
196      *
197              IF F2-OP-STAT = 1
198                  MOVE 0 TO F2-OP-STAT
```

(Continued)

Figure 13.5 *(Continued)*

```
199                      DISPLAY '' AT LINE 24 COLUMN 2 ERASE TO END OF LINE
200                      PERFORM 2540-GET-STATE
201                          UNTIL F2-OP-STAT > 0.
202            *
203               IF F2-OP-STAT = 1
204                  MOVE 0 TO F2-OP-STAT
205                  DISPLAY '' AT LINE 24 COLUMN 2 ERASE TO END OF LINE
206                  PERFORM 2550-GET-ZIP
207                      UNTIL F2-OP-STAT > 0.
208            *
209               IF F2-OP-STAT = 1
210                  MOVE 0 TO F2-OP-STAT
211                  DISPLAY '' AT LINE 24 COLUMN 2 ERASE TO END OF LINE
212                  PERFORM 2560-GET-AREA-CODE
213                      UNTIL F2-OP-STAT > 0.
214            *
215               IF F2-OP-STAT = 1
216                  MOVE 0 TO F2-OP-STAT
217                  DISPLAY '' AT LINE 24 COLUMN 2 ERASE TO END OF LINE
218                  PERFORM 2570-GET-PHONE-FIRST3
219                      UNTIL F2-OP-STAT > 0.
220            *
221               IF F2-OP-STAT = 1
222                  MOVE 0 TO F2-OP-STAT
223                  DISPLAY '' AT LINE 24 COLUMN 2 ERASE TO END OF LINE
224                  PERFORM 2580-GET-PHONE-LAST4
225                      UNTIL F2-OP-STAT > 0.
226            *
227               IF F2-OP-STAT = 1
228                  MOVE 0 TO F2-OP-STAT
229                  DISPLAY '' AT LINE 24 COLUMN 2 ERASE TO END OF LINE
230                  PERFORM 2590-GET-CREDIT-LIMIT
231                      UNTIL F2-OP-STAT > 0.
232            *
233               IF F2-OP-STAT = 1
234                  MOVE 0 TO F2-OP-STAT
235                  DISPLAY '' AT LINE 24 COLUMN 2 ERASE TO END OF LINE
236                  PERFORM 2600-GET-STATUS
237                      UNTIL F2-OP-STAT > 0.
238            *
239               PERFORM 2200-END-A-TRANS.
240        /
241        *-----------------------------------------------------------------
242        *  Begin processing: decide if it will be an add or change:
243        *-----------------------------------------------------------------
244        2100-START-A-TRANS.
245            MOVE WS-OP-ENTRY TO MF-KEY.
246            READ MASTER-FILE.
247            IF WS-MASTFILE-STATUS-BYTE1 = '0'
248               MOVE 'CHG' TO F1-FUNCTION-FLAG
249               PERFORM 3100-MOVE-FIELDS-TO-SCREEN
250               DISPLAY 'OK to change, press <Return> to pass a field, \ to cancel'
251                   AT LINE 24 COLUMN 2 ERASE TO END OF LINE
252             ELSE
253            IF WS-MASTFILE-FS = '23'
254               MOVE 'ADD' TO F1-FUNCTION-FLAG
255               MOVE SPACES TO  MASTER-RECORD  SCREEN-FORMAT-FIELDS
256               MOVE WS-OP-ENTRY TO  MF-KEY  SFF-KEY
257               DISPLAY 'OK to add, enter \ to cancel'
258                   AT LINE 24 COLUMN 2 ERASE TO END OF LINE
259             ELSE
260               MOVE '2100' TO WS-ABORT-PARAGRAPH
261               PERFORM 9999-ABORT.
262            PERFORM 3200-DISPLAY-DATA.
263        /
264        *-----------------------------------------------------------------
265        *  End processing: F2-OP-STAT = 1 record can be added/changed
266        *                  F2-OP-STAT = 2 operator has cancelled trans
267        *-----------------------------------------------------------------
```

Figure 13.5   *(Continued)*

```
268        2200-END-A-TRANS.
269            DISPLAY '' AT LINE 24 COLUMN 2 ERASE TO END OF LINE.
270            IF F2-OP-STAT = 1
271                ADD 1 TO WS-TRANS-COUNT
272                IF F1-FUNCTION-FLAG = 'ADD'
273                    PERFORM 4000-WRITE
274                    MOVE 'Record added; enter another ID or "quit"' TO SCR-MSG
275                ELSE
276                    PERFORM 4100-REWRITE
277                    MOVE 'Record updated; enter another ID or "quit"' TO SCR-MSG
278            ELSE
279                MOVE SPACES TO SCREEN-FORMAT-FIELDS
280                PERFORM 3200-DISPLAY-DATA
281                MOVE 'Action cancelled, enter another ID or "quit"' TO SCR-MSG.
282        *
283            MOVE SPACES TO WS-OP-ENTRY.
284            PERFORM 2700-OP-PROMPT
285                UNTIL WS-OP-ENTRY NOT = SPACES.
286        /
287        *
288        *  Field entry logic -- each field has its own processing logic!
289        *
290        *-------------------------------------------------------------***
291        *  Get MF-FIRM-NAME          Validate: must not be spaces    ***
292        *-------------------------------------------------------------***
293        2510-GET-NAME.
294            DISPLAY SFF-FIRM-NAME
295                REVERSED  AT LINE  5 COLUMN 20.
296            DISPLAY ''    AT LINE  5 COLUMN 20.
297            ACCEPT SFF-FIRM-NAME  PROTECTED SIZE 21 NO BLANK  REVERSED.
298            IF SFF-FIRM-NAME = '\'
299                MOVE 2 TO F2-OP-STAT
300            ELSE
301            IF SFF-FIRM-NAME = SPACES
302                PERFORM 2511-SPACES
303            ELSE
304                PERFORM 2512-FINISH.
305        *   ----------------------------------------------------------
306        2511-SPACES.
307            IF F1-FUNCTION-FLAG = 'CHG'
308                MOVE 1 TO F2-OP-STAT
309                MOVE MF-FIRM-NAME TO SFF-FIRM-NAME
310                DISPLAY SFF-FIRM-NAME AT LINE 5 COLUMN 20
311            ELSE
312                DISPLAY 'E2--Firm name cannot be blank; reenter or \ to quit'
313                    WITH BELL AT LINE 24 COLUMN 2 ERASE TO END OF LINE.
314        *   ----------------------------------------------------------
315        2512-FINISH.
316            MOVE 1 TO F2-OP-STAT.
317            MOVE SFF-FIRM-NAME TO MF-FIRM-NAME.
318            DISPLAY SFF-FIRM-NAME AT LINE 5 COLUMN 20.
319        /
320        *-------------------------------------------------------------***
321        *  Get MF-ADDRESS-STREET    Validate: must not be spaces      ***
322        *-------------------------------------------------------------***
323        2520-GET-ADDRESS.
324            DISPLAY SFF-ADDR-STREET
325                REVERSED  AT LINE  6 COLUMN 20.
326            DISPLAY ''    AT LINE  6 COLUMN 20.
327            ACCEPT SFF-ADDR-STREET  PROTECTED SIZE 20 NO BLANK  REVERSED.
328            IF SFF-ADDR-STREET = '\'
329                MOVE 2 TO F2-OP-STAT
330            ELSE
331            IF SFF-ADDR-STREET = SPACES
332                PERFORM 2521-SPACES
333            ELSE
334                PERFORM 2522-FINISH.
335        *   ----------------------------------------------------------
```

(Continued)

Figure 13.5   (Continued)

```
336        2521-SPACES.
337            IF F1-FUNCTION-FLAG = 'CHG'
338                MOVE 1 TO F2-OP-STAT
339                MOVE MF-ADDR-STREET TO SFF-ADDR-STREET
340                DISPLAY SFF-ADDR-STREET AT LINE 6 COLUMN 20
341            ELSE
342                DISPLAY 'E3--Address cannot be blank; reenter or \ to quit'
343                    WITH BELL AT LINE 24 COLUMN 2 ERASE TO END OF LINE.
344        *  -----------------------------------------------------------
345        2522-FINISH.
346            MOVE 1 TO F2-OP-STAT.
347            MOVE SFF-ADDR-STREET TO MF-ADDR-STREET.
348            DISPLAY SFF-ADDR-STREET AT LINE 6 COLUMN 20.
349        /
350        *-------------------------------------------------------------***
351        *  Get MF-ADDRESS-CITY      Validate: must not be spaces      ***
352        *-------------------------------------------------------------***
353        2530-GET-CITY.
354            DISPLAY SFF-ADDR-CITY
355                REVERSED   AT LINE   7 COLUMN 20.
356            DISPLAY ''     AT LINE   7 COLUMN 20.
357            ACCEPT SFF-ADDR-CITY  PROTECTED SIZE 12 NO BLANK   REVERSED.
358            IF SFF-ADDR-CITY = '\'
359                MOVE 2 TO F2-OP-STAT
360              ELSE
361            IF SFF-ADDR-CITY = SPACES
362                PERFORM 2531-SPACES
363              ELSE
364                PERFORM 2532-FINISH.
365        *  -----------------------------------------------------------
366        2531-SPACES.
367            IF F1-FUNCTION-FLAG = 'CHG'
368                MOVE 1 TO F2-OP-STAT
369                MOVE MF-ADDR-CITY TO SFF-ADDR-CITY
370                DISPLAY SFF-ADDR-CITY AT LINE   7 COLUMN 20
371            ELSE
372                DISPLAY 'E4--City cannot be blank; reenter or \ to quit'
373                    WITH BELL AT LINE 24 COLUMN 2 ERASE TO END OF LINE.
374        *  -----------------------------------------------------------
375        2532-FINISH.
376            MOVE 1 TO F2-OP-STAT.
377            MOVE SFF-ADDR-CITY TO MF-ADDR-CITY.
378            DISPLAY SFF-ADDR-CITY AT LINE   7 COLUMN 20.
379        /
380        *-----------------------------------------------------------***
381        *  Get MF-ADDRESS-STATE   Validate: Call 'PLACNAME' in 2542 ***
382        *-----------------------------------------------------------***
383        2540-GET-STATE.
384            DISPLAY SFF-ADDR-STATE
385                REVERSED   AT LINE   7 COLUMN 34.
386            DISPLAY ''   AT LINE   7 COLUMN 34.
387            ACCEPT SFF-ADDR-STATE  PROTECTED SIZE 2  NO BLANK   REVERSED.
388            IF SFF-ADDR-STATE = '\'
389                MOVE 2 TO F2-OP-STAT
390              ELSE
391            IF SFF-ADDR-STATE = SPACES
392                PERFORM 2541-SPACES
393              ELSE
394                PERFORM 2542-FINISH.
395        *  -----------------------------------------------------------
396        2541-SPACES.
397            IF F1-FUNCTION-FLAG = 'CHG'
398                MOVE 1 TO F2-OP-STAT
399                MOVE MF-ADDR-STATE TO SFF-ADDR-STATE
400                DISPLAY SFF-ADDR-STATE AT LINE   7 COLUMN 34
401            ELSE
402                DISPLAY 'E5A--State/Prov cannot be blank; correct it \'
403                    AT LINE 24 COLUMN 2 ERASE TO END OF LINE.
404        *  -----------------------------------------------------------
```

Figure 13.5   *(Continued)*

```
405    2542-FINISH.
406        MOVE SFF-ADDR-STATE TO PLC-PLACE-ABBREV.
407        CALL 'PLACNAME' USING WS-PLACNAME-FIELDS.
408        IF PLC-STATUS-FLAG = 'Y'
409            MOVE 1 TO F2-OP-STAT
410            MOVE SFF-ADDR-STATE TO MF-ADDR-STATE
411            DISPLAY SFF-ADDR-STATE AT LINE   7 COLUMN 34
412        ELSE
413            DISPLAY 'E5B--Abbrev invalid (must use CAPS); correct it or \'
414                 AT LINE 24 COLUMN 2 ERASE TO END OF LINE.
415    /------------------------------------------------------------***
416    *-------------------------------------------------------------***
417    *  Get MF-ADDRESS-ZIP        Validate: none, okay as spaces   ***
418    *-------------------------------------------------------------***
419    2550-GET-ZIP.
420        DISPLAY SFF-ADDR-ZIP
421            REVERSED  AT LINE   7 COLUMN 38.
422        IF SFF-ADDR-ZIP NOT = SPACES
423            DISPLAY 'W6--Enter new zip or "#" to make zip spaces'
424                 AT LINE 24 COLUMN 2 ERASE TO END OF LINE.
425        DISPLAY ''   AT LINE   7 COLUMN 38.
426        ACCEPT SFF-ADDR-ZIP  PROTECTED SIZE 6  NO BLANK  REVERSED.
427    *   -----------------------------------------------------------
428        IF SFF-ADDR-ZIP = '\'
429            MOVE 2 TO F2-OP-STAT
430        ELSE
431        IF SFF-ADDR-ZIP = SPACES
432            PERFORM 2551-SPACES
433        ELSE
434            PERFORM 2552-FINISH.
435    *   -----------------------------------------------------------
436    2551-SPACES.
437        IF F1-FUNCTION-FLAG = 'CHG'
438            MOVE 1 TO F2-OP-STAT
439            MOVE MF-ADDR-ZIP TO SFF-ADDR-ZIP
440            DISPLAY SFF-ADDR-ZIP AT LINE   7 COLUMN 38
441        ELSE
442            MOVE 1 TO F2-OP-STAT
443            MOVE SPACES TO MF-ADDR-ZIP
444            DISPLAY SFF-ADDR-ZIP AT LINE   7 COLUMN 38.
445    *   -----------------------------------------------------------
446    2552-FINISH.
447        IF SFF-ADDR-ZIP = '#'
448            MOVE 1 TO F2-OP-STAT
449            MOVE SPACES TO  SFF-ADDR-ZIP  MF-ADDR-ZIP
450            DISPLAY SFF-ADDR-ZIP AT LINE   7 COLUMN 38
451        ELSE
452            MOVE 1 TO F2-OP-STAT
453            MOVE SFF-ADDR-ZIP TO MF-ADDR-ZIP
454            DISPLAY SFF-ADDR-ZIP AT LINE   7 COLUMN 38.
455    /------------------------------------------------------------***
456    *-------------------------------------------------------------***
457    *  Get MF-AREA-CODE          Validate: must be numeric        ***
458    *-------------------------------------------------------------***
459    2560-GET-AREA-CODE.
460        DISPLAY SFF-AREA-CODE
461            REVERSED  AT LINE   9 COLUMN 21.
462        DISPLAY ''   AT LINE   9 COLUMN 21.
463        ACCEPT SFF-AREA-CODE  PROTECTED SIZE 3  NO BLANK  REVERSED.
464    *
465        IF SFF-AREA-CODE = '\'
466            MOVE 2 TO F2-OP-STAT
467        ELSE
468        IF SFF-AREA-CODE = SPACES
469            PERFORM 2561-SPACES
470        ELSE
471            PERFORM 2562-FINISH.
472    *   -----------------------------------------------------------
```

(Continued)

Figure 13.5   *(Continued)*

```
473              2561-SPACES.
474                  IF F1-FUNCTION-FLAG = 'CHG'
475                      MOVE 1 TO F2-OP-STAT
476                      MOVE MF-AREA-CODE TO SFF-AREA-CODE
477                      DISPLAY SFF-AREA-CODE AT LINE  9 COLUMN 21
478                  ELSE
479                      PERFORM 2563-ERROR.
480          *   ------------------------------------------------------------
481              2562-FINISH.
482                  IF SFF-AREA-CODE IS NUMERIC
483                      MOVE 1 TO F2-OP-STAT
484                      MOVE SFF-AREA-CODE TO MF-AREA-CODE
485                      DISPLAY SFF-AREA-CODE AT LINE  9 COLUMN 21
486                  ELSE
487                      PERFORM 2563-ERROR.
488          *   ------------------------------------------------------------
489              2563-ERROR.
490                  DISPLAY 'E7--Area code must be entered, numeric, correct it OR
491                      AT LINE 24 COLUMN 2 ERASE TO END OF LINE.
492          /
493          *------------------------------------------------------------***
494          * Get MF-PHONE-FIRST3     Validate: must be numeric        ***
495          *------------------------------------------------------------***
496              2570-GET-PHONE-FIRST3.
497                  DISPLAY SFF-PHONE-FIRST3
498                      REVERSED  AT LINE  9 COLUMN 26.
499                  DISPLAY ''   AT LINE  9 COLUMN 26.
500                  ACCEPT SFF-PHONE-FIRST3  PROTECTED SIZE 3  NO BLANK  REVERSED.
501          *
502                  IF SFF-PHONE-FIRST3 = '\'
503                      MOVE 2 TO F2-OP-STAT
504                  ELSE
505                  IF SFF-PHONE-FIRST3 = SPACES
506                      PERFORM 2571-SPACES
507                  ELSE
508                      PERFORM 2572-FINISH.
509          *   ------------------------------------------------------------
510              2571-SPACES.
511                  IF F1-FUNCTION-FLAG = 'CHG'
512                      MOVE 1 TO F2-OP-STAT
513                      MOVE MF-PHONE-FIRST3 TO SFF-PHONE-FIRST3
514                      DISPLAY SFF-PHONE-FIRST3 AT LINE  9 COLUMN 26
515                  ELSE
516                      PERFORM 2573-ERROR.
517          *   ------------------------------------------------------------
518              2572-FINISH.
519                  IF SFF-PHONE-FIRST3 IS NUMERIC
520                      MOVE 1 TO F2-OP-STAT
521                      MOVE SFF-PHONE-FIRST3 TO MF-PHONE-FIRST3
522                      DISPLAY SFF-PHONE-FIRST3 AT LINE  9 COLUMN 26
523                  ELSE
524                      PERFORM 2573-ERROR.
525          *   ------------------------------------------------------------
526              2573-ERROR.
527                  DISPLAY 'E8--Phone prefix must be entered, numeric; correct it
528                      AT LINE 24 COLUMN 2 ERASE TO END OF LINE.
529          /
530          *------------------------------------------------------------***
531          * Get MF-PHONE-LAST4        Validate: must be numeric       ***
532          *------------------------------------------------------------***
533              2580-GET-PHONE-LAST4.
534                  DISPLAY SFF-PHONE-LAST4
535                      REVERSED  AT LINE  9 COLUMN 30.
536                  DISPLAY ''   AT LINE  9 COLUMN 30.
537                  ACCEPT SFF-PHONE-LAST4  PROTECTED SIZE 4  NO BLANK  REVERSED.
538          *
539                  IF SFF-PHONE-LAST4 = '\'
540                      MOVE 2 TO F2-OP-STAT
541                  ELSE
```

Figure 13.5   *(Continued)*

```
542          IF SFF-PHONE-LAST4 = SPACES
543              PERFORM 2581-SPACES
544          ELSE
545              PERFORM 2582-FINISH.
546 *     -----------------------------------------------------------
547     2581-SPACES.
548          IF F1-FUNCTION-FLAG = 'CHG'
549              MOVE 1 TO F2-OP-STAT
550              MOVE MF-PHONE-LAST4 TO SFF-PHONE-LAST4
551              DISPLAY SFF-PHONE-LAST4 AT LINE  9 COLUMN 30
552          ELSE
553              PERFORM 2583-ERROR.
554 *     -----------------------------------------------------------
555     2582-FINISH.
556          IF SFF-PHONE-LAST4 IS NUMERIC
557              MOVE 1 TO F2-OP-STAT
558              MOVE SFF-PHONE-LAST4 TO MF-PHONE-LAST4
559              DISPLAY SFF-PHONE-LAST4 AT LINE  9 COLUMN 30
560          ELSE
561              PERFORM 2583-ERROR.
562 *     -----------------------------------------------------------
563     2583-ERROR.
564          DISPLAY 'E9--Phone number must be entered, numeric; correct it or \'
565              AT LINE 24 COLUMN 2 ERASE TO END OF LINE.
566 /
567 *-----------------------------------------------------------***
568 *  Get MF-CREDIT-LIMIT     Validate: => 1000 CALL 'NUMCHEK'***
569 *-----------------------------------------------------------***
570     2590-GET-CREDIT-LIMIT.
571          DISPLAY SFF-CREDIT-LIMIT-X
572              REVERSED  AT LINE 11 COLUMN 20.
573          DISPLAY ''   AT LINE 11 COLUMN 20.
574          ACCEPT SFF-CREDIT-LIMIT-X  PROTECTED SIZE 13 NO BLANK  REVERSED.
575 *
576          IF SFF-CREDIT-LIMIT-X = '\'
577              MOVE 2 TO F2-OP-STAT
578          ELSE
579          IF SFF-CREDIT-LIMIT-X = SPACES
580              PERFORM 2591-SPACES
581          ELSE
582              PERFORM 2592-FINISH.
583 *     -----------------------------------------------------------
584     2591-SPACES.
585          IF F1-FUNCTION-FLAG = 'CHG'
586              MOVE 1 TO F2-OP-STAT
587              MOVE MF-CREDIT-LIMIT TO SFF-CREDIT-LIMIT
588              DISPLAY SFF-CREDIT-LIMIT AT LINE 11 COLUMN 20
589          ELSE
590              DISPLAY 'E10A--Credit limit must be specified; correct it or \'
591                  WITH BELL AT LINE 24 COLUMN 2 ERASE TO END OF LINE.
592 *     -----------------------------------------------------------
593     2592-FINISH.
594          MOVE SFF-CREDIT-LIMIT-X TO NUM-INPUT.
595          MOVE 2 TO NUM-RIGHT-OF-DECIMAL.
596          CALL 'NUMCHEK' USING WS-NUMCHEK-FIELDS.
597          IF NUM-STATUS-FLAG = '0'
598              IF NUM-OUTPUT NOT LESS 1000.00
599                  MOVE 1 TO F2-OP-STAT
600                  MOVE NUM-OUTPUT TO  MF-CREDIT-LIMIT  SFF-CREDIT-LIMIT
601                  DISPLAY SFF-CREDIT-LIMIT AT LINE 11 COLUMN 20
602              ELSE
603                  DISPLAY 'E10B--Must be => $1000 with decimal point; correct it or \'
604                      WITH BELL AT LINE 24 COLUMN 2 ERASE TO END OF LINE
605          ELSE
606              DISPLAY 'E10C--Must be numeric, => $1000, with decimal point; correct it or \'
607                  WITH BELL AT LINE 24 COLUMN 2 ERASE TO END OF LINE.
608 /
609 *-----------------------------------------------------------***
610 *  Get MF-STATUS-FLAG       Validate: must be '-' or 'I'    ***
611 *-----------------------------------------------------------***
```

(Continued)

Figure 13.5   *(Continued)*

```
612        2600-GET-STATUS.
613            DISPLAY SFF-STATUS-FLAG
614                REVERSED    AT LINE 11 COLUMN 46.
615            DISPLAY ''     AT LINE 11 COLUMN 46.
616            ACCEPT SFF-STATUS-FLAG   PROTECTED SIZE 1   NO BLANK   REVERSED.
617        *
618            IF SFF-STATUS-FLAG = '\'
619                MOVE 2 TO F2-OP-STAT
620            ELSE  621                    IF SFF-STATUS-FLAG = SPACES
622                PERFORM 2601-SPACES
623            ELSE
624                PERFORM 2602-FINISH.
625        * -------------------------------------------------------------
626        2601-SPACES.
627            IF F1-FUNCTION-FLAG = 'CHG'
628                MOVE 1 TO F2-OP-STAT
629                MOVE MF-STATUS-FLAG TO SFF-STATUS-FLAG
630                DISPLAY SFF-STATUS-FLAG AT LINE 11 COLUMN 46
631            ELSE
632                DISPLAY 'E11--Status flag must be - or I; correct it or \'
633                    AT LINE 24 COLUMN 2 ERASE TO END OF LINE.
634        * -------------------------------------------------------------
635        2602-FINISH.
636            MOVE SFF-STATUS-FLAG TO WS-STATUS-FLAG.
637            PERFORM 3110-INTERP-STATUS.
638            DISPLAY SFF-STATUS-INTERP AT LINE 11 COLUMN 49.
639            IF F3-INTERP-FLAG = 'Y'
640                MOVE 1 TO F2-OP-STAT
641                MOVE SFF-STATUS-FLAG TO MF-STATUS-FLAG
642                DISPLAY SFF-STATUS-FLAG AT LINE 11 COLUMN 46
643            ELSE
644                DISPLAY 'E11--Status flag must be - or I; correct it or \'
645                    AT LINE 24 COLUMN 2 ERASE TO END OF LINE.
646        /
647        *=============================================================
648        *
649        2700-OP-PROMPT.
650            PERFORM 2705-TIME.
651            DISPLAY SCR-MSG   AT LINE 24 COLUMN  2 ERASE TO END OF LINE.
652            DISPLAY '===>'    AT LINE 24 COLUMN 66.
653            ACCEPT WS-OP-ENTRY
654                REVERSED
655                PROTECTED
656                FROM LINE 24 COLUMN 71.
657        *
658            IF WS-OP-ENTRY = SPACES
659                PERFORM 1100-DISPLAY-LABELS
660                PERFORM 3200-DISPLAY-DATA
661            ELSE
662                PERFORM 2705-TIME
663                PERFORM 2710-CONVERT-TO-UPPER-CASE
664                    VARYING OP-IX FROM +1 BY +1
665                        UNTIL OP-IX > +6.
666        *
667            DISPLAY ''          AT LINE 24 COLUMN  2 ERASE TO END OF LINE.
668        *
669        2705-TIME.
670            ACCEPT WS-TIME FROM TIME.
671            MOVE WS-HRS TO WSF-HRS.
672            MOVE WS-MIN TO WSF-MIN.
673            DISPLAY WS-FORMATTED-TIME AT LINE  2 COLUMN 75.
674        *
675        *-------------------------------------------------------------
676        *  This logic shifts lowercase letters to uppercase by
677        *  subtracting 32 from the ASCII value of any byte in the
678        *  ASCII range 97 (a) through 122 (z):
679        *-------------------------------------------------------------
680        2710-CONVERT-TO-UPPER-CASE.
681            MOVE WS-OP-ENTRY-CHAR(OP-IX) TO WS-CHAR
```

Figure 13.5 *(Continued)*

```
682         IF WS-COMP NOT LESS +97 AND NOT GREATER +122
683             SUBTRACT +32 FROM WS-COMP
684             MOVE WS-CHAR TO WS-OP-ENTRY-CHAR(OP-IX).
685     *
686     3100-MOVE-FIELDS-TO-SCREEN.
687         MOVE MF-KEY            TO  SFF-KEY.
688         MOVE MF-FIRM-NAME      TO  SFF-FIRM-NAME.
689         MOVE MF-ADDR-STREET    TO  SFF-ADDR-STREET.
690         MOVE MF-ADDR-CITY      TO  SFF-ADDR-CITY.
691         MOVE MF-ADDR-STATE     TO  SFF-ADDR-STATE.
692         MOVE MF-ADDR-ZIP       TO  SFF-ADDR-ZIP.
693         MOVE MF-AREA-CODE      TO  SFF-AREA-CODE.
694         MOVE MF-PHONE-FIRST3   TO  SFF-PHONE-FIRST3.
695         MOVE MF-PHONE-LAST4    TO  SFF-PHONE-LAST4.
696         MOVE MF-CREDIT-LIMIT   TO  SFF-CREDIT-LIMIT.
697         MOVE MF-STATUS-FLAG    TO  SFF-STATUS-FLAG  WS-STATUS-FLAG.
698         PERFORM 3110-INTERP-STATUS.
699     *
700     3110-INTERP-STATUS.
701         MOVE 'Y' TO F3-INTERP-FLAG.
702         IF WS-STATUS-FLAG = '-'
703             MOVE 'Active'       TO SFF-STATUS-INTERP
704           ELSE
705         IF WS-STATUS-FLAG = 'I'
706             MOVE 'Inactive'     TO SFF-STATUS-INTERP
707           ELSE
708             MOVE 'N' TO F3-INTERP-FLAG
709             MOVE ALL '*'        TO SFF-STATUS-INTERP.
710     *
711     3200-DISPLAY-DATA.
712         DISPLAY SFF-KEY          AT LINE  4 COLUMN 20.
713         DISPLAY SFF-FIRM-NAME    AT LINE  5 COLUMN 20.
714         DISPLAY SFF-ADDR-STREET  AT LINE  6 COLUMN 20.
715         DISPLAY SFF-ADDR-CITY    AT LINE  7 COLUMN 20.
716         DISPLAY SFF-ADDR-STATE   AT LINE  7 COLUMN 34.
717         DISPLAY SFF-ADDR-ZIP     AT LINE  7 COLUMN 38.
718         DISPLAY SFF-AREA-CODE    AT LINE  9 COLUMN 21.
719         DISPLAY SFF-PHONE-FIRST3 AT LINE  9 COLUMN 26.
720         DISPLAY SFF-PHONE-LAST4  AT LINE  9 COLUMN 30.
721         DISPLAY SFF-CREDIT-LIMIT AT LINE 11 COLUMN 20.
722         DISPLAY SFF-STATUS-FLAG  AT LINE 11 COLUMN 46.
723         DISPLAY SFF-STATUS-INTERP AT LINE 11 COLUMN 49.
724         DISPLAY '' AT LINE 24 COLUMN 71 ERASE TO END OF LINE.
725     *
726     *-----------------------------------------------------------
727     * First-byte file status other than '0' indicates index file
728     * failure since read was already done for key at trans begin
729     *-----------------------------------------------------------
730     4000-WRITE.
731         WRITE MASTER-RECORD.
732         IF WS-MASTFILE-STATUS-BYTE1 NOT = '0'
733             MOVE '4100' TO WS-ABORT-PARAGRAPH
734             PERFORM 9999-ABORT.
735     *
736     4100-REWRITE.
737         REWRITE MASTER-RECORD.
738         IF WS-MASTFILE-STATUS-BYTE1 NOT = '0'
739             MOVE '4100' TO WS-ABORT-PARAGRAPH
740             PERFORM 9999-ABORT.
741     /
742     *-----------------------------------------------------------
743     9900-EOJ.
744         DISPLAY '' AT LINE 1, COLUMN 1 ERASE TO END OF SCREEN.
745         CLOSE MASTER-FILE.
746         IF WS-MASTFILE-STATUS-BYTE1 NOT = '0'
747             MOVE '9900' TO WS-ABORT-PARAGRAPH
748             PERFORM 9999-ABORT.
749     *
```

(Continued)

Figure 13.5   *(Continued)*

```
750              9999-ABORT.
751                  DISPLAY '' AT LINE 1, COLUMN 1 ERASE TO END OF SCREEN.
752                  DISPLAY '***************************************************'
753                  DISPLAY 'Program CUPD1 Error E99'.
754                  DISPLAY 'Indexed file failure at paragraph ', WS-ABORT-PARAGRAPH.
755                  DISPLAY 'File Status is ', WS-MASTFILE-FS.
756                  DISPLAY 'Print this screen and contact programming group'.
757                  DISPLAY '***************************************************'
758                  STOP RUN.
```

Figure 13.5   *(Continued)*

You can ACCEPT a number from the screen as a character string of up to 22 bytes. Put this into NUM-INPUT. Program code puts a number into NUM-RIGHT-OF-DECIMAL that represents how many digits should be to the right of the decimal point. You then CALL 'NUMCHEK' USING WS-NUMCHEK-FIELDS. After this CALL, NUM-STATUS-FLAG will be '0' if it was possible to convert NUM-INPUT to numeric form, and the numeric form of the data will be in NUM-OUTPUT.

The NUMCHEK subprogram is fairly smart. It can handle dollar signs and commas. It also allows the terminal operator to enter a number with or without a decimal point and still have it interpreted correctly. For example, assuming 2 is in NUM-RIGHT-OF-DECIMAL, both 1.00 and 100 are correctly interpreted as 1.00. In its present form, however, NUM-CHEK will not handle entry of a negative sign.

I also use a subprogram to validate the two-letter state or province abbreviation which is ACCEPTed at lines 383 to 414. (The CALL to it, named PLACNAME, is at line 407.) While the table lookup in PLAC-NAME gives the actual state or province name when you look up an abbreviation, I really only use the PLC-STATUS-FLAG in CUPD1. If this flag returns as 'Y' the subprogram indicates that the abbreviation entered is valid.

13.8 Overview of Add/Change Program Logic Structure

The logic of a conversational interactive add/change program breaks naturally into the same BOJ/until/EOJ pattern typical of a batch program. Figure 13.6 is the action diagram I prepared to design Program CUPD1. Look over this blueprint and you can grasp the essential logic pattern of the program.

Beginning of job (1000) includes actions to open the indexed file, erase the screen and DISPLAY screen labels, and prompt the terminal operator

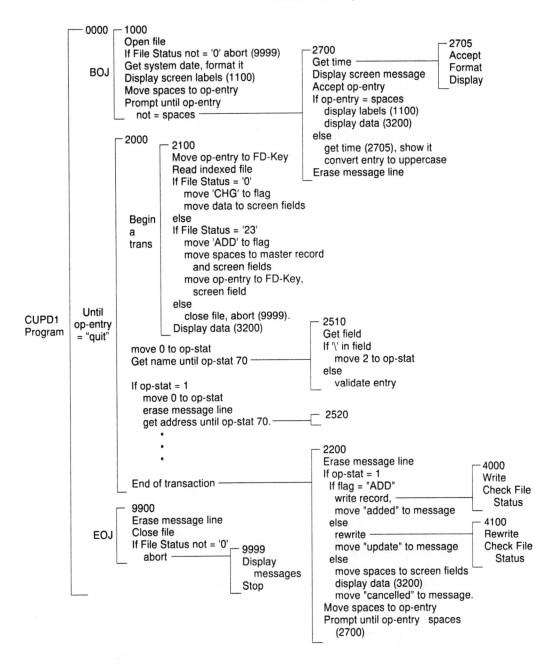

Figure 13.6   Action diagram for the logic of program CUPD1. I built the program after mapping out its logic using this diagram. If you are not familiar with action diagrams you can compare the program logic to this chart to better understand how the program works.

for the entry of a customer ID. I modularized the prompting logic into two units that can be PERFORMed since prompting will be required in BOJ and at the end of each interactive transaction.

Process until (2000) must occur until the operator indicates the desire to end add/change processing. The operator enters the word "quit" at the prompt to do this. If the operator enters anything else it's regarded as a record key and transaction processing starts.

End of job (9900) actions consist of erasing the screen and closing the indexed file.

13.9 Processing a Transaction

The task of processing an add or change transaction (the processing loop, paragraph 2000) itself breaks into three parts:

- **Beginning the transaction** (2100) by READing the indexed file to seek the record matching the key entered by the operator and initializing the screen for an add or change as appropriate. (I use the File Status to see if the key is present in the file at lines 247 and 253.)

- **Obtaining an entry for each field** (lines 181–237 in paragraph 2000) in the record and validating it, or bypassing field entry actions if a cancellation has been indicated by the operator using the backslash \ key.

- **Ending the transaction** (2200) by writing or rewriting the record, as appropriate, if the transaction has not been cancelled.

13.10 Obtaining Data Entries for Fields

The logic to obtain an entry for each data field follows the pattern shown in Figure 13.7. This is the logic to ACCEPT and reDISPLAY the firm name field in a customer record. To get data for this field I perform paragraph 2510 until F2-OP-STAT assumes a value greater than 0. F2-OP-STAT will become 1 if the operator has entered valid data into the field or 2 if the operator cancels the transaction by entering the backslash \ in the first position of a field.

F2-OP-STAT is a just a flag field. In paragraph 2000 I use PERFORM . . . UNTIL and this flag to control cursor movement. I keep the cursor

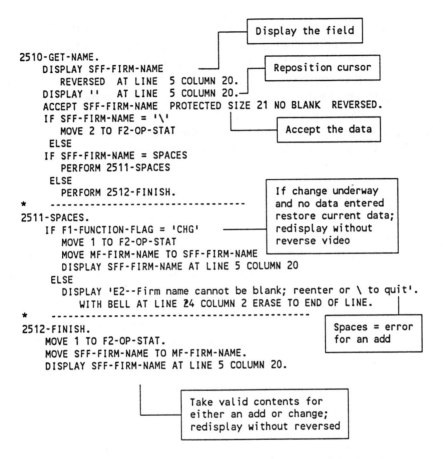

```
2510-GET-NAME.
    DISPLAY SFF-FIRM-NAME                               Display the field
        REVERSED  AT LINE  5 COLUMN 20.
    DISPLAY ''   AT LINE  5 COLUMN 20.                  Reposition cursor
    ACCEPT SFF-FIRM-NAME  PROTECTED SIZE 21 NO BLANK  REVERSED.
    IF SFF-FIRM-NAME = '\'
        MOVE 2 TO F2-OP-STAT                            Accept the data
    ELSE
    IF SFF-FIRM-NAME = SPACES
        PERFORM 2511-SPACES
    ELSE
        PERFORM 2512-FINISH.                         If change underway
*   ----------------------------------               and no data entered
2511-SPACES.                                          restore current data;
    IF F1-FUNCTION-FLAG = 'CHG'                        redisplay without
        MOVE 1 TO F2-OP-STAT                           reverse video
        MOVE MF-FIRM-NAME TO SFF-FIRM-NAME
        DISPLAY SFF-FIRM-NAME AT LINE 5 COLUMN 20
    ELSE
        DISPLAY 'E2--Firm name cannot be blank; reenter or \ to quit'.
            WITH BELL AT LINE 24 COLUMN 2 ERASE TO END OF LINE.
*   ---------------------------------------------        Spaces = error
2512-FINISH.                                             for an add
    MOVE 1 TO F2-OP-STAT.
    MOVE SFF-FIRM-NAME TO MF-FIRM-NAME.
    DISPLAY SFF-FIRM-NAME AT LINE 5 COLUMN 20.
```

Take valid contents for either an add or change; redisplay without reversed

Figure 13.7 The logic to obtain an entry for each data field in the CUPD1 program follows this pattern. (These lines have been extracted from lines 293-318 of CUPD1. The entire program is listed in Figure 13.5.)

in a field until a valid entry is made in it or the operator cancels the transaction. From lines 185 through 233 you see a series of tests on F2-OP-STAT checking to see if it has a value of 1. If the transaction has been cancelled, these tests bypass further field entry actions and take the cancellation straight to its conclusion.

13.11 Ending a Transaction

The value in F2-OP-STAT also controls what happens at the end of a transaction. If its value is 1, it is time to WRITE or REWRITE the master file record; the value of F1-FUNCTION-FLAG (ADD or CHG) dictates which verb is appropriate. I housed these actions in paragraphs 4000 and 4100.

If the value in F2-OP-STAT is not 1, it can only be 2, which indicates that the operator used the backslash \ to cancel the transaction. In this case I erase the data contents of the screen by overwriting each field with spaces and generate "ACTION CANCELLED" as the screen message that will appear next. I move this message to SCR-MSG, which is DISPLAYed at the bottom of the screen when the prompting logic (2700) is invoked.

13.12 Conversion to Uppercase Letters

The terminal operator might enter lowercase letters (a) or uppercase letters (A) into the record key field. Lowercase letters have a different ASCII representation than uppercase letters. This can cause a lot of problems in a key field!

I provided logic in program CUPD1 to automatically convert any lower case letters in the key field to upper case. This is in paragraph 2710 at lines 680 through 684. This logic relies on the fact that the decimal value of the ASCII representation of uppercase letters is 32 less than

```
01  WS-OP-ENTRY.
    12 WS-OP-ENTRY-CHAR  PIC X  OCCURS 6 TIMES   INDEXED BY OP-IX.
    -
01  WS-COMP                          PIC S9(4) COMP  VALUE +0.
01  WS-TWOBYTE  REDEFINES  WS-COMP.
    12 WS-CHAR                       PIC X(1).
    12 FILLER                        PIC X(1).
    -
        PERFORM 2710-CONVERT-TO-UPPER-CASE
           VARYING OP-IX FROM +1 BY +1
              UNTIL OP-IX > +6.
    -
2710-CONVERT-TO-UPPER-CASE.
    MOVE WS-OP-ENTRY-CHAR(OP-IX) TO WS-CHAR.
    IF WS-COMP NOT LESS +97 AND NOT GREATER +122
       SUBTRACT +32 FROM WS-COMP
    MOVE WS-CHAR TO WS-OP-ENTRY-CHAR(OP-IX).
```

Figure 13.8 Fields and logic in program CUPD1 to automatically convert lowercase letters in the prompt entry field for record key to uppercase. This is in paragraph 2710 at lines 680 through 684. This logic relies on the fact that the decimal value of the ASCII representation of uppercase letters is 32 less than that of lowercase letters. (You can also accomplish this using the 1985 COBOL INSPECT verb with the CONVERTING option.)

that of lowercase letters. Look at Figure 13.8, which extracts all the parts of the code that deal with this.

Through the REDEFINES at line 114 I move each character of the entry field one by one to the low order position of a pure binary COMPutation field. (On the VAX the low order position is at the left of a field.) This gives the entire COMP field the decimal value of the ASCII character. I then subtract 32 from this value if it lies in the range 97 to 122, which is a through z. As a result the low order byte contains the uppercase equivalent of the original entry, which I MOVE back to the entry field.

13.13 File Handling in Program CUPD1

Program CUPD1 performs random access to the indexed customer master file. I coded it to rely entirely on File Status checking to receive communication from the indexed file access method. I test File Status after the indexed file OPEN, after each READ, WRITE, or REWRITE, and after the file CLOSE. If indexed file failure occurs the messages coded in paragraph 9999 would appear on the terminal screen to help identify the nature of the problem.

When you use File Status and not INVALID KEY, VAX COBOL requires you to code DECLARATIVES. But since I don't really want to handle file problems in DECLARATIVES this is "dummy" coding in CUPD1, at lines 128 through 33.

13.14 LINK Command With Additional Subprograms

The "real" Program CUPD1 as opposed to testing stub SUPD1 employs CALLs to subprograms PLACNAME and NUMCHEK. The LINK command becomes lengthier when you want to include CUPD1 in the VAXDEMO system.

First, you have to separately compile CUPD1, NUMCHEK, and PLACNAME to create their .OBJ files. Then you can linkage edit all the .OBJ files together:

```
$ LINK VAXDEMO,CINQU1,CUPD1,NUMCHEK,PLACNAME,SDEL1,SBROW1
```

After this command executes you can run VAXDEMO. When you select function 2 from the menu CUPD1 will execute.

13.15 Concurrent Access by Multiple Terminals

Program CUPD1 can be operated by one terminal at a time. But the nature of interactive processing usually requires that multiple terminals be able to use the same transaction program (such as CUPD1) to access the same file at the same time. Such *concurrent access* requires additional logic to keep different users from interfering with each other.

Concurrent access to a file or database by inquiry programs poses little problem of interference, since no user is changing the data to which all have access. Add, change, and delete actions do change stored data. Interference from one user to another may occur if two users try to update the same record at the same time.

The arrangements to handle concurrent access can be complicated. I have deferred discussion of them to Chapter 16. If you plan on implementing an on-line system in which multiple terminals access the same transactions and files at the same time, be sure to read Chapter 16.

13.16 Chapter Summary

An *add/change program* makes the contents of the record visible and accessible to a terminal operator. You can use the same layout for an add/change screen as you do for an inquiry or delete transaction for the same file.

You can combine the add and change functions in one program because they both involve the same field entry and validation logic. This also makes the file maintenance process easier for terminal operators. The program itself determines whether an add or a change is to be handled based on whether the key the terminal operator enters is in the file or not.

If you combine record add and change functions you also need to implement a *transaction cancellation* or *backout* capability. This handles the relatively infrequent instances where the terminal operator enters an incorrect key value and gets into an add or change unintentionally. In my VAXDEMO system the operator cancels a transaction by pressing the backslash key \ at the beginning of any field. The operator might also need to cancel a transaction because valid data for a certain field is not available.

In handling a change to an existing record it's very natural for the terminal operator to "tab through" fields by pressing the **<Return>** key. The CUPD1 program makes this possible by using a comprehensive logic pattern to handle each field entry.

WITH CONVERSION doesn't allow you to enter commas as a part of a number, but many people do want to enter numbers this way. You can use a *de-editing subprogram* such as NUMCHEK (listed in Appendix B) to handle the conversion of numeric data in edited form to purely numeric form.

Add/change program logic has the same three overall parts as any conversational interactive program: beginning of job, process a transaction, and end of job. But the task of processing a transaction also breaks into three parts: Beginning the transaction, obtaining an entry for each field, and ending the transaction.

You have to consider the potential problem of mixed-case letters in record keys. Program CUPD1 includes logic to change lowercase letters to uppercase in the prompt response. This standardizes all key values to capital letters or numbers.

You can use File Status for indexed file conditions such as record-found and record-not-found. If you do this, VAX COBOL requires you to code DECLARATIVES and a dummy section at the start of the PROCEDURE DIVISION.

To replace a testing stub in a menu program with a functional add/change program that itself CALLs subprograms, you first must separately compile the add/change program and its subprograms. Then you link together all of the .OBJ files for the system with a LINK command.

Concurrent access by multiple terminals to the same file imposes some special requirements. You need to provide additional logic to keep different users from interfering with each other. I discuss issues of concurrent access in Chapter 16.

13.17 Important Terms

You can review these terms to check your understanding of this chapter:

File maintenance   The process of adding records to a file, changing the contents of records in a file, or deleting records from a file.

Combined add/change   Grouping the record add and change functions into one interactive program rather than housing them in two separate programs.

Transaction cancellation   The ability to stop work on an add or change transaction after starting it, "backing out" to a screen free of the data you have already entered.

Numeric de-editing subprogram   A subprogram that takes a character string containing a number expressed with dollar sign, commas, and decimal point and converts it to purely numeric (computable) form.

Case conversion   Changing lowercase letters such as a to uppercase (capital) letters such as A to avoid problems with mixed-case data in record keys.

Concurrent use   Access by multiple terminals to the same transaction and file, which carries potential conflicts in simultaneous updates to the same record.

You can find additional questions and exercises for this chapter in Appendix A.

Chapter Fourteen

INTERACTIVE DELETE: PROGRAM CDEL1

Record deletion is sometimes omitted as an on-line function in business systems because it can be especially dangerous. In this chapter I show you how to program an interactive delete for those instances where you do want to provide it. I show you an elementary security mechanism to limit access to this function to authorized personnel. I also illustrate how to preserve deleted records for future reference in an archive file.

If you don't provide record deletion as an on-line function, you can handle it with a batch program that selectively copies records containing obsolete data to another file based on a "last activity" date in records. You might also provide a simple "delete me" flag in each record to control a batch "purge" program. This flag can be set to a value requesting deletion using an add/change change screen.

14.1 A Record Deletion Function

Selection 3 on the VAXDEMO menu lets you delete customer records from the indexed customer master file. I implemented this function in subprogram CDEL1. To this program one transaction is the deletion of one record. As with other VAXDEMO functions you remain within the delete function until you enter "quit" to return to the menu.

14.2 Access Security for the Delete Function

Access to a critical part of an on-line system is usually controlled by requiring the terminal operator to enter an "operator identifier" before being able to use the function. A "password" associated with the identifier can be required as well. In some systems the password is changeable by the operator, but the operator identifier usually remains fixed.

Figure 14.1 illustrates the screen the CDEL1 program displays when the deletion function is selected from the menu. You must enter a four-position operator identifier in response to the initial prompt. I use NO ECHO on the ACCEPT for the response so that it does not appear on the screen. After a valid operator identifier is entered, CDEL1 requests you to enter the password associated with the identifier. I don't present the actual deletion processing screen unless you enter an operator ID and its

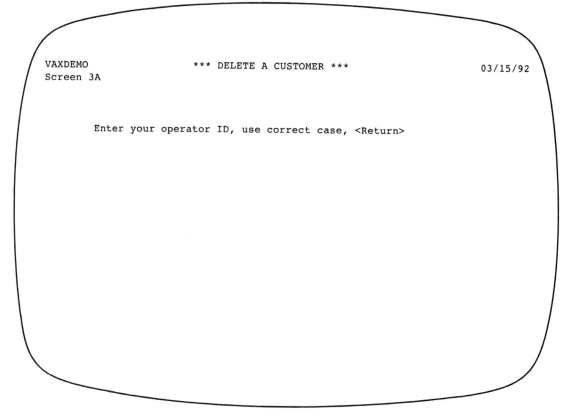

```
VAXDEMO                    *** DELETE A CUSTOMER ***                03/15/92
Screen 3A



        Enter your operator ID, use correct case, <Return>
```

Figure 14.1 This is the screen the CDEL1 program displays when the deletion function is selected from the menu. You must enter a four-position operator identifier in response to the initial prompt. After a valid operator identifier is entered, CDEL1 requests you to enter the password associated with the identifier. If either entry is invalid, control returns to the menu.

password correctly on the first try. If either entry is invalid I immediately send control back to the menu.

14.3 Hardcoded Security Table and Refinements

The operator identifier and password security of program CDEL1 relies on a hardcoded table contained in the program (at lines 119 through 130 in Figure 14.6). Obviously this mechanism is prone to a breach of security by examination of the source code. You could design a more capable mechanism by relying on encrypted passwords stored in a file. As an enhancement over that, a method to allow operators to change their own passwords would be desirable. On-line system security comprises a significant subject area in itself. I demonstrate only a simple (but workable) security mechanism for you here.

14.4 Operation of the Deletion Screen

Figure 14.2 shows you the record deletion screen presented by program CDEL1. It is identical to that of the inquiry and add/change programs. Using the identical screen layout again makes sense. Not only does it reduce the design and programming time, it provides a familiar arrangement of data. As shown in Figure 14.2, we're pretending that you have entered customer ID 437129 to delete this record.

Figure 14.3 illustrates the deletion screen after retrieval of the record intended for deletion. Had no record existed in the file with the specified customer ID, the screen would have remained without data. I would have presented a prompt advising that no such record was found in the file.

At the screen in Figure 14.3 you can proceed with the deletion by entering "DEL" to confirm that the record is the one you want to delete. Alternatively, you can cancel the deletion by entering the backslash \. You'll recognize my use of the backslash as a cancellation entry since I use it consistently for transaction cancellation in the VAXDEMO system.

Figure 14.4 shows you the completion of deletion processing for record 437129. Data from the record remains on the screen, but the prompt changes to indicate that the record has now been deleted. You can enter another customer ID to continue record deletions or enter "quit" to return to the menu.

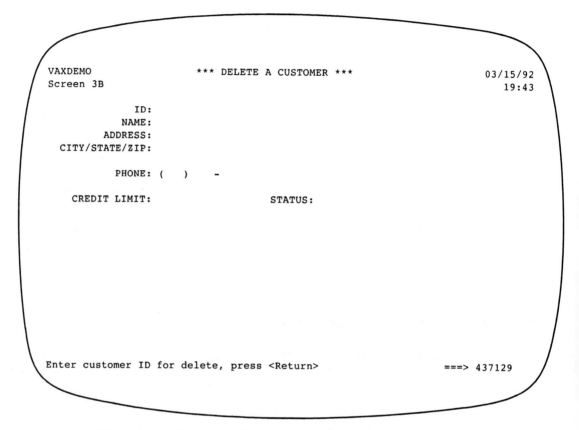

```
VAXDEMO                  *** DELETE A CUSTOMER ***              03/15/92
Screen 3B                                                         19:43

            ID:
          NAME:
       ADDRESS:
 CITY/STATE/ZIP:

         PHONE: (   )    -

   CREDIT LIMIT:                    STATUS:














 Enter customer ID for delete, press <Return>            ===> 437129
```

Figure 14.2   The record deletion screen presented by program CDEL1. It is identical to that of the inquiry and add/change programs. You have entered customer ID 437129 to delete this record.

14.5 Archiving Deleted Records: An Audit Trail

Once deleted, a record cannot be undeleted. If you delete a record by mistake, a copy of it must have been preserved to allow its replacement in the indexed file. Making such a copy is called **archiving** the record.

You can archive a deleted record by writing a copy of it to a sequential file. This was simple for me to do within the framework of program CDEL1 because the record to be deleted is retrieved anyway for confirmation on the screen.

I made the record archival process into an **audit trail** documenting

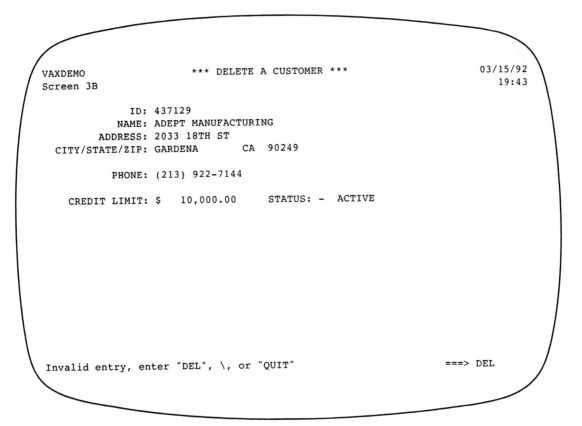

```
VAXDEMO                  *** DELETE A CUSTOMER ***              03/15/92
Screen 3B                                                         19:43

              ID: 437129
            NAME: ADEPT MANUFACTURING
         ADDRESS: 2033 18TH ST
 CITY/STATE/ZIP: GARDENA        CA   90249

           PHONE: (213) 922-7144

    CREDIT LIMIT: $   10,000.00     STATUS: -  ACTIVE




 Invalid entry, enter "DEL", \, or "QUIT"                    ===> DEL
```

Figure 14.3 The CDEL1 deletion screen after retrieval of the record intended for deletion. You have to confirm that this is the record you want to delete by entering "DEL" at the prompt.

record deletion activities by including the operator identifier and system date and time within archived records. An audit trail allows EDP auditors, accounting personnel, and investigators to verify the correct and legitimate operation of a business application system.

Figure 14.5 illustrates the format of archived records I produce with program CDEL1. I append the operator ID, system date, and system time to the 100-byte record, forming a record 118 bytes long. CDEL1 opens the archive file each time you go into the delete function (and closes the file when you quit the delete function). Every time you select the delete function from the menu the VAX creates the next higher version number of the archive file. But a reporting program could be arranged to list the

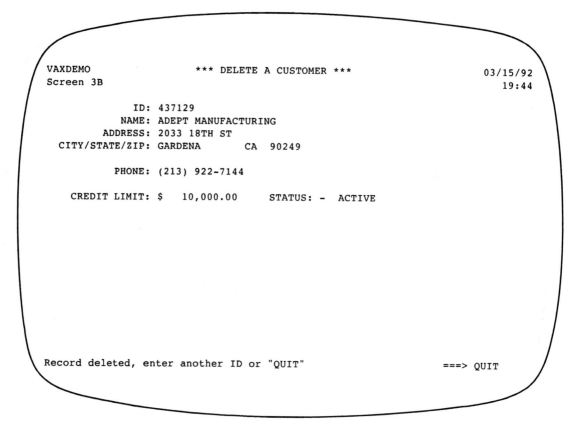

```
VAXDEMO                    *** DELETE A CUSTOMER ***              03/15/92
Screen 3B                                                          19:44

               ID: 437129
             NAME: ADEPT MANUFACTURING
          ADDRESS: 2033 18TH ST
 CITY/STATE/ZIP: GARDENA          CA   90249

           PHONE: (213) 922-7144

   CREDIT LIMIT: $   10,000.00      STATUS: -  ACTIVE




 Record deleted, enter another ID or "QUIT"                ===> QUIT
```

Figure 14.4   Completion of deletion processing for record 437129. Data from the record remains on the screen, but the prompt changes to indicate that the record has now been deleted. You can enter another customer ID to continue record deletions or enter "quit" to return to the menu.

consolidated file of archived records. And a batch or on-line program could replace an archived record in the indexed master file if necessary.

14.6 Program CDEL1 Source Code

I have listed the source code for program CDEL1 for you in Figure 14.6. The action diagram I used to design it before I coded it is shown in Figure 14.7. Using either the source code or the action diagram you can see that the structure of a delete program breaks into the familiar three

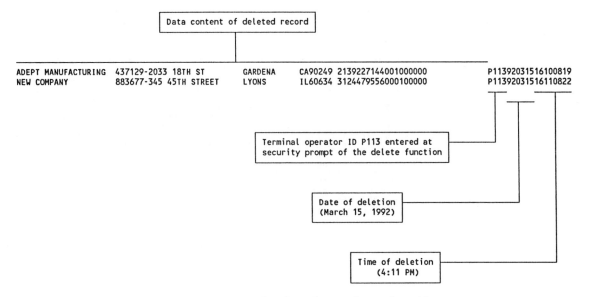

Figure 14.5 The format of archived records produced by program CDEL1. I append the operator ID, system date, and system time to the 100-byte record, forming a record 118 bytes long. You could list these records with a batch reporting program or replace an archived (deleted) record in the indexed master file if necessary.

parts: a beginning (1000), a "process until" the operator no longer desires to do record deletions (2000), and an ending (9900).

In its beginning my CDEL1 deletion program erases the terminal screen and presents top-of-screen labels. But it must also take care of operator ID (1200) and password security (1300) here. If you pass security checks, the beginning-of-job logic can then open files, display screen labels, and get your response to the first prompt for a customer ID.

The processing loop of CDEL1 (2000) executes until you indicate the end of the deletions by entering "quit" at the prompt. Ending the deletion function passes control to end-of-job logic, which erases the screen and closes files.

14.7 Processing a Deletion Transaction

To process a delete transaction you do a random READ of the indexed file to retrieve the record with the specified key. If you find such a record in

```
CDEL1                15-Mar-1992 12:56:09    VAX COBOL V4.3-57
Source Listing       15-Mar-1992 12:56:01    CSC$ROOT:[CSCJGJ.VAXCO]CDEL1.COB;1
     1          IDENTIFICATION DIVISION.
     2          PROGRAM-ID.    CDEL1.
     3          *AUTHOR.        J JANOSSY    INTERNET: JANOSSY@CSCVAX.DEPAUL.EDU
     4          *INSTALLATION.  DEPAUL UNIVERSITY, CHICAGO, IL
     5          *==================================================================
     6          *   Function 3 of VAXDEMO system in VAX COBOL ON-LINE!  3/1/92
     7          *
     8          *   Performs on-line delete to the customer master file.  This
     9          *   program includes primitive extra security in the form of
    10          *   a table of authorized operator IDs and passwords.  Creates
    11          *   an archive file of deleted records.  Caution: This version
    12          *   does not provide for concurrent use by multiple users!  See
    13          *   discussion on record locking you must arrange to allow
    14          *   multiple users to access same file!
    15          *==================================================================
    16          ENVIRONMENT DIVISION.
    17          INPUT-OUTPUT SECTION.
    18          FILE-CONTROL.
    19              SELECT MASTER-FILE              ASSIGN TO MASTER
    20                      ORGANIZATION   IS   INDEXED
    21                      ACCESS MODE    IS   RANDOM
    22                      RECORD KEY     IS   MF-KEY
    23                      ALTERNATE RECORD KEY IS MF-NAME-ALT-KEY
    24                      FILE STATUS    IS   WS-MASTFILE-FS.
    25          *
    26              SELECT ARCHIVE-FILE            ASSIGN TO ARCHIVE.
    27          *------------------------------------------------------------------
    28          DATA DIVISION.
    29          FILE SECTION.
    30          *
    31          FD   MASTER-FILE
    32               RECORD CONTAINS 100 CHARACTERS
    33               LABEL RECORDS ARE STANDARD.
    34          01   MASTER-RECORD.
    35               12 MF-NAME-ALT-KEY.
    36                  15 MF-FIRM-NAME             PIC X(21).
    37                  15 MF-KEY                   PIC X(6).
    38               12 MF-STATUS-FLAG              PIC X(1).
    39                  88 MF-STAT-ACTIVE                       VALUE '-'.
    40                  88 MF-STAT-INACTIVE                     VALUE 'I'.
    41               12 MF-ADDRESS.
    42                  15 MF-ADDR-STREET           PIC X(20).
    43                  15 MF-ADDR-CITY             PIC X(12).
    44                  15 MF-ADDR-STATE            PIC X(2).
    45                  15 MF-ADDR-ZIP              PIC X(6).
    46               12 MF-PHONE-DATA.
    47                  15 MF-AREA-CODE             PIC X(3).
    48                  15 MF-PHONE-FIRST3          PIC X(3).
    49                  15 MF-PHONE-LAST4           PIC X(4).
    50               12 MF-CREDIT-LIMIT             PIC 9(7)V99.
    51               12 FILLER                      PIC X(13).
    52          *
    53          FD   ARCHIVE-FILE
    54               RECORD CONTAINS 118 CHARACTERS
    55               LABEL RECORDS ARE STANDARD.
    56          01   ARCHIVE-RECORD.
    57               12 AR-DATA                     PIC X(100).
    58               12 AR-OPERATOR-ID              PIC X(4).
    59               12 AR-DELETE-DATE              PIC X(6).
    60               12 AR-DELETE-TIME              PIC X(8).
    61          /
    62          *------------------------------------------------------------------
    63          WORKING-STORAGE SECTION.
    64          01   WS-MASTFILE-FS.
    65               12 WS-MASTFILE-STATUS-BYTE1    PIC X(1).
    66               12 FILLER                      PIC X(1).
    67          *
```

Figure 14.6 Source code for program CDEL1. I built this from the action diagram illustrated in Figure 14.7.

```
68    01  WS-STATUS-FLAG                    PIC X(1).
69    01  WS-OP-ID                          PIC X(4).
70    01  WS-PASSWORD                       PIC X(6).
71    01  WS-ABORT-PARAGRAPH                PIC X(4).
72    01  SCR-MSG                           PIC X(64).
73    01  WS-OP-ENTRY.
74        12 WS-OP-ENTRY-CHAR  PIC X  OCCURS 6 TIMES   INDEXED BY OP-IX.
75   *------------------------------------------------------------------
76   *  Screen format fields: a field is coded here carrying the
77   *  display picture for each data field:
78   *------------------------------------------------------------------
79    01  SCREEN-FORMAT-FIELDS.
80        12 SFF-KEY                         PIC X(6).
81        12 SFF-FIRM-NAME                   PIC X(21).
82        12 SFF-ADDR-STREET                 PIC X(20).
83        12 SFF-ADDR-CITY                   PIC X(12).
84        12 SFF-ADDR-STATE                  PIC X(2).
85        12 SFF-ADDR-ZIP                    PIC X(6).
86        12 SFF-AREA-CODE                   PIC X(3).
87        12 SFF-PHONE-FIRST3                PIC X(3).
88        12 SFF-PHONE-LAST4                 PIC X(4).
89        12 SFF-CREDIT-LIMIT                PIC $Z,ZZZ,ZZ9.99.
90        12 SFF-CREDIT-LIMIT-X  REDEFINES
91           SFF-CREDIT-LIMIT                PIC X(13).
92        12 SFF-STATUS-FLAG                 PIC X(1).
93        12 SFF-STATUS-INTERP               PIC X(8).
94   *
95    01  WS-DATE.
96        12 WS-YR                           PIC X(2).
97        12 WS-MO                           PIC X(2).
98        12 WS-DA                           PIC X(2).
99    01  WS-FORMATTED-DATE                  PIC X(8).
100  *
101   01  WS-TIME.
102       12 WS-HRS                          PIC X(2).
103       12 WS-MIN                          PIC X(2).
104       12 FILLER                          PIC X(4).
105   01  WS-FORMATTED-TIME.
106       12 WSF-HRS                         PIC X(2).
107       12 FILLER                          PIC X(1)   VALUE ':'.
108       12 WSF-MIN                         PIC X(2).
109  *
110   01  WS-COMP                            PIC S9(4) COMP   VALUE +0.
111   01  WS-TWOBYTE   REDEFINES  WS-COMP.
112       12 WS-CHAR                         PIC X(1).
113       12 FILLER                          PIC X(1).
114  *------------------------------------------------------------------
115  *  Operator ID and password table for delete processing; a
116  *  better arrangement would place this or a more sophisticated
117  *  mechanism in the menu program itself
118  *------------------------------------------------------------------
119   01  SECURITY-TABLE-SETUP.
120       12 FILLER      PIC X(11)  VALUE 'P112 BBGUM '.
121       12 FILLER      PIC X(11)  VALUE 'P113 POOBAH'.
122       12 FILLER      PIC X(11)  VALUE 'P114 DB2304'.
123       12 FILLER      PIC X(11)  VALUE 'P115 HORSE '.
124       12 FILLER      PIC X(11)  VALUE 'P116 MAGNUM'.
125  *
126   01  SECURITY-TABLE  REDEFINES  SECURITY-TABLE-SETUP.
127       12 ST-ELEMENT   OCCURS 5 TIMES   INDEXED BY ST-INDEX.
128          15 ST-OPERATOR-ID       PIC X(4).
129          15 FILLER               PIC X(1).
130          15 ST-PASSWORD          PIC X(6).
131  *
132  LINKAGE SECTION.
133   01  WS-TRANS-COUNT                     PIC 9(7).
134  /
135  PROCEDURE DIVISION USING WS-TRANS-COUNT.
```

(Continued)

Figure 14.6   *(Continued)*

```
136     *----------------------------------------------------------------
137     *  In VAX COBOL you need declaratives (even in dummy form) to
138     *  avoid abends even when nonzero File Status values such as
139     *  '23' are received for a key-not-found condition.  Since
140     *  DECLARATIVES are a "section" MAIN-PROGRAM must be a section.
141     *----------------------------------------------------------------
142     DECLARATIVES.
143     0000-ERROR    SECTION.
144         USE AFTER STANDARD ERROR PROCEDURE ON MASTER-FILE.
145     0000-DUMMY.   EXIT.
146     *
147     END DECLARATIVES.
148     *----------------------------------------------------------------
149     0000-MAIN-PROGRAM    SECTION.
150     0000-MAINLINE.
151         PERFORM 1000-BOJ.
152         PERFORM 2000-PROCESS
153             UNTIL WS-OP-ENTRY = 'QUIT' or 'quit'.
154         PERFORM 9900-EOJ.
155     0000-EXIT.  EXIT PROGRAM.
156     *
157     1000-BOJ.
158         ACCEPT WS-DATE FROM DATE.
159         STRING WS-MO  '/'  WS-DA  '/'  WS-YR  DELIMITED BY SIZE
160             INTO WS-FORMATTED-DATE.
161         DISPLAY '' AT LINE 1 COLUMN 1 ERASE TO END OF SCREEN.
162         DISPLAY 'VAXDEMO'                   AT LINE  1 COLUMN  2.
163         DISPLAY '*** DELETE A CUSTOMER *** '
164                                      BOLD AT LINE  1 COLUMN 26.
165         DISPLAY WS-FORMATTED-DATE           AT LINE  1 COLUMN 72.
166         DISPLAY 'Screen 3A'                 AT LINE  2 COLUMN  2.
167         PERFORM 1200-OPERATOR-ID.
168         PERFORM 1300-PASSWORD.
169         MOVE WS-DATE TO AR-DELETE-DATE.
170         MOVE WS-OP-ID TO AR-OPERATOR-ID.
171     *
172         OPEN I-O MASTER-FILE.
173         IF WS-MASTFILE-STATUS-BYTE1 NOT = '0'
174             MOVE '1000' TO WS-ABORT-PARAGRAPH
175             PERFORM 9999-ABORT.
176         OPEN OUTPUT ARCHIVE-FILE.
177         PERFORM 1100-DISPLAY-LABELS.
178         MOVE 'Enter customer ID for delete, press <Return>' TO SCR-MSG.
179         PERFORM 2700-OP-PROMPT.
180     *
181     1100-DISPLAY-LABELS.
182         DISPLAY '' AT LINE 1 COLUMN 1 ERASE TO END OF SCREEN.
183         DISPLAY 'VAXDEMO'                   AT LINE  1 COLUMN  2.
184         DISPLAY '*** DELETE A CUSTOMER *** '
185                                      BOLD AT LINE  1 COLUMN 26.
186         DISPLAY WS-FORMATTED-DATE           AT LINE  1 COLUMN 72.
187         DISPLAY 'Screen 3B'                 AT LINE  2 COLUMN  2.
188         DISPLAY 'ID:'              BOLD AT LINE  4 COLUMN 16.
189         DISPLAY 'NAME:'            BOLD AT LINE  5 COLUMN 14.
190         DISPLAY 'ADDRESS:'         BOLD AT LINE  6 COLUMN 11.
191         DISPLAY 'CITY/STATE/ZIP:'  BOLD AT LINE  7 COLUMN  4.
192         DISPLAY 'PHONE: (    )    -' BOLD AT LINE  9 COLUMN 13.
193         DISPLAY 'CREDIT LIMIT:'     BOLD AT LINE 11 COLUMN  6.
194         DISPLAY 'STATUS:'          BOLD AT LINE 11 COLUMN 38.
195     *----------------------------------------------------------------
196     *  Get operator ID and look it up in table.  Operator gets
197     *  only one chance to get it correct; if not valid, control
198     *  returns to the menu.
199     *----------------------------------------------------------------
200     1200-OPERATOR-ID.
201         DISPLAY 'Enter your operator ID, use correct case, <Return>'
202             BOLD AT LINE 4 COLUMN 10 ERASE TO END OF LINE.
203         ACCEPT WS-OP-ID FROM LINE 4 COLUMN 63 WITH NO ECHO.
204     *
```

Figure 14.6   *(Continued)*

```
205              SET ST-INDEX TO 1
206              SEARCH ST-ELEMENT
207                 AT END
208                     MOVE 'B' TO WS-STATUS-FLAG
209                 WHEN ST-OPERATOR-ID(ST-INDEX) = WS-OP-ID
210                     MOVE 'G' TO WS-STATUS-FLAG.
211     *
212              IF WS-STATUS-FLAG = 'B'
213                 DISPLAY 'Operator ID invalid, press <Return>'
214                     AT LINE 24 COLUMN 2 ERASE TO END OF LINE
215                 ACCEPT WS-OP-ID FROM LINE 24 COLUMN 71
216                 EXIT PROGRAM.
217     *-------------------------------------------------------------
218     * Get the password matching the operator ID.  Operator gets
219     * only one chance to get it correct; if not valid, control
220     * returns to the menu.
221     *-------------------------------------------------------------
222      1300-PASSWORD.
223              DISPLAY 'Enter your password, use correct case, <Return>'
224                 BOLD AT LINE 4 COLUMN 10 ERASE TO END OF LINE.
225              ACCEPT WS-PASSWORD FROM LINE 4 COLUMN 63 WITH NO ECHO.
226     *
227              IF WS-PASSWORD NOT = ST-PASSWORD(ST-INDEX)
228                 DISPLAY 'Password invalid, press <Return>'
229                     AT LINE 24 COLUMN 2 ERASE TO END OF LINE
230                 ACCEPT WS-OP-ID FROM LINE 24 COLUMN 71
231                 EXIT PROGRAM.
232     *
233     *=========================================PROCESS A TRANSACTION
234      2000-PROCESS.
235              MOVE WS-OP-ENTRY TO MF-KEY.
236              READ MASTER-FILE.
237              IF WS-MASTFILE-STATUS-BYTE1 = '0'
238                 PERFORM 2100-PROCESS-DELETE
239              ELSE
240              IF WS-MASTFILE-FS = '23'
241                 MOVE SPACES TO SCR-MSG
242                 STRING 'No record with customer ID '   DELIMITED BY SIZE
243                        WS-OP-ENTRY                      DELIMITED BY SIZE
244                        ' on file, reenter ID or "QUIT"' DELIMITED BY SIZE
245                     INTO SCR-MSG
246              ELSE
247                 MOVE '2000' TO WS-ABORT-PARAGRAPH
248                 PERFORM 9999-ABORT.
249              PERFORM 2700-OP-PROMPT.
250     *
251      2100-PROCESS-DELETE.
252              PERFORM 3100-MOVE-FIELDS-TO-SCREEN.
253              PERFORM 3200-DISPLAY-DATA.
254              MOVE 'Enter "DEL" to confirm delete or \ to cancel'  TO SCR-MSG.
255              PERFORM 2700-OP-PROMPT.
256     *
257              IF WS-OP-ENTRY = 'DEL'
258                 PERFORM 4200-ARCHIVE
259                 PERFORM 4300-DELETE
260                 MOVE 'Record deleted, enter another ID or "QUIT"'  TO SCR-MSG
261              ELSE
262              IF WS-OP-ENTRY = '\'
263                 MOVE 'Delete cancelled, enter ID or "QUIT"'   TO SCR-MSG
264              ELSE
265                 MOVE 'Invalid entry, enter "DEL", \, or "QUIT"'   TO SCR-MSG.
266     *
267      2700-OP-PROMPT.
268              PERFORM 2705-TIME.
269              DISPLAY SCR-MSG  AT LINE 24 COLUMN  2 ERASE TO END OF LINE.
270              DISPLAY '===>'   AT LINE 24 COLUMN 66.
271              ACCEPT WS-OP-ENTRY
272                 REVERSED
```

(Continued)

Figure 14.6   *(Continued)*

```
273                      PROTECTED
274                      FROM LINE 24 COLUMN 71.
275              PERFORM 2705-TIME.
276              PERFORM 2710-CONVERT-TO-UPPER-CASE
277                  VARYING OP-IX FROM +1 BY +1
278                      UNTIL OP-IX > +6.
279              DISPLAY ''          AT LINE 24 COLUMN  2 ERASE TO END OF LINE.
280          *
281          2705-TIME.
282              ACCEPT WS-TIME FROM TIME.
283              MOVE WS-HRS TO WSF-HRS.
284              MOVE WS-MIN TO WSF-MIN.
285              DISPLAY WS-FORMATTED-TIME AT LINE  2 COLUMN 75.
286          *-------------------------------------------------------------------
287          *  This logic shifts lowercase letters to uppercase by
288          *  subtracting 32 from the ASCII value of any byte in the
289          *  ASCII range 97 (a) through 122 (z):
290          *-------------------------------------------------------------------
291          2710-CONVERT-TO-UPPER-CASE.
292              MOVE WS-OP-ENTRY-CHAR(OP-IX) TO WS-CHAR.
293              IF WS-COMP NOT LESS +97 AND NOT GREATER +122
294                  SUBTRACT +32 FROM WS-COMP
295                  MOVE WS-CHAR TO WS-OP-ENTRY-CHAR(OP-IX).
296          *
297          3100-MOVE-FIELDS-TO-SCREEN.
298              MOVE MF-KEY             TO  SFF-KEY.
299              MOVE MF-FIRM-NAME       TO  SFF-FIRM-NAME.
300              MOVE MF-ADDR-STREET     TO  SFF-ADDR-STREET.
301              MOVE MF-ADDR-CITY       TO  SFF-ADDR-CITY.
302              MOVE MF-ADDR-STATE      TO  SFF-ADDR-STATE.
303              MOVE MF-ADDR-ZIP        TO  SFF-ADDR-ZIP.
304              MOVE MF-AREA-CODE       TO  SFF-AREA-CODE.
305              MOVE MF-PHONE-FIRST3    TO  SFF-PHONE-FIRST3.
306              MOVE MF-PHONE-LAST4     TO  SFF-PHONE-LAST4.
307              MOVE MF-CREDIT-LIMIT    TO  SFF-CREDIT-LIMIT.
308              MOVE MF-STATUS-FLAG     TO  SFF-STATUS-FLAG   WS-STATUS-FLAG.
309              IF WS-STATUS-FLAG = '-'
310                  MOVE 'ACTIVE'       TO SFF-STATUS-INTERP
311              ELSE
312              IF WS-STATUS-FLAG = 'I'
313                  MOVE 'INACTIVE'     TO SFF-STATUS-INTERP
314              ELSE
315                  MOVE ALL '*'        TO SFF-STATUS-INTERP.
316          *
317          3200-DISPLAY-DATA.
318              DISPLAY SFF-KEY            AT LINE  4 COLUMN 20.
319              DISPLAY SFF-FIRM-NAME      AT LINE  5 COLUMN 20.
320              DISPLAY SFF-ADDR-STREET    AT LINE  6 COLUMN 20.
321              DISPLAY SFF-ADDR-CITY      AT LINE  7 COLUMN 20.
322              DISPLAY SFF-ADDR-STATE     AT LINE  7 COLUMN 34.
323              DISPLAY SFF-ADDR-ZIP       AT LINE  7 COLUMN 38.
324              DISPLAY SFF-AREA-CODE      AT LINE  9 COLUMN 21.
325              DISPLAY SFF-PHONE-FIRST3   AT LINE  9 COLUMN 26.
326              DISPLAY SFF-PHONE-LAST4    AT LINE  9 COLUMN 30.
327              DISPLAY SFF-CREDIT-LIMIT   AT LINE 11 COLUMN 20.
328              DISPLAY SFF-STATUS-FLAG    AT LINE 11 COLUMN 46.
329              DISPLAY SFF-STATUS-INTERP  AT LINE 11 COLUMN 49.
330              DISPLAY '' AT LINE 24 COLUMN 71 ERASE TO END OF LINE.
331          *
332          4200-ARCHIVE.
333              MOVE MASTER-RECORD TO AR-DATA.
334              ACCEPT WS-TIME FROM TIME.
335              MOVE WS-TIME TO AR-DELETE-TIME.
336              WRITE ARCHIVE-RECORD.
337          *-------------------------------------------------------------------
338          *  First-byte File Status other than '0' indicates indexed file
339          *  failure since read was already done for this key at the
340          *  beginning of transaction processing.
341          *-------------------------------------------------------------------
```

Figure 14.6 *(Continued)*

```
342          4300-DELETE.
343              DELETE MASTER-FILE.
344              IF WS-MASTFILE-STATUS-BYTE1 NOT = '0'
345                 MOVE '4300' TO WS-ABORT-PARAGRAPH
346                 PERFORM 9999-ABORT.
347              ADD 1 TO WS-TRANS-COUNT.
348      *
349      *=====================================================END OF JOB
350          9900-EOJ.
351              DISPLAY '' AT LINE 1, COLUMN 1 ERASE TO END OF SCREEN.
352              CLOSE ARCHIVE-FILE.
353              CLOSE MASTER-FILE.
354              IF WS-MASTFILE-STATUS-BYTE1 NOT = '0'
355                 MOVE '9900' TO WS-ABORT-PARAGRAPH
356                 PERFORM 9999-ABORT.
357      *
358          9999-ABORT.
359              DISPLAY '' AT LINE 1, COLUMN 1 ERASE TO END OF SCREEN.
360              DISPLAY '****************************************'
361              DISPLAY 'Program CDEL1 Error E99'.
362              DISPLAY 'Indexed file failure at paragraph ', WS-ABORT-PARAGRAPH.
363              DISPLAY 'File Status is ', WS-MASTFILE-FS.
364              DISPLAY 'Print this screen and contact programming group'.
365              DISPLAY '****************************************'
366              STOP RUN.
```

Figure 14.6   *(Continued)*

the file you can move its data fields to the screen format fields and display them. You then have to prompt for confirmation to proceed with the delete. If you get confirmation, you write the record to the archive file and issue the DELETE verb against the indexed file.

If there is no record in the file with the key specified you have to tell the operator that the key is not valid and seek the entry of another key. If the operator cancels the transaction with the backslash the message is different but the effect is the same: it's time to prompt for another entry.

14.8 Source Code Highlights

I always use File Status to check for record found/not found conditions and I recommend that you do too. You'll notice that the coding at lines 237 to 248 in program CDEL1 (after a random access READ) detects a first-byte File Status of '0' when the record to be deleted is found in the file. A full two-byte File Status value of '23' indicates that the record is not found. No other File Status value is acceptable here. If I receive some other File Status it means that the file has failed. In that case I intentionally abort the program with a descriptive message in 9999-ABORT.

I coded the DELETE verb at line 343 in a separate "deletion" paragraph. The syntax of this verb seems ominous since it makes it look like

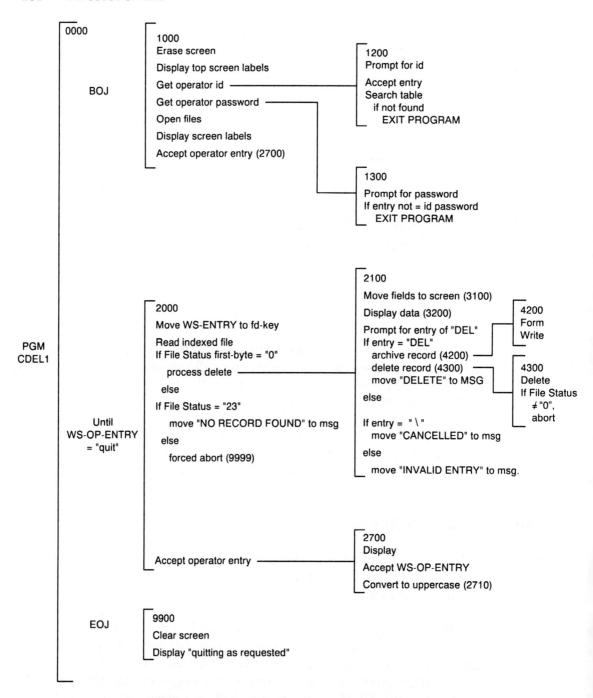

Figure 14.7 The action diagram for program CDEL1. The logic structure of a delete program breaks into the familiar three parts: a beginning (1000), a "process until" the operator no longer desires to do record deletions (2000), and an ending (9900).

the entire file is being deleted! But the DELETE verb just eliminates the record whose key value is in the key field in the File Description (FD). After the DELETE (at lines 344 through 346) I test the File Status for a first-byte value of '0' and regard any other File Status value as an indexed file failure. The only way the program attempts the DELETE is if it actually finds and obtains the record to be deleted. For the DELETE not to succeed could only mean that the indexed file had failed between these actions (see "concurrent access" below).

14.9 Concurrent Access by Multiple Terminals

Program CDEL1 can be operated by one terminal at a time. But the nature of interactive processing usually requires that multiple terminals be able to use the same transaction program such as CDEL1, to access the file at the same time. And isn't there also another program in my VAXDEMO system that affects the contents of the MASTER.DAT indexed file? What about CUPD1, the program that handles interactive add/change transactions?

Concurrent updating access to the same file by multiple terminal users and programs requires additional logic to keep users from interfering with each other. The arrangements to handle concurrent access can be complicated. I have deferred discussion of them to Chapter 16. Be sure to read Chapter 16 before you implement an on-line system in which multiple terminals access the same transactions and files at the same time!

14.10 Chapter Review

If you provide *on-line record deletion* you need to use a security mechanism to limit access to deletion to authorized personnel. A typical security mechanism to control access to a deletion function involves entry of an operator identifier and password. You can use NO ECHO on the ACCEPT for the operator ID and password so that it does not appear on the screen.

A deletion screen can use the same format as the inquiry and add/change programs. This can reduce design and programming time and provide a familiar arrangement of data. When the terminal operator enters the key of a record to be deleted it is retrieved and presented on the screen. This lets the operator confirm that the correct record was specified for deletion. You must provide a way, such as the backslash key used in other parts of the VAXDEMO system, for the terminal operator to cancel the deletion if he or she does not want to confirm the deletion.

You have to save records deleted from a master file in a second file called an *archive file* to be able to restore records deleted by mistake. You can make the archive into an *audit trail* of system activity by including operator ID, date, and time in extra fields appended to archived records. EDP auditors use an archive to periodically check that a business data processing system is being used accurately and legitimately for business purposes.

The logic structure of an interactive deletion program breaks into three parts: a beginning, a "process until" the operator no longer desires to do record deletions, and an ending. Beginning includes screen preparation and entry and checking of operator ID and password. Each deletion transaction causes one iteration of the processing loop. The processing loop executes until the end of deletion transactions is specified by the operator. Ending the deletion function passes control to end-of-job logic, which erases the screen and closes files.

To process a delete transaction you first do a random READ of the indexed file to retrieve the record with the specified key. After the record is presented on the screen and you confirm your intention to delete it, you write the record to the archive file and issue the DELETE verb. File Status tells you whether the READ obtained the record with the key specified and whether DELETE worked or not.

More than one terminal operator may be performing deletes at the same time. An add/change program may also be updating the file when deletions are being done. Concurrent update access to the same file requires additional logic to keep different users from interfering with each other. Chapter 16 considers arrangements needed to protect data integrity in a multiple-user environment.

14.11 Important Terms

You can review these terms to check your understanding of this chapter:

Batch purge A noninteractive program, used instead of an on-line record deletion function, to remove records from a master file based on their last activity date or on a flag field requesting removal from the file.

Access security A mechanism to limit access to sensitive on-line functions such as record deletion to specially authorized personnel.

Operator identifier   A unique code associated with an individual so that each individual can be identified when he or she begins work on an on-line function.

Archive   A file containing records that have been deleted (removed) from a master file.

Audit trail   Evidence remaining after events have taken place that can be examined by auditors or others to understand what actions have occurred.

You can find additional questions and exercises for this chapter in Appendix A.

Chapter Fifteen

INTERACTIVE ALTERNATE KEY BROWSE: PROGRAM CBROW1

You sometimes have to locate a record in an indexed file when you don't know the primary key. Suppose a customer placing an order doesn't know his or her account number? Situations like this arise often throughout the business day.

An alternate key provides access to an indexed file by a field other than the primary key. I defined customer name (firm name) as an alternate key in my customer master file MASTER.DAT. In this chapter I show you how to design and program a browse based on this alternate key. The browse will let you see several records on the screen in customer name order. Using it you can home in on likely records until you locate the one you want. From what you see on the browse screen you can then determine the customer's primary key and proceed to other on-line functions.

15.1 What Is an Alternate Key Browse?

Figure 15.1 shows you my browse screen for customer master file records. Each "detail line" on the screen presents some information from one master file record. I put on the browse screen only selected information that can help you establish the identity of each customer.

My goal for a browse is to allow one line for each customer and provide information from several customer records on the screen. You can't change any customer information on the browse screen, and you can't use this screen to enter new customer records or to delete records.

15.2 Using a Browse Screen

The browse screen lets you tell it where in the sequence of customer names to begin presenting records. You indicate this by entering from

```
VAXDEMO              *** BROWSE CUSTOMERS BY NAME ***          03/15/92
Screen 4                                                         19:45

   ID          NAME                ADDRESS             CITY     ST  ZIP    ACT?

 168857   ACME PRODUCTS CO     8711 HALLDALE AV     LOS ROBLES  CA 90455    -
 415002   ACME PRODUCTS CO     1000 87TH AVE NE     EDMONTON    AB T2E6W5   -
 472293   ACME PRODUCTS CO     9716 HILBORN DR      GRIZZLETOWN GA 30101    -
 600536   ACME PRODUCTS CO     68 ELUSORY WAY       PLEVNA      KS 67568    -
 887633   ACME PRODUCTS CO     76 CRUTCHER CREEK LN CONFLUENCE  KY 41730    I
 267841   ARNOLD ASSOCIATES    1760 N. ASHLAND      CHICAGO     IL 60678    I
 700501   BERNHARD LORING CORP. 9600 SUNSET PKWY    SAN MATEO   CA 94067    -
 419870   BERRY MACHINE TOOLS  12400 N. INDUSTRIAL  LIMA        OH 45801    I
 994365   BERYL AVIATION LTD   1936 W. ATLANTIC PKY ST LAURENT  PQ H4L5E3   -
 258472   BURR & WILLIAMS INC  11100 N. SUFFOLK DR  EAST BEND   WI 53095    -
 700000   DEF CORP.            45 YARDLEY RD        ALGONQUIN   IL 65071    I
 123456   GILMORE TOOL CORP    1775 GLENVIEW RD     GLENDALE    MA 01229    -
 601723   HARRIER METER CORP.  7855 CENTURY PKY     OTTAWA      ON K1G3N3   -
 480114   HILBORN TECHNOLOGIES 215 FERRIS BLVD      CALGARY     AB T2E1H6   -
 521726   HILL ENGINEERING CO  2100 DEWEY AVE       CHARLESTON  SC 29415    I
 437352   JENSEN-SWIFT MFG.    8514 S. PALM DRIVE   RIVERSIDE   CA 92376    -
 882734   JOHNSON MACHINE CORP 68000 TECHNOLOGY WAY RESTON      VA 22070    -

More data exists, press <Return> to continue              ===> h
```

Figure 15.1   The CBROW1 browse screen for customer master file records, starting with the beginning of the customer master file by alternate key. The purpose of a browse screen is to find the ID of a customer when you know only the front part of the customer name. I have entered the letter "h" to begin a new browse screen at the first customer name that starts with this letter.

one to six leading characters of the customer name at the prompt. If you don't enter a starting value, the browse starts at the beginning of the file alphabetically by customer name.

In Figure 15.1 I entered the letter "h" at the prompt to start another browse screen. Like all other programs in the VAXDEMO on-line system, CBROW1 converts lowercase letters to uppercase (capital) letters. My entry of "h" actually starts the browse at the first record with a customer name that starts with "H". That's why in Figure 15.2 you see the record for Harrier Meter Corp. on the first line.

```
VAXDEMO              *** BROWSE CUSTOMERS BY NAME ***           03/15/92
Screen 4                                                          19:45

    ID          NAME                ADDRESS           CITY    ST  ZIP   ACT?

  601723  HARRIER METER CORP.  7855 CENTURY PKY     OTTAWA     ON K1G3N3  -
  480114  HILBORN TECHNOLOGIES 215 FERRIS BLVD      CALGARY    AB T2E1H6  -
  521726  HILL ENGINEERING CO  2100 DEWEY AVE       CHARLESTON SC 29415   I
  437352  JENSEN-SWIFT MFG.    8514 S. PALM DRIVE    RIVERSIDE  CA 92376   -
  882734  JOHNSON MACHINE CORP 68000 TECHNOLOGY WAY  RESTON     VA 22070   -
  695403  NORHOST INSTRUMENT CO 717 HOWARD DRIVE     RED BLUFF  CA 96080   -
  178948  RANGER PRODUCTS, INC. 18 MILL CREEK LANE   NEWHALL    CA 91321   -
  654733  SINCLAIR DRILL WORKS 6750 ARMORY WAY       VANCOUVER  BC V7B1T9  -




End of file, press <Return> to start over, new ID, or "QUIT"    ===>
```

Figure 15.2 The CBROW1 browse screen, showing the first customer record having a name starting with the letter "h". You can enter up to six leading characters of the customer name to begin a browse screen.

15.3 After Finding a Record Using a Browse . . .

A browse function is a "fishing expedition" that succeeds when you find a desired record. In VAXDEMO it's a tool you can use to determine the primary key of a customer record. Once you find out the primary key of the customer record, you'll want to use the regular inquiry, add/change, or delete functions of the on-line system with the record.

In a simple system such as VAXDEMO you have to remember the primary key of a record you learn via a browse if you want to access a record with other on-line system functions. An enhanced system could give you a way to enter the desired primary key and a "transfer" command on the browse screen to traverse directly to another screen. An even more capable system would completely spare you the task of manually entering the primary key value to do more business with the record. Such a system would let you "point" to a record on a browse screen by putting the cursor in front of it. I discuss some of these advanced features and refinements in Chapter 16.

15.4 How a Browse Screen Reflects Updates

A browse screen is like a cross-reference. You can get some of the same functionality that a browse provides by using a printed listing of the

```
VAXDEMO              *** BROWSE CUSTOMERS BY NAME ***           03/15/92
Screen 4                                                           19:47

    ID            NAME              ADDRESS            CITY     ST  ZIP    ACT?

  780000   AAC TEST CORP.       123 N. MAIN STREET   CHICAGO     IL 60604   -
  700000   ABC CORP.            45 YARDLEY RD        ALGONQUIN   IL 65071   I
  168857   ACME PRODUCTS CO     8711 HALLDALE AV     LOS ROBLES  CA 90455   -
  415002   ACME PRODUCTS CO     1000 87TH AVE NE     EDMONTON    AB T2E6W5  -
  472293   ACME PRODUCTS CO     9716 HILBORN DR      GRIZZLETOWN GA 30101   -
  600536   ACME PRODUCTS CO     68 ELUSORY WAY       PLEVNA      KS 67568   -
  887633   ACME PRODUCTS CO     76 CRUTCHER CREEK LN CONFLUENCE  KY 41730   I
  267841   ARNOLD ASSOCIATES    1760 N. ASHLAND      CHICAGO     IL 60678   I
  700501   BERNHARD LORING CORP. 9600 SUNSET PKWY    SAN MATEO   CA 94067   -
  419870   BERRY MACHINE TOOLS  12400 N. INDUSTRIAL  LIMA        OH 45801   I
  994365   BERYL AVIATION LTD   1936 W. ATLANTIC PKY ST LAURENT  PQ H4L5E3  -
  258472   BURR & WILLIAMS INC  11100 N. SUFFOLK DR  EAST BEND   WI 53095   -
  123456   GILMORE TOOL CORP    1775 GLENVIEW RD     GLENDALE    MA 01229   -
  601723   HARRIER METER CORP.  7855 CENTURY PKY     OTTAWA      ON K1G3N3  -
  480114   HILBORN TECHNOLOGIES 215 FERRIS BLVD      CALGARY     AB T2E1H6  -
  521726   HILL ENGINEERING CO  2100 DEWEY AVE       CHARLESTON  SC 29415   I
  437352   JENSEN-SWIFT MFG.    8514 S. PALM DRIVE   RIVERSIDE   CA 92376   -

More data exists, press <Return> to continue                       ===>
```

Figure 15.3 The browse screen for the customer file after I have added two records, one for ABC CORP. and one for AAC TEST CORP. Both of these list on the browse screen before any records for a company named ACME PRODUCT CO. because the browse is in alphabetical name order. What happens to the browse if I use the add/change screen to change the name ABC CORP. to DEF CORP.?

records in the file. With the MASTER.DAT customer file of my VAXDEMO system the records on such a printed listing would be sorted by customer name. But the advantage of an on-line browse screen over other forms of cross-reference is that the browse can immediately reflect updates to records. Changing a customer name in the VAXDEMO on-line system will immediately affect where the record appears in the CBROW1 on-line browse.

Figure 15.3 shows you the browse screen for my customer file after I have added two records, one for ABC CORP. and one for AAC TEST CORP. Both of these list on the browse screen before any records for a company named ACME PRODUCT CO. because the browse is in alpha-

```
VAXDEMO                 *** BROWSE CUSTOMERS BY NAME ***              03/15/92
Screen 4                                                             19:48

   ID           NAME               ADDRESS             CITY     ST  ZIP    ACT?

 780000   AAC TEST CORP.        123 N. MAIN STREET    CHICAGO     IL 60604   -
 168857   ACME PRODUCTS CO      8711 HALLDALE AV      LOS ROBLES  CA 90455   -
 415002   ACME PRODUCTS CO      1000 87TH AVE NE      EDMONTON    AB T2E6W5  -
 472293   ACME PRODUCTS CO      9716 HILBORN DR       GRIZZLETOWN GA 30101   -
 600536   ACME PRODUCTS CO      68 ELUSORY WAY        PLEVNA      KS 67568   -
 887633   ACME PRODUCTS CO      76 CRUTCHER CREEK LN  CONFLUENCE  KY 41730   I
 267841   ARNOLD ASSOCIATES     1760 N. ASHLAND       CHICAGO     IL 60678   I
 700501   BERNHARD LORING CORP. 9600 SUNSET PKWY      SAN MATEO   CA 94067   -
 419870   BERRY MACHINE TOOLS   12400 N. INDUSTRIAL   LIMA        OH 45801   I
 994365   BERYL AVIATION LTD    1936 W. ATLANTIC PKY  ST LAURENT  PQ H4L5E3  -
 258472   BURR & WILLIAMS INC   11100 N. SUFFOLK DR   EAST BEND   WI 53095   -
 700000   DEF CORP.             45 YARDLEY RD         ALGONQUIN   IL 65071   I
 123456   GILMORE TOOL CORP     1775 GLENVIEW RD      GLENDALE    MA 01229   -
 601723   HARRIER METER CORP.   7855 CENTURY PKY      OTTAWA      ON K1G3N3  -
 480114   HILBORN TECHNOLOGIES  215 FERRIS BLVD       CALGARY     AB T2E1H6  -
 521726   HILL ENGINEERING CO   2100 DEWEY AVE        CHARLESTON  SC 29415   I
 437352   JENSEN-SWIFT MFG.     8514 S. PALM DRIVE    RIVERSIDE   CA 92376   -

More data exists, press <Return> to continue                  ===>
```

Figure 15.4   The browse screen after I have changed the name ABC CORP. to DEF CORP. As you would expect, DEF CORP. now lists after all of the "A" and "B" records. This immediate reaction to update is why an interactive browse screen is preferable to a paper cross reference of records in sorted sequence.

betical name order. Suppose after viewing this screen I use the add/change screen to change the name ABC CORP. to DEF CORP. To the add/change program this is just a change in the contents of the firm name field. But to the indexed file access method this is a change in the alternate key of the record with primary key 700000!

Look at Figure 15.4. This is the browse screen after I have changed the name ABC CORP. to DEF CORP. As you would expect, DEF CORP. now lists after all of the "A" and "B" records (there are at present no customer records with name starting with "C").

15.5 Designing a Browse Screen

Figure 15.5 shows you the 80 × 24 grid form I used to lay out the browse screen of Program CBROW1. This layout looks a lot like a printer spacing chart. The screen follows the labeling and message conventions of the other screens in my VAXDEMO on-line system. But the middle area of the screen does not deal with just one record. It has identically formatted detail lines one line after another, a different record on each line.

You should list the primary key of records on a browse screen as the leftmost field in a record line. It's most convenient if you make the alternate key field on which the browse is based the next field on each line. Choose the remaining fields on the line to be those that will best help an operator pinpoint a specific record being sought.

In my customer master file browse I thought that the address would most help distinguish one customer from another if the customers have the same name. The layout you see in Figure 15.5 follows my suggestions. It makes it as easy as possible to find a customer record by name and learn its primary key.

15.6 Browse Program Logic and Source Code

I have provided the action diagram I used to design the CBROW1 browse program in Figure 15.6. This action diagram completely sums up the logic of the program. From it you can see that the higher levels of the program involve the now-familiar beginning of job, "process until," and end of job pattern. But notice that "filling out" a browse screen in program logic involves a loop in itself. Understanding that loop is the key to understanding how interactive browse logic works.

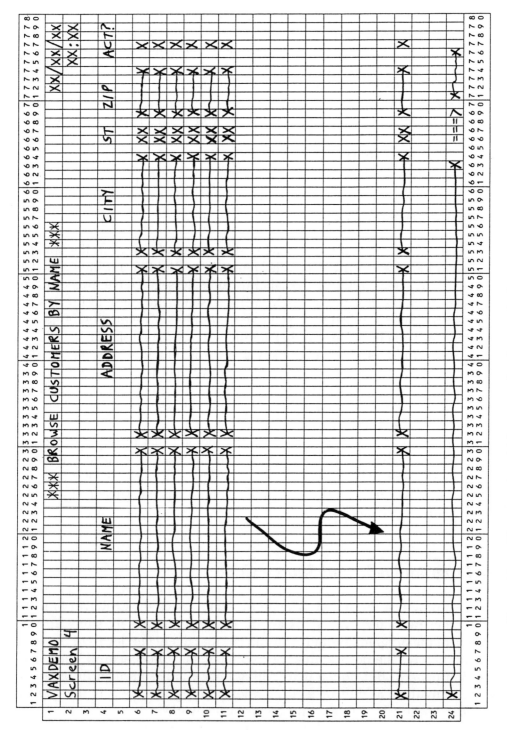

Figure 15.5 The 80 × 24 grid form I used to lay out the browse screen of Program CBROW1. The middle area of the screen does not deal with just one record. It has identically formatted "detail lines" one line after another, a different record on each line.

212

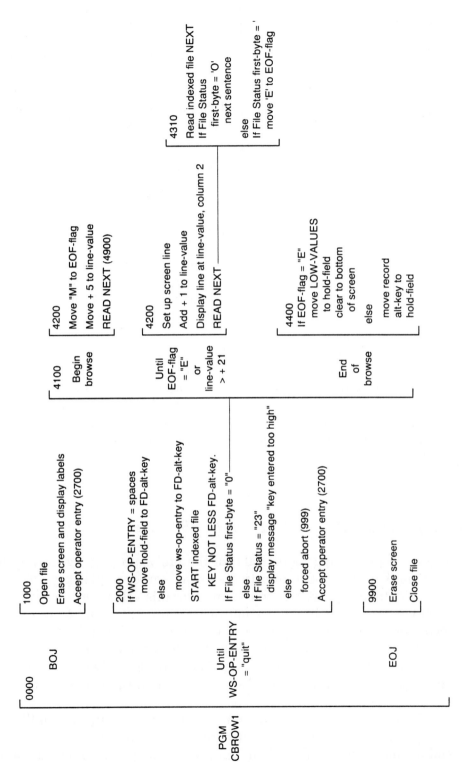

Figure 15.6 This is the action diagram I used to design the CBROW1 browse program. This action diagram completely sums up the logic of the program. You can see that the higher levels of the program involve beginning, "process until," and end of job. But "filling out" a browse screen involves another loop. Understanding that "inner" loop is the key to understanding how interactive browse logic works.

Figure 15.7 shows you the source code for CBROW1. Since I constructed it from the action diagram, you can see that its paragraph numbers correspond one for one with the brackets on the diagram. I especially like and recommend that you use an action diagram as a program logic design tool. Once you have drawn and checked out your action diagram, writing your program is a snap. You just transform every bracket on the diagram into a paragraph of source code!

15.7 How Alternate Key Browse Logic Works

Beginning of job logic in CBROW1 includes actions to open the indexed master file, accept and format the system date for presentation, and display screen labels. I then prompt the operator for the leading portion of a customer name at which the browse should begin. This can be as little as one letter or as many as six letters.

The main processing loop (2000) of the alternate key browse looks like a miniature program within a program. Every time you go through this outer loop the potential exists to produce a screenful or "page" of display. The prompt at the end of this loop seeks operator input to continue browsing or the entry of "quit" to end the browse function.

End of job in the browse erases the screen and closes the indexed file. Control then returns to the menu program.

15.8 Outer Loop PERFORM . . . UNTIL in the Browse

The main processing loop (2000) of the browse begins by loading the alternate key field with a desired starting key or partial key value. In CBROW1 there are two possible sources for this value. The operator may have entered it. Or it may be left over in WS-HOLD-KEY from the last record at the bottom of a previous browse screen. (When I finish writing a browse screen I put the alternate key of the last record on the screen in WS-HOLD-KEY.) If the operator immediately presses **<Return>** instead of entering a new starting browse key I use the hold value to begin the next screen.

Using WS-HOLD-KEY lets me keep browsing right through the file. All the operator has to do is press **<Return>** at the end of one browse screen and the next screen will pick up right where the previous screen left off.

```
CBROW1              15-Mar-1992 18:07:48    VAX COBOL V4.3-57
Source Listing      15-Mar-1992 18:06:51    CSC$ROOT:[CSCJGJ.VAXCO]CBROW1.COB;1
    1           IDENTIFICATION DIVISION.
    2           PROGRAM-ID.    CBROW1.
    3           *AUTHOR.        J JANOSSY    INTERNET: JANOSSY@CSCVAX.DEPAUL.EDU
    4           *INSTALLATION.  DEPAUL UNIVERSITY, CHICAGO, IL
    5           *================================================================
    6           *   Function 4 of VAXDEMO system in VAX COBOL ON-LINE!  3/1/92
    7           *
    8           *   Performs browse on records by alternate key (customer name)
    9           *   Terminal operator enters from 1 to 6 characters of customer
   10           *   name and browse does START then sequential reading at first
   11           *   record with this front part of name.
   12           *================================================================
   13           ENVIRONMENT DIVISION.
   14           INPUT-OUTPUT SECTION.
   15           FILE-CONTROL.
   16               SELECT MASTER-FILE              ASSIGN TO MASTER
   17                   ORGANIZATION   IS   INDEXED
   18                   ACCESS MODE    IS   DYNAMIC
   19                   RECORD KEY     IS   MF-KEY
   20                   ALTERNATE RECORD KEY IS MF-NAME-ALT-KEY
   21                   FILE STATUS    IS   WS-MASTFILE-FS.
   22           *----------------------------------------------------------------
   23           DATA DIVISION.
   24           FILE SECTION.
   25           *
   26           FD  MASTER-FILE
   27               RECORD CONTAINS 100 CHARACTERS
   28               LABEL RECORDS ARE STANDARD.
   29           01  MASTER-RECORD.
   30               12 MF-NAME-ALT-KEY.
   31                   15 MF-FIRM-NAME              PIC X(21).
   32                   15 MF-KEY                    PIC X(6).
   33               12 MF-STATUS-FLAG               PIC X(1).
   34                   88 MF-STAT-ACTIVE                    VALUE '-'.
   35                   88 MF-STAT-INACTIVE                  VALUE 'I'.
   36               12 MF-ADDRESS.
   37                   15 MF-ADDR-STREET           PIC X(20).
   38                   15 MF-ADDR-CITY             PIC X(12).
   39                   15 MF-ADDR-STATE            PIC X(2).
   40                   15 MF-ADDR-ZIP              PIC X(6).
   41               12 MF-PHONE-DATA.
   42                   15 MF-AREA-CODE             PIC X(3).
   43                   15 MF-PHONE-NO              PIC X(7).
   44               12 MF-CREDIT-LIMIT             PIC 9(7)V99.
   45               12 FILLER                      PIC X(13).
   46           /
   47           *----------------------------------------------------------------
   48           WORKING-STORAGE SECTION.
   49           01  WS-MASTFILE-FS.
   50               12 WS-MASTFILE-STATUS-BYTE1    PIC X(1).
   51               12 FILLER                      PIC X(1).
   52           *
   53           01  F1-EOF-FLAG                    PIC X(1).
   54           01  WS-LINE-VAL                    PIC S9(2).
   55           01  WS-ABORT-PARAGRAPH             PIC X(4).
   56           01  WS-HOLD-KEY                    PIC X(27).
   57           01  SCR-MSG                        PIC X(64).
   58           01  WS-OP-ENTRY.
   59               12 WS-OP-ENTRY-CHAR  PIC X  OCCURS 6 TIMES   INDEXED BY OP-IX.
   60           *
   61           01  WS-DATE.
   62               12 WS-YR                        PIC X(2).
   63               12 WS-MO                        PIC X(2).
   64               12 WS-DA                        PIC X(2).
   65           01  WS-FORMATTED-DATE               PIC X(8).
   66           *
```

(Continued)

Figure 15.7   The source code for CBROW1, constructed from the action diagram in Figure 15.6. Paragraph numbers correspond one for one with the brackets on the action diagram.

```
 67            01  WS-TIME.
 68                12  WS-HRS                        PIC  X(2).
 69                12  WS-MIN                        PIC  X(2).
 70                12  FILLER                        PIC  X(4).
 71            01  WS-FORMATTED-TIME.
 72                12  WSF-HRS                       PIC  X(2).
 73                12  FILLER                        PIC  X(1)  VALUE ':'.
 74                12  WSF-MIN                       PIC  X(2).
 75            *-------------------------------------------------------------
 76            *  This is the detail line for the browse.  It is like a
 77            *  print line in that it will be used for several screen lines:
 78            *-------------------------------------------------------------
 79            01  BROWSE-LINE.
 80                12  BL-KEY                        PIC  X(6).
 81                12  FILLER                        PIC  X(2)  VALUE SPACES.
 82                12  BL-FIRM-NAME                  PIC  X(21).
 83                12  FILLER                        PIC  X(1)  VALUE SPACE.
 84                12  BL-ADDR-STREET                PIC  X(20).
 85                12  FILLER                        PIC  X(1)  VALUE SPACE.
 86                12  BL-ADDR-CITY                  PIC  X(12).
 87                12  FILLER                        PIC  X(1)  VALUE SPACE.
 88                12  BL-ADDR-STATE                 PIC  X(2).
 89                12  FILLER                        PIC  X(1)  VALUE SPACE.
 90                12  BL-ADDR-ZIP                   PIC  X(6).
 91                12  FILLER                        PIC  X(2)  VALUE SPACES.
 92                12  BL-STATUS-FLAG                PIC  X(1).
 93            *
 94            01  WS-COMP                           PIC S9(4) COMP  VALUE +0.
 95            01  WS-TWOBYTE   REDEFINES   WS-COMP.
 96                12  WS-CHAR                       PIC  X(1).
 97                12  FILLER                        PIC  X(1).
 98            *
 99            LINKAGE SECTION.
100            01  WS-TRANS-COUNT                    PIC 9(7)V99.
101            /
102            PROCEDURE DIVISION.
103            *-------------------------------------------------------------
104            *  In VAX COBOL you need declaratives (even in dummy form) to
105            *  avoid abends even when nonzero File Status values such as
106            *  '23' are received for a key-not-found condition.  Since
107            *  DECLARATIVES are a "section" MAIN-PROGRAM must be a section.
108            *-------------------------------------------------------------
109            DECLARATIVES.
110            0000-ERROR    SECTION.
111                USE AFTER STANDARD ERROR PROCEDURE ON MASTER-FILE.
112            0000-DUMMY.  EXIT.
113            *
114            END DECLARATIVES.
115            *-------------------------------------------------------------
116            0000-MAIN-PROGRAM    SECTION.
117            0000-MAINLINE.
118                PERFORM 1000-BOJ.
119                PERFORM 2000-PROCESS
120                   UNTIL WS-OP-ENTRY = 'QUIT' OR 'quit'.
121                PERFORM 9900-EOJ.
122            0000-EXIT.  EXIT PROGRAM.
123            *
124            1000-BOJ.
125                MOVE LOW-VALUES TO WS-HOLD-KEY.
126                DISPLAY '' AT LINE 1, COLUMN 1 ERASE TO END OF SCREEN.
127            *
128                OPEN I-O MASTER-FILE.
129                IF WS-MASTFILE-STATUS-BYTE1 NOT = '0'
130                   MOVE '1000' TO WS-ABORT-PARAGRAPH
131                   PERFORM 9999-ABORT.
132            *
133                ACCEPT WS-DATE FROM DATE.
134                STRING  WS-MO  '/'  WS-DA  '/'  WS-YR  DELIMITED BY SIZE
135                   INTO WS-FORMATTED-DATE.
136            *
```

Figure 15.7   *(Continued)*

```
137          DISPLAY 'VAXDEMO'                    AT LINE 1 COLUMN  2.
138          DISPLAY '*** BROWSE CUSTOMERS BY NAME *** '
139             BOLD                              AT LINE 1 COLUMN 25.
140          DISPLAY WS-FORMATTED-DATE            AT LINE 1 COLUMN 72.
141          DISPLAY 'Screen 4'                   AT LINE 2 COLUMN  2.
142          DISPLAY 'ID'               BOLD AT LINE 4 COLUMN  4.
143          DISPLAY 'NAME'             BOLD AT LINE 4 COLUMN 19.
144          DISPLAY 'ADDRESS'          BOLD AT LINE 4 COLUMN 39.
145          DISPLAY 'CITY'             BOLD AT LINE 4 COLUMN 57.
146          DISPLAY 'ST'               BOLD AT LINE 4 COLUMN 66.
147          DISPLAY 'ZIP'              BOLD AT LINE 4 COLUMN 70.
148          DISPLAY 'ACT?'             BOLD AT LINE 4 COLUMN 76.
149      *
150          MOVE SPACES TO WS-OP-ENTRY.
151          MOVE 'Enter up to six letters of firm name for browse, press <Return>'
152             TO SCR-MSG.
153          PERFORM 2700-OP-PROMPT.
154      *
155      *=====================================PROCESS A BROWSE SCREEN
156      *  WS-HOLD-KEY starts as LOW-VALUES so browse begins by default
157      *  at start of file by customer (firm) name.  Holds alternate key
158      *  of last line previously displayed on screen after this time.
159      *  START at this point lets terminal operator continue browsing
160      *  with one line overlap by just pressing <Return>.
161      *-----------------------------------------------------------------
162      2000-PROCESS.
163          IF WS-OP-ENTRY = SPACES
164             MOVE WS-HOLD-KEY TO MF-NAME-ALT-KEY
165           ELSE
166             MOVE WS-OP-ENTRY TO MF-NAME-ALT-KEY.
167      *
168          START MASTER-FILE
169             KEY NOT LESS MF-NAME-ALT-KEY.
170      *
171          IF WS-MASTFILE-STATUS-BYTE1 = '0'
172             PERFORM 4100-BROWSE-A-PAGE
173           ELSE
174          IF WS-MASTFILE-FS = '23'
175             MOVE 'Name too high; press <Return> to start again'
176                TO SCR-MSG
177             MOVE LOW-VALUES TO WS-HOLD-KEY
178           ELSE
179             MOVE '2000' TO WS-ABORT-PARAGRAPH
180             PERFORM 9999-ABORT.
181      *
182          MOVE SPACE TO WS-OP-ENTRY.
183          PERFORM 2700-OP-PROMPT.
184      *-----------------------------------------------------------------
185      2700-OP-PROMPT.
186          ACCEPT WS-TIME FROM TIME.
187          MOVE WS-HRS TO WSF-HRS.
188          MOVE WS-MIN TO WSF-MIN.
189          DISPLAY WS-FORMATTED-TIME AT LINE  2 COLUMN 75.
190          DISPLAY SCR-MSG           AT LINE 24 COLUMN  2.
191          DISPLAY '===>'            AT LINE 24 COLUMN 66.
192          ACCEPT WS-OP-ENTRY
193             REVERSED
194             PROTECTED
195             FROM LINE 24 COLUMN 71.
196          PERFORM 2710-CONVERT-TO-UPPER-CASE
197             VARYING OP-IX FROM +1 BY +1
198                UNTIL OP-IX > +6.
199          DISPLAY ''                AT LINE 24 COLUMN  2
200             ERASE TO END OF LINE.
201      *-----------------------------------------------------------------
202      *  This logic shifts lowercase letters to uppercase by
203      *  subtracting 32 from the ASCII value of any byte in the
204      *  ASCII range 97 (a) to 122 (z):
205      *-----------------------------------------------------------------
```

(Continued)

Figure 15.7   *(Continued)*

```
206            2710-CONVERT-TO-UPPER-CASE.
207                MOVE WS-OP-ENTRY-CHAR(OP-IX) TO WS-CHAR.
208                IF WS-COMP NOT LESS +97 AND NOT GREATER +122
209                    SUBTRACT +32 FROM WS-COMP
210                    MOVE WS-CHAR TO WS-OP-ENTRY-CHAR(OP-IX).
211        *
212        *=================================================================
213            4100-BROWSE-A-PAGE.
214                PERFORM 4200-BEGIN-BROWSE.
215                PERFORM 4300-PROCESS-BROWSE
216                    UNTIL F1-EOF-FLAG = 'E'
217                        OR WS-LINE-VAL > +21.
218                PERFORM 4400-END-BROWSE.
219        *
220            4200-BEGIN-BROWSE.
221                MOVE 'M' TO F1-EOF-FLAG.
222                MOVE +5 TO WS-LINE-VAL.
223                PERFORM 4310-READ-NEXT.
224        *
225            4300-PROCESS-BROWSE.
226                MOVE MF-KEY           TO BL-KEY.
227                MOVE MF-FIRM-NAME     TO BL-FIRM-NAME.
228                MOVE MF-ADDR-STREET   TO BL-ADDR-STREET.
229                MOVE MF-ADDR-CITY     TO BL-ADDR-CITY.
230                MOVE MF-ADDR-STATE    TO BL-ADDR-STATE.
231                MOVE MF-ADDR-ZIP      TO BL-ADDR-ZIP.
232                MOVE MF-STATUS-FLAG   TO BL-STATUS-FLAG.
233                ADD +1 TO WS-LINE-VAL.
234                DISPLAY BROWSE-LINE AT  LINE WS-LINE-VAL  COLUMN 2.
235                PERFORM 4310-READ-NEXT.
236        *
237        *----------------------------------------------------------------
238        *  First-byte File Status other than '0' (OK) or '1' (EOF)
239        *  indicates indexed file failure:
240        *----------------------------------------------------------------
241            4310-READ-NEXT.
242                READ MASTER-FILE NEXT.
243                IF WS-MASTFILE-STATUS-BYTE1 = '0'
244                    NEXT SENTENCE
245                ELSE
246                IF WS-MASTFILE-STATUS-BYTE1 = '1'
247                    MOVE 'E' TO F1-EOF-FLAG
248                ELSE
249                    MOVE '4310' TO WS-ABORT-PARAGRAPH
250                    PERFORM 9999-ABORT.
251        *
252            4400-END-BROWSE.
253                IF F1-EOF-FLAG = 'E'
254                    MOVE 'End of file, press <Return> to start over, new ID, or "QUIT"'
255                        TO SCR-MSG
256                    MOVE LOW-VALUES TO WS-HOLD-KEY
257                    ADD +1 TO WS-LINE-VAL
258                    DISPLAY '' AT  LINE WS-LINE-VAL  COLUMN 2  ERASE TO END OF SCREEN
259                ELSE
260                    MOVE 'More data exists, press <Return> to continue' TO SCR-MSG
261                    MOVE MF-NAME-ALT-KEY TO WS-HOLD-KEY.
262        *
263        *======================================================END OF JOB
264            9900-EOJ.
265                DISPLAY '' AT LINE 1, COLUMN 1 ERASE TO END OF SCREEN.
266                CLOSE MASTER-FILE.
267                IF WS-MASTFILE-STATUS-BYTE1 NOT = '0'
268                    MOVE '9900' TO WS-ABORT-PARAGRAPH
269                    PERFORM 9999-ABORT.
270        *
271            9999-ABORT.
272                DISPLAY '' AT LINE 1, COLUMN 1 ERASE TO END OF SCREEN.
273                DISPLAY '*********************************************'
```

Figure 15.7   *(Continued)*

```
274              DISPLAY 'Program CBROW1 Error E99'.
275              DISPLAY 'Indexed file failure at paragraph ', WS-ABORT-PARAGRAPH.
276              DISPLAY 'File Status is ', WS-MASTFILE-FS.
277              DISPLAY 'Print this screen and contact programming group'.
278              DISPLAY '*************************************************'
279              STOP RUN.
```

Figure 15.7   *(Continued)*

Using a hold key like this to continue a browse is possible because I
forced the alternate key to be unique. I did this by making it a group
name and including the primary key (which must be unique) within it at
its end. Figure 15.8 shows you graphically how this works. When the
previous browse screen hits end-of-file I put LOW–VALUES in WS–HOLD–
KEY. The browse can start over again at the beginning of the file.

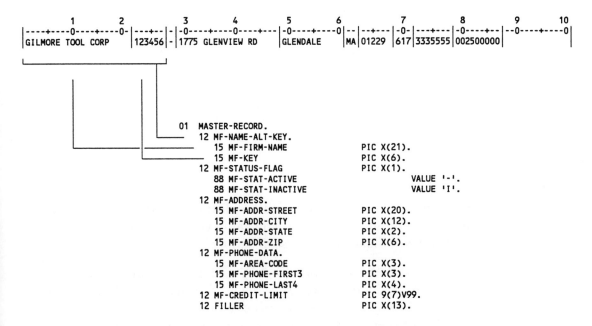

Figure 15.8   Putting the customer ID field (primary key) after the customer name
field lets me define the alternate key as a group name. It includes the customer
name and primary key. This forces the alternate key to be unique in every case and
simplifies continuing the browse from one screen to the next. To continue the
browse I save the MF-NAME-ALT-KEY value from the last line on the browse
screen and use it for a START for the next browse screen.

15.9 START *with Partial Alternate Key*

Look at lines 168 and 169 of CBROW1 and you will see how I use the START verb to begin reading records from the customer file for each browse screen. Notice that I put either WS-HOLD-KEY or the operator's entry value into the alternate key field just before executing the START verb.

When you mention the alternate key field name in a START command you change the indexed file access method to process READ . . . NEXT commands using the alternate index. Technically speaking this changes the **Key of Reference** (KOR) so that it points to the alternate index. START tries to satisfy relation condition specified (KEY NOT LESS MF-NAME-ALT-KEY). In this case it means "position the **Current Record Pointer** (CRP) to point to the first record whose key is equal to or greater than the value now in the alternate key field." START doesn't obtain a record. It sets the CRP, which tells your next READ . . . NEXT which record to get.

Why do I use READ . . . NEXT instead of READ? I could have used READ if I had specified ACCESS MODE IS SEQUENTIAL in the SELECT/ASSIGN statement for MASTER-FILE, but since I coded ACCESS MODE IS DYNAMIC, the READ verb would act as a random mode READ and not sequentially. When you code DYNAMIC you have to use READ (file-name) NEXT to do sequential reading.

15.10 *File Status Checking with* START

You have to check File Status after doing a START just as with any indexed file input/output verb. The value you receive in File Status after the START will dictate the course of action:

- If the START *succeeded* (first-byte File Status value of '0'), you can begin producing a browse screen. I do this at line 172 by performing 4100-BROWSE-A-PAGE (lines 213–218).
- If the START *failed* due to a record-not-found condition (File Status value of '23'), you need to tell the operator that he or she entered a starting value higher than any customer name (entered Z or some other value beyond the last customer name alphabetically).
- If you receive any other File Status value you must terminate the program, because this indicates that the **index file has failed**.

If I got '0' or '23' at the START my main loop ends with moving spaces to the operator entry field and prompting for another entry. The operator can enter "quit" to end the browse or can enter a new starting customer name position. If he or she just presses **<Return>** I continue browsing forward.

15.11 Inner Loop Browse-A-Page Logic

The logic to produce a page (screen) of records is a miniature BOJ/until/EOJ. Look at 4100-BROWSE-A-PAGE (lines 213 to 218) to prove it to yourself.

In beginning of browse you need to reset an end-of-file flag to a value that indicates "more records to browse." In a browse, unlike a once-through-the-file reporting program, you can reach end-of-file many times. You also need to reset a counter to a value that indicates the first screen line to be used for browse output. Then you need to READ . . . NEXT to get the first record for the browse screen.

In the processing loop within 4100-BROWSE-A-PAGE you format and display one detail line on the screen. You then try to get the next record in the file. This is very much like the logic of a reporting program in its main "process until" loop. But notice that my PERFORM . . . UNTIL at lines 215 through 217 has two ending conditions, not one. The browse page ends when I hit end-of-file (reading the customer file sequentially by alternate key) or when I have filled up the screen.

When the browse-a-page inner loop ends you have to do ending tasks. If the loop ended because you reached end-of-file you have to blank out the rest of the screen (it may still have records listed from the previous browse screen). You have to move LOW-VALUES to WS-HOLD-KEY so that the browse can start over at the beginning of the file if the operator presses the **<Return>** key next.

On the other hand, if the inner loop ends because the browse screen is filled you have to prompt the operator with a different message. You also have to move the alternate key of the last record to WS-HOLD-KEY so that you can resume browsing at this point in the file if the operator just presses the **<Return>** key.

You also need to check the File Status of each READ . . . NEXT, of course. I put my READ . . . NEXT into paragraph 4310 (lines 241–250) by itself to make File Status checking easier. Since I'm doing sequential reading I can expect first-byte File Status '0' to indicate that I succeeded in getting a record. First-byte File Status '1' means that I reached end-of-file (see Chapter 10, Figure 10.7, if you need to review File Status values.) A File Status value other than first-byte '0' or '1' means the indexed file has failed.

15.12 Chapter Summary

An *alternate key* provides access to an indexed file by a field other than the primary key. A browse based on an alternate key lets you "home in" on likely records when you don't know the primary key of the record you want. Once you find out the primary key of the record you use the regular inquiry, add/change, or delete functions of the on-line system to work with the record.

A *browse screen* presents a line of information from several records and resembles a page from a printed report. You position the primary key of records as the leftmost field on a line and the alternate key field as the next field. Chose the remaining fields on the line to be those that will best help an operator identify a specific record being sought. When driven by an alternate key, such as customer name, a browse lets you see records listed in customer name order rather than account ID order. You tell a browse screen where in the file to begin presenting records by entering one or more leading characters of the alternate key. The advantage of an on-line browse is that it immediately reflects updates to records. Changing a customer name in the VAXDEMO on-line system will immediately affect where the record appears in the on-line browse.

The higher levels of an interactive browse program involve a beginning of job, "process until," and end of job pattern. The main processing loop (2000) of the alternate key browse looks like a miniature program within a program. Every time you go through this outer loop the potential exists to produce a screenful or "page" of display. The prompt at the end of this loop seeks operator input to continue browsing or the entry of "QUIT" to end the browse function. All the operator has to do is press **<Return>** at the end of one browse screen and the next one will pick up where the former left off.

You use the START verb to position the *Current Record Pointer* (CRP) for sequential reading in a browse program. This can also set the *Key of Reference* (KOR) to the alternate key. You have to check File Status after doing a START just as with any indexed file input/output verb. First-byte

File Status '0' means a successful START. File Status '23' means the START relation condition could not be satisfied. Any other File Status value means that the index file has failed.

The logic to produce a page (screen) of records is a miniature BOJ/until/EOJ. The inner loop of this logic is very much like the logic of a reporting program in its main "process until" loop. The browse page ends when you reach end of file or when you have filled up the screen. If the SELECT/ASSIGN statement for the indexed file is coded ACCESS MODE IS DYNAMIC, you have to use the READ . . . NEXT verb to do sequential reading. (ACCESS MODE IS SEQUENTIAL would let you use the READ verb in this way.) You need to check File Status after each READ . . . NEXT to detect whether you got a record, you reached end-of-file, or the indexed file has failed.

15.13 Important Terms

Browse   A screen that shows you identifying information from several records so that you can pick out the record you want. When it is driven by an alternate key, you can use a browse screen to determine the primary key of a record (such as account ID) using an alternate key (such as customer name).

Partial alternate key   One or a few leading characters from the alternate key field sufficient to point to a location in an indexed file where you want browsing to begin.

Cross-reference   A paper listing of records in a file sorted by name or other alternate key. You can think of a browse screen as a page of such a report.

Outer loop   The main processing loop of a program invoked from its mainline (such as 2000-PROCESS in the programs in this book).

Inner loop   A loop performed inside the main processing loop of a program, such as the loop of a browse program that builds a screen with many records.

Hold key   A WORKING-STORAGE field used to save the alternate key of the last record displayed on a browse screen so that the START that begins the next browse screen can continue listing records from the file at that point.

READ . . . NEXT   The verb you use for sequential reading when you specify ACCESS MODE IS DYNAMIC in your SELECT/ASSIGN statement for an indexed file.

LOW-VALUES   The lowest possible value in a byte, with all eight bits of the byte "off." In hexadecimal this is X'00'. COBOL provides this figurative constant as a convenience. It is lower than any indexed file primary or alternate key value. (The opposite is HIGH-VALUES, all bits "on.")

Chapter Sixteen

ADVANCED FEATURES: DIRECT TRANSFER AND RECORD LOCKING

In this chapter I provide you with some insight on two important advanced aspects of interactive business systems. You should consider both of these topics if you intend to build useful, user-friendly, and reliable interactive systems.

Direct transfer between functions lets experienced system users bypass presentation of a menu when they already know the selection code of the function they want to perform. This feature is simple to install once you understand the philosophy behind it. I discuss this first in this chapter.

Record locking is the second advanced topic you need to understand. When many people use the same interactive system at the same time they share updating functions in the same files. Two or more terminal operators can interfere with each other. They can also unintentionally destroy data integrity by coincidentally updating the same record at the same time. On the VAX you can arrange protection against this using the file sharing features of VMS and Record Management Services.

16.1 Casual and Experienced System Users

A *casual system user* (a person who infrequently uses an interactive system) is best served by a menu-based on-line system architecture. A menu clearly guides this user in gaining access to each on-line function. But having to traverse up and down a menu hierarchy can become irritating to an *experienced system user* since it involves extra time.

For example, suppose you are performing an alternate key browse to identify the customer ID of a record and then wish to go into the add/change function to work with that record. After the browse you have to "quit" it, arrive at the menu, select the add/change, and finally enter the key of the record and bring it up on the screen. If your on-line system is organized into levels of menus (a main menu selection leads to a sub-menu), navigating through the system is even more burdensome.

16.2 Speeding Access in a Menu-Based System

You can speed up access to functions for people already familiar with your menu selections by installing *direct transfer* logic. This involves adding a small amount of logic to the menu and functional subprograms.

```
VAXDEMOX              *** BROWSE CUSTOMERS BY NAME ***              03/15/92
Screen 4                                                              19:48

   ID             NAME              ADDRESS            CITY      ST  ZIP    ACT?

882734   JOHNSON MACHINE CORP  68000 TECHNOLOGY WAY RESTON      VA 22070    -
695403   NORHOST INSTRUMENT CO 717 HOWARD DRIVE      RED BLUFF  CA 96080    -
178948   RANGER PRODUCTS, INC. 18 MILL CREEK LANE    NEWHALL    CA 91321    -
654733   SINCLAIR DRILL WORKS  6750 ARMORY WAY       VANCOUVER  BC V7B1T9   -














End of file, press <Return> to start over, new ID, or "QUIT"    ===> =1
```

Figure 16.1   This is how you could enter a transfer command from the browse screen (CBROW1) directly to the inquiry (CINQU1) in an enhanced system. Enhanced programs would detect the equal sign (=) and give the enhanced menu program your destination code (1). The menu would act as a flow of control router and send control to the inquiry program instead of displaying the menu.

To implement direct transfer, each functional subprogram must be able to accept and detect a special form of prompt response by the operator. You need to designate a special *transfer command* so that an operator can clearly specify a transfer request. A common way to distinguish a transfer command is to preface it with a special symbol such as the equal sign (=). The operator enters this followed by a menu selection code at the prompt instead of "quit."

For example, if you are in the browse function (4) of my VAXDEMO system and want to go directly to the inquiry function (1) you could enter =1 instead of "quit" at the browse screen prompt. The 1 in this command is called the *destination code*. Figure 16.1 shows how you could enter a transfer from the browse screen directly to the inquiry screen.

16.3 Bad and Good Ways to Implement Direct Transfer

Your first inclination in considering direct transfer may be to have each functional subprogram pass control directly to another functional subprogram as illustrated in the top part of Figure 16.2. While this seems simple and appealing it has two fatal drawbacks:

- It forces each functional subprogram to "know" the menu selection code and name of all of the other subprograms in the system.
- If you use CALL to accomplish such transfers you will inevitably have recursion problems. With enough transfers you'll wind up having a program involved in a chain of CALLs that winds back on itself.

Even if the second problem did not exist the first of these drawbacks poses problems of practicality when an on-line system provides more than a few menu selections. For n selectable functions you must anticipate n × (n − 1) transfer paths (sets of transfer logic). For my VAXDEMO system this means 4 × 3 = 12 transfers. For a system with 10 selections on the menu it would mean 10 × 9 = 90 paths. And if you add new functions to an interactive system you have to modify all of the existing programs to maintain complete direct transfer capability. That's far too burdensome. And it's not necessary to introduce this complexity. You can provide direct transfer with much simpler logic!

A practical means to provide direct transfer involves enhancement of the menu program to play the role of *control flow router* and to have it

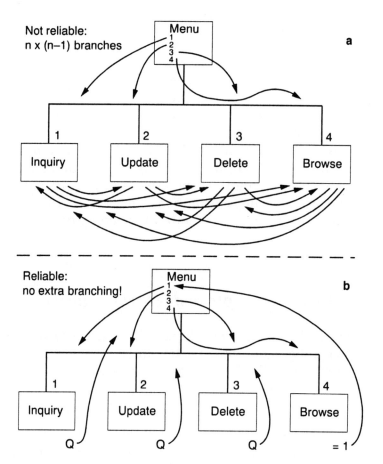

Figure 16.2 (a) Placing logic to handle direct transfers in each functional subprogram forces each functional program to "know" the menu selection code and name of all of the other programs in the system. This results in n x (n–1) sets of transfer logic and creates a program maintenance nightmare. (b) Making the menu program into a router provides direct transfer capabilities to all functions with a negligible amount of standard (unchanging) logic in each program.

only incidentally display a menu. This reduces the level of complexity to a minimum. Only the menu program needs to "know" the identities of your functional subprograms. Each subprogram needs to include only the identical few lines of additional code to communicate a transfer request to the menu. And no subprogram ever needs to know the names of any other programs! Figure 16.2(b) shows you the way I suggest that you implement direct transfer.

16.4 Implementing Direct Transfer

Figure 16.3 lists the source code for Program VAXDEMOX, my VAXDEMO program with direct transfer logic installed. I made two changes in VAXDEMO to support direct transfer:

- I expanded the memory shared by VAXDEMO with functional subprograms. The menu now shares the selection code for the current menu selection, the code for the next menu selection (from a direct transfer command), and the operator entry field (lines 24–31).
- I modified the processing loop in VAXDEMO following the EVALUATE statement to determine if control has reached this point with a menu selection already present. This lets me present the menu screen only when a direct transfer is *not* underway.

With these changes VAXDEMOX functions as a flow of control router more than a menu displayer. When VAXDEMOX receives control and a valid destination code is contained in WS-NEXT-MENU-SELECTION I do not display the menu. Instead, I pass control to the functional subprogram for the destination code just as if you had entered this code at the menu screen.

As a side benefit you should realize that the menu program also passes to each functional subprogram the menu selection code by which it (the subprogram) received control. This is powerful! The subprogram (such as CINQU1, CUPD1, CDEL1, or CBROW1) can use this selection code to label its own screen. This way the terminal operator can always see where he or she is in the hierarchy of screens not only by name but by the selection code chosen to get there. But the individual functional subprogram screens don't have to be hardcoded to know their own selection codes! You can change menu selection codes or add new ones without changing subprogram screens.

16.5 Direct Transfer Logic in Functional Subprograms

Figure 16.4 lists the source code for Program SINQU1X, a direct transfer version of SINQU1, the stub testing program for function 1 (the customer inquiry). I made these changes in SINQU1 to implement direct transfer:

- I expanded its LINKAGE SECTION to receive the several memory fields to be shared with it by the VAXDEMO menu program.

```
VAXDEMOX              15-Mar-1992 00:11:20     VAX COBOL V4.3-57
Source Listing        15-Mar-1992 00:07:56     CSC$ROOT:[CSCJGJ.VAXCO]VAXDEMOX.COB;1
        1             IDENTIFICATION DIVISION.
        2             PROGRAM-ID.     VAXDEMOX.
        3            *AUTHOR.         J JANOSSY    INTERNET: JANOSSY@CSCVAX.DEPAUL.EDU
        4            *INSTALLATION.   DEPAUL UNIVERSITY, CHICAGO, ILLINOIS, USA
        5            *===============================================================
        6            *     Main Menu Program in VAXDEMO System in VAX COBOL ON-LINE!
        7            *
        8            *     Presents menu screen and allows terminal operator to
        9            *     select a function or quit.  Originally set to CALL stub
       10            *     programs for testing (see paragraph 2000-PROCESS).
       11            *
       12            *     **  Contains enhancements to share more fields with CALLed  **
       13            *     **  subprogram and to receive "=" as direct transfer router. **
       14            *
       15            *===============================================================
       16             ENVIRONMENT DIVISION.
       17            *---------------------------------------------------------------
       18             DATA DIVISION.
       19             WORKING-STORAGE SECTION.
       20             01  WS-FORMATTED-COUNT                PIC Z,ZZZ,ZZ9.
       21             01  WS-VALID-CHOICE                   PIC X(1).
       22             01  SCR-MSG                           PIC X(58).
       23            *
       24             01  WS-SHARED-FIELDS.
       25                 12  WS-TRANS-COUNT                PIC 9(7).
       26                 12  WS-MENU-SELECTION             PIC X(1).
       27                 12  WS-NEXT-MENU-SELECTION        PIC X(1).
       28                 12  WS-SCREEN-NOW-DISPLAYED       PIC X(15).
       29                 12  WS-OP-ENTRY.
       30                     15  WS-OP-ENTRY-BYTE1         PIC X(1).
       31                     15  WS-OP-ENTRY-BYTE2-END     PIC X(5).
       32            *
       33             01  WS-DATE.
       34                 12  WS-YR                         PIC X(2).
       35                 12  WS-MO                         PIC X(2).
       36                 12  WS-DA                         PIC X(2).
       37             01  WS-FORMATTED-DATE                 PIC X(8).
       38            *
       39             01  WS-TIME.
       40                 12  WS-HRS                        PIC X(2).
       41                 12  WS-MIN                        PIC X(2).
       42                 12  FILLER                        PIC X(4).
       43             01  WS-FORMATTED-TIME.
       44                 12  WSF-HRS                       PIC X(2).
       45                 12  FILLER                        PIC X(1)  VALUE ':'.
       46                 12  WSF-MIN                       PIC X(2).
       47            /
       48             PROCEDURE DIVISION.
       49             0000-MAINLINE.
       50                 PERFORM 1000-BOJ.
       51                 PERFORM 2000-PROCESS
       52                     UNTIL WS-OP-ENTRY = 'Q' OR 'q'.
       53                 PERFORM 3000-EOJ.
       54                 STOP RUN.
       55            *
       56             1000-BOJ.
       57                 MOVE SPACE TO WS-NEXT-MENU-SELECTION.
       58                 ACCEPT WS-DATE FROM DATE.
       59                 STRING  WS-MO  '/'  WS-DA  '/'  WS-YR  DELIMITED BY SIZE
       60                     INTO WS-FORMATTED-DATE.
```

Figure 16.3 Source code for VAXDEMOX, the VAXDEMO menu program with logic added to handle direct transfers. Memory shared with subprograms is expanded so that the destination code from a transfer request can be passed back from a subprogram to the menu program. A small amount of logic is added after the EVALUATE so that the program can avoid presenting the menu screen when a valid menu selection (destination code) is already present.

```
61              MOVE 'Enter a selection code and press <Return>' TO SCR-MSG.
62              PERFORM 2600-DISPLAY-MENU.
63              PERFORM 2700-OP-PROMPT.
64       * - - - - - - - - - - - - - - - - - - - - - - - - - - - -
65          2000-PROCESS.
66              MOVE WS-OP-ENTRY TO WS-MENU-SELECTION.
67              MOVE 'Y' TO WS-VALID-CHOICE.
68       *
69              EVALUATE WS-OP-ENTRY
70                  WHEN '1'  CALL 'SINQU1X' USING WS-TRANS-COUNT
71                  WHEN '2'  CALL 'SUPD1X'  USING WS-TRANS-COUNT
72                  WHEN '3'  CALL 'SDEL1X'  USING WS-TRANS-COUNT
73                  WHEN '4'  CALL 'SBROW1X' USING WS-TRANS-COUNT
74                  WHEN OTHER
75                      MOVE 'N' TO WS-VALID-CHOICE.
76       *
77              IF WS-VALID-CHOICE = 'Y'
78                  IF WS-NEXT-MENU-SELECTION = SPACE
79                      PERFORM 2800-GET-NEW-SELECTION
80                  ELSE
81                      MOVE WS-NEXT-MENU-SELECTION TO WS-OP-ENTRY
82                  ELSE
83                      PERFORM 2900-INVALID-SELECTION.
84       * - - - - - - - - - - - - - - - - - - - - - - - - - - - -
85          2600-DISPLAY-MENU.
86              DISPLAY '' AT LINE 1 COLUMN 1 ERASE TO END OF SCREEN.
87              DISPLAY 'VAXDEMOX' AT LINE 1 COLUMN 2.
88              DISPLAY '*** CUSTOMER MASTER FILE SYSTEM MENU *** '
89                  BOLD AT LINE 1 COLUMN 21.
90              DISPLAY WS-FORMATTED-DATE AT LINE 1 COLUMN 72.
91              DISPLAY 'Screen 0X' AT LINE 2 COLUMN 2.
92              DISPLAY 'ENTER FUNCTION CODE AND PRESS RETURN' AT LINE 4 COLUMN 23.
93              DISPLAY '1   Inquire about a customer'  AT LINE  7 COLUMN 27.
94              DISPLAY '2   Add/change customer data'  AT LINE  7 COLUMN 27.
95              DISPLAY '3   Delete a customer'         AT LINE  9 COLUMN 27.
96              DISPLAY '4   Browse customers by name'  AT LINE 11 COLUMN 27.
97              DISPLAY 'Q   Quit (end VAXDEMO)'        AT LINE 15 COLUMN 27.
98              MOVE 'Screen 0X' TO WS-SCREEN-NOW-DISPLAYED.
99       *
100         2700-OP-PROMPT.
101             ACCEPT WS-TIME FROM TIME.
102             MOVE WS-HRS TO WSF-HRS.
103             MOVE WS-MIN TO WSF-MIN.
104             DISPLAY WS-FORMATTED-TIME AT LINE  2 COLUMN 75.
105             DISPLAY SCR-MSG           AT LINE 24 COLUMN  2.
106             DISPLAY '===>'            AT LINE 24 COLUMN 66.
107             ACCEPT WS-OP-ENTRY       FROM LINE 24 COLUMN 71.
108             IF WS-OP-ENTRY-BYTE1 = '='
109                 MOVE WS-OP-ENTRY-BYTE2-END TO WS-OP-ENTRY.
110             DISPLAY ''                AT LINE 24 COLUMN  2 ERASE TO END OF LINE.
111         *
112         2800-GET-NEW-SELECTION.
113             MOVE 'Enter a selection code and press <Return>' TO SCR-MSG.
114             PERFORM 2600-DISPLAY-MENU.
115             PERFORM 2700-OP-PROMPT.
116         *
117         2900-INVALID-SELECTION.
118             IF WS-SCREEN-NOW-DISPLAYED NOT = 'Screen 0X'
119                 PERFORM 2600-DISPLAY-MENU.
120             MOVE 'Invalid selection!  Re-enter a choice' TO SCR-MSG.
121             PERFORM 2700-OP-PROMPT.
122         *
123         *=================================================================
124         3000-EOJ.
125             DISPLAY '' AT LINE 1 COLUMN 1 ERASE TO END OF SCREEN.
126             DISPLAY 'Quitting as requested'                 AT LINE 1 COLUMN 2.
127             MOVE WS-TRANS-COUNT TO WS-FORMATTED-COUNT.
128             DISPLAY 'Number of transactions processed = '   AT LINE 2 COLUMN 2.
129             DISPLAY WS-FORMATTED-COUNT                      AT LINE 2 COLUMN 37.
130             DISPLAY 'Enter any VMS command now...'          AT LINE 4 COLUMN 2.
```

Figure 16.3 *(Continued)*

```
SINQU1X            15-Mar-1992 00:11:40    VAX COBOL V4.3-57
Source Listing     15-Mar-1992 00:08:52    CSC$ROOT:[CSCJGJ.VAXCO]SINQU1X.COB;1
       1           IDENTIFICATION DIVISION.
       2           PROGRAM-ID.    SINQU1X.
       3          *AUTHOR.        J JANOSSY    INTERNET: JANOSSY@CSCVAX.DEPAUL.EDU
       4          *INSTALLATION.  DEPAUL UNIVERSITY, CHICAGO, ILLINOIS, USA
       5          *=================================================================
       6          *    Testing Stub for VAXDEMOX Program CINQU1X in VAX COBOL ON-LINE!
       7          *
       8          *    This program receives control from the VAXDEMO menu program
       9          *    and just presents a simple message saying that it has been
      10          *    accessed.  After another <Return> it ends and control goes
      11          *    back to the menu program.
      12          *
      13          *    **  Enhancement added to allow direct transfer from this     **
      14          *    **  program through menu as "router" to any other function   **
      15          *    **  in the system.                                           **
      16          *
      17          *=================================================================
      18           ENVIRONMENT DIVISION.
      19          *-----------------------------------------------------------------
      20           DATA DIVISION.
      21           WORKING-STORAGE SECTION.
      22           01  SCR-MSG                       PIC X(58).
      23          *
      24           LINKAGE SECTION.
      25           01  WS-SHARED-FIELDS.
      26               12 WS-TRANS-COUNT             PIC 9(7).
      27               12 WS-MENU-SELECTION          PIC X(1).
      28               12 WS-NEXT-MENU-SELECTION     PIC X(1).
      29               12 WS-SCREEN-NOW-DISPLAYED     PIC X(15).
      30               12 WS-OP-ENTRY.
      31                  15 WS-OP-ENTRY-BYTE1       PIC X(1).
      32                  15 WS-OP-ENTRY-BYTE2-END   PIC X(5).
      33          /
      34          *-----------------------------------------------------------------
      35           PROCEDURE DIVISION USING WS-SHARED-FIELDS.
      36           0000-MAINLINE.
      37               MOVE SPACES TO  WS-OP-ENTRY  WS-NEXT-MENU-SELECTION.
      38               PERFORM 2000-STAY-HERE
      39                   UNTIL WS-OP-ENTRY = 'QUIT'.
      40           0000-EXIT.  EXIT PROGRAM.
      41          *
      42           2000-STAY-HERE.
      43               ADD 1 TO WS-TRANS-COUNT.
      44               DISPLAY '' AT LINE 1 COLUMN 1 ERASE TO END OF SCREEN.
      45               DISPLAY 'Control passed to SINQU1X'.
      46               DISPLAY 'Menu selection code that got here = ', WS-MENU-SELECTION.
      47               DISPLAY '(You could DISPLAY this code on the screen to label it)'.
      48               DISPLAY ' '.
      49               DISPLAY 'Press <Return> to remain in this function'.
      50               DISPLAY 'Enter "QUIT" <Return> to return to menu'.
      51               DISPLAY 'To tRansfer directly to another function without menu'.
      52               DISPLAY '    enter = and menu selection code, such as =2 or =Q <RETURN>'.
      53               MOVE 'Screen 1X' TO WS-SCREEN-NOW-DISPLAYED.
      54          *
      55               ACCEPT WS-OP-ENTRY
      56                   REVERSED
      57                   PROTECTED
      58                   FROM LINE 24 COLUMN 71.
      59               IF WS-OP-ENTRY-BYTE1 = '='
      60                   MOVE WS-OP-ENTRY-BYTE2-END TO WS-NEXT-MENU-SELECTION
      61                   MOVE 'QUIT' TO WS-OP-ENTRY.
```

Figure 16.4 Source code for Program SINQU1X, an direct transfer version of SINQU1, the stub testing program for function 1 (the customer inquiry). The changes in SINQU1 to implement direct transfer include expanding its LINKAGE SECTION, logic to initialize the shared memory fields WS-OP-ENTRY and WS-NEXT-MENU-SELECTION to spaces, and logic to recognize a direct transfer command at the prompt response.

- I installed logic to initialize the shared memory fields WS-OP-ENTRY and WS-NEXT-MENU-SELECTION to spaces in beginning of job, since these fields may contain data left there by another program.
- I added logic to recognize a direct transfer command at the prompt response (lines 59–61).

A direct transfer command is handled by a functional subprogram such as SINQU1X by moving the destination code (only) to WS-NEXT-MENU-SELECTION and replacing the operator's prompt response with "QUIT." This ends the processing loop as if the terminal operator had entered "QUIT" but gives the desired destination code to the menu program.

16.6 Installing Direct Transfer in the VAXDEMO System

To experiment with direct transfer you can install direct transfer capabilities in all of the VAXDEMO stub testing programs. You can then experiment with the demonstration system. Note that the logic you put into each testing stub to implement direct transfer is exactly the same! Just make the simple changes outlined in topic 16.4 in your menu program. Then install the logic I described in topic 16.5 in each functional subprogram.

Figure 16.5 shows you how the direct transfer enhancement handles a situation where an incorrect destination code has been entered in a transfer command. The menu program detects the invalid menu selection and shows the menu and an error message just as if the invalid selection had been made at the menu screen itself.

Figure 16.6 depicts an added benefit of direct transfer. With the program logic I have illustrated for you it is possible to log off from the interactive system from any place within it. By entering the menu selection for logoff in a direct transfer command (=Q in the case of my VAXDEMOX system) the menu program receives control and ends.

16.7 File Sharing and Record Locking

It's quite likely that you have not (until now) had to worry about multiple programs accessing the same file at the same time. Batch programs typically read entire files and make exclusive use of them during execution. But an on-line system is most often used by many people simultane-

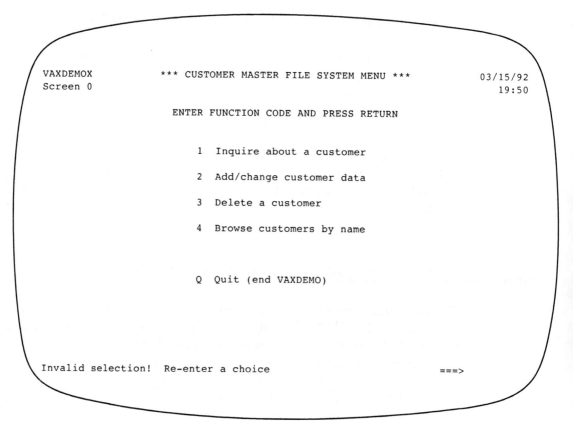

```
VAXDEMOX              *** CUSTOMER MASTER FILE SYSTEM MENU ***           03/15/92
Screen 0                                                                  19:50

                         ENTER FUNCTION CODE AND PRESS RETURN


                    1    Inquire about a customer

                    2    Add/change customer data

                    3    Delete a customer

                    4    Browse customers by name



                    Q    Quit (end VAXDEMO)






Invalid selection!  Re-enter a choice                              ===>
```

Figure 16.5 How the direct transfer enhancement handles a situation where an incorrect destination code has been entered in a transfer command. The menu program detects the invalid menu selection and shows the menu and an error message just as if the invalid selection had been made at the menu screen itself.

ously, and any one person accesses only one or a few records at a time. Multiple users share access to the files supporting the on-line system.

Consider the on-line system by which a small business takes orders for products and keeps track of its inventory. Two or more personnel may be on the telephone entering new orders into the system at the same time that personnel in the warehouse are updating files to reflect stock removed from inventory. Someone elsewhere may be changing customer information while another person is also putting new customer records into the system. All of these people will be accessing the same files!

```
VAXDEMOX              *** BROWSE CUSTOMERS BY NAME ***              03/15/92
Screen 4                                                             19:50

   ID          NAME                ADDRESS            CITY      ST   ZIP   ACT?

  780000   AAC TEST CORP.        123 N. MAIN STREET   CHICAGO     IL 60604   -
  168857   ACME PRODUCTS CO      8711 HALLDALE AV     LOS ROBLES  CA 90455   -
  415002   ACME PRODUCTS CO      1000 87TH AVE NE     EDMONTON    AB T2E6W5  -
  472293   ACME PRODUCTS CO      9716 HILBORN DR      GRIZZLETOWN GA 30101   -
  600536   ACME PRODUCTS CO      68 ELUSORY WAY       PLEVNA      KS 67568   -
  887633   ACME PRODUCTS CO      76 CRUTCHER CREEK LN CONFLUENCE  KY 41730   I
  267841   ARNOLD ASSOCIATES     1760 N. ASHLAND      CHICAGO     IL 60678   I
  700501   BERNHARD LORING CORP. 9600 SUNSET PKWY     SAN MATEO   CA 94067   -
  419870   BERRY MACHINE TOOLS   12400 N. INDUSTRIAL  LIMA        OH 45801   I
  994365   BERYL AVIATION LTD    1936 W. ATLANTIC PKY ST LAURENT  PQ H4L5E3  -
  258472   BURR & WILLIAMS INC   11100 N. SUFFOLK DR  EAST BEND   WI 53095   -
  700000   DEF CORP.             45 YARDLEY RD        ALGONQUIN   IL 65071   I
  123456   GILMORE TOOL CORP     1775 GLENVIEW RD     GLENDALE    MA 01229   -
  601723   HARRIER METER CORP.   7855 CENTURY PKY     OTTAWA      ON K1G3N3  -
  480114   HILBORN TECHNOLOGIES  215 FERRIS BLVD      CALGARY     AB T2E1H6  -
  521726   HILL ENGINEERING CO   2100 DEWEY AVE       CHARLESTON  SC 29415   I
  437352   JENSEN-SWIFT MFG.     8514 S. PALM DRIVE   RIVERSIDE   CA 92376   -

More data exists, press <Return> to continue                ===> =q
```

Figure 16.6 With the direct transfer feature installed you can log off from the interactive system from any place within it. When you enter =q at any subprogram prompt the menu program receives control. Since "q" is the menu selection to "quit" execution of the application, the system ends.

16.8 Potential Problems in Shared File Access

When multiple users run the same interactive system some conflicts can arise. Let's talk about these in terms of terminal operators John, Wendy, Dennis, Karen, Mike, and Suzanne.

- John begins an on-line change to customer 123456 to change the credit limit as a part of a normal accounting review. At the same time Wendy receives a call from this customer asking to change the telephone number and shipping address. Wendy starts her on-line action after John but finishes it before he does; her copy of the record is rewritten with the new address and telephone number. When John finishes his update, his copy of the record is rewritten. What's the address and telephone number on the record now? It's the old one. Wendy updated the record on disk but John's rewrite replaced it with the old copy he read first!

- Dennis begins a delete action on customer 876545. He enters this key, sees the record on the screen, and the screen prompts him to confirm the deletion. But Dennis gets sidetracked on a telephone call. Meanwhile Karen, not knowing that Dennis started the delete, begins, confirms, and completes the delete on her terminal. Dennis finishes his telephone call and confirms the delete. But his program abends! By the time he confirmed his delete there was no such record in the file!

- Both Mike and Suzanne, unknown to each other, enter the same nonexistent record key into the CUPD1 program. Both get into "add" processing. But Suzanne finishes her work first and completes the record addition. When Mike finishes his add transaction, his program abends because he is trying to WRITE a record with a duplicate key!

These situations may seem farfetched to you. But you have to consider concurrent access such as this when you program an interactive business application. Multiple-user business systems are vulnerable to events like this that can disrupt work and damage data integrity. Every multiple-user interactive system has to take measures to keep one user from interfering with another.

On the VAX the potentially conflicting demands of shared file access are addressed as four issues:

- Disk residency.
- File access privileges (VMS file protection).
- File sharing (handled by the file system of VMS).
- Record locking (handled by RMS, Record Management Services).

These issues form a hierarchy. To arrange record locking you have to enjoy file sharing. To do file sharing you have to arrange file access privileges. And to arrange file access privileges you have to establish disk residency.

16.9 Disk Residency

The issue of disk residency is a simple one. For multiple users to access files concurrently the files must reside on disk. You cannot arrange to share tape files. But since tape is almost useless for on-line systems (except as a data backup medium) this issue is very nearly moot.

16.10 File Access Security

The second issue of concurrent access is file access privileges. You need to grant every user who will run an on-line system the privilege to exe-

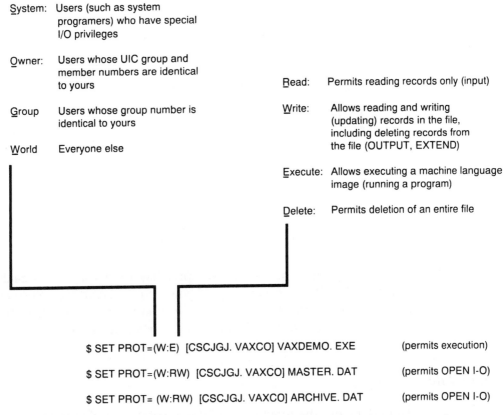

System: Users (such as system programers) who have special I/O privileges

Owner: Users whose UIC group and member numbers are identical to yours

Group   Users whose group number is identical to yours

World   Everyone else

Read: Permits reading records only (input)

Write: Allows reading and writing (updating) records in the file, including deleting records from the file (OUTPUT, EXTEND)

Execute: Allows executing a machine language image (running a program)

Delete: Permits deletion of an entire file

$ SET PROT=(W:E) [CSCJGJ. VAXCO] VAXDEMO. EXE   (permits execution)

$ SET PROT=(W:RW) [CSCJGJ. VAXCO] MASTER. DAT   (permits OPEN I-O)

$ SET PROT= (W:RW) [CSCJGJ. VAXCO] ARCHIVE. DAT   (permits OPEN I-O)

Figure 16.7   Summary of VAX VMS user categories and file access privileges. You use the $ SET PROT command to grant various privileges to different groups of VAX system users.

cute the `.EXE` file that contains the machine language of the system. You also need to give these users appropriate access to every data file that supports the system.

The VMS operating system normally limits access to files to the programmer who creates them. You can use the `$ SET PROT` command as described in Figure 16.7 to open up access to these files. Note that you need to give users both **R**ead and **W**rite access to allow them to use a program (such as add/change CUPD1 or delete CDEL1) that opens a file `I-O`.

By coordinating the assignment of "UIC" identifiers and group numbers with a system programmer you can designate a **G**roup of users that you can permit to access files. If you can't coordinate UICs and group numbers, you can open file access to **W**orld.

You can use the `DIR` command to check on the security currently associated with any file. Here is an example of a `DIR/PROT`, a `SET PROT` to give read and write access to "world" users, and a `DIR/PROT` to confirm that access security has been changed:

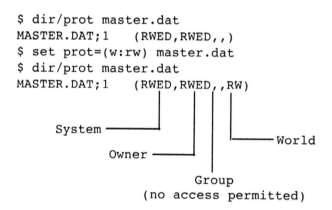

```
$ dir/prot master.dat
MASTER.DAT;1    (RWED,RWED,,)
$ set prot=(w:rw) master.dat
$ dir/prot master.dat
MASTER.DAT;1    (RWED,RWED,,RW)
```

```
        System ───────────┐
            Owner ──────────┐ │ │ ┌──── World
                     Group ──┘
            (no access permitted)
```

Keep in mind that file access privileges are specific to each *version number* of a file. For example, if you again `$ LINK VAXDEMO`, creating a new `.EXE` file, the new file will be limited to owner access until you use `$ SET PROT` to open it up for group or world access.

16.11 File Sharing

To understand the third issue of concurrent access, you need to know the term **access stream**. An access stream is the series of file and record operations being performed by a single user. A single COBOL program can define one or more access streams. Each `OPEN` verb creates (initializes) an access stream. The CLOSE verb or program ending terminates it. Multiple access streams (created by other users executing the same program or other programs) can access the same file. When multiple access streams can access the same file, *file sharing* is occurring.

Figure 16.8 shows you four concurrent access streams sharing access to the MASTER.DAT file. User 1 is executing CUPD1, user 2 is also executing CUPD1, user 3 is executing CDEL1, and user 4 is executing CINQU1. A rule you can think of as "first in time, first in right" characterizes file sharing. The first access stream to access a file determines how other access streams can concurrently access the file or if they can access it at all.

You code the extra clause ALLOWING in the OPEN for a file to specify file sharing. How you OPEN a file (INPUT, OUTPUT, I-O, or EXTEND) determines what *you* can do with the file. How you code ALLOWING determines what *other* (subsequent) access streams can do with it concurrently. At the time the second and subsequent access streams try to OPEN the file the system makes these checks:

- The new stream's ALLOWING specification is compared to the ALLOWING specifications of the previous access streams.
- The OPEN mode of the new stream is checked against the ALLOWING specification of the previous access streams.

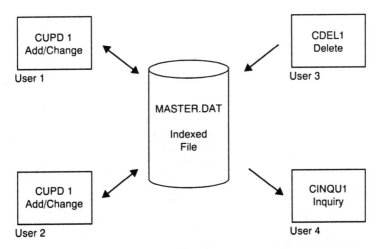

Figure 16.8 Multiple "access streams" can use the same file concurrently. You can think of each access stream as a program. To arrange file sharing like this you need to specify the ALLOWING clause in your OPEN statement as ALLOWING READERS, ALLOWING WRITERS, or ALLOWING UPDATERS. Without ALLOWING, the default for a program updating a file is exclusive use (no file sharing).

The new access stream doesn't get access unless it ALLOWS what the previous streams are already doing. The new stream fails to gain access if it is trying to OPEN the file in a way that the previous ALLOWING specifications prohibit. Figure 16.9 summarizes what the OPEN mode and ALLOWING specifications let your program and other access streams do.

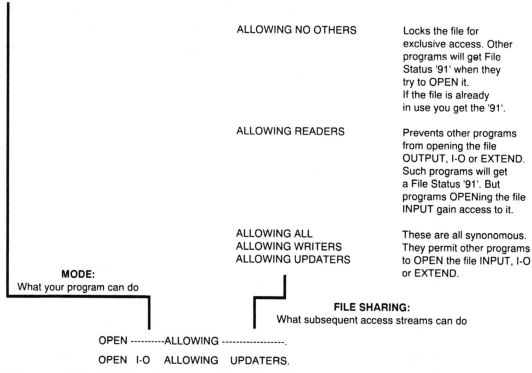

OPEN Mode	SELECT/ASSIGN Access Mode	You can:
INPUT	Any	READ, START
OUTPUT	Any	WRITE
I-O	SEQUENTIAL	READ, START, REWRITE, DELETE
I-O	RANDOM or DYNAMIC	READ, START, REWRITE, DELETE, WRITE
EXTEND	SEQUENTIAL	WRITE

ALLOWING NO OTHERS — Locks the file for exclusive access. Other programs will get File Status '91' when they try to OPEN it. If the file is already in use you get the '91'.

ALLOWING READERS — Prevents other programs from opening the file OUTPUT, I-O or EXTEND. Such programs will get a File Status '91'. But programs OPENing the file INPUT gain access to it.

ALLOWING ALL
ALLOWING WRITERS
ALLOWING UPDATERS — These are all synonomous. They permit other programs to OPEN the file INPUT, I-O or EXTEND.

MODE:
What your program can do

FILE SHARING:
What subsequent access streams can do

OPEN ----------ALLOWING ------------------.

OPEN I-O   ALLOWING   UPDATERS.

Figure 16.9   Summary of OPEN statement file modes and file sharing specifications. If you don't code ALLOWING, the default for a program doing updating is ALLOWING NO OTHERS, which prevents any concurrent file use.

If you don't specify the ALLOWING clause on the OPEN statement different defaults apply depending on your OPEN mode:

OPEN INPUT	filename	*defaults to* ALLOWING READERS
OPEN I-O	filename	*defaults to* ALLOWING NO OTHERS
OPEN OUTPUT	filename	*defaults to* ALLOWING NO OTHERS
OPEN EXTEND	filename	*defaults to* ALLOWING NO OTHERS

If your program tries to open a file in a mode that conflicts with the ALLOWING specification of an existing access stream you will receive a File Status value of '91' for your OPEN. This means "file locked by another user." So you can see that the default locks entire files to other users once one access stream is active. This is why you need to specify ALLOWING to permit file sharing.

16.12 Record Locking

A *record lock* makes just one record (not an entire file) inaccessible to all but one concurrent file user. VAX Record Management Services provides two types of record locking: automatic and manual. To get *automatic record locking* you just specify the ALLOWING clause of the OPEN statement to permit file sharing. (Unless you specify ALLOWING, the defaults just shown preclude file sharing and make record locking unnecessary). To get *manual record locking* you have to use the clause APPLY LOCK-HOLDING in a special I-O-CONTROL SECTION (following your FILE-CONTROL SECTION), use ALLOWING on the OPEN, and use ALLOWING on each READ, WRITE, REWRITE, or START verb.

The names *automatic* and *manual record locking* are really very descriptive. If you use OPEN . . . ALLOWING UPDATERS you automatically get a record lock on each record as you READ it. If you use the extra clauses to do manual record locking, then OPEN . . . ALLOWING UPDATERS gives you no record locking; you have to apply locks yourself.

Automatic record locking locks one record per access stream at a time. The lock is applied when you READ the record. This gives you exclusive access to the record: no other program (access stream) can access it until you release the lock. During the time that the lock is in effect any other access stream that tries to access the record will receive either File Status '90' or '92' for READ, DELETE, or START.

The lock on a record is released when you READ another record, you

REWRITE the record, you DELETE it, or you CLOSE the file. You can also execute the UNLOCK RECORD statement to release a record without doing additional input/output actions:

```
FILE-CONTROL.
SELECT MY-FILE ASSIGN TO 'SOME.DAT'
    ORGANIZATION IS INDEXED
    ACCESS MODE IS RANDOM
    RECORD KEY IS MR-FD-KEY
    FILE STATUS IS WS-MASTERFILE-FS.
    -
    -
```

> This example shows manual record locking. For automatic record locking omit the I-O-CONTROL paragraph and just code your OPEN for the file with "ALLOWING . . ."

```
I-O CONTROL.
    APPLY LOCK-HOLDING ON MY-FILE.
DATA DIVISION.
FILE SECTION.
FD MY-FILE
    RECORD CONTAINS 100 CHARACTERS
    LABEL RECORDS ARE STANDARD.
01 MY-RECORD.
    05 MR-FD-KEY      PIC X(8).
    -
    -

PROCEDURE DIVISION.
    -
    OPEN I-O MY-FILE ALLOWING UPDATERS.
    -
    READ MY-FILE ALLOWING NO OTHERS.
    -
    REWRITE MR-RECORD ALLOWING NO OTHERS.
    -
    UNLOCK MY-FILE ALL RECORDS.
    -
    CLOSE MY-FILE.
```

16.13 File Status Values '90' and '92'

When file sharing and automatic record locking are in effect your programs may receive File Status values '90' or '92' in the normal course of operation.

File Status '90' indicates a "soft" record lock. It means that the record you are trying to access is held (locked) by another access stream but that you did get a copy of the record in your FD. In other words, you do have the record in memory and you can use the data in it.

File Status '92' indicates a "hard" record lock. Another access stream has locked the record you are trying to access and you did not get a copy of it in your FD.

In a multiple-user environment you shouldn't regard File Status '90' or '92' as grounds for program abort but instead as grounds just for transaction cancellation. If your program receives either of these values, you should notify the terminal operator that the record involved is in use by another terminal operator and automatically cancel the transaction. Prompt the user to wait a short time and retry the transaction.

16.14 Suggestions for Handling Multiple-User Access

The VAXDEMO system, like most interactive business applications, includes functions to add records to an indexed file, change records in it, and delete records from it. These are the types of operations that are susceptible to conflict between concurrent users. You can modify the programs in VAXDEMO in these ways to make the system capable of multiple-user access:

1. Change the OPEN statement for MASTER.DAT to include the ALLOW-ING UPDATERS clause. This provides file sharing update capabilities to multiple access streams with record locking.

2. Expand File Status checking in all programs to recognize receipt of values '90' and '92' as nonabort situations. You'll need to provide a prompt such as RECORD IN USE; TRY AGAIN LATER when a program encounters a locked record. It's appropriate to cancel the transaction in these cases.

3. Change CUPD1 so that receiving File Status '22' on a WRITE is not regarded as grounds for an abend. Instead, develop logic to tell the operator (Mike in the example in section 16.8) that someone assigned the key to a new record during the time he or she was busy composing a new record with it!

4. Recompile and relink the programs.

5. Grant Execute privileges to group or world users for VAXDEMO.EXE. (You can't do this before changing the programs because security is specific to each version number of a file!)

6. Grant **R**ead and **W**rite privileges to group or world users for MASTER.DAT.

ARCHIVE.DAT is currently a sequential file OPENed for OUTPUT by program CDEL1. This makes it impossible to share access to it. If I were going to set up VAXDEMO for multiple users, I would change the organization of ARCHIVE.DAT to indexed. To prevent the possibility of duplicate keys on records in the file I would rearrange fields in the archive record format so that the primary key became a group name that encompassed the customer ID, date, and time fields. With these changes ARCHIVE.DAT could be shared among multiple users just as is MASTER.DAT is, and all deleted records would be in one file.

16.15 Additional Information on File Sharing

You can find additional information about file sharing and record locking in Chapter 13 of *VAX Cobol User Manual*, order number AA-H632E-TE. I have put information about this and other Digital Equipment Corporation manuals in Appendix C.

16.16 Chapter Summary

Direct transfer between functions lets experienced system users bypass presentation of a menu when they already know the selection code of the function they want to perform. Installing direct transfer capabilities does not detract from the activities of a *casual system user*, since normal menu use remains.

To implement direct transfer, each functional subprogram must be able to accept and detect a special form of prompt response by the operator. You need to designate a special *transfer command* such as the equal sign (=) to preface prompt responses that request direct transfer.

You should implement direct transfer by making the menu program into a *flow of control router* rather than by putting branching logic into all functional subprograms. This minimizes the amount of code needed to accomplish direct transfer and greatly reduces program maintenance. As a router the menu program always receives control from all subprograms, even when a direct transfer is requested. If the menu program detects a valid direct transfer request it omits presentation of the menu screen and routes control to another function, just as if it had been selected from the menu screen.

File sharing and *record locking* are advanced topics that you must consider in most interactive VAX business applications. When multiple people use the same interactive system at the same time they share updating functions in the same files. Two or more users trying to update the same record at the same time can conflict with each other and damage data integrity.

Concurrent file use is addressed on the VAX as four issues in a hierarchy: disk residency, file access privileges, file sharing, and record locking. To arrange record locking you have to consider the three other issues first.

Disk residency is the first concurrent file use issue. This just means that for file sharing to be possible, files have to be on disk.

The second issue of concurrent use is *file access privileges*. The VMS operating system normally limits access to these files to the programmer who creates them. You can use the $ SET PROT command to open up access to these files. You need to give users both **R**ead and **W**rite access to allow users to update files (to enjoy I-O access). You can check current file security settings using the $ DIR/PROT command. File access privileges are specific to each version number of a file. For example, if you create a new .EXE file, the new file will be limited to owner access until you grant other users file access privileges to execute it.

The third issue of concurrent access is file sharing. An *access stream* is the series of file and record operations being performed by a single user. Each OPEN verb creates an access stream and the CLOSE verb terminates it. How you OPEN a file (INPUT, OUTPUT, I-O, or EXTEND) determines what you can do with the file. How you code ALLOWING on the OPEN statement (NO OTHERS, READERS, WRITERS, or UPDATERS) determines what other (subsequent) access streams can do with the file concurrently. If you don't specify the ALLOWING clause on the OPEN I-O statement, the default ALLOWING NO OTHERS applies. This locks the entire file to others while you are using it. When a program tries to open a file in a mode that conflicts with the ALLOWING specification of an existing access stream, it receives a File Status value of '91' for the OPEN.

Record locking is the final concurrent access issue. A record lock makes just one record (not an entire file) inaccessible to all but one file user. The VAX provides *automatic record locking* and *manual record locking*. To get automatic record locking you just specify the ALLOWING clause of the OPEN statement to permit file sharing. To get manual record locking you have to use the clause APPLY LOCK-HOLDING in a special

I-O-CONTROL SECTION, use ALLOWING on your OPEN statement, and use ALLOWING on *each* READ, WRITE, REWRITE, or START.

Automatic record locking locks one record per access stream at a time. The lock is applied when you READ the record. During the time that the lock is in effect, any other access stream that tries to access the record will receive either File Status '90' or '92' for READ, DELETE, or START. The lock on a record is released when you READ another record, you REWRITE the record, you DELETE it, you CLOSE the file, or you execute the UNLOCK RECORD statement.

File Status '90' indicates a "soft" record lock. It means that the record you are trying to access is held ("locked") by another access stream but that you did get a copy of the record in your FD. File Status '92' indicates a "hard" record lock. Another access stream has locked the record and you did not get a copy of it in your FD. In a multiple-user environment you shouldn't regard File Status '90' or '92' as grounds for program abort but instead as grounds just for transaction cancellation.

You can install direct transfer in my VAXDEMO demonstration system to experiment with it. Begin by copying the SINQU1X stub testing program and creating testing stubs for all functional programs. Fully test VAXDEMOX, a version of the menu with direct transfer logic installed. Then add similar direct transfer to the functional subprograms and replace stubs with real programs testing each one individually.

You can also modify VAXDEMO to make the system capable of multiple-user access. Change OPEN statements to include the ALLOWING UPDATERS clause and expand File Status checking in all programs to recognize receipt of values '90' and '92' as nonabort situations. You'll also have to change CUPD1 so that receiving File Status '22' on a WRITE is not regarded as grounds for an abend. Recompile and linkage edit the programs and grant appropriate execute, read, and write file access privileges to categories of users. You should also make ARCHIVE.DAT an indexed file instead of a sequential one so that you can able to share it among multiple users just like MASTER.DAT.

16.17 Important Terms

Casual system user   A person who uses a system infrequently and is best served by making function selections from a menu.

Experienced system user   A person who uses a system frequently enough to remember the selection codes for functions. This type of user often finds direct transfer more convenient than selecting functions from a menu.

Direct transfer   Transfer of control from one interactive program to another without viewing a menu screen.

Direct transfer command   A special character such as the equal sign used in front of a destination code to request a direct transfer.

Destination code   The menu selection code, entered with a direct transfer command, that indicates what function you want to transfer to.

Control flow router   The way a menu program operates when logic to handle direct transfer is included in it.

Concurrent file use   Access to a disk file by more than one program (access stream) at a time.

Access stream   The series of file and record operations being performed by a single user. Each OPEN verb creates an access stream, and the CLOSE verb terminates it.

Disk residency   Existing on random access disk as opposed to magnetic tape.

File access privileges   The four categories of actions recognized by VAX file system security: execute, read, write, and delete access.

File sharing   Access to a disk file by more than one program (access stream) at a time; a synonym for concurrent file use.

Record locking   One access stream preventing another access stream from accessing an individual record in a file.

Automatic record locking   Record locking provided by Record Management Services when you READ a record, a service you can obtain just by allowing file sharing with the OPEN . . . ALLOWING clause.

Manual record locking   Record locking you must arrange for yourself using the ALLOWING clause on READ, WRITE, REWRITE, and DELETE verbs.

ALLOWING   An optional clause of the OPEN and input/output verbs that establishes file sharing for automatic record locking and the locks themselves for manual record locking.

Soft record lock   Associated with File Status '90', this means that a record is locked by another access stream but you can read the data in the record (it is in the FD in your program).

Hard record lock   Associated with File Status '92', this means that a record is locked by another access stream and you can't even read it.

Appendix A

REVIEW QUESTIONS, EXERCISES, AND SELECTED ANSWERS

This appendix contains fill-in-the-blank review questions, problems, and exercises arranged by chapter. *You can find answers to the even-numbered items at the end of this appendix.*

An economically priced student workbook paralleling *VAX COBOL On-Line* is available from Stipes Publishing Company, 10-12 Chester Street, Champaign, Illinois 61824, telephone (217) 356-8391. The workbook contains teaching and lecture materials and a complete series of student lab exercises suitable for college course use. Appendix E describes how to get the source code for all programs in this book on diskette, as an aid in running them for these exercises.

CHAPTER 1: INTRODUCTION TO INTERACTIVE PROCESSING

REVIEW QUIZ

In all review questions fill in each blank with the appropriate word. In all cases each underscore is intended to be replaced by a single word. (Question and problem numbers relate to chapters but the numbering is *not* tied to section numbers.)

    1.1 First generation (vacuum tube) and second generation (transistorized) computers of the 1950–1964 era were designed to operate as _____ machines, not to support _____ processing.

    1.2 Batch processing is typified by a " _____ / _____ / _____ " work flow.

    1.3 Technological advances in disk storage and video terminal technology in the late 1960s paved the way for the advent of _____ processing.

1.4   The term *on-line* came to be associated with interactive process-ing because this form of processing required _____ _____ to be on-line rather than off-line when process-ing was underway.

1.5   When parts of computer applications that had been processed in a batch mode were adapted to on-line processing, these ele-ments were sometimes said to be examples of _____ _____.

1.6   Terminals communicating with a computer system over tele-phone lines are said to be accomplishing _____.

1.7   A common data transmission rate over ordinary telephone lines is _____ bits per second.

1.8   The purpose of a modem is to _____ digital computer signals into _____ for conveyance by the telephone network.

1.9   In modern business data processing systems, _____ and _____ processing modes coexist, each providing part of the processing support.

1.10   Modern on-line business data processing systems usually require information to be stored in _____ _____ such as those supported by RMS on the VAX or VSAM on IBM main-frames.

PROBLEMS FOR CHAPTER 1

1.11   Define how batch processing and interactive processing differ in the scheduling of work for processing by the computer system.

1.12   Explain how the term *on-line* came to be associated with inter-active data processing.

1.13   In what significant way does a *real-time* processing situation dif-fer from interactive processing?

1.14   What purpose does a modem serve and why is it a necessary component of many teleprocessing systems?

1.15   Did on-line processing replace batch processing? Explain why or why not.

1.16   A certain data screen contains 1,015 characters. How long (in seconds accurate to tenths) will it take to transmit this screen using a 1200 bits per second modem?

1.17 A particular business application requires the uploading of about 130,000 characters of data from a spreadsheet to a mini-computer every month. Assume that a 2400 bits per second modem costs $179 and a 1200 bits per second modem costs $99. Suppose you were trying to justify buying the higher speed modem. How long would you have to use the 2400 bits per second modem to save as much on telephone line charges as the difference in price between the modems? Assume that telephone line charges are 5.7 cents per minute.

1.18 Explain what ISDN stands for and how this modern telephone system development may change the configuration of telepro-cessing equipment.

CHAPTER 2: COMPARING VAX AND IBM/CICS ON-LINE PROCESSING

REVIEW QUIZ

2.1 In the _____ environment on-line programming usually involves the use of the _____ and _____ verbs.

2.2 In the _____ environment CICS (Customer Information Control System) is used with COBOL to program on-line applications.

2.3 An on-line COBOL program is the _____ between a computer terminal user and information stored in disk files.

2.4 In the VAX environment an on-line program deals with _____ in the same way a batch program does.

2.5 Under _____ on-line programming the computer program is inactive when the terminal operator is entering information into a screen.

2.6 Under *conversational* on-line programming the interactive program is _____ during the time that a terminal operator enters data into a screen.

2.7 _____ is an example of a teleprocessing monitor program that deals with terminals and files on behalf of application programs.

2.8   A COBOL program that deals with CICS is really a _____, since it is _____ by CICS.

2.9   Graduating from batch to interactive programming in the VAX environment requires learning about extensions to the _____ and _____ verbs.

2.10   Moving from batch to interactive programming on an IBM mainframe using CICS requires learning _____ _____.

PROBLEMS FOR CHAPTER 2

2.11   Explain some of the reasons why minicomputer vendors decided to have operating systems directly support interactive processing instead of adopting a "batch-oriented" philosophy.

2.12   What historical factor affects the IBM mainframe and its approach to interactive processing?

2.13   Why is a teleprocessing monitor program such as CICS necessary on an IBM mainframe but not on a VAX?

2.14   In the VAX environment, which COBOL verbs handle communication between your program and a computer terminal?

2.15   In a VAX program when does each keystroke entered at a terminal reach the operating system? When does it reach the program?

2.16   Identify some factors that complicate on-line programming on IBM mainframes.

CHAPTER 3: MENU-BASED INTERACTIVE SYSTEMS

REVIEW QUIZ

3.1   The acronym ACID can be used to describe the generic functions of an interactive business data processing system. The letters of this acronym stand for _____, _____, _____, and _____.

3.2   The menu of a menu-based on-line system allows the computer terminal operator to _____ a desired _____.

3.3   The structure of a menu-based on-line system can be depicted with a _____ _____.

3.4 The three generic or "geographic" areas of a formatted on-line screen are _____, _____, _____, and they are usually used for _____, _____, and _____.

3.5 A message from an interactive program to the computer terminal operator is often called a _____.

3.6 Some menu-based on-line systems provide the means to _____ directly between functions without having to go through _____.

3.7 Help screens are a modern innovation of on-line data processing systems. If a terminal operator receives information specific to the task being performed, as opposed to general information, the help screen is said to be _____ _____.

3.8 With a paging display each screen completely _____ another, whereas with scrolling displays each new line entered appears at the screen _____.

3.9 On-line system security may require the entry of an _____ and a _____ before an operator can begin work.

3.10 Terminal operators require much more _____ to use a command-based interactive system than to use a menu-based system.

PROBLEMS FOR CHAPTER 3

3.11 List the generic functions of an interactive business data processing system and describe what these functions allow you to do.

3.12 Explain the difference between a paging display and a scrolling display.

3.13 Design a menu screen for the system you thought about in question 11 and sketch it out. Your sketch can be informal and does not need to be done on a grid chart, but follow the guidelines presented in this chapter for use of screen geography.

3.14 A certain on-line screen is used to enter data about a customer's name, address, and balance due in payment for orders. Identify the kinds of information a general help screen should give a terminal operator. Contrast this with the information a context-sensitive help screen might provide for this function.

3.15 Describe why you might choose to use a command-based structure for a certain on-line application as opposed to a menu-based structure. Mention what benefit this would bring to the terminal operator as well as how it might penalize him or her.

3.16 Sketch a hierarchy chart for a small on-line system that will allow you to maintain information about your checking account. Identify functions such as adding new check records to a file (for checks written), inquiring about a check, updating a check to show that it has been cashed, and so forth. Assume that each function will be handled by a separate program. Arrange the hierarchy chart with a menu program at the top.

CHAPTER 4: DESIGNING COMPUTER TERMINAL SCREENS

REVIEW QUIZ

4.1 The most common screen size for computer terminals is _____ characters by _____ lines.

4.2 Screen field attributes affect how characters are displayed on the terminal screen; the three common screen field display attributes are _____, _____, and _____.

4.3 VAX COBOL and the VT-100 family of computer terminals support advanced screen field display attributes, including _____ video, _____, and _____.

4.4 When a word processor is used to design the field layout of an on-line screen you should include a _____ _____ at the top and bottom to facilitate programming.

4.5 Three general areas exist on an on-line screen; the top part is commonly used for _____, the middle is used for _____, and the bottom is used for _____.

4.6 Computer screen titles and labeling are usually kept simple and plain because the _____ required to _____ each character of data affects the responsiveness of an interactive system.

4.7 Screen field labels should not include _____ because it clutters the screen and words should be used _____.

4.8 Communication from an interactive program to the computer terminal operator is usually called a _____ because it informs the operator either to correct an error with a correct entry or to take some other action.

4.9 Error messages produced by an on-line screen should be free of

_____ and should not _____ the terminal operator.

4.10 While it is not a requirement of VAX COBOL for the cursor to move from _____ to _____, and from the _____ side of the screen to the _____, this is often arranged because it is the way in which the English language is read.

PROBLEMS FOR CHAPTER 4

4.11 Why is it a good idea to design interactive business applications for a screen size of 80 characters per line and 24 lines?

4.12 Assume that an average 80 × 24 screen will be 60% full of characters that have to be transmitted to the terminal. How long will this data transmission take using a 2400 bit per second modem?

4.13 A systems analyst designed an 80 × 24 screen including ornate borders of asterisks on many titles and fields. The screen is now at 82% of its maximum character capacity. The terminal user is complaining about poor response time. If we remove excess ornamentation so that the screen consists of 55% of its maximum capacity, what will be the transmission time savings? (Assume use of a 2400 bits per second modem.)

4.14 Using an 80 × 24 screen design form or a word processor design a screen that will let you enter information about your friends and associates, such as name, address, telephone number, and birthday. Use screen geography as suggested in Chapter 4, including appropriate screen titles and labels. Neatly circle anything that should appear bright on the screen. Think through the operation of this screen. List criteria for field validations and compose a list of prompts that will be needed to program it. Make sure each prompt will fit on the screen.

4.15 Using an 80 × 24 screen design form or a word processor, design a screen that will let you enter information from your checking account (each check). Use screen geography as suggested in Chapter 4, including appropriate screen titles and labels. Neatly circle anything that should appear bright on the screen. Think through the operation of this screen. List criteria for field validations and compose a list of prompts that will be needed to program the screen. Make sure each prompt will fit on the screen.

CHAPTER 5: VAX FILE COMMANDS AND THE EDT TEXT EDITOR

REVIEW QUIZ

5.1   When you log onto the VAX you first enter your _____
       _____ and when asked, enter your _____.

5.2   To log off the VAX you enter the command $ _____.

5.3   Files on the VAX are named with a front part of one to
       _____ characters followed by a period and one to
       _____ characters in a suffix.

5.4   The $ TYPE command _____ a file while the $ DIR
       command gives you a _____ _____ files.

5.5   To make a copy of a file you use the $ COPY command and state
       first the _____ file and after it the _____ file.

5.6   When you use the $ APPEND command you copy one file to the
       _____ of another file.

5.7   When you copy a file to a filename that already exists the new
       filename is one _____ _____ higher.

5.8   To delete all but the current version of a file you use the $
       _____ command.

5.9   To delete all copies of CALC1.COB you have to code the com-
       mand $ _____ _____.

5.10   You want to tell VMS to temporarily stop sending data to your
       terminal. You press *<Ctrl>/*_____ to do this; to
       resume transmission you press *<Ctrl>/*_____.

PROBLEMS FOR CHAPTER 5

5.11   Explain the difference between VAX and VMS, and describe
       how the acronym DCL fits into this environment.

5.12   Describe how EDT keypad mode and line editing mode differ.

5.13   Enter this text into a file named ALICE.DAT using EDT:

               The time has come,
               the walrus said,
               to talk of many things.
               Sailing ships, and sealing wax,
               and cabbages and kings.

After entering in the text, end your EDT editing session and print the file. Then rename this file OYSTER.DAT and print it again.

5.14 Make a list of eight people by writing the name of each on a different line. Then next to each name write the person's birthday (not including year), favorite color, and favorite animal. For example, you can start with this information about me:

```
JIM JANOSSY 09-09 BLUE WOMBAT
```

Then use EDT keypad or line editing mode to enter this information into a file named FOLKS.DAT. When you have finished the entry process, end your EDT session and print the file.

5.15 After completing problems 5.13 and 5.14 append your OYSTER.DAT file to your FOLKS.DAT file. Then print FOLKS.DAT and explain how it is different than when you created it.

5.16 Copy OYSTER.DAT to a file named X.DAT. Then copy X.DAT to OYSTER.DAT three times. Do a directory listing, and explain why it shows multiple copies of OYSTER.DAT and how VMS tells them apart.

CHAPTER 6: COMPILING, LINKAGE EDITING, AND RUNNING ON THE VAX

REVIEW QUIZ

6.1 To process the source code for a program named ABCD.COB into executable form you have to _____ it then _____ _____ it.

6.2 To get a listing file of your source code from the VAX COBOL compiler you invoke it with the option _____.

6.3 If you use the COPY compiler directive in your program to copy in lines from a copy library, you will not see them in your .LIS file from the compiler unless you use the compiler's _____ option.

6.4 To linkage edit a single program named ABCD.OBJ you enter the command $ _____ _____.

6.5 To linkage edit the .OBJ files of main program WIZARD and subprograms BOING and BOUNCE that are CALLed by it you enter the command $ _____.

6.6 To execute main program WIZARD on the VAX you enter the command $ _____ _____.

6.7 You can view the .LIS file produced by the VAX COBOL compiler using the $ _____ command or _____.

6.8 On the VAX you name a command file with the suffix _____.

6.9 To execute a command file you preface its name with the symbol _____.

6.10 VMS stores your last 20 commands (which you entered at the dollar sign prompt). To retrieve these commands you press the <_____ _____> key.

PROBLEMS FOR CHAPTER 6

Due to the skills-building nature of this chapter you should do problems 6.11 through 6.15 in sequence, since they refer to one another.

6.11 Enter the following small program into the VAX system using EDT. It is in VAX terminal format: no COBOL line numbers and no need to indent column 8 to distinguish it from comment column 7. When you have entered the program print it with your local $ PR command:

```
IDENTIFICATION DIVISION.
PROGRAM-ID.     CH6Q11.
*
ENVIRONMENT DIVISION.
*
DATA DIVISION.
WORKING-STORAGE SECTION.
 01 WS-SUB       PIC 9(2) VALUE 0.
*
PROCEDURE DIVISION.
0000-MAINLINE.
    DISPLAY '' AT LINE 1 COLUMN 1 ERASE TO END
    OF SCREEN.
    PERFORM
      VARYING WS-SUB FROM 8 BY 1
```

```
      UNTIL WS-SUB > 20
        DISPLAY 'VAX COBOL IS FUN!'
            AT LINE WS-SUB COLUMN WS-SUB
   END-PERFORM.
   STOP RUN.
```

6.12 Compile Program CH6Q11 using the appropriate compiler option to get a source code listing. Then use your local command to print the compiler listing.

6.13 Use the $ LINK command to linkage edit your CH6Q11.OBJ file. What happens on the screen after you execute the $ LINK command?

6.14 Use the $ RUN command to execute your CH6Q11.EXE file. Describe what happens on the screen and explain why this happens as a result of the in-line PERFORM statement in the program.

6.15 This program presents 14 lines on the screen all at the same intensity. After completing problems 6.11 through 6.14 see if you can modify this program to present the even-numbered lines at bright intensity but the odd-numbered lines at normal intensity blinking. (*Hint*: Think about using two different PERFORMs to do this, with different FROM and BY values. You don't have to DISPLAY the lines in strict ascending sequence. Peek ahead and look at the beginning of Chapter 7.)

CHAPTER 7: ACCEPT AND DISPLAY IN VAX COBOL

REVIEW QUIZ

7.1 VAX COBOL provides the _____ and _____ verbs to support program-to-terminal communication.

7.2 If ACCEPT is coded without the word FROM, or with FROM and a LINE and COLUMN specification, it seeks input from the _____ _____.

7.3 Keystrokes you enter when ACCEPT is being executed are placed into the receiving field when you press the _____ key.

7.4 In the VAX environment, information output with DISPLAY is automatically assigned to the _____.

7.5 The _____ and _____ specifications of DISPLAY position the data to be presented at specific screen locations.

7.6 The terminal screen can be completely erased by coding (fill in the complete program statement) _____.

7.7 In order to DISPLAY a field at bright intensity with a short warning tone you code _____ and _____ _____.

7.8 If you ACCEPT a field with the REVERSED option it appears as _____ characters on a _____ background.

7.9 The ACCEPT option PROTECTED limits the entry of characters in a field to the _____ _____.

7.10 The WITH CONVERSION option is often used when numeric data is being input via the keyboard to insure that the data received is _____, to remove an explicit _____ _____ and to supply leading _____.

PROBLEMS FOR CHAPTER 7

7.11 The ACCEPT verb gives your COBOL program the ability to receive communication from a computer terminal. Explain *when* the program receives the data being entered in response to ACCEPT. Does the program get the data keystroke by keystroke or the entire field at once?

7.12 Explain what an interactive program must do in numeric field de-editing.

7.13 What do you accomplish by coding the WITH CONVERSION option of the ACCEPT verb and what are its limitations?

7.14 Code a DISPLAY verb to completely clear your terminal screen. Follow this with a second DISPLAY verb that puts your name centered at the top of the screen in extra-bright characters.

7.15 We want to present this message on a clear screen on a computer terminal: ** THIS IS A TEST **. Code *one* VAX COBOL DISPLAY statement that will present this message in the middle of an 80 × 24 screen that has been cleared of any other information. Make the terminal beep when the text is sent to it.

7.16 In VAX COBOL you can ACCEPT a field PROTECTED. How does the PROTECTED option change the way the ACCEPT verb works?

CHAPTER 8: CALC1: YOUR FIRST CONVERSATIONAL PROGRAM

REVIEW QUIZ

8.1 A conversational interactive program in the VAX environment has a logic structure that contains a _____, a "_____ . . . _____", and an _____, just as does a batch program.

8.2 Every time control passes through the main processing loop in a conversational interactive program a _____ has been processed.

8.3 At the end of the main processing loop in a conversational interactive program the operator controls processing in the way he or she responds to a _____.

8.4 DISPLAYs executed once at the beginning of an interactive program present _____ on the screen that need to be written _____ no matter how many _____ are to be processed.

8.5 In a conversational interactive program, statements at the start of the processing loop can display _____ in screen entry fields to eliminate data left by a previous transaction.

8.6 Unless you use special programming VAX COBOL's ACCEPT does not allow the use of the cursor movement _____ keys or the _____ key.

8.7 If you enter no data in response to an ACCEPT . . . WITH CONVERSION and immediately press the **<Return>** key, a numeric receiving field is given a value of _____.

8.8 If you enter no data in response to an ACCEPT and you immediately press the **<Return>** key, an alphanumeric receiving field is given a value of _____.

8.9 The _____ option of ACCEPT can be used to give a field a standard value when the terminal operator does not enter one, but the value does not show on the screen.

8.10 If you enter fewer characters into a screen field than an alphanumeric receiving field can accommodate, the value entered is

_____ _____ in the receiving field and the remaining positions are filled with _____.

PROBLEMS FOR CHAPTER 8

These problems require you to actually compile, link, and run the CALC1 program discussed in Chapter 8. You can key-enter this program from Figure 8.4 or upload it to your VAX system from the ASCII files available on diskette as described in Appendix E. It's assumed that you will do task 8.11 before answering questions 8.12 to 8.16.

8.11 Use the $ COBOL/LIST command to compile the CALC1 program. Print the .LIS file so that you can see its source code. Then use the $ LINK command to linkage edit it. With its source code next to your terminal, use the $ RUN command to execute CALC1. Put in several combinations of numbers and see how the program responds to your entries. Try entering some data that is not numeric or is too large or too small for the field.

Answer these questions only after running and "playing with" CALC1:

8.12 Describe what actions are accomplished one time in BOJ in CALC1.

8.13 Explain what condition ends the processing loop of CALC1.

8.14 Describe what WITH CONVERSION coded at line 51 of CALC1 does (Figure 8.4), and give some of its limitations.

8.15 Run CALC1 and enter QUANTITY as 2,496, then press **<Return>**. Explain what happens and why.

8.16 Run CALC1, press **<Return>** without entering a value for QUANTITY, and press **<Return>** without entering a value for PRICE. Explain what happens and why.

CHAPTER 9: CALC2 AND CALC3: MORE EFFECTIVE SCREEN HANDLING

REVIEW QUIZ

9.1 Video DISPLAY options (attributes) of VT-100 and similar terminals include _____, _____, _____, _____, _____, and _____.

9.2 Making a field on a screen _____ can draw operator attention to an error but can produce a harsh and unpleasant screen if overused.

9.3 Screen labels are often DISPLAYed with _____ intensity so that they stand out from data entry fields.

9.4 When WITH CONVERSION is used on a DISPLAY statement and a PIC S9(5)V99 field containing -12345v67 is presented, the field appears with _____ _____ and _____ but without a _____.

9.5 When a column of numbers must be presented on a screen WITH CONVERSION on, DISPLAY statements cannot arrange to _____ _____ their decimal points.

9.6 Instead of using WITH CONVERSION on a DISPLAY statement, a numeric field can be shown in a formatted manner by moving it to a _____ _____ _____ and then DISPLAYing that field.

9.7 A field can be _____ after entry in order to present it in a formatted manner.

9.8 The customary way to DISPLAY the negative sign on a signed numeric field (according to accounting conventions) is _____ the number.

9.9 If a PIC 999V99 value is entered, MOVEd to a PIC ZZZ.99 field, and the PIC ZZZ.99 field redisplayed, you can describe the PIC ZZZ.99 field as a _____ _____ _____.

9.10 The WITH CONVERSION clause on an ACCEPT statement with a PIC 9(5)V99 receiving field will not allow entry of a _____ as part of a valid numeric entry.

PROBLEMS FOR CHAPTER 9

These problems require you to actually compile, link, and run the CALC2 and CALC3 programs discussed in Chapter 9. You can key-enter these programs or upload them to your VAX system from the ASCII files available on diskette as described in Appendix E. It's assumed that you will do task 9.11 before answering questions 9.12 to 9.16.

9.11 Use the $ COBOL/LIST command to compile the CALC2 program. Print the .LIS file so that you can see the source code.

Then use the $ LINK command to linkage edit it. With its source code next to your terminal, use the $ RUN command to execute CALC2. Put in several combinations of numbers and see how the program responds to your entries. Try entering some data that is not numeric or is too large or small for the field. Then repeat the same actions for the CALC3 program.

Answer these questions only after running and "playing with" CALC1 (Chapter 8), CALC2, and CALC3:

9.12 Run CALC2 and identify things it does differently than CALC1. Which version of the program is more pleasing to work with? Give some specific reasons to support your statements.

9.13 Run CALC3, then explain the benefit of redisplaying an entry field without reverse video, using (if the field is numeric) a numeric formatted field.

9.14 The Podunk Power Company operates two coal-fired electric power plants and a nuclear reactor to serve a small region. The company needs a computational screen to enter customer name and billing information. Meter readers examine each customer's electric meter each month and record the number on the dial. When the previous month's meter reading is subtracted from the present reading, the resulting value indicates how many units of electricity the customer used in the billing period. Design a screen for the Podunk Power Company following good screen design practices. This screen should carry the following information and data:

- Title at the top including the company name.
- Entry fields for customer name, present electric meter reading (5 digits), and previous meter reading.
- A field for the difference between present and previous meter reading (not entered, but to be computed by the program).
- A field for cost per unit of electricity, which will be fixed at 87.5 cents.
- Computed cost of electricity used, which can be as large as $99,999,999.99.
- The prompt field at the bottom of the screen.

9.15 After completing the screen design indicated in problem 9.14, develop a program that will use your Podunk Power Company screen to allow entry of the customer name, present electric meter reading, and previous meter reading. The program should:

a. Accept entry of the customer name, present reading, and previous reading.
b. Compute the units of electricity used by subtracting the previous meter reading from the current reading and display the number of units used. (*Note:* "Rollover" may occur if, for example, the previous reading was 99998 and the current reading is 00005. Your logic has to handle this!)
c. Calculate the cost of the electricity used at a fixed rate of $ 0.875 per unit and display the cost on the screen. Your answer may need rounding.

Code and test your program using CALC3 as a guide. Then enter a present meter reading of 00012 and previous meter reading of 99997. If your program does not return a value of 15 units of electricity used, for a cost of $13.13, go back and check your logic! (Have you coded computations with COMPUTE result-field ROUNDED = qty-units * .875?)

CHAPTER 10: CREATING AND USING INDEXED FILES

REVIEW QUIZ

10.1 Because of their construction, disk devices permit _____ _____ to individual records in a file.

10.2 When you store information in a file and you expect to access individual records in it, you have to be able to _____ _____ each record.

10.3 The _____ _____ of a record in an indexed file must be unique.

10.4 A _____ _____ tells where the data is physically stored on disk.

10.5 A _____ _____ is just a unique identifier and has nothing to do with where the data is stored.

10.6 To access records in a sequential file you have to READ them _____ _____ _____.

10.7   For a relative file the key of each record is a _____ key.

10.8   For an indexed file the key of each record is a _____ key.

10.9   An indexed file is composed of a _____ component and an _____.

10.10 An alternate key _____ _____ have to be unique to one record.

10.11 If you OPEN a file for I-O you can use the _____ verb to put records into it, the _____ verb to obtain records from it, and the _____ verb to replace records in it after you have updated them.

CODING EXERCISES FOR CHAPTER 10

10.12 Complete the following SELECT/ASSIGN statement for a program that will access an indexed file of payroll data using RANDOM access:

```
SELECT PAYROLL-FILE   ASSIGN TO PAYFILE
            _____ IS _____
            _____ IS _____
            _____ IS _____
            _____ IS _____
            _____ IS _____.
```

The key of the record is called PD-EMPLOYEE-ID in the file description. An alternate key is employee social security number, called PR-EMPLOYEE-SSN in the file description. Make up any other names that you need to code this SELECT/ASSIGN statement. (*Note: Is the alternate key unique? What if it is not a required field?*)

10.13 Compose a SELECT/ASSIGN statement for a program that will access an indexed file of credit card payments using RANDOM access. The key of the record is a group name PYMT-ID in the file description, which has these two fields coded under it: PYMT-ID-ACCT-NO and PYMT-ID-DATE. PYMT-ID-DATE is also an alternate key. Make up any other names you need to code this SELECT/ASSIGN statement.

```
SELECT CRED-PAY-FILE ASSIGN TO PYMTFILE
_____ IS _____
_____ IS _____
_____ IS _____
_____ IS _____
_____ IS _____ .
```

PROBLEMS FOR CHAPTER 10

These work items require you to actually compile, link, and run the IND-LOAD program. You can key-enter this program or upload it to your VAX system from the ASCII files available on diskette as described in Appendix E. It's assumed that you will do task 10.14 before answering questions 10.15 to 10.17.

10.14 Use the $ COBOL/LIST command to compile the INDLOAD program listed in Figure 10.6. Print the .LIS file so that you can see the source code. Then linkage edit the program using the $ LINK command. Compile the LISTALT program (Figure 10.7) and print its .LIS file. Linkage edit it with the $ LINK command.

Answer these questions only after preparing the INDLOAD and LISTALT programs as described in problem 10.14:

10.15 Make sure you have a copy of the CUSTOMER.DAT file in your VAX account. RUN the INDLOAD program. Use the $ DIR command to make sure you have created the MASTER.DAT indexed file. Use $ TYPE to see the contents of MASTER.DAT.

10.16 Run the LISTALT program. Compare your output to that shown in Figure 10.9 to make sure the program works properly. Then comment out lines 71 through 77 of the program and compile and linkage edit it again. Run it in its modified form and compare the output you receive for the second run to the output from the first. Explain how the outputs differ and why.

10.17 Delete your MASTER.DAT indexed file (you can always re-create it by running INDLOAD):

```
$ DELETE MASTER.DAT;*
```

Now run the LISTALT program again (for this exercise it doesn't matter whether lines 71–77 are active in it or not). What happens when you run LISTALT now? Use the chart of File Status values in Figure 10.7 to analyze your result.

10.18 Make a copy of the CUSTOMER.DAT file, naming it CUST2.DAT. Then use EDT to change the primary key value of Hilborn Technologies from 480114 to 080114. This will put the record out of ascending key sequence. Make a copy of INDLOAD.COB, naming it INDLOAD2.COB. Modify the SELECT/ASSIGN statements in INDLOAD2.COB so that the program reads your CUST2 sequential file and creates MASTER2.DAT. Compile, linkage edit, and run INDLOAD2 and see what information it displays on the screen. Use Figure 10.7 to help analyze your results.

CHAPTER 11: VAXDEMO: A COMPLETE MENU-BASED ON-LINE SYSTEM

REVIEW QUIZ

11.1 The name of the menu program is often the name of the _____ _____.

11.2 The heart of processing in a menu program is the identification of the operator's _____ of _____ _____ and passage of control to the correct subprogram to handle it.

11.3 When CALL is used in an interactive menu program, the subprogram invoked to handle a function remains active until all _____ the operator wishes to process with it are _____.

11.4 System date can be obtained once by a menu program in its _____ _____ _____ logic, but if _____ is to be DISPLAYed on the screen you have to obtain it frequently, since it changes continuously.

11.5 You can use the 1985 COBOL _____ verb instead of a serial "case-type" _____/_____ to identify the operator's menu selection.

11.6 Housing the DISPLAY statements that place the menu on the screen in a paragraph allows you to perform this logic in _____ _____ _____ and at the bottom of the _____ _____.

11.7 To limit redundant coding you can house the logic to DISPLAY the operator _____ and ACCEPT a _____ in a paragraph.

11.8 To test a menu program apart from functional subprograms you can code _____ programs that _____ control and then return it.

11.9 You prepare and compile menu and functional subprograms _____, producing an _____ _____ for each.

11.10 A single VAX command to linkage edit a menu and functional programs contains the_____ program name followed by each subprogram name, with names separated by _____.

PROBLEMS FOR CHAPTER 11

These problems require you to actually compile, link, and run the VAXDEMO menu program and four stub testing programs. You can key-enter these programs or upload them to your VAX system from the ASCII files available on diskette as described in Appendix E. It's assumed that you will do task 11.11 before answering questions 11.12 to 11.16.

11.11 Use the $ COBOL/LIST command to compile the VAXDEMO program. Print the .LIS file so that you can see the source code. Then compile the SINQU1, SUPD1, SDEL1, and SBROW1 stub testing programs and print the .LIS file for each. Use the appropriate $ LINK command to linkage edit these into one executable file.

Answer these questions only after preparing the VAXDEMO menu program and stub testing programs as described in problem 11.11:

11.12 Run VAXDEMO, make a menu selection of 2, and press *<Return>*. Then press *<Return>* again. Make several other valid (1, 2, 3, 4) menu choices. Make some invalid menu choices, such as 4, 5, T, K, and so forth. Keep track of how many valid and invalid choices you make. When you have made at least 10 choices, choose menu selection Q to quit. Compare your manually tabulated counts to the end-of-job messages produced by VAXDEMO and describe what the WS-TRANS-COUNT field actually tells you.

11.13 Run VAXDEMO again and over the course of three minutes press the *<Return>* key several times without making any menu choices. Then explain why I put the ACCEPT and DISPLAY of the system time in paragraph 2700 instead of in paragraph 2600 and what effect this has on program operation.

11.14 What is the purpose of the EVALUATE statement at lines 62 through 68 of VAXDEMO? With what other COBOL syntax could you code this?

11.15 Lines 70 through 74 of VAXDEMO contain an IF/ELSE statement. Why is 2600-DISPLAY-MENU performed in one case and not the other?

11.16 Explain why I coded the compound condition OR at line 46 in VAXDEMO.

CHAPTER 12: INTERACTIVE INQUIRY: PROGRAM CINQU1

REVIEW QUIZ

12.1 An interactive inquiry program gives you "_____" access to information stored in an indexed file or database.

12.2 When you start an interactive inquiry program the _____ _____ are present but no data is on the screen.

12.3 If you enter a nonexistent key value at the prompt in an interactive inquiry program, you'll get a prompt on the screen that indicates "_____ _____ _____."

12.4 On an action diagram each bracket represents _____ _____ of COBOL source code.

12.5 On an action diagram the highest level of program logic is shown at the _____ side while the lowest level of logic is at the _____ side.

12.6 In beginning of job, an interactive inquiry program has to _____ the indexed file and obtain your first _____ _____ .

12.7 When you code the SELECT/ASSIGN statement for an indexed file with ACCESS MODE IS _____ the READ verb will never reach _____ _____ _____ .

12.8 You will get a first-byte File Status value of _____ for a random mode READ when you obtain the record you were seeking.

12.9   You will get a File Status value of _____ for a random mode READ when there is no record in the indexed file with the key you indicated.

12.10 You must check for a File Status value of _____ when you OPEN or CLOSE an indexed file as an indication of successful processing.

PROBLEMS FOR CHAPTER 12

These problems require you to actually compile, link, and run the VAXDEMO menu program, CINQU1 inquiry program, and SUPD1, SDEL1, and SBROW1 stub testing programs. You can key-enter these programs or upload them to your VAX system from the ASCII files available on diskette as described in Appendix E. It's assumed that you will do task 12.11 before answering questions 12.12 to 12.16, and that you will have already accomplished all but the tasks involving CINQU1 in the exercises following Chapters 10 (loading your indexed file) and 11 (VAXDEMO menu program).

12.11 Use the $ COBOL/LIST command to compile the CINQU1 program. Print the .LIS file so that you can see the source code. Change line 63 of the VAXDEMO program so that it CALLS 'CINQU1' instead of 'SINQU1'. Then compile VAXDEMO again. Finally, use the $ LINK command to link together the menu, functional program CINQU1, and the stub programs SUPD1, SDEL1, and SBROW1.

Answer these questions only after preparing the VAXDEMO menu program and others as described in problem 12.11:

12.12 Use the VMS $ TYPE command to look at the contents of your MASTER.DAT indexed file. (As created and loaded in Chapter 10 this will have 20 records in it.) Write down some of the key values, then run VAXDEMO and select function 1. Explain what happens if you enter a key value at the CINQU1 prompt and a record exists in the customer master file with that key.

12.13 Explain what happens if you enter a key value at the CINQU1 prompt and no record exists in the customer master file with that key.

12.14 Start VAXDEMO, select function 1, and inquire about five records (one at a time). Use four record keys that exist and one that does not exist. Immediately afterward enter "quit" at the CINQU1 prompt, then choose the "q" menu selection from VAXDEMO. Explain why the transaction count (shown last by VAXDEMO end-of-job logic) is shown with the value that it is.

12.15 When viewing a record on the CINQU1 screen try using the arrow keys to move the cursor to the customer name field to change the data value in it. Explain what happens.

12.16 Try entering only part of a key value at the CINQU1 prompt, such as 60053 (the actual record key is 600536). Press *<Return>* and explain what happens and why.

CHAPTER 13: INTERACTIVE ADD/CHANGE: PROGRAM CUPD1

REVIEW QUIZ

13.1 Since the processing of an add transaction and the processing of a change transaction involve identical field _____ actions, combining the handling of these functions eliminates _____ coding.

13.2 A combined interactive add/change program determines for itself whether an add or change is underway by doing a _____ _____ of the indexed file or database using the _____ entered by the terminal operator.

13.3 If a record add is underway, processing of the transaction should conclude with a _____ to the indexed file.

13.4 If a record change is underway, processing of the transaction should conclude with a _____ to the indexed file.

13.5 The ability for a terminal operator to end processing of a transaction before completing it is known as _____ _____ and is initiated in Program CUPD1 by entering a _____ in a field.

13.6 You can move data to _____ _____ _____ to format it for DISPLAY on the screen; you can also ACCEPT data into these fields.

13.7 Processing an add or change transaction involves three parts: _____ actions, _____ of _____ for each field, and _____ actions.

13.8 A terminal operator using the CUPD1 program to process a change transaction presses **<Return>** in a field without entering any data. This means that the operator intends the existing data in the field to be _____ .

13.9 Validation of data entered into a field, such as state abbreviation, is sometimes done by _____ a _____ .

13.10 Since _____ _____ cannot handle entry of a dollar sign or commas, you can receive the data for a numeric field as a character string and CALL a subprogram such as NUM-CHEK to _____ it.

PROBLEMS FOR CHAPTER 13

These problems require you to actually compile, link, and run the VAXDEMO menu program, CINQU1 inquiry program, CUPD1 add/change program, subprograms NUMCHEK and PLACNAME, and three stub testing programs. You can key-enter these programs or upload them to your VAX system from the ASCII files available on diskette as described in Appendix E. It's assumed that you will do task 13.11 before answering questions 13.12 to 13.16 and that you will have already accomplished all but the tasks involving CUPD1 in the exercises following Chapters 10, 11, and 12.

13.11 Use the $ COBOL/LIST command to compile the CUPD1 program. Print the .LIS file so that you can see the source code. Compile subprograms NUMCHEK and PLACNAME using $ COBOL/LIST. Print the .LIS file for each of these three new programs. Change line 64 of the VAXDEMO program so that it CALLs 'CUPD1' instead of 'SUPD1'. Then compile VAXDEMO again. Finally, use the $ LINK command discussed in this chapter to link together the menu, functional subprograms CINQU1 and CUPD1, NUMCHEK, PLACNAME, and the stub programs SDEL1 and SBROW1.

Answer these questions only after preparing the VAXDEMO menu program and others as described in item 13.11. It is assumed that you have created and loaded an indexed file named MASTER.DAT as described in Chapter 10. For problems 13.12 to 13.16 $ RUN VAXDEMO as you answer the questions.

13.12 Use the VMS $ TYPE command to look at the contents of your MASTER.DAT indexed file. (As created and loaded in Chapter

10 this will have 20 records in it.) Write down some of the key values, then run VAXDEMO and select function 2. Explain what happens if you enter a key value at the CUPD1 prompt and a record already exists in the customer master file with that key.

13.13 Explain what happens if you enter a key value at the CUPD1 prompt and no record exists in the customer master file with that key.

13.14 Begin a change transaction using CUPD1. Change the name in an existing record, then press *<Return>* a few times to move the cursor to the zip code field. At the first position in the zip code field enter the backslash \ and press *<Return>*. Explain what happens. Then check on the contents of the record again and see if the name field has the original contents or the contents you changed it to.

13.15 Add a record to the customer master file using key value 500123. When you reach the state abbreviation field, enter ZZ, which is not the abbreviation of any province or state. Explain what happens and tell what two courses of action are available to you to continue working.

13.16 Attempt to change the record with key value 415002, entering a new value of 1600 for the credit limit. Describe what happens. Try entering this new credit limit as 1600.00 and indicate what happens with that. Then try entering a credit limit exactly twice this amount as 320000 and see if that works.

CHAPTER 14: INTERACTIVE DELETE: PROGRAM CDEL1

REVIEW QUIZ

14.1 A deletion function immediately _____ a record from an _____ _____, an action that is not _____.

14.2 Access to a delete function can be made more difficult or impossible for unauthorized personnel by requiring the entry of an _____ _____ and a _____.

14.3 A simple mechanism for access security can be implemented using a _____ to house _____ _____ and _____.

14.4   A security mechanism installed in the _____ program can be used to control access to the entire on-line system.

14.5   A hardcoded table-stored security mechanism is prone to a breach of security if an unauthorized person _____ the _____ _____.

14.6   When a deletion transaction is being processed you display the record to be deleted on the screen so that the operator can _____ that it is to be _____.

14.7   If you want to be able to restore a record deleted by mistake, the record can be _____ to a _____ _____ before the DELETE verb is executed.

14.8   EDP auditors, accounting personnel, and/or investigators may periodically examine the way a business data processing system works to verify that it operates _____ and is being used only for _____ purposes.

14.9   You can include an operator ID and the system date and time in the archived copy of a deleted record to establish an _____ _____ of deletion activities.

14.10 Many of the source code elements of a deletion program exist in an interactive _____ / _____ program, and you can rapidly build a deletion program from it.

PROBLEMS FOR CHAPTER 14

These problems require you to actually compile, link, and run the VAXDEMO menu program, CINQU1 inquiry program, CUPD1 add/change program, subprograms NUMCHEK and PLACNAME, the CDEL1 program, and stub testing program SBROW1. You can key-enter these programs or upload them to your VAX system from the ASCII files available on diskette as described in Appendix E. It's assumed that you will do task 14.11 before answering questions 14.12 to 14.16.

14.11 Use the $ COBOL/LIST command to compile the CDEL1 program. Print the .LIS file so that you can see the source code. Change line 65 of the VAXDEMO program so that it CALLs 'CDEL1' instead of 'SDEL1'. Then compile VAXDEMO again. Finally, use the $ LINK command discussed in this chapter to link together the menu, functional subprograms CINQU1,

CUPD1, NUMCHEK, PLACNAME, CDEL1, and the stub program and SBROW1.

Answer these questions only after preparing the VAXDEMO menu program and others as described in item 14.11. It is assumed that you have created and loaded an indexed file named MASTER.DAT as described in Chapter 10. For problems 14.12 to 14.16, $ RUN VAXDEMO as you answer the questions.

14.12 Select 3 from the main menu. To gain access to the delete function you can enter P113 and POOBAH. Explain what these things are and why the delete function asks for them before allowing you to delete records.

14.13 Explain (referring to lines of source code in the program) what happens if you enter a key value for CDEL1 and no record with that key exists in the customer master file.

14.14 Go to the add/change function and examine the record with key value 415002. Then go to the delete function and delete the record. Go back to the add/change function and seek record 415002. Explain what the result is.

14.15 After performing item 14 go to the add/change function and add a new record with the key 415002, filling in the name and address of DePaul University (243 S. Wabash, Chicago, IL, 60604) with a credit limit of $50,000.00. Then go to the delete function and try to delete this record. Explain why you can or cannot delete it now.

14.16 Examine lines 26, 53–60, 169–170, 258, and 332–336 of CDEL1. Explain what purpose is served by these lines in the deletion function. Could the deletion function operate if you commented out these lines?

CHAPTER 15: INTERACTIVE ALTERNATE KEY BROWSE: PROGRAM CBROW1

REVIEW QUIZ

15.1 An alternate key browse function is useful for identifying the ＿＿＿＿＿＿＿＿＿ ＿＿＿＿＿＿＿＿＿ of a record when you know only the alternate key (such as customer name).

15.2   A browse arranged by primary key would not usually be useful because the purpose of a browse is to locate a record for which the _____ _____ is not known.

15.3   Each detail line on a browse screen presents _____ information from _____ _____ .

15.4   You can tell the browse the point at which to begin accessing a file by specifying a _____ _____ of an alternate key.

15.5   After finding a desired record with a browse you can go to _____ functions to do inquiries or updates using the _____ key value.

15.6   If an alternate key field value is changed on-line, a browse based on the field will be _____ .

15.7   Each detail line on an alternate key browse screen usually carries the _____ _____ at the left, followed by the _____ _____ and other identifying information.

15.8   For an alternate key browse to continue automatically from page (screen) to page, the alternate key on the screen's _____ _____ must be retained by the program in a _____ _____ .

15.9   You code a START at the beginning of the alternate key browse processing loop to change the _____ _____ _____ and set the _____ _____ _____ .

15.10 The inner loop within a browse that builds and DISPLAYs each "detail line" of the screen ends when you reach _____ - _____ - _____ or when the screen is _____ .

PROBLEMS FOR CHAPTER 15

These problems require you to actually compile, link, and run the VAXDEMO menu program, CINQU1 inquiry program, CUPD1 add/change program, subprograms NUMCHEK and PLACNAME, the CDEL1 program, and program CBROW1. You can key-enter these programs or upload them to your VAX system from the ASCII files available on diskette as described in Appendix E. It's assumed that you will do task 15.11 before answering questions 15.12 to 15.16.

15.11 Use the COBOL/LIST command to compile the CBROW1 program. Print the .LIS file so that you can see the source code. Change line 66 of the VAXDEMO program so that it CALLs 'CBROW1' instead of 'SBROW1'. Then compile VAXDEMO again. Finally, use the LINK command discussed in this chapter to link together the menu and the functional subprograms CINQU1, CUPD1, NUMCHEK, PLACNAME, CDEL1, and CBROW1. This completes your entire VAXDEMO system!

Answer these questions only after preparing the VAXDEMO menu program and others as described in item 15.11. It is assumed that you have created and loaded an indexed file named MASTER.DAT as described in Chapter 10. For problems 15.12 to 15.16, $ RUN VAXDEMO as you answer the questions.

15.12 When you view the records presented by the browse screen, in what order do they appear? Explain how this is accomplished.

15.13 Examine lines 217 and 222 of CBROW1. Explain why +21 and +5 are coded in these lines.

15.14 Execute the browse function and enter JO when asked for a browse starting value. Describe what record lists first on the screen and why.

15.15 After seeing the first screen of the browse press *<Return>* to continue "paging forward." After examining the code for paragraphs 2000, 4200, 4300, and 4400 explain how the logic arranges to resume the browse at the appropriate place in the file.

15.16 View the first screen of the browse (beginning of the file according to alternate key). Then use the add/change function to change the name of the record with key 600536 from ACME PRODUCTS CO. to HAZARD ENGINEERING CO. View the first screen of the browse again, and explain where the listing for this record now appears and why.

CHAPTER 16: ADVANCED FEATURES: DIRECT TRANSFER AND RECORD LOCKING

REVIEW QUIZ

16.1 A casual on-line system user is a person who _____ uses the system.

16.2 A person just learning how to use an on-line system is best served by a _____-_____ system architecture.

16.3 _____ _____ allows experienced system users to bypass presentation of a menu when they already know the selection code of the function they want to perform.

16.4 In the command =1 the = is known as a _____ _____.

16.5 When a menu program acts as a router it presents the _____ only when necessary and passes several _____ to each functional subprogram.

16.6 When an on-line business system supports multiple terminal operators, you have to make provision to allow _____ _____.

16.7 An access stream is the series of _____ _____ _____ operations being performed by a single user.

16.8 A _____ _____ makes just one record (not an entire file) inaccessible to all but one file user.

16.9 On the VAX you can arrange for either _____ record locking or _____ record locking.

16.10 File Status values _____ and _____ are associated with "soft" and "hard" record locks.

PROBLEMS FOR CHAPTER 16

These problems require you to actually compile, link, and run the VAXDEMOX menu program and "direct transfer" version of the SINQU1X stub testing program. You can key-enter these programs or upload them to your VAX system from the ASCII files available on diskette as described in Appendix E. It's assumed that you will do task 16.11 before answering questions 16.12 to 16.16.

16.11 Use the $ COBOL/LIST command to compile the VAXDEMOX and SINQU1X programs. Print the .LIS file so that you can see the source code. Copy SINQU1X to make versions of it for all the stub testing programs you need. Modify those copies so that they contain SUPD1X, SDEL1X, and SBROW1X in their IDENTIFICATION DIVISION and messages. Compile these other three testing stub programs. Finally, use the $ LINK command to link together the menu and direct transfer testing stubs. $ RUN VAXDEMOX to experiment with direct transfer in the following work items.

16.12 When you run VAXDEMOX, select 4 from the menu to get into the SBROW1 browse testing stub. Enter =1 as a prompt response. Explain what comes up on your screen and why.

16.13 Run VAXDEMOX and get into the add/change stub testing program (function 2). Enter =7 as a prompt response. Describe what happens and why.

16.14 Start running VAXDEMOX and get into the browse function (4). Make a note of the keys of three records. Then do a direct transfer to the delete function (3). Delete each of the three records. Go back directly to the browse. Then enter =Q at the browse screen prompt. Explain what screen appears next and why, and explain why the transaction count is as you find it.

16.15 Modify the testing stub programs so that each has a regular top-of-screen appearance, including system and screen name, title, and system date and time. Include in the centered title the menu selection code by which you get to the function from the menu. Don't make this value hardcoded. Instead, make it a data field that gets its value from the shared field named WS-MENU-SELECTION. Compile, link, and run VAXDEMOX with this version of the stub testing programs. Explain why you don't need to "hardcode" any functional subprogram with its menu selection code but can still provide it on the screen in this way. Test to see if the subprogram works when you arrive at a function using direct transfer. Does it?

16.16 Your copy of VAXDEMOX is all set for use in a real on-line application system that provides direct transfer. Modify the CINQU1, CUPD1, CDEL1, and CBROW1 programs to include the small amount of logic necessary for them to support direct transfer. Separately compile these modified programs. Then linkage edit the VAXDEMOX menu program and the functional programs together as you did in the exercises in Chapter 15. Finally, test your complete VAXDEMOX system, which includes all of the same record access as VAXDEMO and which provides direct transfer, too! *When you have completed this task you have at your fingertips a powerful model for interactive business data processing using VAX COBOL!*

ANSWERS FOR EVEN-NUMBERED QUESTIONS AND EXERCISES

CHAPTER 1

1.2 BOJ/process/EOJ

1.4 disk drives

1.6 teleprocessing

1.8 convert, tones

1.10 indexed files

1.12 For interactive processing disk drives had to be on-line for access as opposed to off-line for maintenance; interactive processing came to be associated with the term *on-line.*

1.14 A modem converts digital square-wave pulse signals to audio tones and vice versa. Modems are necessary because ordinary telephone circuits were designed to handle the audio signals of voice communication and can't handle digital signals.

1.16 A 1200 bit per second modem transmits 1200 bits per second ÷ 10 bits per character = 120 characters per second. Transmitting a screen containing 1015 characters will take $1,015 \div 120 = 8.5$ seconds.

1.18 ISDN stands for Integrated Digital Services Network. It is a new form of telephone signal transmission in which voice is converted to digital form. ISDN circuits are designed to carry digital signals. ISDN will ultimately make modems unnecessary.

CHAPTER 2

2.2 pseudoconversational

2.4 files

2.6 active

2.8 subprogram, CALLed

2.10 CICS commands

2.12 IBM mainframe architecture and the MVS and DOS/VSE operating systems were designed before on-line processing became common. Therefore, on-line processing is not directly supported by mainframe operating systems. It must be provided by separate software, CICS.

2.14 In the VAX environment ACCEPT and DISPLAY handle communication between your program and a computer terminal.

2.16 These factors complicate on-line programming in the IBM mainframe environment: (a) a mainframe interactive program is really a subroutine to CICS and not a freestanding program; (b) the program must use special CICS commands to ask CICS to do terminal and file access; (c) much coordination is required because CICS is controlled by external tables that only a system programmer can update; (4) pseudoconversational logic is more complex than the conversational logic of VAX interactive programs.

CHAPTER 3

3.2 select, function

3.4 top, middle, bottom, titles, data, messages

3.6 transfer, menus

3.8 replaces, bottom

3.10 training

3.12 A paging display uses formatted screens. You move the cursor between fields on the screen to access data. One formatted screen replaces another as you "move around" in a system. A scrolling display acts like a typewriter. Lines follow one another until the cursor reaches the bottom of the screen. Then new lines continue to appear at the bottom. The top line scrolls off the screen as each new line appears at the bottom.

3.14 A general help screen for a screen used to enter customer name, address, and balance due might give information about how the keys of the keyboard work and a table of contents showing detailed topics you could request information about. You would get the same general help screen no matter where you were within the on-line system. Context-sensitive help would "know" that you were performing a customer add/change function and could tell you the criteria for valid contents in each of the fields on the add/change screen.

3.16

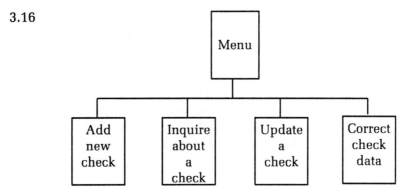

CHAPTER 4

4.2 bright, normal, dark

4.4 column ruler

4.6 time, transmit

4.8 prompt

4.10 top, bottom, left, right

4.12 A full screen is 1,920 characters; 60% of this is 1,152 characters. Since a 2400 bits per second modem transmits 2400 ÷ 10 bits per character = 240 characters per second, it will take 1152 ÷ 240 = 4.8 seconds to transmit the screen.

4.14 Refer to Figure 4.2 and use it as a guide.

CHAPTER 5

5.2 LOGOUT

5.4 displays, list of

5.6 end

5.8 PURGE

5.10 S, Q

5.12 EDT keypad mode offers full screen editing whereas line edit mode lets you work with one line at a time. Keypad mode requires a terminal such as a VT-100 (or emulation by a microcomputer), but you could use line editing mode even on an "ancient" (and slow printing!) hardcopy terminal.

5.14 To do this assignment you need to enter original data into a file using EDT and then print it. Review this chapter for information on the VMS and EDT commands you need to do this work.

5.16 VMS tells the several copies of file apart by managing the version number which is at the end of the name. Each version of the file has a different version number.

CHAPTER 6

6.2 /LIST

6.4 $ LINK ABCD

6.6 $ RUN WIZARD

6.8 .COM

6.10 *<Up arrow>*

6.12 Compile with the command $ COBOL/**LIST** ch6q11

6.14 You get 12 copies of the line on the screen. Each line is indented farther to the right because WS-SUB changes in value and is used as the COLUMN value.

CHAPTER 7

7.2 terminal keyboard

7.4 screen

7.6 DISPLAY ' ' AT LINE 1 COLUMN 1 ERASE TO END OF SCREEN

7.8 dark, light

7.10 numeric, decimal point, zeros

7.12 To de-edit entered numeric data the program has to convert the entry into a pure COBOL number. This means eliminating any dollar sign, leading spaces, commas, explicit decimal points, and leading or trailing signs.

7.14 For the first line see answer 6. For the centered name you need to count the letters in your name, subtract this from the width of the screen (80), and divide the answer in half. This will tell you the starting column of your name centered on the screen. Code

LINE 2 and COLUMN appropriately. Use the BOLD video attribute with the DISPLAY statement.

7.16 PROTECTED makes the cursor stop at the end of the field so that you can't continue entering data beyond this point. It protects the part of the screen that follows the field so that you can't accidentally obliterate other information already on the screen.

CHAPTER 8

8.2 transaction

8.4 labels, once, transactions

8.6 *<Arrow>*, *<Backspace>*

8.8 spaces

8.10 left justified, spaces

8.12 The screen is cleared and labels are presented. See the source code listed in Figure 8.4.

8.14 WITH CONVERSION de-edits the value entered for WS-QUANTITY to remove explicit decimal point and leading spaces. It cannot accept a comma or dollar sign.

8.16 When you don't enter a value into a numeric field that is being ACCEPTed WITH CONVERSION the field receives a value of zero. If CALC1 gets zeros for quantity and price it computes zero for the total before tax, the sales tax, and the grand total.

CHAPTER 9

9.2 blink

9.4 decimal point, sign, comma

9.6 numeric edited field

9.8 after

9.10 comma

9.12 CALC2 uses reverse video on all fields, uses the WITH BELL option a great deal, and uses BLINKING to flash the prompt line. This "overuse" of features produces a distracting and hard-to-look-at screen.

9.14 Use Figure 8.1 as a pattern to develop a layout for the screen for

Podunk Power Company. Review Chapter 4 for guidelines on the effective placement of fields on a screen.

CHAPTER 10

10.2   uniquely identify

10.4   pointer key

10.6   one after another

10.8   symbolic

10.10 does not

10.12

```
SELECT PAYROLL-FILE ASSIGN TO PAYFILE
ORGANIZATION IS INDEXED
ACCESS MODE IS RANDOM
RECORD KEY IS PD-EMPLOYEE-ID
ALTERNATE RECORD KEY IS PR-EMPLOYEE-SSN (WITH
    DUPLICATES?)
FILE STATUS IS WS-STATUS.
```

If employee social security number is a required field, the alternate key would be unique. But if this field is not required, most likely more than one record would have spaces in it, making the alternate key nonunique.

10.14 This problem requires you to do some VAX COBOL compiles and linkage edits. Review Chapter 6 if you need guidance in these tasks.

10.16 When you run LISTALT as coded it will produce a listing of the records in alternate key sequence. If you comment out the START in beginning of job, there is nothing in the program to change the key of reference to the alternate key and the data lists in primary key sequence.

10.18 You get a File Status value of 21 when you follow the steps in this problem. The record that you have intentionally put out of sequence in the sequential file is not loaded.

CHAPTER 11

11.2   choice, menu selection

11.4   beginning of job, time

11.6   beginning of job, processing loop

11.8   stub, receive

11.10 main, commas

11.12 The WS-TRANS-COUNT field accumulates a count of the times each functional subprogram went through its processing loop. VAXDEMO displays this field when you end it.

11.14 The EVALUATE determines the meaning of the menu selection code that the terminal operator entered and associates it with the subprogram to be called to deliver the service. You could also use a serial "case" type of IF/ELSE statement for this.

11.16 The compound OR is coded at line 46 to allow you to enter either "QUIT" (uppercase letters) or "quit" (lowercase letters) to end program execution.

CHAPTER 12

12.2   screen labels

12.4   one paragraph

12.6   open, prompt response

12.8   '0'

12.10 '00'

12.12 When you enter an existing value to the CINQU1 inquiry program, the program finds the value in the indexed file and puts the data from the file on the screen.

12.14 The VAXDEMO transaction count tabulates the number of transactions processed. When you enter a key to the CINQU1 inquiry program and find that the key is not on file, it is counted as a transaction.

12.16 The prompt response key field is six bytes alphanumeric. If you enter only part of a key to CINQU1, it appears as a six-byte field with trailing spaces. The key will not be found in the file and you'll get a message indicating this.

CHAPTER 13

13.2   random read, key

13.4   WRITE

13.6   screen format fields

13.8   unchanged

13.10 WITH CONVERSION, de-edit

13.12 If you enter a key into the CUPD1 add/change program and that key exists in the indexed file, the program assumes that you want to change data in the record. It sets the record up on the screen for you to change.

13.14 Entering the backslash \ at the start of any field tells CUPD1 to cancel the transaction. None of the changes you have made on the screen to an existing record are rewritten to the file when you cancel the transaction.

13.16 Your entry of 1600 for the credit limit will be rejected. Since the entry has no explicit decimal point, NUMCHEK will regard it as $16.00, which is lower than the $1000 lower bound of the credit limit. If you enter 320000, NUMCHEK will regard the entry as $3,200.00 and accept it. CUPD1 will format it for redisplay on the screen with dollar sign, comma, and explicit decimal point.

CHAPTER 14

14.2   operator identifier, password

14.4   menu

14.6   confirm, deleted

14.8   accurately, legitimate

14.10 add/change

14.12 P113 is an operator identifer and POOBAH is the password associated with it. CDEL1 asks you to enter these things before giving you access to delete capabilities as a measure of security. This helps prevent unauthorized people (who would not know these codes) from deleting records from the master file.

14.14 When you delete a record using CDEL1 it is deleted immediately. You can see the record on the system by using CINQU1 or CUPD1 before the deletion. After the deletion the record is gone and you can no longer find it.

14.16 The indicated source code lines deal with archiving a copy of the deleted record. If you commented them out, CDEL1 would still work but deleted records would not be saved in a file.

CHAPTER 15

15.2   primary key

15.4   leading part

15.6   affected

15.8   last line, hold field

15.10 end-of-file, filled

15.12 The records appear as if they were sorted in ascending sequence of the alternate key (customer name) field. This is because the START at the top of the processing loop changes the Key of Reference (KOR) of the indexed file to the alternate key. You are now automatically reading the records in the alternate index and using them to guide your access to the actual data records. Your sequential READ (or READ . . . NEXT) is coded no differently, since the access method handles this use of the alternate index records itself.

15.14 When you enter JO the first record on the screen is for JOHNSON MACHINE CORP. since this is the first record that has "JO" (or something later in sort sequence) at the beginning of its name field.

15.16 When you change the name of ACME PRODUCTS CO. to HAZARD ENGINEERING CO. its position on the browse screen changes. Now the record lists after the record for HARRIER METER CORP. and before HILBORN TECHNOLOGIES, since this is where HAZARD sorts alphabetically by name.

CHAPTER 16

16.2   menu-based

16.4   transfer command

16.6   file sharing

16.8   record lock

16.10 '90', '92'

16.12 Your entry of =1 takes you directly to the inquiry program testing stub without having the menu presented.

16.14 Your entry of =Q at the end of the actions I have indicated logs you off the VAXDEMOX system as if you had selected "Q" from the menu. The transaction count is 5 because you did a browse, then did 3 delete transactions, then did another browse before finally ending VAXDEMOX execution.

16.16 You make the identical modification in each functional subprogram to provide it with direct transfer capabilities. These are located in the LINKAGE SECTION and in processing of the operator prompt response. (See lines 24–32 and 59–61 of SINQU1X, Figure 16.4, for guidance.) Keep in mind how simple it is to provide direct transfer in this way when you build real-life on-line systems. Your VAXDEMOX menu already provides what you need in any menu program for any system you create!

Appendix B

NUMCHEK And PLACNAME Subprogram Source Code

Subprograms provide a convenient way to modularize logic. Some data validation service routines are a natural candidate to be housed in subprograms. This appendix provides you with the source code for two subprograms CALLed by the interactive add/change program CUPD1 discussed in Chapter 13.

You can ACCEPT numeric fields as character strings and de-edit them with the NUMCHEK subprogram shown in Figure B.1. It is more capable than the WITH CONVERSION option of ACCEPT, since it will handle commas and dollar signs in the input. Its LINKAGE SECTION is described by copy library member NUMLINK.LIB, which appears in its listing.

The PLACNAME subprogram, shown in Figure B.2, looks up a PIC X(2) field carrying a state or province postal code and tells you whether or not the code is valid. It does this by table lookup, which also provides the country (CAN or USA) and place name (state or province, spelled out). Its LINKAGE SECTION is described by copy library member PLACLINK.LIB.

See the documentary comments at the top of each of these subprograms for more information on their use. I coded them with copy library members for the descriptions of memory that CALLing programs share with them. This is a common technique to make sure that CALLing and CALLed programs both define shared memory identically. (I didn't use COPY in CUPD1, although I could have. I tried to keep that program as simple as possible for example purposes.)

A VAX copy library member is just a fragment source code that exists in a file with a name ending with .LIB. If these are in the same subdirectory as your program, a statement such as COPY NUMLINK in line 51 of NUMCHEK copies in NUMLINK.LIB. If you put your copy library members in other subdirectories or name them with a suffix other than .LIB, your COPY statements have to specify full names. For example, if I had named the description of the linkage record for NUMCHEK as NUM-LINK.COB and had stored it in subdirectory [CSCJGJ.CSC360], I would code the copy at line 51 as:

```
COPY "[CSCJGJ.CSC360]NUMLINK.COB".
```

```
NUMCHEK               15-Mar-1992 20:51:07      VAX COBOL V4.3-57
Source Listing        15-Mar-1992 20:34:57
CSC$ROOT:[CSCJGJ.VAXCO]NUMCHEK.COB;1

     1          IDENTIFICATION DIVISION.
     2          PROGRAM-ID.     NUMCHEK.
     3         *AUTHOR.         J JANOSSY    INTERNET: JANOSSY@CSCVAX.DEPAUL.EDU
     4         *INSTALLATION.   DEPAUL UNIVERSITY, CHICAGO, IL
     5         *=================================================================
     6         *   Numeric De-editing Subprogram in VAX COBOL ON-LINE!  3/1/92
     7         *
     8         *   This subprogram accepts a PIC X(22) field named NUM-INPUT
     9         *   and a value for the intended number of digits right of a
    10         *   decimal point. It accepts any customary rendition of the
    11         *   input as a character string and provides the numeric form
    12         *   of the input in a pic 9(11)V9(6) field named NUM-OUTPUT.
    13         *   The following codes result at NUM-STATUS-FLAG:
    14         *
    15         *       0     Input valid, transformed to PIC 9(11)V9(6)
    16         *       1     CALLing program did not specify
    17         *             NUM-RIGHT-OF-DECIMAL in the range 0 - 6
    18         *       2     Input contained alphanumeric symbols other
    19         *             than one $, commas, one period serving
    20         *             as a decimaL POINT
    21         *       3     Input value has fewer or more digits right
    22         *             of the explicit decimal point than the
    23         *             CALLing program stated in NUM-RIGHT-OF-
    24         *             DECIMAL.  Input need not carry an explicit
    25         *             decimal point but if it does it must
    26         *             agree in positioning with the value in
    27         *             NUM-RIGHT-OF-DECIMAL.
    28         *=================================================================
    29          ENVIRONMENT DIVISION.
    30         *-----------------------------------------------------------------
    31          DATA DIVISION.
    32          WORKING-STORAGE SECTION.
    33          01  W1-AREA.
    34              12 W1-BYTE   OCCURS 22 TIMES  PIC X(1).
    35         *
    36          01  W2-AREA.
    37              12 W2-BYTE   OCCURS 22 TIMES  PIC X(1).
    38         *
    39          01  W1-SUB                        PIC S9(4) COMP.
    40          01  W2-SUB                        PIC S9(4) COMP.
    41          01  W3-SUB                        PIC S9(4) COMP.
    42          01  WS-DOLLAR-SIGNS-COUNTED       PIC S9(4) COMP.
    43          01  WS-DEC-POINTS-COUNTED         PIC S9(4) COMP.
    44          01  WS-COMPUTED-DEC-PLACES        PIC S9(4) COMP.
    45         *
    46          01  WS-ALMOST-DONE-X              PIC X(17)  JUSTIFIED RIGHT.
    47          01  WS-ALMOST-DONE-9    REDEFINES
    48              WS-ALMOST-DONE-X              PIC 9(17).
    49         *-----------------------------------------------------------------
    50          LINKAGE SECTION.
    51          01  NUMCHEK-LINKAGE-RECORD.   COPY NUMLINK.
    52L        *****************************************************************
    53L        *  LINKAGE RECORD FOR NUMCHEK DE-EDITING SUBPROGRAM            *
    54L        *****************************************************************
```

Figure B.1   Source code for NUMCHEK numeric de-editing subprogram.

```
55L                12 NUM-INPUT                 PIC X(22).
56L                12 NUM-RIGHT-OF-DECIMAL       PIC 9(1).
57L                12 NUM-STATUS-FLAG            PIC X(1).
58L                12 NUM-OUTPUT                 PIC 9(11)V9(6).
59         *=================================================================
60         PROCEDURE DIVISION USING NUMCHEK-LINKAGE-RECORD.
61         0000-MAINLINE.
62             MOVE ' '          TO NUM-STATUS-FLAG.
63             MOVE ZEROS        TO NUM-OUTPUT.
64             MOVE NUM-INPUT    TO W1-AREA.
65         *
66             IF NUM-RIGHT-OF-DECIMAL NOT NUMERIC
67                 MOVE '1' TO NUM-STATUS-FLAG
68             ELSE
69             IF NUM-RIGHT-OF-DECIMAL > 6
70                 MOVE '1' TO NUM-STATUS-FLAG
71             ELSE
72                 PERFORM 1000-PROCESS.
73         0000-EXIT.  EXIT PROGRAM.
74         *---------------------------------------------------------------
75         *  Replace first $ with a space, all commas with spaces:
76         *---------------------------------------------------------------
77         1000-PROCESS.
78             MOVE +0 TO WS-DOLLAR-SIGNS-COUNTED.
79             PERFORM 2100-DOLLAR-SIGN-DELETE
80                 VARYING W1-SUB FROM +1 BY +1
81                     UNTIL W1-SUB > +22
82                         OR WS-DOLLAR-SIGNS-COUNTED = +1.
83         *
84             PERFORM 2200-COMMA-REPLACE
85                 VARYING W1-SUB FROM +1 BY +1
86                     UNTIL W1-SUB > +22.
87         *---------------------------------------------------------------
88         *  Move W1-AREA to W2-AREA byte-by-byte from right to left,
89         *  eliminating imbedded spaces and providing leading zeros:
90         *---------------------------------------------------------------
91             MOVE +23      TO W2-SUB.
92             MOVE ZEROS    TO W2-AREA.
93             PERFORM 2300-SQUISH-RIGHT
94                 VARYING W1-SUB FROM +22 BY -1
95                     UNTIL W1-SUB < +1.
96         *---------------------------------------------------------------
97         *  Find explicit decimal point(s) if present, make W3-SUB
98         *  hold the position from right of the first decimal point:
99         *---------------------------------------------------------------
100            MOVE +0 TO WS-DEC-POINTS-COUNTED.
101            PERFORM 2400-DEC-POINT-SCAN-FROM-RT
102                VARYING W2-SUB FROM +22 BY -1
103                    UNTIL W2-SUB < +1.
104        *
105            IF WS-DEC-POINTS-COUNTED = +0
106                PERFORM 1120-CONCLUSION
107            ELSE
108            IF WS-DEC-POINTS-COUNTED = +1
109                PERFORM 1100-EXPLICIT-DECIMAL-WORK
110            ELSE
111                MOVE '2' TO NUM-STATUS-FLAG.
112        *---------------------------------------------------------------
113        1100-EXPLICIT-DECIMAL-WORK.
114            COMPUTE WS-COMPUTED-DEC-PLACES = 22 - W3-SUB.
115            IF WS-COMPUTED-DEC-PLACES = NUM-RIGHT-OF-DECIMAL
116                PERFORM 1110-ELIMINATE-DECIMAL
117                PERFORM 1120-CONCLUSION
118            ELSE
119                MOVE '3'  TO NUM-STATUS-FLAG.
120        *
121        1110-ELIMINATE-DECIMAL.
122            MOVE ' '       TO W2-BYTE(W3-SUB).
123            MOVE W2-AREA   TO W1-AREA.
124            MOVE ZEROS     TO W2-AREA.
125            MOVE +23 TO W2-SUB.
```

(Continued)

Figure B.1   *(Continued)*

```
126                  PERFORM 2300-SQUISH-RIGHT
127                      VARYING W1-SUB FROM +22 BY -1
128                          UNTIL W1-SUB < +1.
129          *
130              1120-CONCLUSION.
131                  IF W2-AREA IS NUMERIC
132                      PERFORM 1130-FINAL-MOVE
133                      MOVE '0' TO NUM-STATUS-FLAG
134                  ELSE
135                      MOVE '2' TO NUM-STATUS-FLAG.
136          *
137              1130-FINAL-MOVE.
138                  MOVE W2-AREA TO WS-ALMOST-DONE-X.
139                  IF NUM-RIGHT-OF-DECIMAL = 0
140                      MOVE WS-ALMOST-DONE-9 TO NUM-OUTPUT
141                  ELSE
142                      COMPUTE NUM-OUTPUT =
143                          WS-ALMOST-DONE-9 / ( 10.000 ** NUM-RIGHT-OF-DECIMAL ).
144          *================================================================
145          *  Performed character string routines (used instead of the
146          *  INSPECT verb so this routine also works with IBM CICS):
147          *================================================================
148              2100-DOLLAR-SIGN-DELETE.
149                  IF W1-BYTE(W1-SUB) = '$'
150                      MOVE ' ' TO W1-BYTE(W1-SUB)
151                      ADD +1 TO WS-DOLLAR-SIGNS-COUNTED.
152          *
153              2200-COMMA-REPLACE.
154                  IF W1-BYTE(W1-SUB) = ','
155                      MOVE ' ' TO W1-BYTE(W1-SUB).
156          *
157              2300-SQUISH-RIGHT.
158                  IF W1-BYTE(W1-SUB) NOT = ' '
159                      SUBTRACT +1 FROM W2-SUB
160                      MOVE W1-BYTE(W1-SUB) TO W2-BYTE(W2-SUB).
161          *
162              2400-DEC-POINT-SCAN-FROM-RT.
163                  IF W2-BYTE(W2-SUB) = '.'
164                      ADD +1 TO WS-DEC-POINTS-COUNTED
165                      IF WS-DEC-POINTS-COUNTED = +1
166                          MOVE W2-SUB TO W3-SUB.
```

Figure B.1   *(Continued)*

```
PLACNAME                15-Mar-1992 20:51:26    VAX COBOL V4.3-57
Source Listing          15-Mar-1992 20:35:57
CSC$ROOT:[CSCJGJ.VAXCO]PLACNAME.COB;1

      1             IDENTIFICATION DIVISION.
      2             PROGRAM-ID.      PLACNAME.
      3            *AUTHOR.          J JANOSSY    INTERNET: JANOSSY@CSCVAX.DEPAUL.EDU
      4            *INSTALLATION.    DEPAUL UNIVERSITY, CHICAGO, IL
      5            *=================================================================
      6            *    State/Province Lookup Subprogram in VAX COBOL ON-LINE! 3/1/92
      7            *
      8            *    If you CALL this subprogram with a PIC X(2) field it looks
      9            *    up the contents and returns the county as PIC X(3), state
     10            *    or province name as PIC X(20), and PLC-STATUS-FLAG as 'Y'
     11            *    for valid code or 'N' for invalid code.  Uses binary search.
     12            *=================================================================
     13             ENVIRONMENT DIVISION.
     14            *-----------------------------------------------------------------
     15             DATA DIVISION.
     16             WORKING-STORAGE SECTION.
     17             01  PLACE-TABLE-SETUP.
     18                 12 FILLER  PIC X(27)   VALUE 'AB CAN ALBERTA            '.
     19                 12 FILLER  PIC X(27)   VALUE 'AK USA ALASKA             '.
     20                 12 FILLER  PIC X(27)   VALUE 'AL USA ALABAMA            '.
     21                 12 FILLER  PIC X(27)   VALUE 'AR USA ARKANSAS           '.
     22                 12 FILLER  PIC X(27)   VALUE 'AZ USA ARIZONA            '.
     23                 12 FILLER  PIC X(27)   VALUE 'BC CAN BRITISH COLUMBIA   '.
     24                 12 FILLER  PIC X(27)   VALUE 'CA USA CALIFORNIA         '.
     25                 12 FILLER  PIC X(27)   VALUE 'CN USA CONNECTICUT        '.
     26                 12 FILLER  PIC X(27)   VALUE 'CO USA COLORADO           '.
     27                 12 FILLER  PIC X(27)   VALUE 'DC USA DISTRICT OF COLUMBIA'.
     28                 12 FILLER  PIC X(27)   VALUE 'DE USA DELAWARE           '.
     29                 12 FILLER  PIC X(27)   VALUE 'FL USA FLORIDA            '.
     30                 12 FILLER  PIC X(27)   VALUE 'GA USA GEORGIA            '.
     31                 12 FILLER  PIC X(27)   VALUE 'HI USA HAWAII             '.
     32                 12 FILLER  PIC X(27)   VALUE 'IA USA IOWA               '.
     33                 12 FILLER  PIC X(27)   VALUE 'ID USA IDAHO              '.
     34                 12 FILLER  PIC X(27)   VALUE 'IL USA ILLINOIS           '.
     35                 12 FILLER  PIC X(27)   VALUE 'IN USA INDIANA            '.
     36                 12 FILLER  PIC X(27)   VALUE 'KS USA KANSAS             '.
     37                 12 FILLER  PIC X(27)   VALUE 'KY USA KENTUCKY           '.
     38                 12 FILLER  PIC X(27)   VALUE 'LA USA LOUISIANA          '.
     39                 12 FILLER  PIC X(27)   VALUE 'MA USA MASSACHUSETTS      '.
     40                 12 FILLER  PIC X(27)   VALUE 'MB CAN MANITOBA           '.
     41                 12 FILLER  PIC X(27)   VALUE 'MD USA MARYLAND           '.
     42                 12 FILLER  PIC X(27)   VALUE 'ME USA MAINE              '.
     43                 12 FILLER  PIC X(27)   VALUE 'MI USA MICHIGAN           '.
     44                 12 FILLER  PIC X(27)   VALUE 'MN USA MINNESOTA          '.
     45                 12 FILLER  PIC X(27)   VALUE 'MO USA MISSOURI           '.
     46                 12 FILLER  PIC X(27)   VALUE 'MS USA MISSISSIPPI        '.
     47                 12 FILLER  PIC X(27)   VALUE 'MT USA MONTANA            '.
     48                 12 FILLER  PIC X(27)   VALUE 'NB CAN NEW BRUNSWICK      '.
     49                 12 FILLER  PIC X(27)   VALUE 'NC USA NORTH CAROLINA     '.
     50                 12 FILLER  PIC X(27)   VALUE 'ND USA NORTH DAKOTA       '.
     51                 12 FILLER  PIC X(27)   VALUE 'NE USA NEBRASKA           '.
     52                 12 FILLER  PIC X(27)   VALUE 'NF CAN NEWFOUNDLAND       '.
     53                 12 FILLER  PIC X(27)   VALUE 'NH USA NEW HAMPSHIRE      '.
     54                 12 FILLER  PIC X(27)   VALUE 'NJ USA NEW JERSEY         '.
     55                 12 FILLER  PIC X(27)   VALUE 'NM USA NEW MEXICO         '.
     56                 12 FILLER  PIC X(27)   VALUE 'NS CAN NOVA SCOTIA        '.
     57                 12 FILLER  PIC X(27)   VALUE 'NT CAN NORTH WEST TERR.   '.
     58                 12 FILLER  PIC X(27)   VALUE 'NV USA NEVADA             '.
     59                 12 FILLER  PIC X(27)   VALUE 'NY USA NEW YORK           '.
     60                 12 FILLER  PIC X(27)   VALUE 'OH USA OHIO               '.
     61                 12 FILLER  PIC X(27)   VALUE 'OK USA OKLAHOMA           '.
     62                 12 FILLER  PIC X(27)   VALUE 'ON CAN ONTARIO            '.
     63                 12 FILLER  PIC X(27)   VALUE 'OR USA OREGON             '.
     64                 12 FILLER  PIC X(27)   VALUE 'PA USA PENNSYLVANIA       '.
```

(Continued)

Figure B.2   Source code for PLACNAME state/province abbreviation lookup and validation subprogram.

```
65                  12 FILLER   PIC X(27)   VALUE 'PE CAN PRINCE EDWARD ISLAND'.
66                  12 FILLER   PIC X(27)   VALUE 'PQ CAN QUEBEC              '.
67                  12 FILLER   PIC X(27)   VALUE 'PR USA PUERTO RICO         '.
68                  12 FILLER   PIC X(27)   VALUE 'RI USA RHODE ISLAND        '.
69                  12 FILLER   PIC X(27)   VALUE 'SC USA SOUTH CAROLINA      '.
70                  12 FILLER   PIC X(27)   VALUE 'SD USA SOUTH DAKOTA        '.
71                  12 FILLER   PIC X(27)   VALUE 'SK CAN SASKATCHEWAN        '.
72                  12 FILLER   PIC X(27)   VALUE 'TN USA TENNESSEE           '.
73                  12 FILLER   PIC X(27)   VALUE 'TX USA TEXAS               '.
74                  12 FILLER   PIC X(27)   VALUE 'UT USA UTAH                '.
75                  12 FILLER   PIC X(27)   VALUE 'VA USA VIRGINIA            '.
76                  12 FILLER   PIC X(27)   VALUE 'VT USA VERMONT             '.
77                  12 FILLER   PIC X(27)   VALUE 'WA USA WASHINGTON          '.
78                  12 FILLER   PIC X(27)   VALUE 'WI USA WISCONSIN           '.
79                  12 FILLER   PIC X(27)   VALUE 'WV USA WEST VIRGINIA       '.
80                  12 FILLER   PIC X(27)   VALUE 'WY USA WYOMING             '.
81                  12 FILLER   PIC X(27)   VALUE 'YU CAN YUKON               '.
82            *
83            01   PLACE-TABLE REDEFINES PLACE-TABLE-SETUP.
84                  12 PLACE-TABLE-ELEMENT   OCCURS 64 TIMES
85                                           ASCENDING KEY IS PT-ABBREV
86                                           INDEXED BY PT-INDEX.
87                     15 PT-ABBREV            PIC X(2).
88                     15 FILLER               PIC X(1).
89                     15 PT-COUNTRY           PIC X(3).
90                     15 FILLER               PIC X(1).
91                     15 PT-NAME              PIC X(20).
92            *-------------------------------------------------------------
93            LINKAGE SECTION.
94            01   LS-LINKAGE-RECORD.   COPY PLACLINK.
95L           ***********************************************************
96L           *   LINKAGE RECORD FOR PLACE NAME SUBPROGRAM           *
97L           ***********************************************************
98L                  12 PLC-PLACE-ABBREV      PIC X(2).
99L                  12 PLC-COUNTRY           PIC X(3).
100L                 12 PLC-PLACE-NAME        PIC X(20).
101L                 12 PLC-STATUS-FLAG       PIC X(1).
102           *-------------------------------------------------------------
103           PROCEDURE DIVISION USING LS-LINKAGE-RECORD.
104           0000-MAINLINE.
105               SEARCH ALL PLACE-TABLE-ELEMENT
106                   AT END
107                       MOVE ALL '*'   TO  PLC-COUNTRY   PLC-PLACE-NAME
108                       MOVE 'N' TO PLC-STATUS-FLAG
109                   WHEN PT-ABBREV(PT-INDEX) = PLC-PLACE-ABBREV
110                       MOVE PT-COUNTRY(PT-INDEX) TO PLC-COUNTRY
111                       MOVE PT-NAME(PT-INDEX) TO PLC-PLACE-NAME
112                       MOVE 'Y' TO PLC-STATUS-FLAG.
113           0000-EXIT.  EXIT PROGRAM.
```

Figure B.2   *(Continued)*

Appendix C

Digital Equipment Corporation VAX COBOL Bibliography

I have listed for your convenience the DEC manuals that I have found to be most useful in working with VAX COBOL interactive programs. If you are in the United States call 1-800-DIGITAL (that is, 1-800-344-4825) to order any of these publications from DEC. If you are in Puerto Rico call 1-809-754-7575, and if you are in Canada call 1-800-267-6215. You can order any of these by telephone using a credit card and the order numbers I have listed here.

VAX COBOL User Manual, order number AA-H632E-TE. This is a well-written publication that gives you examples of DEC's VAX COBOL syntax. It includes detailed coverage of ACCEPT and DISPLAY, file locking, the VAX debugger, control key handling, and compiler options.

VAX COBOL Reference Manual, order number AA-H631E-TE. This manual is a language reference and explains standard COBOL features. An appendix in it called (for some odd reason) "Extension Marking" gives you a standard COBOL language syntax chart. I find this manual less useful than the user manual.

VAX COBOL Quick Reference Guide, order number AA-PAKQA-TE. A superb little paperback reference guide that gathers together the VAX COBOL language syntax chart, charts of codes and File status values, and other similar materials.

VMS Debugger Manual, order number AA-LA59B-TE. This is the standard publication for the VAX symbolic debugger, which is applicable to most DEC-supported languages including COBOL, PL/I, Fortran, assembly language, and others.

Guide to VMS File Applications, order number AA-LA78A-TE. This large publication contains information on file performance measurement and tuning, including File Definition Language (FDL) concepts and commands. You need this manual if you will create large indexed files that you must design to be efficient in supporting many concurrent terminal users.

VAX-11 TDMS Summary Description, order number AA-M056A-TE. This small publication provides an overview of DEC's Terminal Data Management System, an optional software product that works with several different languages and the optional VAX Common Data Dictionary (CDD). TDMS lets you define screens apart from programs using the Form Definition Utility (FDU) and store their images in the data dictionary. The publication is a good starting point to explore TDMS.

Appendix D

Converting VAX COBOL to Ryan McFarland RM/COBOL-85

If you have used *Structured COBOL Programming, 6th Edition* by Nancy and Robert Stern (John Wiley & Sons, Inc., 1991) you may have used the Ryan McFarland RM/COBOL-85 compiler. An inexpensive educational version of it is available with that introductory text. This compiler meets 1985 COBOL standards and runs on any level of MS-DOS microcomputer. ***You can easily adapt all of the programs in this book to RM/COBOL-85!***

As you learned in Chapter 1 of *VAX COBOL On-Line*, interactive processing developed after COBOL was invented. There is no standard syntax for screen handling in COBOL. RM/COBOL-85 uses slightly different syntax than VAX COBOL. I have documented the differences in comments at the top of several of the programs that follow.

I have listed for you in Figures D.1 through D.4 the source code for these programs, which I converted from VAX COBOL to RM/COBOL-85:

- •CALC3 — My best demonstration of screen handling.
- •INDLOAD — Loads an indexed file from a sequential file.
- •VAXDEMO — Menu program for my demonstration system.
- •SINQU1 — A sample stub testing program.

I have tested my converted programs on a Gateway-2000 PC (25 MHz 386, MS-DOS 4.01) and they run fine. But I have also used RM/COBOL-85 on machines as slow as an original 8088 microcomputer running at 4.77 MHz. The compiler and each converted program work very well (and quickly) even on that modest level of machine!

RM/COBOL-85 accepts source code as ASCII files. If you obtain the source code for the programs in this book on diskette as described in Appendix E, you can modify them using any word processor to convert the entire VAXDEMO system to RM/COBOL-85. Give your source code code files the suffix `.CBL` rather than `.COB`.

RM/COBOL-85 does not support VAX terminal format. You have to give it source code that actually has the comment asterisk in column 7 and the "A" margin in column 8. I've included on my distribution diskette a program I wrote named TERMTORM ("**TERM**inal **TO RM**") that takes VAX terminal format code and converts it to the "normal" format that RM/COBOL-85 requires. I've also included on the diskette another utility named RENUM that just renumbers source code in columns 1 through 6 to help you originate COBOL code on a microcomputer. (I wrote both utilities in COBOL, of course, but used a noneducational compiler that creates self contained .EXE files. You execute these utility programs by name without the word RUN. The source code for RENUM is listed in an appendix to another of my books, *VS COBOL II: Highlights and Techniques*, published by John Wiley & Sons, Inc., 1992.)

RM/COBOL-85 does not require a linkage editor; it produces code executed by a runtime program. If you convert VAXDEMO to RM/COBOL-85, just compile the menu program and all subprograms in the same subdirectory. Your CALLs from the menu program to subprograms will be handled dynamically by the runtime environment. Execute your converted VAXDEMO system by entering RUN VAXDEMO.

```
000100 IDENTIFICATION DIVISION.
000200 PROGRAM-ID.      CALC1.
000300*AUTHOR.          J JANOSSY    INTERNET: JANOSSY@CSCVAX.DEPAUL.EDU
000400*INSTALLATION.    DEPAUL UNIVERSITY, CHICAGO, ILLINOIS, USA
000500*================================================================
000600*REMARKS.           ONLINE VAX PROGRAM CALC1 ADAPTED TO WORK
000700*                   WITH THE RM/COBOL-85 MICROCOMPUTER COMPILER
000800*
000900*   Major differences between VAX COBOL and RM/COBOL-85:
001000*
001100*      COLUMN                   is coded  POSITION
001200*      ERASE TO END OF SCREEN   is coded  EOS
001300*      ERASE TO END OF LINE     is coded  EOL
001400*      REVERSED                 is coded  REVERSE
001500*      BLINKING                 is coded  BLINK
001600*      AT and FROM are eliminated
001700*      WITH CONVERSION is not coded
001800*      ACCEPT with REVERSE does not show reverse video
001900*            until entry; DISPLAY spaces reversed before
002000*            the ACCEPT to show length of your entry field
002100*      PROTECT is not required to prevent entry beyond field
002200*      Cursor automatically skips to next field when
002300*            entry fills up a field
002400*
002500*================================================================
002600 ENVIRONMENT DIVISION.
002700*
002800 DATA DIVISION.
002900 WORKING-STORAGE SECTION.
003000 01  WS-QUANTITY                       PIC 9(5).
003100 01  WS-PRICE                          PIC 99V99.
```

Figure D.1   CALC3 program converted to Ryan McFarland RM/COBOL-85.

```
003200 01  WS-TOTAL                        PIC 9(7)V99.
003300 01  WS-TAX-AMOUNT                    PIC 9(7)V99.
003400 01  WS-GRAND-TOTAL                   PIC 9(8)V99.
003500 01  WS-MONEY-FORMATTED               PIC ZZ,ZZZ,ZZ9.99.
003600 01  WS-RESPONSE                      PIC X(4).
003700/
003800 PROCEDURE DIVISION.
003900 0000-MAINLINE.
004000     PERFORM 1000-BOJ.
004100     PERFORM 2000-PROCESS
004200        UNTIL WS-RESPONSE = 'QUIT'.
004300     PERFORM 3000-EOJ.
004400     STOP RUN.
004500*
004600 1000-BOJ.
004700     DISPLAY ' ' LINE 1 POSITION 1 ERASE EOS.
004800     DISPLAY 'QUANTITY      PRICE              TOTAL'
004900        LINE 5 POSITION 20.
005000     DISPLAY '8% TAX'        LINE 10 POSITION 35.
005100     DISPLAY '============' LINE 12 POSITION 43.
005200     DISPLAY 'GRAND TOTAL'   LINE 14 POSITION 30.
005300*
005400 2000-PROCESS.
005500     DISPLAY '        '       LINE  7 POSITION 21.
005600     DISPLAY '        '       LINE  7 POSITION 33.
005700     DISPLAY '        '  LINE  7 POSITION 43.
005800     DISPLAY '        '  LINE 10 POSITION 43.
005900     DISPLAY '        '  LINE 14 POSITION 43.
006000     DISPLAY 'ENTER VALUE (NO COMMAS) AND PRESS RETURN'
006100        LINE 24 POSITION 1 ERASE EOL.
006200*
006300     ACCEPT WS-QUANTITY  LINE 7 POSITION 21.
006400     ACCEPT WS-PRICE     LINE 7 POSITION 33.
006500*
006600     COMPUTE WS-TOTAL = WS-QUANTITY * WS-PRICE.
006700     MOVE WS-TOTAL TO WS-MONEY-FORMATTED.
006800     DISPLAY WS-MONEY-FORMATTED LINE 7 POSITION 43.
006900*
007000     COMPUTE WS-TAX-AMOUNT = WS-TOTAL * .08.
007100     MOVE WS-TAX-AMOUNT TO WS-MONEY-FORMATTED.
007200     DISPLAY WS-MONEY-FORMATTED LINE 10 POSITION 43.
007300*
007400     COMPUTE WS-GRAND-TOTAL = WS-TOTAL + WS-TAX-AMOUNT.
007500     MOVE WS-GRAND-TOTAL TO WS-MONEY-FORMATTED.
007600     DISPLAY WS-MONEY-FORMATTED LINE 14 POSITION 43.
007700*
007800     DISPLAY 'PRESS RETURN TO CONTINUE, OR ENTER "QUIT" TO END '
007900        LINE 24 POSITION 1.
008000     ACCEPT WS-RESPONSE LINE 24 POSITION 60.
008100*
008200 3000-EOJ.
008300     DISPLAY 'QUITTING AS REQUESTED' LINE 1 POSITION 1
008400        ERASE EOS.
```

Figure D.1   (*Continued*)

```
000100 IDENTIFICATION DIVISION.
000200 PROGRAM-ID.    INDLOAD.
000300*AUTHOR.        J JANOSSY    INTERNET: JANOSSY@CSCVAX.DEPAUL.EDU
000400*INSTALLATION.  DEPAUL UNIVERSITY, CHICAGO, ILLINOIS, USA
000500*===============================================================
000600*    Program to Create/Load Indexed File in VAX COBOL On-Line!
000700*       General Purpose Indexed File Loader  6-1-91
000800*       ** ADAPTED TO RM/COBOL-85 MICROCOMPUTER COMPILER **
000900*
001000*    Reads records from a sequential file and copies them to
001100*    an indexed file.  Once this program has been run the
001200*    indexed file exists and can be accessed.
001300*
001400*    Major differences between this version and VAX COBOL:
001500*
001600*        Source code can't extend beyond column 72 (like IBM)
001700*        SELECT/ASSIGN differs after "ASSIGN TO"
001800*        SEQUENTIAL files are coded as LINE SEQUENTIAL
001900*
002000*===============================================================
002100 ENVIRONMENT DIVISION.
002200 INPUT-OUTPUT SECTION.
002300 FILE-CONTROL.
002400     SELECT SEQ-FILE              ASSIGN TO DISK 'CUSTOMER.DAT'
002500         ORGANIZATION IS  LINE SEQUENTIAL.
002600     SELECT IND-FILE              ASSIGN TO DISK 'MASTER.DAT'
002700         ORGANIZATION  IS  INDEXED
002800         ACCESS MODE   IS  SEQUENTIAL
002900         RECORD KEY    IS  IR-IND-KEY
003000         ALTERNATE RECORD KEY IS IR-ALT-KEY
003100         FILE STATUS   IS  WS-STATUS.
003200*---------------------------------------------------------------
003300 DATA DIVISION.
003400 FILE SECTION.
003500*
003600 FD  SEQ-FILE
003700     LABEL RECORDS ARE STANDARD
003800     RECORD CONTAINS 100 CHARACTERS.
003900 01  SEQ-RECORD                    PIC X(100).
004000*
004100 FD  IND-FILE
004200     LABEL RECORDS ARE STANDARD
004300     RECORD CONTAINS 100 CHARACTERS.
004400 01  IND-RECORD.
004500     12 IR-ALT-KEY.
004600        15 IR-FIRM-NAME            PIC X(21).
004700        15 IR-IND-KEY              PIC X(6).
004800     12 FILLER                     PIC X(73).
004900/
005000*---------------------------------------------------------------
005100 WORKING-STORAGE SECTION.
005200 01  WS-STATUS.
005300     12 WS-STATUS-BYTE1            PIC X(1).
005400     12 FILLER                     PIC X(1).
005500*
005600 01  WS-INPUT-COUNT                PIC 9(5)   VALUE 0.
005700 01  WS-REC-LOADED                 PIC 9(5)   VALUE 0.
005800 01  WS-REC-NOT-LOADED             PIC 9(5)   VALUE 0.
005900 01  F1-EOF-FLAG                   PIC X(1)   VALUE 'M'.
006000/
006100 PROCEDURE DIVISION.
006200*---------------------------------------------------------------
006300*  In RM/COBOL-85 you need declaratives (even in dummy form) to
006400*  avoid abends even when non-zero File Status values such as
006500*  '23' are received for a key-not-found condition.  Since
006600*  DECLARATIVES are a "section" MAIN-PROGRAM must be a section.
006700*---------------------------------------------------------------
006800 DECLARATIVES.
006900 0000-ERROR    SECTION.
007000     USE AFTER STANDARD ERROR PROCEDURE ON IND-FILE.
007100 0000-DUMMY.  EXIT.
007200*
```

Figure D.2   INDLOAD program converted to Ryan McFarland RM/COBOL-85.

```
007300 END DECLARATIVES.
007400*------------------------------------------------------------------
007500 0000-MAIN-PROGRAM    SECTION.
007600 0000-MAINLINE.
007700     PERFORM 1000-BOJ.
007800     PERFORM 2000-PROCESS
007900         UNTIL F1-EOF-FLAG = 'E'.
008000     PERFORM 3000-EOJ.
008100     STOP RUN.
008200*
008300 1000-BOJ.
008400     DISPLAY '*** Start of program INDLOAD'.
008500     OPEN OUTPUT  IND-FILE.
008600     IF WS-STATUS-BYTE1 NOT = '0'
008700         DISPLAY '*** Error opening indexed file, program ended'
008800         DISPLAY '    File Status = ', WS-STATUS
008900         STOP RUN.
009000     OPEN  INPUT  SEQ-FILE.
009100     PERFORM 2700-READ.
009200*
009300 2000-PROCESS.
009400     WRITE IND-RECORD FROM SEQ-RECORD.
009500     IF WS-STATUS-BYTE1 = '0'
009600         DISPLAY IND-RECORD(1:27)
009700         ADD 1 TO WS-REC-LOADED
009800      ELSE
009900     IF WS-STATUS = '21'
010000         DISPLAY '*** Err next rec    File Status = ', WS-STATUS
010100         DISPLAY IND-RECORD(1:27)
010200         ADD 1 TO WS-REC-NOT-LOADED
010300      ELSE
010400         DISPLAY '*** Loading failed!   File Status = ', WS-STATUS
010500         DISPLAY IND-RECORD(1:27)
010600         STOP RUN.
010700     PERFORM 2700-READ.
010800*------------------------------------------------------------------
010900 2700-READ.
011000     READ SEQ-FILE
011100       AT END
011200         MOVE 'E' TO F1-EOF-FLAG.
011300     IF F1-EOF-FLAG NOT = 'E'
011400         ADD 1 TO WS-INPUT-COUNT.
011500*
011600 3000-EOJ.
011700     CLOSE  SEQ-FILE  IND-FILE.
011800     DISPLAY 'File status at INDFILE close = ', WS-STATUS.
011900     DISPLAY 'Seq file records read  ',
012000         WS-INPUT-COUNT.
012100     DISPLAY 'Records loaded         ',
012200         WS-REC-LOADED.
012300     DISPLAY 'Records not loaded     ',
012400         WS-REC-NOT-LOADED.
012500     DISPLAY '*** Program ended normally'.
```

Figure D.2   *(Continued)*

```
000100 IDENTIFICATION DIVISION.
000200 PROGRAM-ID.     VAXDEMO.
000300*AUTHOR.          J JANOSSY   INTERNET: JANOSSY@CSCVAX.DEPAUL.EDU
000400*INSTALLATION.  DEPAUL UNIVERSITY, CHICAGO, ILLINOIS, USA
000500*================================================================
000600*    Main Menu Program in VAXDEMO System in VAX COBOL ON-LINE!
000700*        ** ADAPTED TO RM/COBOL-85 MICROCOMPUTER COMPILER **
000800*
000900*    Presents menu screen and allows terminal operator to
001000*    select a function or quit.  Originally set to CALL stub
001100*    programs for testing (see paragraph 2000-PROCESS).
001200*
001300*  Major differences between VAX COBOL and RM/COBOL-85:
001400*
001500*       Source code can't extend beyond column 72 (like IBM)
001600*       COLUMN              is coded POSITION
001700*       ERASE TO END OF SCREEN  is coded ERASE EOS
001800*       ERASE TO END OF LINE    is coded ERASE EOL
001900*       REVERSED            is coded REVERSE
002000*       BLINKING            is coded BLINK
002100*       NO ECHO             is coded LOW
002200*       BOLD                is coded HIGH
002300*       AT and FROM are eliminated
002400*       WITH CONVERSION is not coded
002500*       ACCEPT with REVERSE does not show reverse video
002600*            until entry; DISPLAY spaces reversed before
002700*            the ACCEPT to show length of your entry field
002800*       PROTECTED is not required to prevent entry beyond field
002900*       Cursor automatically skips to next field when entry
003000*            fills up a field (like VAX AUTOTERMINATE)
003100*       You can't display a null literal '' so display a
003200*            space ' ' instead
003300*
003400*================================================================
003500 ENVIRONMENT DIVISION.
003600*----------------------------------------------------------------
003700 DATA DIVISION.
003800 WORKING-STORAGE SECTION.
003900 01  WS-TRANS-COUNT              PIC 9(7)  VALUE 0.
004000 01  WS-FORMATTED-COUNT          PIC Z,ZZZ,ZZ9.
004100 01  WS-OP-ENTRY                 PIC X(1)  VALUE SPACES.
004200 01  WS-VALID-CHOICE             PIC X(1).
004300 01  SCR-MSG                     PIC X(58).
004400*
004500 01  WS-DATE.
004600     12 WS-YR                    PIC X(2).
004700     12 WS-MO                    PIC X(2).
004800     12 WS-DA                    PIC X(2).
004900 01  WS-FORMATTED-DATE.
005000     12 WSF-MO                   PIC X(2).
005100     12 FILLER                   PIC X(1)  VALUE '/'.
005200     12 WSF-DA                   PIC X(2).
005300     12 FILLER                   PIC X(1)  VALUE '/'.
005400     12 WSF-YR                   PIC X(2).
005500*
005600 01  WS-TIME.
005700     12 WS-HRS                   PIC X(2).
005800     12 WS-MIN                   PIC X(2).
005900     12 FILLER                   PIC X(4).
006000 01  WS-FORMATTED-TIME.
006100     12 WSF-HRS                  PIC X(2).
006200     12 FILLER                   PIC X(1)  VALUE ':'.
006300     12 WSF-MIN                  PIC X(2).
006400*----------------------------------------------------------------
006500 PROCEDURE DIVISION.
006600 0000-MAINLINE.
006700     PERFORM 1000-BOJ.
006800     PERFORM 2000-PROCESS
006900         UNTIL WS-OP-ENTRY = 'Q' OR 'q'.
007000     PERFORM 3000-EOJ.
007100     STOP RUN.
007200*
```

Figure D.3   VAXDEMO program converted to Ryan McFarland RM/COBOL-85.

```
007300 1000-BOJ.
007400      ACCEPT WS-DATE FROM DATE.
007500      MOVE WS-MO TO WSF-MO.
007600      MOVE WS-DA TO WSF-DA.
007700      MOVE WS-YR TO WSF-YR.
007800      MOVE 'Enter a selection code and press <Return>' TO SCR-MSG.
007900      PERFORM 2600-DISPLAY-MENU.
008000      PERFORM 2700-OP-PROMPT.
008100* - - - - - - - - - - - - - - - - - - - - - - - - - - - - - -
008200 2000-PROCESS.
008300      MOVE 'Y' TO WS-VALID-CHOICE.
008400*
008500      EVALUATE WS-OP-ENTRY
008600         WHEN '1' CALL 'SINQU1' USING WS-TRANS-COUNT
008700         WHEN '2' CALL 'SUPD1'  USING WS-TRANS-COUNT
008800         WHEN '3' CALL 'SDEL1'  USING WS-TRANS-COUNT
008900         WHEN '4' CALL 'SBROW1' USING WS-TRANS-COUNT
009000         WHEN OTHER
009100            MOVE 'N' TO WS-VALID-CHOICE.
009200*
009300      IF WS-VALID-CHOICE = 'Y'
009400         PERFORM 2600-DISPLAY-MENU
009500         MOVE 'Enter a selection code and press <Return>'
009600            TO SCR-MSG
009700       ELSE
009800         MOVE 'Invalid selection!  Re-enter a choice' TO SCR-MSG.
009900*
010000      PERFORM 2700-OP-PROMPT.
010100* - - - - - - - - - - - - - - - - - - - - - - - - - - - - -
010200 2600-DISPLAY-MENU.
010300      DISPLAY ' ' LINE 1 POSITION 1 ERASE EOS.
010400      DISPLAY 'VAXDEMO' LINE 1 POSITION 2.
010500      DISPLAY '*** CUSTOMER MASTER FILE SYSTEM MENU *** '
010600         HIGH LINE 1 POSITION 21.
010700      DISPLAY WS-FORMATTED-DATE LINE 1 POSITION 72.
010800      DISPLAY 'SCREEN 0' LINE 2 POSITION 2.
010900      DISPLAY 'ENTER FUNCTION CODE AND PRESS RETURN'
011000         LINE 4 POSITION 23.
011100      DISPLAY '1  Inquire about a customer' LINE  7 POSITION 27.
011200      DISPLAY '2  Add/change customer data' LINE  9 POSITION 27.
011300      DISPLAY '3  Delete a customer'        LINE 11 POSITION 27.
011400      DISPLAY '4  Browse customers by name' LINE 13 POSITION 27.
011500      DISPLAY 'Q  Quit (end VAXDEMO)'       LINE 17 POSITION 27.
011600*
011700 2700-OP-PROMPT.
011800      ACCEPT WS-TIME FROM TIME.
011900      MOVE WS-HRS TO WSF-HRS.
012000      MOVE WS-MIN TO WSF-MIN.
012100      DISPLAY WS-FORMATTED-TIME   LINE  2 POSITION 75.
012200      DISPLAY SCR-MSG             LINE 24 POSITION  2.
012300      DISPLAY '===>'             LINE 24 POSITION 66.
012400      ACCEPT WS-OP-ENTRY          LINE 24 POSITION 71.
012500      DISPLAY ' '                 LINE 24 POSITION  2 ERASE EOL.
012600*
012700 3000-EOJ.
012800      DISPLAY ' ' LINE 1 POSITION 1  ERASE EOS.
012900      DISPLAY 'Quitting as requested'        LINE 1 POSITION 2.
013000      MOVE WS-TRANS-COUNT TO WS-FORMATTED-COUNT.
013100      DISPLAY 'Number of transactions processed = '
013200         LINE 2 POSITION 2.
013300      DISPLAY WS-FORMATTED-COUNT             LINE 2 POSITION 37.
013400      DISPLAY 'Enter any DOS command now...' LINE 4 POSITION 2.
```

Figure D.3   *(Continued)*

```
000100 IDENTIFICATION DIVISION.
000200 PROGRAM-ID.    SINQU1.
000300*AUTHOR.        J JANOSSY    INTERNET: JANOSSY@CSCVAX.DEPAUL.EDU
000400*INSTALLATION.  DEPAUL UNIVERSITY, CHICAGO, ILLINOIS, USA
000500*=================================================================
000600*   Testing Stub for VAXDEMO Program CINQU1 in VAX COBOL ON-LINE!
000700*        ** ADAPTED TO RM/COBOL-85 MICROCOMPUTER COMPILER **
000800*
000900*   This program receives control from the VAXDEMO menu program
001000*   and just presents a simple message saying that it has been
001100*   accessed.  After another <Return> it ends and control goes
001200*   back to the menu program.
001300*=================================================================
001400 ENVIRONMENT DIVISION.
001500*-----------------------------------------------------------------
001600 DATA DIVISION.
001700 WORKING-STORAGE SECTION.
001800 01  WS-OP-ENTRY                     PIC X(1).
001900 01  SCR-MSG                         PIC X(58).
002000*
002100 LINKAGE SECTION.
002200 01  WS-TRANS-COUNT                  PIC 9(7).
002300*-----------------------------------------------------------------
002400 PROCEDURE DIVISION USING WS-TRANS-COUNT.
002500 0000-MAINLINE.
002600     ADD 1 TO WS-TRANS-COUNT.
002700     DISPLAY ' ' LINE 1 POSITION 1 ERASE EOS.
002800     DISPLAY 'Control passed to SINQU1'          LINE 1 POSITION 2.
002900     DISPLAY 'Press <Return> to continue...'     LINE 2 POSITION 2.
003000     ACCEPT WS-OP-ENTRY                           LINE 3 POSITION 2.
003100 0000-EXIT.  EXIT PROGRAM.
```

Figure D.4   SINQU1 stub testing program converted to Ryan McFarland
RM/COBOL-85.

Appendix E

Obtaining Program Source Code On Diskette

You can obtain all of the programs in this book in VAX terminal format as ASCII files on MS-DOS diskette by sending $35 (US) in check or money order form to:

Practical Distribution Diskettes
P.O. Box 46078
Chicago, Illinois 60646

The diskette includes the NUMCHECK and PLACNAME subprograms, and the TERMTORM VAX to RM/COBOL-85 conversion utility. Please specify whether you want a 360K, 5-1/4" diskette or 720K, 3-1/2" diskette. Please allow four weeks for delivery.

Special Note to College and University Instructors:

The source code diskette is free to instructors. Just send a brief note to the above address using your institution's letterhead, and mention the course for which you are considering using the book.

An economically priced student workbook paralleling *VAX COBOL On-Line* is available from Stipes Publishing Company, 10-12 Chester Street, Champaign, Illinois 61824, telephone (217) 356-8391. The workbook contains teaching and lecture materials and additional student lab exercises suitable for college course use.

Index